The Glory of TORAH!

ALL THE COMMANDMENTS ORGANIZED

OlivePress
צהר זית

THE GLORY OF TORAH! All the Commandments organized

2nd Edition

ISBN 978-1-941173-26-8

Published by

Olive Press Messianic and Christian Publisher

www.olivepresspublisher.com

olivepressbooks@gmail.com

Our prayer at Olive Press is that we may help make the Word of Adonai fully known, that it spread rapidly and be glorified everywhere. We hope our books help open people's eyes so they will turn from darkness to Light and from the power of the adversary to יהוה (God) and to trust in ישוע Yeshua (Jesus). (From II Thess. 3:1; Col. 1:25; and Acts 26:18,15, NRSV, CJB, and SNB.)

This whole book is all Scripture, with very little commentary. So the author is really יהוה Himself.

Except in a couple sections, all Scripture unless otherwise noted are taken from the *Sacred Name Bible*, which is the King James Version with these words changed to Hebrew: LORD to יהוה (YHVH, God's Sacred Name, which in Hebrew letter pictographs means "behold hand, behold nail"), Jesus to ישוע (Yeshua, which means Salvation), Christ to Messiah; and in this book we changed: law to Torah, Ghost to Spirit, Testament to Covenant, vail to veil, occasionally Lord to Adonai, and in the first section: God to Elohim. We also capitalized some words like Name and Jubilee, etc. On the back cover, we changed "thou" and "thee" to "you," etc. Copyright ©2011 by Olive Press Messianic and Christian Publisher. All rights reserved.

Why KJV ? *Because it is public domain. Other versions charge to use their versions so extensively.*

With "Gospel" capitalized in all of them and pronouns referring to the Trinity in some,
Scriptures marked:

SNB are taken from our *Sacred Name Bible*. See above.

Great SHALOM have those who
love Your Torah;
nothing can make them stumble.

Psalm 119:165 [(NRSV) ("shalom" and "Torah" from the Hebrew)]

He that keepeth the Torah, happy is he.

Prov. 29:18

TORAH תּוֹרָה Instruction

(Torah in Hebrew means Instruction, not law.)
(It's our Creator's instructions on how best to live our lives.)

NOTE: *For a **spiral bound** copy of this book, go to* olivepresspublisher.com/gloryofTorah

Table of Contents

NOTE: *For a **spiral bound** copy of this book, go to* olivepresspublisher.com/gloryofTorah

Think not that I am come to destroy
the Torah or the prophets:
I am not come to destroy, but to fulfill.
Matt. 5:17

Wherefore the Torah is holy,
and the commandment holy, and just, and good ...
For we know that the
Torah is spiritual:
Rom. 7:12,14

For I delight in the Torah of God after the inward man:
But I see another law in my members.....
Rom. 7:22-23a

So then with the mind I myself serve the Torah of God;
but with the flesh the law of sin.
Rom. 7:25b

For the Torah of the Spirit of life in Messiah יֵשׁוּעַ
hath made me free from the law of sin and death.
For what the Torah [alone] could not do,
in that it was weak through the flesh,
God sending His own Son
in the likeness of sinful flesh, and for sin,
condemned sin in the flesh:
That the *righteousness* of the **Torah**
might be fulfilled in us,
who walk not after the flesh, but after the Spirit.
Rom. 8:2-4

We say we love the LORD and His Word, but then we choose to ignore or neglect one part, His Torah—the Law. We tend to shy away from it. Nonetheless, the Torah came from the very mouth of the Most High God! It is part of the very WORD which in the beginning was with God, which is Jesus (ישוע Yeshua**) (John 1:1-3). So there has to be life and power and beauty in His Laws as there is in all His Word. Therefore it behooves us to take a closer look.

To help us find the jewels and gems and life-giving spiritual nourishment in the Torah, this book has all the verses on the same instruction grouped together. For example, something is said about giving to the poor in one verse here and a little more about it in another verse there. Then it is repeated or further explained in yet several more places. We gathered them all together (at least that was our goal), so we can study everything יהוה (God, the LORD*) said about that particular commandment, along with some important verses about it from the rest of Scripture. It is all categorized. (The category titles are given in the margins and are listed generally in the order that they first appear in the Torah.)

*Many believers are against the Torah because the Bible says we "are not under the law" (Rom.6:14; Gal.5:18), but we ask ourselves: If we are supposed to toss out the Torah, then is it okay to ignore the poor and starving? How about orphans and the disabled? Is it okay now to look down on them and not take care of them as in some cultures? How about destruction of property, dishonest business deals, biased court decisions, and rape, and child molesting—are they not crimes anymore? These and much more are all against **specific** guidelines in the **Torah**, which we all surely want the world to still follow! So maybe when it says "ye are not under the law, but under grace," it doesn't mean to never learn from or obey the Torah. Therefore, let's open our minds and not miss the amazing treasures of Heaven contained within it.*

Why KJV ? *Because it is public domain. Other versions charge to use their versions so extensively.*

A note *from the compiler/editor: I created this book so I can spend time pondering on and drinking in every Word יהוה said about each commandment in the Torah and how ישוע and the Apostles built upon each one in the New Covenant, then meditating on it, letting the meaning and message and intention sink into my spirit, reflecting on it while waiting for יהוה, through His Holy Spirit, to reveal the design and purpose for that particular teaching for us today. It draws me closer to ישוע and my joy is filled more and more as I do this. If this is helpful to you also, than I am blessed even further.*

***NOTE:** *The Hebrew word: יהוה—YHVH—is God's Majestic, Holy Name used throughout the Hebrew Bible, which no one today knows how to pronounce. Hebrew letters were originally pictographs. יהוה in pictures says, "Behold hand, behold nail." It speaks of He who "was and is and is to come," of the great I AM, of existence and the breath of Life. It is God's most Awe-inspiring, Powerful Name.*

** *ישוע (Yeshua) is Jesus' Hebrew Name which means Salvation, and is pronounced exactly the same as ישועה (yeshuah)—salvation. Notice that ישוע has seven flames atop the letters just like the Menorah, the Temple Lampstand. ישוע is the Light of the World.*

These Hebrew Names are used throughout this book—beauty for our spiritual eyes to behold.

Open Thou mine eyes,
that I may behold *wondrous* things
out of Thy Torah.

Psalms 119:18

But whoso looketh into
the perfect Torah of **liberty**,
and continueth therein …
shall be blessed in his deed [in what he does].

James 1:25

I **delight** to do Thy will, O my God:
yea, Thy Torah is within my heart.

Psalms 40:8

And I will walk at **liberty**: for I seek Thy precepts.

Psalms 119:45

O how love I Thy Torah!
It is my meditation all the day. Thou through Thy
commandments hast made me wiser than mine enemies:
... I understand more than the ancients,
because I keep Thy precepts.
Psalm 119:97-98, 100

He who turns away his ear from listening to
the law [Torah], even his prayer is an abomination.
Prov 28:9 (NASB)

His delight is in the Torah of יהוה; and in His
Torah doth he meditate day and night. 3 And he shall
be like a tree planted by the rivers of water, ... and
whatsoever he doeth shall prosper.
Psalm 1:2-3

For the commandment is a lamp;
and the Torah is light
Prov. 6:23

1. THE FIRST AND GREATEST COMMANDMENT

שמע ישראל יהוה אלהינו יהוה אחד

Shema Yisrael ADONAI Elohenu ADONAI echad.

Here [O] Israel יהוה our Elohim, יהוה [is] one.

Deut. 6:4-6 **Hear, O Israel:** יהוה **our Elohim,** יהוה *is* **one: And thou shalt love** יהוה **thy Elohim with all thine heart, and with all thy soul, and with all thy might.**

Matt. 22:36-38 Master, which is the great[est] commandment in the Torah? 37 ישוע said unto him, **Thou shalt love** יהוה **thy Elohim with all thy heart, and with all thy soul, and with all thy mind.** 38 This is the first and great[est] commandment.

Mark 12:28-30 And one of the scribes came, and ... asked Him, Which is the first commandment of all? 29 And ישוע answered him, **The first of all the commandments is, Hear, O Israel;** יהוה **our Elohim** יהוה **is one:** 30 **And thou shalt love** יהוה **thy Elohim with all thy heart, and with all thy soul, and with all thy mind, and with all thy strength: this is the first commandment.**

Observant Jewish people do hold this commandment above all others. They recite it every week in the Synagogue and every day at home. During the Holocaust, many were reciting it as they entered the gas chambers.

2. THE SECOND GREATEST COMMANDMENT

Lev. 19:18 ...thou shalt love thy neighbour as thyself: I am יהוה.

Matt. 22: 39-40 *(cont. from above)* And the second is like unto it, Thou shalt love thy neighbour as thyself. 40 **On these two commandments hang all the Torah and the prophets.**

Rom. 13:9b-10 Thou shalt love thy neighbour as thyself. 10 Love worketh no ill to his neighbour: therefore love is the fulfilling of the Torah.

Gal. 5:14 For all the Torah is fulfilled in one word, even in this; Thou shalt love thy neighbour as thyself.

I Pet. 4:8 (ASV) ...love covereth a multitude of sins. **Prov. 10:12b** ...love covereth all sins.

***Yeshua** elevated these two commandments as the first and greatest ones (even though they don't appear until Leviticus and Deuteronomy), therefore we put them here first. By His Grace, we live them.*

(See much more about the first commandment on pages 238-240 where it is listed again in the general order that it appears in the Torah. "Love thy neighbor" is on page 94-96.)

3. I AM יהוה YOUR GOD

Ex. 20:2 I *am* יהוה thy God [Elohim], which have brought thee out of the land of Egypt, out of the house of bondage.

The Jewish people consider this the first of the Ten Words (Hebrew "debar" דבר which means "word" not "commandment.") As you can see below, God said "I am יהוה your Elohim" many times before He came down on Mt. Sinai, and He continued to say it myriads more times afterwards. Why? Perhaps because He wants to establish for us first and foremost who He is.

We will look at some verses where He is really explaining and expounding on who He is. Then we will look at the long list of verses all through the Tenakh (Old Testament) containing God's I Am statements. [Elohim, Elohi (pronounced Elohee), or EL are used in place of God.] Hebrew is included for some of it in case you're interested. If not, no problem, it will still bless you to just read the English.

BEFORE SINAI

Ex. 3:14 I AM THAT I AM אֶהְיֶה אֲשֶׁר אֶהְיֶה [Eh-h-yeh a-sher Eh-h-yeh]: and He said, Thus shalt thou say unto the children of Israel, I AM אֶהְיֶה hath sent me unto you.

Ex. 6:2-3 And Elohim spake unto Moses, and said unto him, I *am* יהוה: And I appeared unto Abraham, unto Isaac, and unto Jacob, by the Name of EL Almighty [El Shaddai אֵל שַׁדַּי], but by My Name יהוה was I not known to them.

Ex. 6:6-7 Wherefore say unto the children of Israel, I *am* יהוה, and I will bring you out from under the burdens of the Egyptians, and I will rid you out of their bondage, and I will redeem you with a stretched out arm, and with great judgments: 7 And I will take you to Me for a people, and I will be to you a Elohim: and ye shall know that I *am* יהוה your Elohim, which bringeth you out from under the burdens of the Egyptians.

Ex. 6:8 And I will bring you in unto the land, concerning the which I did swear to give it to Abraham, to Isaac, and to Jacob; and I will give it you for an heritage: I *am* יהוה.

Ex. 7:5 And the Egyptians shall know that I *am* יהוה, when I stretch forth mine hand upon Egypt, and bring out the children of Israel from among them.

Ex. 14:4 And I will harden Pharaoh's heart, that he shall follow after them; and I will be honoured upon Pharaoh, and upon all his host; that the Egyptians may know that I *am* יהוה. And they did so.

Ex. 34:6-7 And יהוה passed by before him, and proclaimed, יהוה, יהוה אֵל (EL), merciful and gracious, longsuffering, and abundant in goodness and truth, 7 Keeping mercy for thousands, forgiving iniquity and transgression and sin, and that will by no means clear *the guilty*; visiting the iniquity of the fathers upon the children, and upon the children's children, unto the third and to the fourth *generation*.

AFTER SINAI

Ex. 23:25 And ye shall serve יהוה your Elohim, and He shall bless thy bread, and thy water; and I will take sickness away from the midst of thee.

Lev. 26:12-13 And I will walk among you, and will be your Elohim, and ye shall be My people. 13 I *am* יהוה your Elohim, which brought you forth out of the land of Egypt, that ye should not be their bondmen; and I have broken the bands of your yoke, and made you go upright.

Deut. 4:10 Gather Me the people together, and I will make them hear My Words, that they may learn to fear Me all the days that they shall live upon the earth, and that they may teach their children. [also in Teach your children, p. 194]

Deut. 5:6 I *am* יהוה thy Elohim, which brought thee out of the land of Egypt, from the house of bondage.

Deut. 6:12-13 Then beware lest thou forget יהוה, which brought thee forth out of the land of Egypt, from the house of bondage. Thou shalt fear יהוה thy Elohim, and serve Him, and shalt swear by His Name. [also in No other gods, p. 31 and Name in vain, p. 40]

Deut. 10:17-18 For יהוה your Elohim is Elohi of gods, and Lord of lords, a great EL, a mighty, and a terrible, which regardeth not persons, nor taketh reward: He doth execute the judgment of the fatherless and widow, and loveth the stranger, in giving him food and raiment. [also in No other gods, p. 31]

I AM STATEMENTS OF GOD

Be blessed as you read these aloud to yourself and meditate on them

BEFORE SINAI (with some Hebrew)

Gen. 15:1 I *am* אָנֹכִי thy shield, [and] thy exceeding great reward. אָנֹכִי מָגֵן לָךְ שְׂכָרְךָ הַרְבֵּה מְאֹד

Gen. 15:7 I *am* יהוה that brought thee out of Ur of the Chaldees, to give thee this land to inherit it.

Gen. 17:1 I *am* אֲנִי the Almighty EL אֵל שַׁדַּי; walk before Me, and be thou perfect. אֲנִי אֵל שַׁדַּי

Gen. 26:24 [to Jacob] I *am* אָנֹכִי the Elohi of Abraham thy father: fear not, for I *am* with thee, and will bless thee, and multiply thy seed for My servant Abraham's sake.

Gen. 28:13 [to Jacob] I *am* יהוה Elohi of Abraham thy father, and the Elohi of Isaac: the land whereon thou liest, to thee will I give it, and to thy seed;

Gen. 28:15 [to Jacob] And, behold, I *am* with thee, and will keep thee in all [places] whither thou goest, and will bring thee again into this land; for I will not leave thee, until I have done *that* which I have spoken to thee of.

Gen. 31:13 [to Jacob] I *am* אָנֹכִי the EL of Bethel, where thou anointedst the pillar, *and* where thou vowedst a vow unto Me: now arise, get thee out from this land, and return unto the land of thy kindred.

11

I AM

Gen. 35:11 I *am* אֲנִי EL Almighty אֵל שַׁדַּי: be fruitful and multiply; a nation and a company of nations shall be of thee, and kings shall come out of thy loins;

Gen. 46:3 I *am* אָנֹכִי Elohim, the EL of thy father: fear not to go down into Egypt; for I will there make of thee a great nation:

Ex. 3:6 I *am* אָנֹכִי the Elohi of thy father, the Elohi of Abraham, the Elohi of Isaac, and the Elohi of Jacob.

Ex. 3:8 And I am come down to deliver them out the hand of the Egyptians,

Ex. 6:2,8; 7:5; 14:4 I *am* יְהוָֹה; [אֲנִי יְהוָֹה] (*Most times when it says, I am* יְהוָֹה *it uses* אֲנִי)]

Ex. 7:17 In this thou shalt know that I am יְהוָֹה:

Ex. 8:22 And I will sever in that day the land of Goshen, in which My people dwell, that no swarms [of flies] shall be there; <u>to the end thou mayest know that I *am* יְהוָֹה in the midst of the earth.</u>

Ex. 10:2 And that thou mayest tell in the ears of thy son, and of thy son's son, what things I have wrought in Egypt, and My signs which I have done among them; that ye may know how that I *am* יְהוָֹה.

Ex. 14:4 ...that the Egyptians may know that I *am* יְהוָֹה.

Ex. 14:18 And the Egyptians shall know that I *am* יְהוָֹה,

Ex. 15:26 ...for I *am* יְהוָֹה that healeth thee. [also in Keep All, p. 20]

Ex. 16:12 ...and ye shall know that I *am* יְהוָֹה your Elohim.

FROM MT. SINAI

Ex. 20:2 I *am* יְהוָֹה; [אֲנִי יְהוָֹה] thy Elohim, which have brought thee out of … bondage.

AFTER SINAI

Ex. 22:27 ...and it shall come to pass, when he crieth unto Me, that I will hear; for I *am* gracious.

Ex. 29:46 And they shall know that I *am* יְהוָֹה their Elohim, that brought them forth out of the land of Egypt, that I may dwell among them: I *am* יְהוָֹה their Elohim.

Ex. 33:19 And He said, I will make all My goodness pass before thee, and I will proclaim the Name of יְהוָֹה before thee; and will be gracious to whom I will be gracious, and will shew mercy on whom I will shew mercy.

Lev. 11:44 For I am יְהוָֹה your Elohim: ye shall therefore sanctify yourselves, and ye shall be holy; for I *am* holy:

Lev. 11:45 For I *am* יְהוָֹה that bringeth you up out of the land of Egypt, to be your Elohim: ye shall therefore be holy, for I *am* holy.

Lev. 18:2 I am יְהוָֹה your Elohim.

Lev. 18:5 Ye shall therefore keep My statutes, and My judgments: which if a man do, he shall live in them: I *am* יְהוָֹה.

Lev. 18:4,5,6,21,30; 19:4,37; 22:31; & many more!!! I *am* יְהוָֹה your Elohim. Or I am יְהוָֹה.

Lev. 20:8 And ye shall keep My statutes, and do them: I *am* יהוה which sanctify you.

Lev. 20:24 ...and I will give it unto you to possess it, a land that floweth with milk and honey: I *am* יהוה your Elohim, which have separated you from [other] people.

Lev. 22:32 Neither shall ye profane My Holy Name; but I will be hallowed among the children of Israel: I *am* יהוה which hallow you, [also in Name in vain, p. 40]

Lev. 26:12-13 And I will walk among you, and will be your Elohim, and ye shall be My people. 13 I am יהוה your Elohim, which brought you forth out of the land of Egypt, that ye should not be their bondmen; and I have broken the bands of your yoke, and made you go upright.

Num. 18:20 I *am* thy part [portion] and thine inheritance.

Deut. 29:6 ...that ye might know that I *am* יהוה your Elohim.

Deut. 32:39 See now that I, *even* I, *am* He, and *there is* no god with [besides] Me: I kill, and I make alive; I wound, and I heal: neither *is there any* that can deliver out of My hand.

AFTER TORAH

Judges 6:10 I *am* יהוה your Elohim; fear not the gods of the Amorites, in whose land ye dwell:

1 Kings 20:13 Hast thou seen all this great multitude? Behold, I will deliver it into thine hand this day; and thou shalt know that I *am* יהוה.

1 Kings 20:28 ...therefore will I deliver all this great multitude into thine hand, and ye shall know that I *am* יהוה.

Psalms 50:7 I *am* Elohim, *even* thy Elohim.

Psalms 81:10 I *am* יהוה thy Elohim, which brought thee out of the land of Egypt: open thy mouth wide, and I will fill it.

Prov. 8:14 Counsel *is* mine, and sound wisdom: I *am* understanding;

Isaiah 1:11,14 I am full of burnt offerings.... Your New Moons and your Appointed Feasts My soul hateth: they are a trouble unto Me; I am weary to bear *them. [Because they were sinful and rebellious and there was blood on their hands (verses 4, 5, 15).]*

Isaiah 41:10 Fear thou not; for I *am* with thee: be not dismayed; for I *am* thy Elohim: I will strengthen thee; yea, I will help thee; yea, I will uphold thee with the right hand of My righteousness.

Isaiah 42:8 I *am* יהוה: that [is] My Name: and My Glory will I not give to another, neither My praise....

Isaiah 43:3 For I *am* יהוה thy Elohim, the Holy One of Israel, thy Saviour: ....

Isaiah 43:5 Fear not: for I *am* with thee: I will bring thy seed from the east, and gather thee from the west....

Isaiah 43:11 I, *even* I, *am* יהוה; and beside Me [there is] no saviour.

Isaiah 43:12 I have declared, and have saved, and I have shewed, when *there was* no strange *god* among you: therefore ye *are* My witnesses, saith יהוה, that I *am* Elohim.

Isaiah 43:13 Yea, before the day *was* I *am* He; and *there is* none that can deliver out of My hand: ….

Isaiah 43:15 I *am* יהוה, your Holy One, the Creator of Israel, your King.

Isaiah 43:25 I, *even* I, *am* He that blotteth out thy transgressions for Mine own sake, and will not remember thy sins.

Isaiah 44:6 Thus saith יהוה the King of Israel, and his Redeemer יהוה of hosts; I *am* the first, and I *am* the last; and beside Me *there is* no Elohim.

Isiaah 44:24 Thus saith יהוה, thy Redeemer, and He that formed thee from the womb, I *am* יהוה that maketh all *things*; that stretcheth forth the heavens alone; that spreadeth abroad the earth by Myself;

Isaiah 45:5 I *am* יהוה, and *there is* none else, *there is* no Elohim beside Me: I girded thee, though thou hast not known Me:

Isaiah 45:6 That they may know from the rising of the sun, and from the west, that [there is] none beside Me. I *am* יהוה, and *there is* none else.

Isaiah 45:18 For thus saith יהוה that created the heavens; Elohim Himself that formed the earth and made it; He hath established it, He created it not in vain, He formed it to be inhabited: I *am* יהוה; and *there is* none else.

Isaiah 45:22 Look unto Me, and be ye saved, all the ends of the earth: for I *am* Elohim, and [there is] none else.

Isaiah 46:4 And *even* to *your* old age I *am* He; and *even* to hoar hairs will I carry [you]: I have made, and I will bear; even I will carry, and will deliver *you*.

Isaiah 46:9-10 Remember the former things of old: for I *am* Elohim, and *there is* none else; [I am] Elohim, and *there is* none like Me, 10 Declaring the end from the beginning, and from ancient times [the things] that are not [yet] done, saying, My counsel shall stand, and I will do all My pleasure:….

Isaiah 48:12 Hearken unto Me, O Jacob and Israel, My called; I *am* He; I *am* the first, I also *am* the last.

Isaiah 48:17 Thus saith יהוה, thy Redeemer, the Holy One of Israel; I *am* יהוה thy Elohim which teacheth thee to profit, which leadeth thee by the way *that* thou shouldest go.

Isaiah 49:23 …and thou shalt know that I *am* יהוה: for they shall not be ashamed that wait for Me.

Isaiah 51:12 I, *even* I, *am* He that comforteth you: who [art] thou, that thou shouldest be afraid of a man *that* shall die, ….

Isaiah 51:15 But I *am* יהוה thy Elohim, that divided the sea, whose waves roared: יהוה of hosts *is* His Name.

Isaiah 52:6 Therefore My people shall know My Name: therefore [they shall know] in that day that I *am* He that doth speak: behold, *it is* I.

Isaiah 58:9 Then shalt thou call, and יהוה shall answer; thou shalt cry, and He shall say, Here I *am*.

Isaiah 65:1 I am sought of *them that* asked not [for Me]; I am found of *them that* sought Me not: ….

Jer. 1:8 Be not afraid of their faces: for I *am* with thee to deliver thee, saith יהוה.

I Am Statements of God (cont.)

Jer. 3:12 Return, thou backsliding Israel, saith יהוה; [and] I will not cause Mine anger to fall upon you: for I *am* merciful, saith יהוה, [and] I will not keep *anger* forever.

Jer. 3:14 Turn, O backsliding children, saith יהוה; for I am married unto you: ….

Jer. 9:23-24 (NRSV with יהוה) Do not let the wise boast in their wisdom, do not let the mighty boast in their might, do not let the wealthy boast in their wealth; but let those who boast boast in this, that they understand and know Me, that I am יהוה; I act with steadfast love, justice, and righteousness in the earth, for in these things I delight, says יהוה.

Jer. 15:20 And I will make thee unto this people a fenced brasen wall: and they shall fight against thee, but they shall not prevail against thee: for I *am* with thee to save thee and to deliver thee, saith יהוה.

Jer. 23:30 I *am* against the *[false]* prophets, says יהוה, "who steal My Words…. (See also 21:13, 23:31,32)

Jer. 24:7 And I will give them an heart to know Me, that I *am* יהוה: and they shall be My people, and I will be their Elohim: for they shall return unto Me with their whole heart. [also in Love יהוה, p. 239]

Jer. 30:11 For I *am* with thee, saith יהוה, to save thee: … but I will correct thee in measure, and will not leave thee altogether unpunished.

Jer. 31:9 They shall come with weeping, and with supplications will I lead them: I will cause them to walk by the rivers of waters in a straight way, wherein they shall not stumble: for I am a father to Israel….

Jer. 32:27 Behold, I *am* יהוה, the Elohi of all flesh: is there any thing too hard for Me?

Ezek. 12:25 For I *am* יהוה: I will speak, and the Word that I shall speak shall come to pass; it shall be no more prolonged: for in your days, O rebellious house, will I say the Word, and will perform it, saith Adonai יהוה.

Ezek. 16:62 And I will establish My covenant with thee; and thou shalt know that I *am* יהוה:

Ezek. 20:7 Then said I unto them, Cast ye away every man the abominations of his eyes, and defile not yourselves with the idols of Egypt: I am יהוה your Elohim. [also in No Idols, p. 37]

Ezek. 20:12 Moreover also I gave them My Sabbaths, to be a sign between Me and them, that they might know that I *am* יהוה that sanctify them. [also in Sabbath, p. 44]

Ezek. 20:19-20 I *am* יהוה your Elohim; walk in My statutes, and keep My judgments, and do them; 20 And hallow My Sabbaths; and they shall be a sign between Me and you, that ye may know that I am יהוה your Elohim. [also in Sabbath, p. 44]

Ezek. 20:42 And ye shall know that I *am* יהוה, when I shall bring you into the land of Israel, into the country for the which I lifted up Mine hand to give it to your fathers.

Ezek. 37:13 And ye shall know that I *am* יהוה, when I have opened your graves, O My people, and brought you up out of your graves,

Ezek. 38:23 Thus will I magnify Myself, and sanctify Myself; and I will be known in the eyes of many nations, and they shall know that I *am* יהוה.

Ezek. 39:6-7 And I will send a fire on Magog, and among them that dwell carelessly in the isles: and they shall know that I *am* יהוה. 7 So will I make My Holy Name known in the midst of My people

Israel; and I will not let them pollute My Holy Name any more: and the heathen shall know that I *am* יהוה, the Holy One in Israel.

Ezek. 39:22 So the house of Israel shall know that I *am* יהוה their Elohim from that day and forward.

Ezek. 39:28 Then shall they know that I *am* יהוה their Elohim, which caused them to be led into captivity among the heathen: but I have gathered them unto their own land, and have left none of them any more there.

Hosea 13:4 Yet I *am* יהוה thy Elohim from the land of Egypt, and thou shalt know no god but Me: for there is no Saviour beside Me.

Joel 2:27 And ye shall know that I am in the midst of Israel, and that I *am* יהוה your Elohim, and none else: and My people shall never be ashamed.

Joel 3:17 So shall ye know that I *am* יהוה your Elohim dwelling in Zion, My holy mountain: then shall Jerusalem be holy, and there shall no strangers pass through her any more.

Zech 10:6 And I will strengthen the house of Judah, and I will save the house of Joseph, and I will bring them again to place them; for I have mercy upon them: and they shall be as though I had not cast them off: for I *am* יהוה their Elohim, and will hear them.

Mal. 3:6 For I *am* יהוה, I change not; therefore ye sons of Jacob are not consumed.

NEW COVENANT

Matt. 3:17 And lo a voice from heaven, saying, This is My beloved Son, in whom **I am well pleased**.

Matt. 17:5 While He yet spake, behold, a bright cloud overshadowed them: and behold a voice out of the cloud, which said, This is My beloved Son, in whom **I am well pleased**; hear ye Him. [Also in Prophet like Moses, p. 225]

Mark 1:11 And there came a voice from heaven, saying, Thou art My beloved Son, in whom **I am well pleased**.

Luke 3:22 And the Holy Spirit descended in a bodily shape like a dove upon Him, and a voice came from heaven, which said, Thou art My beloved Son; in Thee **I am well pleased**.

Mark 12:26 And as touching the dead, that they rise: have ye not read in the book of Moses, how in the bush יהוה spake unto him, saying, I *am* the Elohi of Abraham, and the Elohi of Isaac, and the Elohi of Jacob?

YESHUA'S I AM STATEMENTS

Matt. 11:29 Take My yoke upon you, and learn of Me; for **I am meek and lowly in heart:** and ye shall find rest unto your souls.

John 6:32-35 Then יֵשׁוּעַ said unto them, Verily, verily, I say unto you, Moses gave you not that Bread from Heaven; but My Father giveth you the true Bread from Heaven. 33 For the Bread of God is He which cometh down from Heaven, and giveth Life unto the world. 34 Then said they unto Him, Lord, evermore give us this bread. 35 And יֵשׁוּעַ said unto them, **I am the Bread of Life**: he that cometh to Me shall never hunger; and he that believeth on Me shall never thirst.

John 6:41 The Jews then murmured at Him, because He said, **I am the Bread which came down from Heaven**.

John 6:48 **I am that Bread of Life**.

John 6:51 **I am the Living Bread** which came down from Heaven: if any man eat of this Bread, he shall live **forever**: and the Bread that I will give is My flesh, which I will give for the Life of the world.

John 7:28-29 Then cried יֵשׁוּעַ in the Temple as He taught, saying, Ye both know Me, and ye know whence I am: and I am not come of Myself, but He that sent Me is true, whom ye know not. 29 But I know Him: for **I am from Him**, and He hath sent Me.

John 7:34 Ye shall seek Me, and shall not find Me: and where **I am**, thither ye cannot come.

John 8:12 Then spake יֵשׁוּעַ again unto them, saying, **I am the Light of the world:** He that followeth Me shall not walk in darkness, but shall have the Light of Life.

John 8:16 And yet if I judge, My judgment is true: for **I am not alone,** but I *[am with]* the Father that sent Me.

John 8:18 **I am** one that bear witness of Myself, and the Father that sent Me beareth witness of Me.

John 8:23-24   And He said unto them, Ye are from beneath; **I am from above:** ye are of this world; **I am not of this world.** 24 I said therefore unto you, that ye shall die in your sins: for if ye believe not that **I am** *He*, ye shall die in your sins.

John 8:28 Then said יֵשׁוּעַ unto them, When ye have lifted up the Son of man, then shall ye know that **I am** *He*, and *that* I do nothing of Myself; but as My Father hath taught Me, I speak these things.

John 8:58 יֵשׁוּעַ said unto them, Verily, verily, I say unto you, Before Abraham was, **I am.**

John 9:5   As long as I am in the world, **I am the Light of the world.**

John 10:7 Then said יֵשׁוּעַ unto them again, Verily, verily, I say unto you, **I am the door of the sheep.**

John 10:9 **I am the door:** by Me if any man enter in, he shall be saved, and shall go in and out, and find pasture.

John 10:10 The thief cometh not, but for to steal, and to kill, and to destroy: **I am** come that they might have life, and that they might have it more abundantly.

John 10:11 **I am the Good Shepherd**: the Good Shepherd giveth his Life for the sheep.

John 10:14 **I am the Good Shepherd**, and know My sheep, and am known of Mine.

John 10:36 Say ye of Him, whom the Father hath sanctified, and sent into the world, Thou blasphemest; because I said, **I am the Son of God**?

John 11:25 ישוע said unto her, **I am the Resurrection, and the Life**: he that believeth in Me, though he were dead, yet shall he live:

John 12:46 **I am come a Light into the world**, that whosoever believeth on Me should not abide in darkness.

John 13:13 Ye call Me Master and Lord: and ye say well; for so **I am.**

John 13:19 Now I tell you before it come, that, when it is come to pass, ye may believe that **I am** *He*.

John 14:6 ישוע saith unto him, **I am the Way, the Truth, and the Life:** no man cometh unto the Father, but by Me.

John 14:10-11 Believest thou not that **I am in the Father, and the Father in Me**? The Words that I speak unto you I speak not of Myself: but the Father that dwelleth in Me, He doeth the works. 11 Believe Me that **I am in the Father, and the Father in Me**: or else believe Me for the very works' sake.

John 14:20 At that day ye shall know that **I am in My Father, and ye in Me, and I in you**.

John 15:1 **I am the True Vine**, and My Father is the husbandman.

John 15:5 **I am the Vine**, ye are the branches: He that abideth in Me, and I in him, the same bringeth forth much fruit: for without Me ye can do nothing.

John 16:32 Behold, the hour cometh, yea, is now come, that ye shall be scattered, every man to his own, and shall leave Me alone: and yet **I am not alone**, because the Father is with Me.

John 17:10 And all Mine are Thine, and Thine are Mine; and **I am glorified in them**.

John 17:14-16 I have given them Thy Word; and the world hath hated them, because they are not of the world, even as **I am not of the world**. 15 I pray not that thou shouldest take them out of the world, but that thou shouldest keep them from the evil. 16 They are not of the world, even as **I am not of the world.**

John 18:4-6 ישוע therefore, knowing all things that should come upon Him, went forth, and said unto them, Whom seek ye? 5 They answered Him, ישוע of Nazareth. ישוע saith unto them, **I am** *He*. And Judas also, which betrayed Him, stood with them. 6 As soon then as He had said unto them, **I am** *He*, they went backward, and fell to the ground.

John 18:8 ישוע answered, I have told you that **I am** *He*: if therefore ye seek Me, let these go their way:

Mark 14:61-62 But He held His peace, and answered nothing. Again the high priest asked Him, and said unto Him, Art thou the Messiah, the Son of the Blessed? 62 And ישוע said, **I am**: and ye shall see the Son of man sitting on the right hand of power, and coming in the clouds of heaven.

John 18:37 Pilate therefore said unto Him, Art thou a king then? ישוע answered, Thou sayest that **I am a King.** To this end was I born, and for this cause came I into the world, that I should bear witness unto the Truth. Every one that is of the Truth heareth My voice.

Matt. 27:43 He trusted in God; let Him deliver Him now, if He will have Him: for He said, **I am the Son of God.**

Matt. 28:20 Teaching them to observe all things whatsoever I have commanded you: and, lo, **I am with you alway**, even unto the end of the world. Amen.

Acts 9:5 And he said, Who art thou, Lord? And the Lord said, **I am** ישוע whom thou persecutest: it is hard for thee to kick against the pricks.

Acts 18:9-10 Then spake the Lord to Paul in the night by a vision, Be not afraid, but speak, and hold not thy peace: 10 For **I am with thee**, and no man shall set on thee to hurt thee: for I have much people in this city.

4. YOU SHALL KEEP ALL HIS COMMANDMENTS

Exodus 15:26 And said, If thou wilt diligently hearken to the voice of יהוה thy God, and wilt do that which is right in His sight, and wilt give ear to His commandments, and <u>keep all His statutes</u>, I will put none of these diseases upon thee, which I have brought upon the Egyptians: for I am יהוה that healeth thee. [last part also in God's I AM, p. 12]

Lev. 19:37 Therefore shall ye <u>observe all My statutes, and all My judgments</u>, and do them: I am יהוה.

Lev. 20:22 Ye shall therefore <u>keep all My statutes, and all My judgments</u>, and do them: that the land, whither I bring you to dwell therein, spue you not out.

Lev. 26:14-17 But if ye will not hearken unto Me, and will not <u>do all these commandments</u>; 15 And if ye shall despise My statutes, or if your soul abhor My judgments, so that ye will not <u>do all My commandments</u>, but that ye break My covenant: 16 I also will do this unto you; I will even appoint over you terror, consumption, and the burning ague, that shall consume the eyes, and cause sorrow of heart: and ye shall sow your seed in vain, for your enemies shall eat it. 17 And I will set My face against you, and ye shall be slain before your enemies: they that hate you shall reign over you; and ye shall flee when none pursueth you.

Num. 1:54 And the children of Israel did <u>according to all</u> that יהוה commanded Moses...

Num. 15:22-24 And if ye have erred, and not <u>observed all these commandments</u>, which יהוה hath spoken unto Moses, 23 Even all that יהוה hath commanded you by the hand of Moses, from the day that יהוה commanded Moses, and henceforward among your generations; 24 Then it shall be, ... [sacrifices for cleansing from disobedience are listed]

Num. 15:39 And it shall be unto you for a fringe, that ye may look upon it, and <u>remember all the commandments</u> of יהוה, and do them; and that ye seek not after your own heart and your own eyes, after which ye use to go a whoring: [also in Fringe/Tzit-tzit, p. 191]

Deut. 5:31 [God to Moses] But as for thee, stand thou here by Me, and I will speak unto thee <u>all the commandments, and the statutes, and the judgments</u>, which thou shalt teach them, that they may do them in the land which I give them to possess it.

Deut. 6:2 That thou mightest fear יהוה thy God, <u>to keep all His statutes and His command-ments</u>, which I command thee, thou, and thy son, and thy son's son, all the days of thy life; and that thy days may be prolonged.

Deut. 6:25 And it shall be our righteousness, if we observe to <u>do all these commandments</u> before יהוה our God, as He hath commanded us.

Deut. 8:1 <u>All the commandments</u> which I command thee this day shall ye observe to do, that ye may live, and multiply, and go in and possess the land which יהוה sware unto your fathers.

Deut. 11:8-9 Therefore shall ye keep all the commandments which I command you this day, that ye may be strong, and go in and possess the land, whither ye go to possess it; 9 And that ye may prolong your days in the land, which יהוה sware unto your fathers to give unto them and to their seed, a land that floweth with milk and honey.

Deut. 11:22-24 For if ye shall diligently <u>keep all these commandments</u> which I command you, to do them, to love יהוה your God, to <u>walk in all His ways</u>, and to cleave unto Him; 23 Then will יהוה drive out all these nations from before you, and ye shall possess greater nations and mightier than yourselves. 24 Every place whereon the soles of your feet shall tread shall be yours.... [also in Blessings for Obedience, p. 227 and verse 22 also in Love יהוה, p. 238]

Deut. 11:32 And ye shall observe to <u>do all the statutes and judgments</u> which I set before you this day.

Deut. 12:28 Observe and hear <u>all these words which I command thee</u>, that it may go well with thee, and with thy children after thee **forever**, when thou doest that which is good and right in the sight of יהוה thy God. [also in That it May Go Well, p. 257]

Deut. 13:17-18 ...that יהוה may ... have compassion upon thee, and multiply thee ... [w]hen thou shalt hearken to the voice of יהוה thy God, to <u>keep all His commandments</u> which I command thee this day, to do that which is right in the eyes of יהוה thy God.

Deut. 15:5-6 Only if thou carefully hearken unto the voice of יהוה thy God, to observe to <u>do all these commandments</u> which I command thee this day. 6 For יהוה thy God blesseth thee, as He promised thee: and thou shalt lend unto many nations, but thou shalt not borrow; and thou shalt reign over many nations, but they shall not reign over thee. [also in Lending,p. 125]

Deut. 19:9 If thou shalt <u>keep all these commandments</u> to do them, which I command thee this day, to love יהוה thy God, and to walk ever in His ways; then shalt thou add three cities more for thee, beside these three: [also in Love יהוה your God, p. 238]

Deut. 26:16-end This day יהוה thy God hath commanded thee to do these statutes and judgments: thou shalt therefore keep and do them **with all thine heart, and with all thy soul**. 17 Thou hast avouched יהוה this day to be thy God, and to walk in His ways, and to keep His statutes, and His commandments, and His judgments, and to hearken unto His voice: 18 And יהוה hath avouched thee this day to be His peculiar people, as He hath promised thee, and that thou shouldest <u>keep all His commandments</u>; 19 And to make thee high above all nations which He hath made, in praise, and in name, and in honour; and that thou mayest be an holy people unto יהוה thy God, as He hath spoken. [also in Obey יהוה, p. 26]]

Deut. 27:1 And Moses with the elders of Israel commanded the people, saying, <u>Keep all the commandments</u> which I command you this day.

Deut. 27:26 Cursed be He that confirmeth not <u>all the words of this Torah</u> to do them. And all the people shall say, Amen.

Deut. 28:1-3 and on. And it shall come to pass, if thou shalt hearken diligently unto the voice of יהוה thy God, to observe and to <u>do all His commandments</u> which I command thee this day, that יהוה thy God will set thee on high above all nations of the earth: 2 And all these blessings shall come on thee, and overtake thee, if thou shalt hearken unto the voice of יהוה thy God. 3 Blessed shalt thou be in the city, and blessed shalt thou be in the field. ...[also in Blessings, p.227]

Deut. 28:15-17 But it shall come to pass, if thou wilt **not** hearken unto the voice of יהוה thy God, to observe to <u>do all His commandments and His statutes</u> which I command thee this day; that all these curses shall come upon thee, and overtake thee: 16 Cursed shalt thou be in the city, and cursed shalt thou be in the field. 17 Cursed shall be thy basket and thy store.... [*Many more curses listed.*] [also in Punishment for Disobeying, p. 230]

Deut. 28:58-60, 63 If thou wilt **not** observe to <u>do all the Words of this Torah</u> that are written in this book, that thou mayest fear this glorious and fearful Name, יהוה THY GOD; 59 Then יהוה will make thy plagues wonderful, and the plagues of thy seed, even great plagues, and of long continuance, and sore sicknesses, and of long continuance. 60 Moreover He will bring upon thee all the diseases of Egypt, which thou wast afraid of; and they shall cleave unto thee. ... 63 And it shall come to pass, that as יהוה rejoiced over you to do you good, and to multiply you; so יהוה will rejoice over you to destroy you, and to bring you to nought; and ye shall be plucked from off the land whither thou goest to possess it. 64 And יהוה shall scatter thee among all people, from the one end of the earth even unto the other.... [also in Punishment for Disobeying, p. 230]

Deut. 29:29 The secret things belong unto יהוה our God: but those things which are revealed belong unto us and to our children **forever**, that we may <u>do all the Words of this Torah</u>.

Deut. 30:8-10 And thou shalt return and obey the voice of יהוה, and <u>do all His commandments</u> which I command thee this day. 9 And יהוה thy God will make thee plenteous in every work of thine hand, in the fruit of thy body, and in the fruit of thy cattle, and in the fruit of thy land, for good: for יהוה will again rejoice over thee for good, as He rejoiced over thy fathers: 10 If thou shalt hearken unto the voice of יהוה thy God, to keep His commandments and His statutes which are written in this book of the Torah, and if thou turn unto יהוה thy God **with all thine heart, and with all thy soul.** [also in Blessings, p. 228; Love יהוה p. 238]

Deut. 31:10-13 And Moses commanded them, saying, At the end of every seven years, in the solemnity of the year of release, in the Feast of Tabernacles [Sukkot], 11 When all Israel is come to appear before יהוה thy God in the place which He shall choose, thou shalt read this Torah before all Israel in their hearing. 12 Gather the people together, men, and women, and children, and thy stranger that is within thy gates, that they may hear, and that they may learn, and fear יהוה your God, and observe to <u>do all the Words of this Torah</u>: 13 And that their children, which have not known any thing, may hear, and learn to fear יהוה your God, as long as ye live in the land whither ye go over Jordan to possess it. [also in Shmitah, p. 156; Sukkot, p. 180; and in Teach Your Children, p. 194]

Deut. 32:45-47 And Moses made an end of speaking all these Words to all Israel: 46 And He said unto them, Set your hearts unto <u>all the Words</u> which I testify among you this day, which ye shall command your children to observe to do, <u>all the Words of this Torah</u>. 47 For it is not a vain thing for you; because it is your life: and through this thing ye shall prolong your days in the land, whither ye go over Jordan to possess it. [also in Teach Your Children, p. 194]

YESHUA יֵשׁוּעַ

Matt. 5:17- 20 Think not that I am come to destroy the Torah, or the Prophets: I am not come to destroy, but to fulfill. 18 For verily I say unto you, till heaven and earth pass, one jot or one tittle shall in no wise pass from the Torah, till all be fulfilled. 19 <u>Whosoever therefore shall break one of these least commandments,</u> and shall teach men so, he <u>shall be called the least in the Kingdom of Heaven</u>: but whosoever shall do and teach them, the same shall be called great in the Kingdom of Heaven. 20 For I say unto you, That except your righteousness shall exceed the righteousness of the scribes and Pharisees, ye shall in no case enter into the Kingdom of Heaven. [also in Blessings, p. 228 and Punishment, p. 233]

Matt. 28:20 Teaching them <u>to observe all things whatsoever I have commanded you</u>: and, lo, I am with you alway, even unto the end of the world. Amen.

APOSTLES

Rom. 2:23 You who make your boast in the Torah, do you dishonor God through breaking the Torah?

James 1:25 But whoso looketh into the <u>perfect Torah of liberty, and continueth therein</u>, he being not a forgetful hearer, but a doer of the work, this man shall be blessed in his deed. [also in Blessings, p. 228]

James 2:10-12 For whosoever shall <u>keep the whole Torah</u>, and yet offend in one point, he is guilty of all. 11 For he that said, Do not commit adultery [*which Yeshua said is also just lusting*], said also, Do not kill [*which Yeshua said is also just being angry*]. Now if thou commit no adultery, yet if thou kill, thou art become a transgressor of the Torah. 12 So speak ye, and so do, as they that shall be judged by the Torah of liberty.

5. OBEY יהוה,
KEEP HIS COMMANDMENTS

Lev. 18:4-5 Ye shall do my judgments, and keep mine ordinances, to walk therein: I am יהוה your God. 5 Ye shall therefore keep My statutes, and My judgments: which if a man do, he shall live in them: I am יהוה.

Lev. 20:8 And ye shall keep My statutes, and do them: I am יהוה which sanctify you.

Lev. 22:31 Therefore shall ye keep My commandments, and do them: I am יהוה.

Lev. 26:3-6 If ye walk in My statutes, and keep My commandments, and do them; 4 Then I will give you rain in due season, and the land shall yield her increase, and the trees of the field shall yield their fruit. 5 And your threshing shall reach unto the vintage, and the vintage shall reach unto the sowing time: and ye shall eat your bread to the full, and dwell in your land safely. 6 And I will give peace in the land, and ye shall lie down, and none shall make you afraid: ...

Lev. 26:18-20 And if ye will not yet for all this hearken unto Me, then I will punish you seven times more for your sins. 19 And I will break the pride of your power; and I will make your heaven as iron, and your earth as brass: 20 And your strength shall be spent in vain: for your land shall not yield her increase, neither shall the trees of the land yield their fruits.

Lev. 26:21-22 And if ye walk contrary unto Me, and will not hearken unto Me; I will bring seven times more plagues upon you according to your sins. 22 I will also send wild beasts among you, which shall rob you of your children, and destroy your cattle, and make you few in number; and your high ways shall be desolate.

Lev. 26:23-26 And if ye will not be reformed by Me by these things, but will walk contrary unto Me; 24 Then will I also walk contrary unto you, and will punish you yet seven times for your sins. 25 And I will bring a sword upon you, that shall avenge the quarrel of my covenant: and when ye are gathered together within your cities, I will send the pestilence among you; and ye shall be delivered into the hand of the enemy. 26 And when I have broken the staff of your bread, ten women shall bake your bread in one oven, and they shall deliver you your bread again by weight: and ye shall eat, and not be satisfied.

Lev. 26:27-29 And if ye will not for all this hearken unto Me, but walk contrary unto Me; 28 Then I will walk contrary unto you also in fury; and I, even I, will chastise you seven times for your sins. 29 And ye shall eat the flesh of your sons, and the flesh of your daughters shall ye eat.

Lev. 26:40-43 If they shall confess their iniquity, and the iniquity of their fathers, with their trespass which they trespassed against Me, and that also they have walked contrary unto Me; 41 And that I also have walked contrary unto them, and have brought them into the land of their enemies; if then their uncircumcised hearts be humbled, and they then accept of the punishment of their iniquity: 42 Then will I remember My covenant with Jacob, and also

My covenant with Isaac, and also My covenant with Abraham will I remember; and I will remember the land. 43 The land also shall be left of them, and shall enjoy her Sabbaths, while she lieth desolate without them: and they shall accept of the punishment of their iniquity: because, even because they despised my judgments, and because their soul abhorred my statutes. [also in Punishment (Repentance), p. 233]

Num 14:20-23 And יהוה said, I have pardoned according to thy word: 21 But as truly as I live, all the earth shall be filled with the glory of יהוה. 22 Because all those men which have seen My glory, and My miracles, which I did in Egypt and in the wilderness, and have tempted Me now these ten times, and have not hearkened to My voice; 23 Surely they shall not see the land which I sware unto their fathers, neither shall any of them that provoked Me see it:

Num. 15:30-31 But the soul that doeth ought presumptuously, whether he be born in the land, or a stranger, the same reproacheth יהוה; and that soul shall be cut off from among his people. 31 Because he hath despised the Word of יהוה, and hath broken His commandment, that soul shall utterly be cut off; his iniquity shall be upon him. [verse 30 in One Torah, p. 87]

Deut. 4:6 Keep therefore and do them; for this is your wisdom and your understanding in the sight of the nations, which shall hear all these statutes, and say, Surely this great nation is a wise and understanding people.

Deut. 5:1-2, 4 ... Hear, O Israel, the statutes and judgments which I speak in your ears this day, that ye may learn them, and keep, and do them. 2 יהוה our God made a covenant with us in Horeb. ... 4 יהוה talked with you face to face in the mount out of the midst of the fire...

Deut. 6:17 Ye shall diligently keep the commandments of יהוה your God, and His testimonies, and His statutes, which He hath commanded thee.

Deut. 7:11-15 Thou shalt therefore keep the commandments, and the statutes, and the judgments, which I command thee this day, to do them. 12 Wherefore it shall come to pass, if ye hearken to these judgments, and keep, and do them, that יהוה thy God shall keep unto thee the covenant and the mercy which He sware unto thy fathers: 13 And He will love thee, and bless thee, and multiply thee: He will also bless the fruit of thy womb, and the fruit of thy land, thy corn, and thy wine, and thine oil, the increase of thy kine, and the flocks of thy sheep, in the land which he sware unto thy fathers to give thee. 14 Thou shalt be blessed above all people: there shall not be male or female barren among you, or among your cattle. 15 And יהוה will take away from thee all sickness, and will put none of the evil diseases of Egypt, which thou knowest, upon thee; but will lay them upon all them that hate thee.

Deut. 12:1 These are the statutes and judgments, which ye shall observe to do in the land, which יהוה God of thy fathers giveth thee to possess it, all the days that ye live upon the earth.

Deut. 13:4 Ye shall walk after יהוה your God, and fear Him, and keep His commandments, and obey His voice, and ye shall serve him, and cleave unto Him.

KEEP ALL

25

5. Obey יהוה, Keep His commandments (cont.)

Deut. 26:16, 18-19 This day יהוה thy God hath commanded thee to do these statutes and judgments: thou shalt therefore keep and do them **with all thine heart, and with all thy soul**. ... 18 (to end NRSV with יהוה**:**) Today יהוה has obtained your agreement: to be His treasured people, as He promised you, and to keep His commandments; 19 for Him to set you high above all nations that He has made, in praise and in fame and in honor; and for you to be a people holy to יהוה your God, as He promised. [also in Keep All, p. 21]

Deut. 27:9-10 And Moses and the priests the Levites spake unto all Israel, saying, Take heed, and hearken, O Israel; this day thou art become the people of יהוה thy God. 10 Thou shalt therefore obey the voice of יהוה thy God, and do His commandments and His statutes, which I command thee this day.

Deut. 28:9-11 יהוה shall establish thee an holy people unto Himself, as He hath sworn unto thee, if thou shalt keep the commandments of יהוה thy God, and walk in His ways. 10 And all people of the earth shall see that thou art called by the Name of יהוה; and they shall be afraid of thee. 11 And יהוה shall make thee plenteous in goods.... [*lists more blessings.*] [also in Blessings for Obeying, p. 228]

Deut. 28:45-51 Moreover all these curses shall come upon thee, and shall pursue thee, and overtake thee, till thou be destroyed; because thou hearkenedst **not** unto the voice of יהוה thy God, to keep His commandments and His statutes which He commanded thee: 46 And they shall be upon thee for a sign and for a wonder, and upon thy seed **forever**. 47 Because thou servedst **not** יהוה thy God with joyfulness, and with gladness of heart, for the abundance of all things; 48 Therefore shalt thou serve thine enemies which יהוה shall send against thee, in hunger, and in thirst, and in nakedness, and in want of all things: and He shall put a yoke of iron upon thy neck, until He have destroyed thee. 49 יהוה shall bring a nation against thee from far, from the end of the earth, as swift as the eagle flieth; a nation whose tongue thou shalt not understand; 50 A nation of fierce countenance, which shall not regard the person of the old, nor shew favour to the young: 51 And he shall eat the fruit of thy cattle, and the fruit of thy land, until thou be destroyed: ... [also in Punishment for Disobeying, p. 231-232; verse 47 also in Rejoice, p. 186]]

Deut. 29:9 Keep therefore the words of this Covenant, and do them, that ye may **prosper in all that ye do**. [also in Go Well, p. 257]

Deut. 30:1-7 And it shall come to pass, when all these things are come upon thee, the blessing and the curse, which I have set before thee, and thou shalt call them to mind among all the nations, whither יהוה thy God hath driven thee, 2 And shalt return unto יהוה thy God, and shalt obey His voice according to all that I command thee this day, thou and thy children, **with all thine heart, and with all thy soul;** 3 That then יהוה thy God will turn thy captivity, and have compassion upon thee, and will return and gather thee from all the nations, whither יהוה thy God hath scattered thee. 4 If any of thine be driven out unto the outmost parts of heaven, from thence will יהוה thy God gather thee, and from thence will He fetch thee: 5 And יהוה thy God will bring thee into the land which thy fathers possessed, and thou shalt possess it; and He will do thee good, and multiply thee above thy fathers. 6 ... 7 And יהוה thy God will put all these curses upon thine enemies, and on them that hate thee, which persecuted thee. [also in Punishment (Repentance), p. 233; verse 2 in Love יהוה, p. 238]

Deut. 30:15-18 See, I have set before thee this day life and good, and death and evil; 16 In that I command thee this day to love יהוה thy God, to walk in His ways, and to keep His commandments and His statutes and His judgments, that thou mayest live and multiply: and יהוה thy God shall bless thee in the land whither thou goest to possess it. 17 But if thine heart turn away, so that thou wilt not hear, but shalt be drawn away, and worship other gods, and serve them; 18 I denounce unto you this day, that ye shall surely perish, and that ye shall not prolong your days upon the land, whither thou passest over Jordan to go to possess it. [[also in Punishment, p. 233; Choose Life, p. 235; verse 16 in Love יהוה, p. 238]

Deut. 30:19-20 I call heaven and earth to record this day against you, that I have set before you life and death, blessing and cursing: therefore choose life, that both thou and thy seed may live: 20 That thou mayest love יהוה thy God, and that thou mayest obey His voice, and that thou mayest cleave unto Him: for He is thy life, and the length of thy days: that thou mayest dwell in the land which יהוה sware unto thy fathers, to Abraham, to Isaac, and to Jacob, to give them. [also in Choose Life, p. 235-36; verse 20 in Love יהוה, p. 238]

PSALMS

Ps. 94:12-13a Blessed is the man whom thou chastenest, O יהוה, and teachest him out of Thy Torah; That Thou mayest give him rest from the days of adversity....

Ps. 119:5 O that my ways were directed to keep Thy statutes!

Ps. 119:10 With my whole heart have I sought Thee: O let me not wander from Thy commandments. [also in Love יהוה, p. 239]

Ps. 119:18 Open Thou mine eyes, that I may behold wondrous things out of Thy Torah.

Ps. 119:33 HEY ה Teach me, O יהוה, the way of Thy statutes; and I shall keep it unto the end.

Ps. 119:34 Give me understanding, and I shall keep Thy Torah; yea, I shall observe it with my whole heart. [also in Love יהוה, p. 239]

Ps. 119:35 Make me to go in the path of Thy commandments; for therein do I delight.

Ps.119:47 And I will delight myself in Thy commandments, which I have loved.

Ps. 119:51 (NKJV) The proud have me in great derision, Yet I do not turn aside from Your law [Torah].

Ps. 119:60 (NKJV) I made haste, and did not delay To keep Your commandments.

Ps. 119:63 I am a companion of all them that fear thee, and of them that keep Thy precepts.

Ps. 119:69-70 The proud have forged a lie against me: but I will keep Thy precepts with my whole heart. ... I delight in Thy Torah. [also in Love יהוה, p. 239]

Ps. 119:72 The Torah of Thy mouth is better unto me than thousands of gold and silver.

Ps. 119:73 JOD [YOD] י. Thy hands have made me and fashioned me: give me understanding, that I may learn Thy commandments.

Ps. 119:77b ...Thy Torah is my delight.

Ps. 119:97 MEM מ. O how love I Thy Torah! it is my meditation all the day.

Ps. 119:100 I understand more than the ancients, because I keep Thy precepts.

Ps 119:113 SAMECH ס. I hate vain thoughts: but Thy Torah do I love.

Ps. 119:104 Through Thy precepts I get understanding: therefore I hate every false way.

Ps. 119:127 Therefore I love Thy commandments above gold; yea, above fine gold.

Ps. 119:142b ... Thy Torah is the truth.

Psa 119:163 I hate and abhor lying: but Thy Torah do I love.

Ps. 119:165 (NKJV) Great peace have those who love Your law [Torah], And nothing causes them to stumble. [also in Covenant of Peace, p. 237]

THE PROPHETS

Ezek. 20:19-20 I am יהוה your God; walk in My statutes, and keep My judgments, and do them....

YESHUA ישוע

Matt. 19:17b ...if thou wilt **enter into life**, keep the commandments. [also in Go Well, p. 257]

John 14:21-24 (NKJV) He who **has My commandments and keeps them,** it is he who loves Me. And he who loves Me will be loved by My Father, and I will love him and manifest Myself to him. ... "If anyone loves Me, he will **keep My Word**; and My Father will love him, and We will come to him and make Our home with him. 24 He who does not love Me does not keep My Words; and the Word which you hear is not Mine but the Father's who sent Me. [also in Love יהוה, p. 240]

John 15:7-8 If ye abide in Me, and **My Words abide in you**, ye shall ask what ye will, and it shall be done unto you. 8 Herein is My Father glorified, that ye bear much fruit; so shall ye be My disciples.

John 17:6 (NKJV) I have manifested Your Name to the men whom You have given Me out of the world. They were Yours, You gave them to Me, and they have **kept Your Word.**

APOSTLES

Acts 5:32b ...the Holy [Spirit] whom God hath given to them that **obey Him.**

I John 2:3-6 And hereby we do know that we know Him, if we **keep His commandments.** 4 He that saith, I know Him, and keepeth not His commandments, is a liar, and the truth is not in him. 5 But whoso keepeth His word, in him verily is the love of God perfected: hereby know we that we are in Him. 6 He that saith he abideth in Him ought himself also so to walk, even as He walked.

I John 3:24 (RSV) All who **keep His commandments** abide in Him, and He in them. And by this we know that He abides in us, by the Spirit which He has given us.

2 John 1:6 And this is love, that we **walk after His commandments**. [also in Love יהוה, p. 238]

6. DO NOT ADD OR TAKE AWAY

Deut. 4:2 Ye shall not add unto the Word which I command you, neither shall ye diminish ought from it, that ye may keep the commandments of יהוה your God which I command you.

Deut. 12:32 What thing soever I command you, observe to do it: thou shalt not add thereto, nor diminish from it.

AFTER TORAH

Prov. 30:5-6 Every Word of God is pure: He is a shield unto them that put their trust in Him. 6 Add thou not unto His Words, lest He reprove thee, and thou be found a liar.

1 Cor. 4:6 (RSV) ...that you may learn by us not to go beyond what is written....

2 John 1:9 (NRSV) Everyone who does not abide in the teaching of Christ, but goes beyond it, does not have God....

Rev. 22:18-19 For I testify unto every man that heareth the Words of the prophecy of this book, If any man shall add unto these things, God shall add unto him the plagues that are written in this book: 19 And if any man shall take away from the Words of the book of this prophecy, God shall take away his part out of the Book of Life, and out of the Holy City, and from the things which are written in this book.

7. DO NOT TEMPT OR TEST יהוה

Ex. 17:7 And he called the name of the place Massah, and Meribah, because of the chiding of the children of Israel, and because they **tempted** יהוה, saying, Is יהוה among us, or not?

Num 14:22 Because all those men which have seen My glory, and My miracles, which I did in Egypt and in the wilderness, and have **tempted** Me now these ten times, and have not hearkened to My voice;

Deut. 6:16 Ye shall not tempt יהוה your God, as ye tempted Him in Massah.

PSALMS

Psa 78:18 And they tempted God in their heart by asking meat for their lust.

Psa 78:41 Yea, they turned back and tempted God, and limited the Holy One of Israel.

Psa 78:56 Yet they tempted and provoked the most high God, and kept not His testimonies:

Psa 95:8-11 Harden not your heart, as in the provocation, and as in the day of temptation in the wilderness: 9 When your fathers tempted Me, proved Me, and saw My work. 10 Forty years long was I grieved with this generation, and said, It is a people that do err in their heart, and they have not known My ways: 11 Unto whom I sware in My wrath that they should not enter into My rest.

Psa 106:14 But lusted exceedingly in the wilderness, and tempted God in the desert.

YESHUA ישוע and APOSTLES

Matt. 4:7 ישוע said unto him, It is written again, Thou shalt not **tempt** יהוה thy God.

Hebrews 3:7-19 Wherefore (as the Holy Spirit saith, Today if ye will hear His voice, 8 Harden not your hearts, as in the provocation, in the day of temptation in the wilderness: 9 When your fathers tempted Me, proved Me, and saw My works forty years. 10 Wherefore I was grieved with that generation, and said, They do alway err in their heart; and they have not known My ways. 11 So I swear in My wrath, They shall not enter into My rest.) 12 Take heed, brethren, lest there be in any of you an evil heart of unbelief, in departing from the living God. 13 But exhort one another daily, while it is called Today; lest any of you be hardened through the deceitfulness of sin. 14 For we are made partakers of Messiah, if we hold the beginning of our confidence steadfast unto the end; 15 While it is said, Today if ye will hear His voice, harden not your hearts, as in the provocation. 16 For some, when they had heard, did provoke: howbeit not all that came out of Egypt by Moses. 17 But with whom was He grieved forty years? Was it not with them that had sinned, whose carcases fell in the wilderness? 18 And to whom swear He that they should not enter into His rest, but to them that believed not? 19 So we see that they could not enter in because of unbelief.

8. THOU SHALT HAVE NO OTHER GODS BEFORE ME

Ex. 20:3 Thou shalt have no other gods before Me.

Ex. 22:20 He that sacrificeth unto any god, save unto יהוה only, he shall be utterly destroyed.

Ex. 22:28a Thou shalt not revile God (Elohim),

Ex. 23:13 And in all things that I have said unto you be circumspect: and make no mention of the name of other gods, neither let it be heard out of thy mouth. [also in Don't mention the names of other gods, p. 100]

Ex. 34:13-14 But ye shall destroy their altars, break their images, and cut down their groves: For thou shalt worship no other god: for יהוה, whose name is Jealous, is a jealous God:...

Deut. 4:35 Unto thee it was shewed, that thou mightest know that יהוה He *is* God; *there is* **none else** beside Him.

Deut. 4:39 Know therefore this day, and consider *it* in thine heart, that יהוה He *is* God in heaven above, and upon the earth beneath: *there is* none else.

Deut. 5:7 Thou shalt have none other gods before Me.

Deut. 6:12-13 Then beware lest thou forget יהוה, which brought thee forth out of the land of Egypt, from the house of bondage. Thou shalt fear יהוה thy God, and serve Him, and shalt swear by His Name. [also in I am יהוה p. 11, and Name in vain, p. 40]

Deut. 6:14-15 Ye shall not go after other gods, of the gods of the people which are round about you; (For יהוה thy God is a jealous God among you) lest the anger of יהוה thy God be kindled against thee, and destroy thee from off the face of the earth.

Deut. 7:4 For they will turn away thy son from following Me, that they may serve other gods: so will the anger of יהוה be kindled against you, and destroy thee suddenly.

Deut. 7:16 And thou shalt consume all the people which יהוה thy God shall deliver thee; thine eye shall have no pity upon them: neither shalt thou serve their gods; for that will be a snare unto thee. [also in Destroy heathen nations in Canaan, p. 111]

Deut. 8:19 And it shall be, if thou do at all forget יהוה thy God, and walk after other gods, and serve them, and worship them, I testify against you this day that ye shall surely perish.

Deut. 10:17-18 For יהוה your God is God of gods, and Lord of lords, a great God, a mighty, and a terrible, which regardeth not persons, nor taketh reward: He doth execute the judgment of the fatherless and widow, and loveth the stranger, in giving him food and raiment. [also in I am יהוה p. 11]

Deut. 10:20-21 Thou shalt fear יהוה thy God; Him shalt thou serve, and to Him shalt thou cleave, and swear by His Name. He is thy praise, and He is thy God, that hath done for thee these great and terrible things, which thine eyes have seen. [also in Name in vain, p. 40]

8. No other gods before Me (cont.)

Deut. 12:30 Take heed to thyself that thou be not snared..., after that they be destroyed from before thee; and that thou <u>inquire not after their gods</u>, saying, How did these nations serve their gods? Even so will I do likewise. Thou shalt not do so unto יהוה thy God: for every abomination to יהוה, which He hateth, have they done unto their gods; for even their sons and their daughters they have burnt in the fire to their gods. [also in Do not Inquire, p. 102]

Deut. 13:2-3 And the sign or the wonder come to pass, whereof he spake unto thee, saying, Let us go after other gods, which thou hast not known, and let us serve them; Thou shalt not hearken unto the words of that prophet, or that dreamer of dreams: for יהוה your God proveth you, to know whether ye love יהוה your God with all your heart and with all your soul. [also in False prophets, p. 106]

Deut. 13:6b-8, 9...entice thee secretly, saying, Let us go and serve other gods, which thou hast not known, thou, nor thy fathers; Namely, of the gods of the people which are round about you, nigh unto thee, or far off from thee, from the one end of the earth even unto the other end of the earth; Thou shalt not consent unto him, nor hearken unto him; ... But thou shalt surely kill him; thine hand shall be first upon him to put him to death, and afterwards the hand of all the people.

Deut. 13:12-17 If thou shalt hear say in one of thy cities, which יהוה thy God hath given thee to dwell there, saying, 13 Certain men, the children of Belial, are gone out from among you, and have withdrawn the inhabitants of their city, saying, Let us go and serve other gods, which ye have not known; 14 Then shalt thou inquire, and make search, and ask diligently; and, behold, if it be truth, and the thing certain, that such abomination is wrought among you; 15 Thou shalt surely smite the inhabitants of that city with the edge of the sword, destroying it utterly, and all that is therein, and the cattle thereof, with the edge of the sword. 16 And thou shalt gather all the spoil of it into the midst of the street thereof, and shalt burn with fire the city, and all the spoil thereof every whit, for יהוה thy God: and it shall be an heap **forever**; it shall not be built again. 17 And there shall cleave nought of the cursed thing to thine hand: that יהוה may turn from the fierceness of His anger, and shew thee mercy, and have compassion upon thee, and multiply thee, as He hath sworn unto thy fathers;

Deut. 17:2-5 If there be found among you, within any of thy gates which יהוה thy God giveth thee, man or woman, that hath wrought wickedness in the sight of יהוה thy God, in transgressing His covenant, And hath gone and served other gods, and worshipped them, either the sun, or moon, or any of the host of heaven, which I have not commanded; And it be told thee, and thou hast heard of it, and enquired diligently, and, behold, it be true, and the thing certain, that such abomination is wrought in Israel: Then shalt thou bring forth that man or that woman, which have committed that wicked thing, unto thy gates, even that man or that woman, and shalt stone them with stones, till they die.

Deut. 29:23-28 And that the whole land thereof is brimstone, and salt, and burning, that it is not sown, nor beareth, nor any grass groweth therein, like the overthrow of Sodom, and Gomorrah, Admah, and Zeboim, which יהוה overthrew in his anger, and in his wrath: 24 Even all nations shall say, Wherefore hath יהוה done thus unto this land? what meaneth the heat of this great anger? 25 Then men shall say, <u>Because they have forsaken the covenant of יהוה God of their fathers,</u> which He made with them when He brought them forth out of the land of Egypt: 26 <u>For they went and served other gods,</u> and worshipped them, gods whom they knew not, and whom He had not given unto them: 27 And the anger of יהוה was kindled against this land, to bring upon it all the curses that are written in this book: 28 And יהוה rooted them out of their land in anger, and in wrath, and in great indignation, and cast them into another land, as it is this day.

Deut. 30:17-18 But if thine heart turn away, so that thou wilt not hear, but shalt be drawn away, and worship other gods, and serve them; 18 I denounce unto you this day, that ye shall surely perish, and that ye shall not prolong your days upon the land, whither thou passest over Jordan to go to possess it. [also in Obey, p. 27]

Deut. 31:16-17 And יהוה said unto Moses, Behold, thou shalt sleep with thy fathers; and this people will rise up, and go a whoring after the gods of the strangers of the land, whither they go to be among them, and will forsake Me, and break My covenant which I have made with them. 17 Then My anger shall be kindled against them in that day, and I will forsake them, and I will hide My face from them, and they shall be devoured, and many evils and troubles shall befall them; so that they will say in that day, Are not these evils come upon us, because our God is not among us?

Deut. 31:18-21 And I will surely hide My face in that day for all the evils which they shall have wrought, in that they are turned unto other gods. 19 Now therefore write ye this song for you, and teach it the children of Israel: put it in their mouths, that this song may be a witness for Me against the children of Israel. 20 For when I shall have brought them into the land which I sware unto their fathers, that floweth with milk and honey; and they shall have eaten and filled themselves, and waxen fat; then will they turn unto other gods, and serve them, and provoke Me, and break My covenant. 21 And it shall come to pass, when many evils and troubles are befallen them, that this song shall testify against them as a witness; for it shall not be forgotten out of the mouths of their seed: for I know their imagination which they go about, even now, before I have brought them into the land which I sware.

Deut. 32:17,19 They <u>sacrificed unto devils, not to God</u>; to gods whom they knew not, <u>to new gods that came newly up,</u> whom your fathers feared not. ... 19 And when יהוה saw it ... He said, I will hide My face from them, I will see what their end shall be: ... they have provoked Me to anger.... *[See 1 Cor. 10:20, next page.]*

AFTER TORAH

I Kings 8:60 That all the people of the earth may know that יהוה *is* God, *and that there is* **none else**.

Isaiah 45:21 Tell ye, and bring *them* near; yea, let them take counsel together: who hath declared this from ancient time? *Who* hath told it from that time? *Have* not I יהוה? And *there is* no God **else** beside Me; a just God and a Saviour; *there is* **none** beside Me.

Jer. 7:6-7 If ye oppress not the stranger, the fatherless, and the widow, and shed not innocent blood in this place, neither walk after other gods to your hurt: Then will I cause you to dwell in this place, in the Land that I gave to your fathers, **forever and ever.** [also in No killing, p. 49, Strangers, p. 86, and Widows, p. 88]

YESHUA יֵשׁוּעַ

Matt. 6:24 and Luke 16:13 No man can serve two masters: for either he will hate the one, and love the other; or else he will hold to the one, and despise the other. Ye cannot serve God and mammon *[money]*.

Matt. 10:32-39 (NKJV) "Therefore whoever confesses Me before men, him I will also confess before My Father who is in heaven. 33 But whoever denies Me before men, him I will also deny before My Father who is in heaven. 34 "Do not think that I came to bring peace on earth. I did not come to bring peace but a sword. 35 For I have come to 'set a man against his father, a daughter against her mother, and a daughter-in-law against her mother-in-law'; 36 and 'a man's enemies will be those of his own household.' 37 He who loves father or mother more than Me is not worthy of Me. And he who loves son or daughter more than Me is not worthy of Me. 38 And he who does not take his cross and follow after Me is not worthy of Me. 39 He who finds his life will lose it, and he who loses his life for My sake will find it."

Matt. 19:17 and Mark 10:18 and Luke 18:19 ...there is none good but one, that is, God....

Mark 12: 29 And יֵשׁוּעַ answered him, The first of all the commandments is, Hear, O Israel; The Lord our God is one Lord.

APOSTLES

1 Cor. 8:4b-6 ...there is none other God but one. 5 For though there be that are called gods, whether in heaven or in earth, (as there be gods many, and lords many,) 6 But to us there is but one God, the Father, of whom are all things, and we in Him; and one Lord יֵשׁוּעַ Messiah, by whom are all things, and we by Him.

1 Cor. 10:20 But I say, that the things which the Gentiles sacrifice, they sacrifice to devils, and not to God: and I would not that ye should have fellowship with devils.

Gal. 3:20 Now a mediator is not a mediator of one, but God is one.

Eph. 4:4-6 There is one body, and one Spirit, even as ye are called in one hope of your calling; 5 One Lord, one faith, one baptism, 6 One God and Father of all, who is above all, and through all, and in you all.

1 Tim. 2:3b-6 ...God our Saviour; 4 Who will have all men to be saved, and to come unto the knowledge of the truth. 5 For there is one God, and one mediator between God and men, the man Messiah יֵשׁוּעַ; 6 Who gave himself a ransom for all, to be testified in due time.

James 2:19-20 Thou believest that there is one God; thou doest well: the devils also believe, and tremble. 20 But wilt thou know, O vain man, that faith without works is dead?

9. NO IDOLS

Ex. 20:4 Thou shalt not make unto thee any graven image, or any likeness of any thing that is in heaven above, or that is in the earth beneath, or that is in the water under the earth:

Ex. 20:23 Ye shall not make with me gods of silver, neither shall ye make unto you gods of gold.

Ex. 34:17 Thou shalt make thee no molten gods.

Lev. 19:4 Turn ye not unto idols, nor make to yourselves molten gods: I am יהוה your God.

Lev. 26:1 Ye shall make you no idols nor graven image, neither rear you up a standing image, neither shall ye set up any image of stone in your land, to bow down unto it: for I am יהוה your God.

Lev. 26:30-32 And I will destroy your high places, and cut down your images, and cast your carcases upon the carcases of your idols, and my soul shall abhor you. 31 And I will make your cities waste, and bring your sanctuaries unto desolation, and I will not smell the savour of your sweet odours. 32 And I will bring the land into desolation: and your enemies which dwell therein shall be astonished at it....

Num. 33:51-52 Speak unto the children of Israel, and say unto them, When ye are passed over Jordan into the land of Canaan; 52 Then ye shall drive out all the inhabitants of the land from before you, and destroy all their pictures, and destroy all their molten images, and quite pluck down all their high places: [also in Destroy heathen..., p. 113]

Deut. 4:15-16 Take ye therefore good heed unto yourselves; for ye saw no manner of similitude on the day that יהוה spake unto you in Horeb [Mt. Sinai] out of the midst of the fire: Lest ye corrupt yourselves, and make you a graven image, the similitude of any figure, the likeness of male or female, The likeness of any beast that is on the earth, the likeness of any winged fowl that flieth in the air, The likeness of any thing that creepeth on the ground, the likeness of any fish that is in the waters beneath the earth: And lest thou lift up thine eyes unto heaven, and when thou seest the sun, and the moon, and the stars, even all the host of heaven, shouldest be driven to worship them, and serve them, which יהוה thy God hath divided [NRSV: alloted] unto all nations under the whole heaven.

Deut. 4:23-24 Take heed unto yourselves, lest ye forget the covenant of יהוה your God, which He made with you, and make you a graven image, or the likeness of any thing, which יהוה thy God hath forbidden thee. For יהוה thy God is a consuming fire, even a jealous God.

Deut. 5:8 Thou shalt not make thee any graven image, or any likeness of any thing that is in heaven above, or that is in the earth beneath, or that is in the waters beneath the earth:

Deut. 7:5 But thus shall ye deal with them; ye shall destroy their altars, and break down their images, and cut down their groves, and burn their graven images with fire.

Deut. 7:25-26 The graven images of their gods shall ye burn with fire: thou shalt not desire the silver or gold that is on them, nor take it unto thee, lest thou be snared therein: for it is an abomination to יהוה thy God. Neither shalt thou bring an abomination into thine house, lest thou be a cursed thing like it: but thou shalt utterly detest it, and thou shalt utterly abhor it; for it is a cursed thing.

Deut. 12:2-3 Ye shall utterly destroy all the places, wherein the nations which ye shall possess served their gods, upon the high mountains, and upon the hills, and under every green tree: And ye shall overthrow their altars, and break their pillars, and burn their groves with fire; and ye shall hew down the graven images of their gods, and destroy the names of them out of that place.

Deut. 16:21-22 Thou shalt not plant thee a grove of any trees near unto the altar of יהוה thy God, which thou shalt make thee. 22 Neither shalt thou set thee up any image (NRSV says "stone pillar"); which יהוה thy God hateth. [also in Trees, p. 133 and No Trees, p. 39]

Deut. 27:15 Cursed be the man that maketh any graven or molten image, an abomination unto יהוה, the work of the hands of the craftsman, and putteth it in a secret place.

Deut. 29:17-20 And ye have seen their abominations, and their idols, wood and stone, silver and gold, which were among them:) 18 Lest there should be among you man, or woman, or family, or tribe, whose heart turneth away this day from יהוה our God, to go and serve the gods of these nations; lest there should be among you a root that beareth gall and wormwood; 19 And it come to pass, when he heareth the words of this curse, that he bless himself in his heart, saying, I shall have peace, though I walk in the imagination of mine heart, to add drunkenness to thirst: 20 יהוה will not spare him, but then the anger of יהוה and his jealousy shall smoke against that man, and all the curses that are written in this book shall lie upon him, and יהוה shall blot out his name from under heaven.

AFTER TORAH *[There are 100s of verses against idolatry. Here are a few.]*

2 Kings 17:12 For they served idols, whereof יהוה had said unto them, Ye shall not do this thing.

1 Chron. 16:26; Psalm 96:5 For all the gods of the nations are idols: but יהוה made the heavens.

Psalm 106:36 And they served their idols: which were a snare unto them.

Psalm 115:2-8 (also Psalm 135:15-18) Wherefore should the heathen say, Where is now their God? 3 But our God is in the heavens: He hath done whatsoever He hath pleased. 4 Their idols are silver and gold, the work of men's hands. 5 They have mouths, but they speak not: eyes have they, but they see not: 6 They have ears, but they hear not: noses have they, but they smell not: 7 They have hands, but they handle not: feet have they, but they walk not: neither speak they through their throat. 8 They that make them are like unto them; so is every one that trusteth in them.

Isaiah 31:7 For in that day every man shall cast away his idols of silver, and his idols of gold, which your own hands have made unto you for a sin.

Isaiah 45:16 They shall be ashamed, and also confounded, all of them: they shall go to confusion together that are makers of idols.

Ezek. 14:6; 20:7 Thus saith יהוה; Repent, and turn yourselves from your idols; and turn away your faces from all your abominations. ... Cast ye away every man the abominations of his eyes, and defile not yourselves with the idols of Egypt: I am יהוה your Elohim.

Ezek. 14:7-10 For every one ... which separateth himself from Me, and setteth up his idols in his heart, ... and cometh to a prophet to enquire of him concerning Me; I יהוה will answer him by Myself: 8 And I will set My face against that man, and will make him a sign and a proverb, and I will cut him off from the midst of My people; and ye shall know that I am יהוה. 9 And if the prophet be deceived when he hath spoken a thing, I יהוה have deceived that prophet, and I will stretch out My hand upon him, and will destroy him from the midst of My people Israel. 10 ...the punishment of the prophet shall be even as the punishment of him that seeketh unto him....

Hos. 13:2 And now they sin more and more, and have made them molten images of their silver, and idols according to their own understanding, all of it the work of the craftsmen: they say of them, Let the men that sacrifice kiss the calves.

Hab. 2:18 What profiteth the graven image that the maker thereof hath graven it; the molten image, and a teacher of lies, that the maker of his work trusteth therein, to make dumb idols?

APOSTLES

Acts 15:20; 21:25 But that we write unto them, that they abstain from pollutions of idols, and from fornication, and from things strangled, and from blood. ... 29 That ye abstain from meats offered to idols, ... from which if ye keep yourselves, ye shall do well. 21:25 ...that they keep themselves from things offered to idols....

Rom. 2:22b ...thou that abhorrest idols, dost thou commit sacrilege?

1 Cor. 8:4 As concerning therefore the eating of those things that are offered in sacrifice unto idols, we know that an idol is nothing in the world, and that there is none other God but one.

1 Cor. 10:20-21 But I say, that the things which the Gentiles sacrifice, they sacrifice to devils, and not to God: and I would not that ye should have fellowship with devils. 21 Ye cannot drink the cup of the Lord, and the cup of devils: ye cannot be partakers of the Lord's table, and of the table of devils.

1 Cor. 12:2 Ye know that ye were Gentiles, carried away unto these dumb idols, even as ye were led.

2 Cor. 6:16 And what agreement hath the Temple of God with idols? For ye are the Temple of the living God; as God hath said, I will dwell in them, and walk in them; and I will be their God, and they shall be My people.

Eph. 5:5b ...nor covetous man, who is an idolater, hath any inheritance in the Kingdom of Messiah and of God.

1 Thess. 1:9b-10 ...how ye turned to God from idols to serve the living and true God; 10 And to wait for His Son from heaven, whom He raised from the dead, even ישוע, which delivered us from the wrath to come.

1 John 5:21 Little children, keep yourselves from idols. Amen.

Rev. 2:14, 20 But I have a few things against thee, because thou hast there them that hold the doctrine of Balaam, who taught Balac to cast a stumblingblock before the children of Israel, to eat things sacrificed unto idols, and to commit fornication. ... 20 Notwithstanding I have a few things against thee, because thou sufferest that woman Jezebel, which calleth herself a prophetess, to teach and to seduce my servants to commit fornication, and to eat things sacrificed unto idols.

Rev. 21:8 But ... idolaters, ... shall have their part in the lake which burneth with fire....

Rev. 22:14-15 Blessed are they that ... enter in through the gates into the city. 15 For without are ... murderers, and idolaters.....

10. DON'T BOW DOWN TO IDOLS

Ex. 20:5-6 Thou shalt not bow down thyself to them, nor serve them: for I יהוה thy God am a jealous God, visiting the iniquity of the fathers upon the children unto the third and fourth generation of them that hate me; And shewing mercy unto thousands of them that love me, and keep my commandments.

Ex. 23:24 Thou shalt not bow down to their gods, nor serve them, nor do after their works: but thou shalt utterly overthrow them, and quite break down their images.

Ex. 23:32 Thou shalt make no covenant with them, nor with their gods

Deut. 5:9-10 Thou shalt not bow down thyself unto them, nor serve them: for I יהוה thy God am a jealous God, visiting the iniquity of the fathers upon the children unto the third and fourth generation of them that hate Me, And shewing mercy unto thousands of them that love Me and keep My commandments.

Deut. 7:5,9 But thus shall ye deal with them; ye shall destroy their altars, and break down their images, and cut down their groves, and burn their graven images with fire. ... 9 Know therefore that יהוה thy God, He is God, the faithful God, which keepeth covenant and mercy with them that love Him and keep His commandments **to a thousand generations;** And repayeth them that hate Him to their face, to destroy them: He will not be slack to him that hateth Him, He will repay him to his face.

AFTER TORAH

I Sam. 15:23 For rebellion is as the sin of witchcraft, and <u>stubbornness is as iniquity and idolatry.</u>

Elijah stood against idol worshipers (I Kings 18:20-40)

King Josiah destroyed idols that were in the Temple and all over Israel (2 Kings 23:1-20).

Isaiah 45:23 I have sworn by Myself, the Word is gone out of My mouth in righteousness, and shall not return, That unto Me every knee shall bow, every tongue shall swear.

Daniel and friends wouldn't bow down to Nebuchadnezzar's golden image (Dan. 3).

APOSTLES

Rom. 2:22b   ...thou that abhorrest idols, dost thou commit sacrilege?

Rom. 14:11 For it is written, As I live, saith the Lord, every knee shall bow to Me, and every tongue shall confess to God.

1 Cor. 10:14 Wherefore, my dearly beloved, flee from idolatry. [NRSV: ...flee from the worship of idols.]

Eph. 5:5-6 For this ye know, that no whoremonger, nor unclean person, nor <u>covetous man, who is an idolater,</u> hath any inheritance in the Kingdom of Messiah and of God. 6 Let no man deceive you with vain words: for because of these things cometh the wrath of God upon the children of disobedience.

Phil. 2:10-11 That at the Name of ישוע every knee should bow, of things in heaven, and things in earth, and things under the earth; 11 And that every tongue should confess that ישוע Messiah is Lord, to the Glory of God the Father.

Rev. 9:20 And the rest of the men which were not killed by these plagues yet repented not of the works of their hands, that they should not worship devils, and idols of gold, and silver, and brass, and stone, and of wood: which neither can see, nor hear, nor walk:

11. NO TREES IN THE TEMPLE?

Deut. 16:21-22 Thou shalt not plant thee a grove of any trees near unto the altar of יהוה thy God, which thou shalt make thee.

AFTER TORAH

Psalm 52:8   But I am like a green olive tree in the house of God.

This verse is talking about making idols out of a tree:

Jer. 10:2-5 Thus saith יהוה, Learn not the way of the heathen.... 3 For the customs of the people are vain: for one **cutteth a tree out of the forest,** the **work of the hands** of the workman, with the axe. 4 T**hey deck it with silver and with gold**; they fasten it with nails and with hammers, that it move not. 5 T**hey are upright as the palm tree, <u>but speak not:</u> they must needs be borne, because <u>they cannot go.</u> Be not afraid of them; for <u>they cannot do evil,</u>** neither also is it in them to do good.

In this vision of the new Temple that God gave Ezekiel, there are palm trees carved into the wall:

Ezek. 41:15,17b-20 ...with the **inner Temple** ... by all the wall round about within and without, by measure. 18 And it was made with cherubims and **palm trees**, so that a **palm tree** was between a cherub and a cherub; and every cherub had two faces; 19 So that the face of a man was toward the **palm tree** on the one side, and the face of a young lion toward the **palm tree** on the other side: it was made through all the house round about. 20 From the ground unto above the door were cherubims and **palm trees** made, and **on the wall of the Temple.**

12. NAME IN VAIN

Ex. 20:7 Thou shalt not take the Name of יהוה thy God in vain; for יהוה will not hold him guiltless that taketh His Name in vain.

Lev. 18:21 ...neither shalt thou profane the Name of thy God: I am יהוה. [also in Don't pass children thro fire, p. 104]

Lev. 19:12 And ye shall not swear by My Name falsely, neither shalt thou profane the Name of thy God: I am יהוה.

Lev. 20:3 ...because he hath given of his seed unto Molech, to defile my sanctuary, and to **profane** My Holy **Name**.

Lev. 21:6 They shall be holy unto their God, and not profane the Name of their God:

Lev. 22:2 Speak unto Aaron and to his sons, that they separate themselves from the holy things of the children of Israel, and that they profane not My Holy Name *in those things* which they hallow unto Me: I *am* יהוה.

Lev. 22:32 Neither shall ye profane My Holy Name; but I will be hallowed among the children of Israel: I am יהוה which hallow you, 33 That brought you out of the land of Egypt, to be your God: I am יהוה.

Lev. 24:10-16, 23 And the son of an Israelitish woman, whose father was an Egyptian, went out among the children of Israel: [he] and a man of Israel strove together in the camp; 11 And the Israelitish woman's son blasphemed the Name of יהוה, and cursed. And they brought him unto Moses: (and his mother's name was Shelomith, the daughter of Dibri, of the tribe of Dan:) 12 And they put him in ward, that the mind of יהוה might be shewed them. 13 And יהוה spake unto Moses, saying, 14 Bring forth him that hath cursed without the camp; and let all that heard him lay their hands upon his head, and let all the congregation stone him. 15 And thou shalt speak unto the children of Israel, saying, Whosoever curseth his God shall bear his sin. 16 And he that blasphemeth the Name of יהוה, he shall surely be put to death, and all the congregation shall certainly stone him: as well the stranger, as he that is born in the land, when he blasphemeth the Name of יהוה, shall be put to death. ... 23 ... And the children of Israel did as יהוה commanded Moses.

Deut. 5:11 Thou shalt not take the Name of יהוה thy God in vain: for יהוה will not hold him guiltless that taketh His Name in vain.

Deut. 6:12-13 Then beware lest thou forget יהוה, which brought thee forth out of the land of Egypt, from the house of bondage. Thou shalt fear יהוה thy God, and serve Him, and shalt swear by His Name. [also in I am יהוה, p. 11, and No other gods, p. 31]

Deut. 10:20-21 Thou shalt fear יהוה thy God; Him shalt thou serve, and to Him shalt thou cleave, and swear by His Name. He is thy praise, and He is thy God, that hath done for thee these great and terrible things, which thine eyes have seen. [also in No other Gods, p. 31]

Ezek. 39:7 So will I make My Holy Name known in the midst of My people Israel; and I will not let them pollute My Holy Name any more: and the heathen shall know that I am יהוה, the Holy One in Israel.

Amos. 2:7 That pant after the dust of the earth on the head of the poor, and turn aside the way of the meek: and a man and his father will go in unto the *same* maid, to **profane** My Holy **Name**:

YESHUA ישוע

John 14:12-14 Verily, verily, I say unto you, He that believeth on Me, the works that I do shall he do also; and greater works than these shall he do; because I go unto My Father. 13 And whatsoever ye shall ask **in My Name,** that will I do, that the Father may be glorified in the Son. 14 If ye shall ask any thing in My Name, I will do it.

Mark 16:17-18 And these signs shall follow them that believe; **In My Name** shall they cast out devils; they shall speak with new tongues; 18 They shall take up serpents; and if they drink any deadly thing, it shall not hurt them; they shall lay hands on the sick, and they shall recover.

APOSTLES

Acts 4:12 Neither is there salvation in any other: for there is **none other Name under heaven** given among men, whereby we must be saved.

Rom. 2:23-24 You who make your boast in the Torah, do you dishonor God through breaking the Torah? 24 For "the Name of God is blasphemed among the Gentiles because of you," as it is written.

Phil. 2:9-12 Wherefore God also hath highly exalted Him, and given Him a Name which is above every name: 10 That at the Name of ישוע every knee should bow, of things in heaven, and things in earth, and things under the earth; 11 And that every tongue should confess that ישוע Messiah is Lord, to the glory of God the Father.

I John 2:12 ... your sins are forgiven you **for His Name's sake**.

Rev. 14:1 And I looked, and, lo, a Lamb stood on the mount Zion, and with Him an hundred forty and four thousand, having His Father's Name written in their foreheads.

Rev. 22:3-4 And there shall be no more curse: but the throne of God and of the Lamb shall be in it; and His servants shall serve Him: 4 And they shall see His face; and His Name shall be in their foreheads.

13. SABBATH

BEFORE TORAH

Gen. 2:2-3 2 And on the seventh day God ended His work which He had made; and He rested on the seventh day from all His work which He had made. 3 And God blessed the seventh day, and sanctified it: because that in it He had rested from all His work....

BEFORE SINAI

Ex. 16:23-29 And he said unto them, This is that which יהוה hath said, To morrow is the rest of the holy Sabbath unto יהוה: bake that which ye will bake to day, and seethe that ye will seethe; and that which remaineth over lay up for you to be kept until the morning. ... 26 Six days ye shall gather it; but on the seventh day, which is the Sabbath, in it there shall be none. ... 29 See, for that יהוה hath given you the Sabbath, therefore he giveth you on the sixth day the bread of two days; abide ye every man in his place, let no man go out of his place on the seventh day.

AT SINAI AND AFTER

Ex. 20:8-11 Remember the Sabbath day, to keep it holy. Six days shalt thou labour, and do all thy work: But the seventh day is the Sabbath of יהוה thy God: in it thou shalt not do any work, thou, nor thy son, nor thy daughter, thy manservant, nor thy maidservant, nor thy cattle, nor thy stranger that is within thy gates: For in six days יהוה made heaven and earth, the sea, and all that in them is, and rested the seventh day: wherefore יהוה blessed the Sabbath day, and hallowed it.

Ex. 23:12 Six days thou shalt do thy work, and on the seventh day thou shalt rest: that thine ox and thine ass may rest, and the son of thy handmaid, and the stranger, may be refreshed.

Ex. 34:21 Six days thou shalt work, but on the seventh day thou shalt rest: in earing time and in harvest thou shalt rest.

Ex. 35:3 Ye shall kindle no fire throughout your habitations upon the Sabbath day.

Lev. 19:3b and keep My Sabbaths: I am יהוה your God.

Lev. 23:3 Six days shall work be done: but the seventh day is the Sabbath of rest, **an holy convocation;** ye shall do no work therein: it is the Sabbath of יהוה in all your dwellings.

Lev. 26:2 Ye shall keep My Sabbaths, and reverence My Sanctuary: I am יהוה.

Num. 15:32-36 And while the children of Israel were in the wilderness, they found a man that gathered sticks upon the Sabbath day. 33 And they that found him gathering sticks brought him unto Moses and Aaron, and unto all the congregation. 34 And they put him in ward, because it was not declared what should be done to him. 35 And יהוה said unto Moses, The man shall be surely put to death: all the congregation shall stone him with stones without the camp. 36 And all the congregation brought him without the camp, and stoned him with stones, and he died; as יהוה commanded Moses.

Num. 28:9-10 And on the Sabbath day two lambs of the first year without spot, and two tenth
deals of flour for a meat offering, mingled with oil, and the drink offering thereof: 10 This is
the burnt offering of every Sabbath, beside the continual (daily/tamid) burnt offering, and
his drink offering.

Deut. 5:12-15 Keep the Sabbath day to sanctify it, as יהוה thy God hath commanded thee.
13 Six days thou shalt labour, and do all thy work: 14 But the seventh day is the Sabbath of
יהוה thy God: in it thou shalt not do any work, thou, nor thy son, nor thy daughter, nor
thy manservant, nor thy maidservant, nor thine ox, nor thine ass, nor any of thy cattle, nor
thy stranger that is within thy gates; that thy manservant and thy maidservant may rest as well
as thou. 15 And remember that thou wast a servant in the land of Egypt, and that יהוה thy
God brought thee out thence through a mighty hand and by a stretched out arm: therefore
יהוה thy God commanded thee to keep the Sabbath day.

AFTER TORAH

Nehemiah 13:15-22 In those days saw I in Judah some treading wine presses on the Sabbath, and
bringing in sheaves, and lading asses; as also wine, grapes, and figs, and all manner of burdens,
which they brought into Jerusalem on the Sabbath day: and I testified against them in the day
wherein they sold victuals. 16 There dwelt men of Tyre also therein, which brought fish, and
all manner of ware, and sold on the Sabbath unto the children of Judah, and in Jerusalem. 17
Then I contended with the nobles of Judah, and said unto them, What evil thing is this that
ye do, and profane the Sabbath day? 18 Did not your fathers thus, and did not our God bring
all this evil upon us, and upon this city? yet ye bring more wrath upon Israel by profaning the
Sabbath. 19 And it came to pass, that when the gates of Jerusalem began to be dark before
the Sabbath, I commanded that the gates should be shut, and charged that they should not
be opened till after the Sabbath: and some of my servants set I at the gates, that there should
no burden be brought in on the Sabbath day. 20 So the merchants and sellers of all kind of
ware lodged without Jerusalem once or twice. 21 Then I testified against them, and said unto
them, Why lodge ye about the wall? if ye do so again, I will lay hands on you. From that time
forth came they no more on the Sabbath. 22 And I commanded the Levites that they should
cleanse themselves, and that they should come and keep the gates, to sanctify the Sabbath day.

Isaiah 56:2,6-7 Blessed is the man that... keepeth the Sabbath from polluting it, ... every one
that keepeth the Sabbath from polluting it, and taketh hold of my covenant; 7 Even them will
I bring to my holy mountain, and make them joyful in my house of prayer:

Isaiah 58:13-14 If thou turn away thy foot from the Sabbath, from doing thy pleasure on my
holy day; and call the Sabbath a delight, the holy of יהוה, honourable; and shalt honour
him, not doing thine own ways, nor finding thine own pleasure, nor speaking thine own
words: 14 Then shalt thou delight thyself in יהוה; and I will cause thee to ride upon the
high places of the earth, and feed thee with the heritage of Jacob thy father: for the mouth of
יהוה hath spoken it.

Jer. 17:21-22 Thus saith יהוה; Take heed to yourselves, and bear no burden on the Sabbath day, nor bring it in by the gates of Jerusalem; 22 Neither carry forth a burden out of your houses on the Sabbath day, neither do ye any work, but hallow ye the Sabbath day, as I commanded your fathers.

Ezek. 20:12 Moreover also I gave them My Sabbaths, to be a sign between Me and them, that they might know that I am יהוה that sanctify them. [also in God's I am statements, p. 15]

Ezek. 20:19-20 I am יהוה your God; walk in My statutes, and keep My judgments, and do them; 20 And hallow My Sabbaths; and they shall be a sign between Me and you, that ye may know that I am יהוה your God.

YESHUA ישוע

Matt. 12:1-8 At that time ישוע went on the Sabbath day through the corn; and His disciples were an hungred, and began to pluck the ears of corn, and to eat. 2 But when the Pharisees saw it, they said unto Him, Behold, thy disciples do that which is not lawful to do upon the Sabbath day. 3 But He said unto them, Have ye not read what David did, when he was an hungred, and they that were with him; 4 How he entered into the house of God, and did eat the shewbread, which was not lawful for him to eat, neither for them which were with him, but only for the priests? 5 Or have ye not read in the Torah, how that on the Sabbath days the priests in the Temple profane the Sabbath, and are blameless? 6 But I say unto you, That in this place is One greater than the Temple. 7 But if ye had known what this meaneth, I will have mercy, and not sacrifice, ye would not have condemned the guiltless. 8 For the Son of man is Lord even of the Sabbath day.

Matt. 12:10-12 … they asked Him, saying, Is it lawful to heal on the Sabbath days? that they might accuse Him. 11 And He said unto them, What man shall there be among you, that shall have one sheep, and if it fall into a pit on the Sabbath day, will he not lay hold on it, and lift it out? 12 How much then is a man better than a sheep? Wherefore it is lawful to do well on the Sabbath days.

Luke 14:5 …Which of you shall have an ass or an ox fallen into a pit, and will not straightway pull him out on the Sabbath day?

Luke 13:14-16 And the ruler of the synagogue answered with indignation, because that ישוע had healed on the Sabbath day, and said unto the people, There are six days in which men ought to work: in them therefore come and be healed, and not on the Sabbath day. 15 The Lord then answered him, and said, Thou hypocrite, doth not each one of you on the Sabbath loose his ox or his ass from the stall, and lead him away to watering? 16 And ought not this woman, being a daughter of Abraham, whom Satan hath bound, lo, these eighteen years, be loosed from this bond on the Sabbath day?

Luke 6:5 And He said unto them, That the Son of man is Lord also of the Sabbath.

Luke 6:9-11 Then said ישוע unto them, I will ask you one thing; Is it lawful on the Sabbath days to do good, or to do evil? to save life, or to destroy it? 10 And looking round about upon them all, he said unto the man, Stretch forth thy hand. And he did so: and his hand was restored whole as the other. 11 And they were filled with madness; and communed one with another* what they might do to יֵשׁוּעַ .

Mark 2:27 And He said unto them, The Sabbath was made for man, and not man for the Sabbath:

Matt 24:20 But pray ye that your flight be not in the winter, neither on the Sabbath day:

John 5:10 -11, 16-17 [They] said unto him that was cured, It is the Sabbath day: it is not lawful for thee to carry thy bed. 11 He answered them, He that made me whole, the same said unto me, Take up thy bed, and walk. ... 16 And therefore did the Jews persecute Jesus, and sought to slay him, because he had done these things on the Sabbath day. 17 But יֵשׁוּעַ answered them, My Father worketh hitherto, and I work.

John 2:16 ...make not My Father's House an house of merchandise.

Luke 4:16 And He came to Nazareth, where He had been brought up: and, as His custom was, He went into the synagogue on the Sabbath day, and stood up for to read.

APOSTLES

Act. 13:27 For they that dwell at Jerusalem, and their rulers, because they knew Him not, nor yet the voices of the prophets which are read every Sabbath day,

Acts 15:21 For Moses of old time hath in every city them that preach him, being read in the synagogues every Sabbath day.

Acts 13:42, 44 And when the Jews were gone out of the synagogue, the Gentiles besought that these words might be preached to them the next Sabbath. ... And the next Sabbath day came almost the whole city together to hear the Word of God.

Acts 16:13 And on the Sabbath we went out of the city by a river side, where prayer was wont to be made; and we sat down, and spake unto the women which resorted thither.

Acts 17:1b-2 ... they came to Thessalonica, where was a synagogue of the Jews: And Paul, as his manner was, went in unto them, and three Sabbath days reasoned with them out of the Scriptures.

Acts 18:4 And he reasoned in the synagogue every Sabbath, and persuaded the Jews and the Greeks.

Romans 14:4-6 Who art thou that judgest another man's servant? to his own master he standeth or falleth. Yea, he shall be holden up: for God is able to make him stand. 5 One man esteemeth one day above another: another esteemeth every day alike. Let every man be fully persuaded in his own mind. 6 He that regardeth the day, regardeth it unto the Lord; and he that regardeth not the day, to the Lord he doth not regard it.

Col 2:16 Let no man therefore judge you in meat, or in drink, or in respect of an holyday, or of the new moon, or of the Sabbath days:

Heb. 10:25 Not forsaking the assembling of ourselves together, as the manner of some is; but exhorting one another: and so much the more, as ye see the day approaching.

14. HONOR FATHER AND MOTHER

Ex. 20:12 Honour thy father and thy mother: that thy days may be long upon the land which יהוה thy God giveth thee.

Ex. 21:15 And he that smiteth his father, or his mother, shall be surely put to death.

Ex. 21:17 And he that curseth his father, or his mother, shall surely be put to death.

Ex. 22:28b: nor curse the ruler of thy people.

Lev. 19:3a Ye shall fear every man his mother, and his father,

Lev. 20:9 For every one that curseth his father or his mother shall be surely put to death: he hath cursed his father or his mother; his blood shall be upon him.

Deut. 5:16 Honour thy father and thy mother, as יהוה thy God hath commanded thee; that thy days may be prolonged, and that it may go well with thee, in the land which יהוה thy God giveth thee.

Deut. 27:16 Cursed be he that setteth light by his father or his mother. And all the people shall say, Amen.

YESHUA ישוע

Matt. 15:3-9 But he answered and said unto them, Why do ye also transgress the commandment of God by your tradition? 4 For God commanded, saying, Honour thy father and mother: and, He that curseth father or mother, let him die the death. 5 But ye say, Whosoever shall say to his father or his mother, It is a gift, by whatsoever thou mightest be profited by me; 6 And honour not his father or his mother, he shall be free. Thus have ye made the commandment of God of none effect by your tradition. 7 Ye hypocrites, well did Esaias prophesy of you, saying, 8 This people draweth nigh unto me with their mouth, and honoureth me with their lips; but their heart is far from me. 9 But in vain they do worship me, teaching for doctrines the commandments of men.

Matt. 10:37 He who loves father or mother more than Me is not worthy of Me.

APOSTLES

Eph. 6:1-3 Children, obey your parents in the Lord: for this is right. 2 Honour thy father and mother; which is the first commandment with promise; 3 That it may be well with thee, and thou mayest live long on the earth. [also in That it May Go Well, p. 257]

2 Tim. 3:2 For men shall be lovers of their own selves, covetous, boasters, proud, blasphemers, **disobedient to parents,** unthankful, unholy....

I Tim. 5:8 But if any provide not for his own, and specially for those of his own house, he hath denied the faith, and is worse than an infidel. *[He's talking about taking care of widows, so a person's widowed mother or mother-in-law would be of his own household.]*

15. NO KILLING

BEFORE TORAH

Gen. 4:1-16 *Cain is exiled for murdering his brother.*

Gen. 9:6 Whoso sheddeth man's blood, by man shall his blood be shed: for in the image of God made he man.

TORAH

Ex. 20:13 Thou shalt not kill.

Ex. 21:12 He that smiteth a man, so that he die, shall be surely put to death.

Ex. 21:13 And if a man lie not in wait, but God deliver him into his hand; then I will appoint thee a place whither he shall flee.

Ex. 21:14 But if a man come presumptuously upon his neighbour, to slay him with guile; thou shalt take him from mine altar, that he may die.

Ex. 21:20 And if a man smite his servant, or his maid, with a rod, and he die under his hand; he shall be surely punished. [also in Don't Mistreat Slaves, p. 71]

Ex. 22:2-3 If a thief be found breaking up [*in?*], and be smitten that he die, there shall no blood be shed for him. 3 If the sun be risen upon him [if he steals in the daytime?], there shall be blood shed for him; for he should make full ʀestitution; if he have nothing, then he shall be sold for his theft. [also in Thou shalt not steal, p. 52]

Lev. 24:17 And he that killeth any man shall surely be put to death.

Lev. 24:21b...: and he that killeth a man, he shall be put to death.

EXAMPLE CASES: Num. 35:16-19 And if he smite him with an instrument of iron, so that he die, he is a murderer: the murderer shall surely be put to death. 17 And if he smite him with throwing a stone, wherewith he may die, and he die, he is a murderer: the murderer shall surely be put to death. 18 Or if he smite him with an hand weapon of wood, wherewith he may die, and he die, he is a murderer: the murderer shall surely be put to death. 19 **The revenger of blood himself shall slay the murderer**: when he meeteth him, he shall slay him.

Num. 35:20-21...if he thrust him of hatred, or hurl at him by laying of wait, that he die; 21 Or in enmity smite him with his hand, that he die: he ... shall surely be put to death; for he is a murderer: **the revenger of blood shall slay the murderer,** when he meeteth him.

ACCIDENTAL MANSLAUGHTER: Num. 35:22-29 But if he thrust him suddenly without enmity, or have cast upon him any thing without laying of wait, 23 Or with any stone, wherewith a man may die, seeing him not, and cast it upon him, that he die, and was not his enemy, neither sought his harm: 24 Then the congregation shall judge between the slayer and the revenger of blood according to these judgments: 25 And the congregation shall deliver the slayer out of the hand of the revenger of blood, and the congregation shall restore him to the city of his refuge, whither he was fled: and he shall abide in it unto the death of the high priest, which was anointed with the holy oil. 26 But if the slayer shall at any time come without the border of the city of his refuge, whither he was fled; 27 And the revenger of blood find him without the borders of the city of his refuge, and the revenger of blood kill the slayer; he shall not be guilty of blood: 28 Because he should have remained in the city of his refuge until the death of the high priest: but after the death of the high priest the slayer shall return into the land of his possession. 29 So these things shall be for a **statute of judgment** unto you **throughout your generations in all your dwellings**. [also in Cities of Refuge, p. 50]

Num. 35:30-31 Whoso killeth any person, the murderer shall be put to death by the mouth of witnesses: but **one witness shall not testify against any person** to cause him to die. 31 Moreover ye shall take no satisfaction for the life of a murderer, which is guilty of death: but he shall be surely put to death. [also in Two or three witnesses, p. 123]

Num. 35:33-34 So ye shall not pollute the land wherein ye are: for blood it defileth the land: and the **land cannot be cleansed** of the blood that is shed therein, **but by the blood of him that shed it**. 34 Defile not therefore the land which ye shall inhabit, wherein I dwell: for I יהוה dwell among the children of Israel. [also in Cities of Refuge, p. 50 and Defile not, p. 68]

Deut. 5:17 Thou shalt not kill.

Deut. 19:11-13 But if any man **hate his neighbour, and lie in wait for him**, and rise up against him, **and smite him** mortally **that he die**, and fleeth into one of these cities: Then the elders of his city shall send and fetch him thence, and deliver him into the hand of the avenger of blood, that he may die. Thine eye shall not pity him, but thou shalt put away the guilt of innocent blood from Israel, that it may go well with thee. [also in Cities of Refuge, p. 50]

UNSOLVED MURDER, CLEANSE THE LAND: Deut. 21:1-9 If one be found slain in the land which יהוה thy God giveth thee to possess it, lying in the field, and it be not known who hath slain him: 2 Then thy elders and thy judges shall come forth, and they shall measure unto the cities which are round about him that is slain: 3 And it shall be, that the city which is next unto the slain man, even the elders of that city shall take an heifer, which hath not been wrought with, and which hath not drawn in the yoke; 4 And the elders of that city shall bring down the heifer unto a rough valley, which is neither eared nor sown, and shall strike off the heifer's neck there in the valley: 5 And the priests the sons of Levi shall come near; for them יהוה thy God hath chosen to minister unto him, and to bless in the Name of יהוה; and by their word shall every controversy and every stroke be tried: 6 And all the elders of that city, that are next unto the slain man, shall wash their hands over the heifer that is beheaded in the valley: 7 And they shall answer and say, Our hands have not shed this blood, neither have our eyes seen it. 8 Be merciful, O יהוה, unto thy people Israel, whom thou hast redeemed, and lay not innocent blood unto thy people of Israel's charge. And the blood shall be forgiven them. 9 So shalt thou put away the guilt of innocent blood from among you, when thou shalt do that which is right in the sight of יהוה. [also in Defile not the land, p. 68]

MURDER FOR HIRE: Deut. 27:25 Cursed be he that taketh reward to slay an innocent person. And all the people shall say, Amen.

AFTER TORAH

2 Kings 24:3-4 Surely at the commandment of יהוה came this upon Judah, to remove them out of his sight, for the sins of Manasseh, according to all that he did; And also for the innocent blood that he shed: for he filled Jerusalem with innocent blood; which יהוה would not pardon.

Psalm 106:38,40 And shed innocent blood, even the blood of their sons and of their daughters...: and the land was polluted with blood. ... Therefore was the wrath of יהוה kindled against his people.... [*How much more for our nation shedding the blood of the pre-born?*]

Jer. 7:6-7 If ye oppress not the stranger, the fatherless, and the widow, and shed not innocent blood in this place, neither walk after other gods to your hurt: Then will I cause you to dwell in this place, in the Land that I gave to your fathers, **forever and ever**. [also in No other gods, p. 34, Strangers, p. 86, and Widows, p. 88]

Jer. 22:3,5 Thus saith יהוה; Execute ye judgment and righteousness, and deliver the spoiled out of the hand of the oppressor: and do no wrong, do no violence to the stranger, the fatherless, nor the widow, neither shed innocent blood in this place. ... 5 But if ye will not hear these words, I swear by myself, saith יהוה, that this house shall become a desolation. [also in Strangers, p. 86, and Widows, p. 88]

Joel 3:19 Egypt shall be a desolation, and Edom shall be a desolate wilderness, for the violence against the children of Judah, because they have shed innocent blood in their land.

YESHUA ישוע

Matt. 5:21-24 Ye have heard that it was said by them of old time, Thou shalt not kill; and whosoever shall kill shall be in danger of the judgment: 22 But I say unto you, That whosoever is angry with his brother without a cause shall be in danger of the judgment: and whosoever shall say to his brother, Raca, shall be in danger of the council: but whosoever shall say, Thou fool, shall be in danger of hell fire. 23 Therefore if thou bring thy gift to the altar, and there rememberest that thy brother hath ought against thee; 24 Leave there thy gift before the altar, and go thy way; first be reconciled to thy brother, and then come and offer thy gift.

John 8:44 Ye are of your father the devil, and the lusts of your father ye will do. He was a murderer from the beginning....

APOSTLES

Eph. 4:26 Be ye angry, and sin not: let not the sun go down upon your wrath.

Eph. 4:31 (CJB) Get rid of all bitterness, rage, anger, violent assertiveness and slander, along with all spitefulness.

Heb. 12:15 Looking diligently lest any man fail of the Grace of God; lest any root of bitterness springing up trouble you, and thereby many be defiled;

1 Pet. 4:15 But let none of you suffer as a murderer....

I John 2:11 But he that hateth his brother is in darkness, and walketh in darkness, and knoweth not whither he goeth, because that darkness hath blinded his eyes.

Rev. 21:7-8 He that overcometh shall inherit all things; and I will be his God, and he shall be my son. 8 But the fearful,... and murderers, ... and idolaters ... shall have their part in the lake which burneth with fire and brimstone: which is the second death.

Rev. 22:14-15a Blessed are they that do his commandments, that they may have right to the tree of life, and may enter in through the gates into the city. 15 For without are dogs, and ... murderers and idolaters....

16. CITIES OF REFUGE

(For the one who accidentally kills)

(MERCY in the TORAH!)

Num. 35:9-15 And יהוה spake unto Moses, saying, 10 Speak unto the children of Israel, and say unto them, When ye be come over Jordan into the land of Canaan; 11 Then ye shall appoint you cities to be cities of refuge for you; that the slayer may flee thither, which **killeth any person at unawares**. 12 And they shall be unto you **cities for refuge** from the avenger; that the manslayer die not, until he stand before the congregation in judgment. 13 And of these cities which ye shall give **six cities** shall ye have for refuge. 14 Ye shall give **three** cities on this side Jordan, **and three** cities shall ye give in the land of Canaan, which shall be cities of refuge. 15 These six cities shall be a refuge, both for the children of Israel, and for the stranger, and for the sojourner among them: that **every one that killeth any person unawares** may flee thither.   [verse 15 also in Strangers, p. 86]

EXAMPLE CASES: Num. 35:22-25 But if he thrust him suddenly without enmity, or have cast upon him any thing without laying of wait, 23 Or with any stone, wherewith a man may die, seeing him not, and cast it upon him, that he die, and was not his enemy, neither sought his harm: 24 Then the congregation shall judge between the slayer and the revenger of blood according to these judgments: 25 And the congregation shall deliver the slayer out of the hand of the revenger of blood, and the congregation shall restore him to the city of his refuge, whither he was fled: and he shall abide in it **unto the death of the high priest,** which was anointed with the holy oil. [also in No killing, p. 47]

MUST NOT LEAVE THE CITY OF REFUGE: Num. 35:26-29 But if the slayer shall at any time come without the border of the city of his refuge, whither he was fled; 27 And the revenger of blood find him without the borders of the city of his refuge, and the revenger of blood kill the slayer; he shall not be guilty of blood: 28 Because he should have **remained in the city of his refuge until the death of the high priest:** but after the death of the high priest the slayer shall return into the land of his possession. 29 So these things shall be for a statute of judgment unto you **throughout your generations** in all your dwellings. [also in No killing, p. 47]

Num. 35:32-34 *[Verses 30-31 speak of executing murders]* And ye shall take no satisfaction for him that is fled to the city of his refuge, that he should come again to dwell in the land, until the death of the priest. 33 **So ye shall not pollute the land** wherein ye are: for blood it defileth the land: and the land cannot be cleansed of the blood that is shed therein, but by the blood of him that shed it. 34 **Defile not therefore the land** which ye shall inhabit, wherein I dwell: for I יהוה dwell among the children of Israel. [also in No killing, p. 48 and Defile not the Land, p. 68]

Deut. 19:1-4 When יהוה thy God hath cut off the nations, whose land יהוה thy God giveth thee, and thou succeedest them, and dwellest in their cities, and in their houses; 2 Thou shalt **separate three cities** for thee in the midst of thy land, which יהוה thy God giveth thee to possess it. 3 Thou shalt prepare thee a way, and divide the coasts of thy land, which יהוה thy God giveth thee to inherit, into three parts, **that every slayer may flee thither.** 4 And this is the case of the slayer, which shall flee thither, that he may live: **Whoso killeth his neighbour ignorantly**, whom he hated not in time past;

EXAMPLE CASE: Deut. 19:5-7 As when a man goeth into the wood with his neighbour to hew wood, and his hand fetcheth a stroke with the axe to cut down the tree, and the head slippeth from the helve, and lighteth upon his neighbour, that he die; he shall flee unto one of those cities, and live: 6 Lest the avenger of the blood pursue the slayer, while his heart is hot, and overtake him, because the way is long, and slay him; whereas he was not worthy of death, inasmuch as he hated him not in time past. 7 Wherefore I command thee, saying, Thou shalt separate three cities for thee.

Deut. 19:8-10 **And if** יהוה thy God **enlarge thy coast**, as he hath sworn unto thy fathers, and give thee all the land which he promised to give unto thy fathers; 9 If thou shalt keep all these commandments to do them, which I command thee this day, to love יהוה thy God, and to walk ever in his ways; then shalt thou **add three cities more** for thee, beside these three: 10 That innocent blood be not shed in thy land, which יהוה thy God giveth thee for an inheritance, and so blood be upon thee.

EXAMPLE CASE THAT DOES NOT APPLY: Deut. 19:11-13 But if any man hate his neighbour, and lie in wait for him, and rise up against him, and smite him mortally that he die, and fleeth into one of these cities: Then the elders of his city shall send and fetch him thence, and deliver him into the hand of the avenger of blood, that he may die. Thine eye shall not pity him, but thou shalt put away the guilt of innocent blood from Israel, that it may go well with thee. [also in No killing, p. 48]

17. NO STEALING
(INCLUDES NO KIDNAPPING)

Ex. 21:16 Thou shalt not steal.

Ex. 22:1 If a man shall steal an ox, or a sheep, and kill it, or sell it; he shall restore five oxen for an ox, and four sheep for a sheep.

Ex. 22:2 If a thief be found breaking up *[in?]*, and be smitten that he die, there shall no blood be shed for him. [also in No killing, p. 47]

Ex. 22:3 If the sun be risen upon him, there shall be blood shed for him; for he should make full restitution; if he have nothing, then he shall be sold for his theft. [also in No killing, p. 47]

Ex. 22:4 If the theft be certainly found in his hand alive, whether it be ox, or ass, or sheep; he shall restore double.

Lev. 19:11a, 13 Ye shall not steal.... Thou shalt not defraud thy neighbour, neither rob him: the wages of him that is hired shall not abide with thee all night until the morning.

Deut. 5:19 Neither shalt thou steal.

DEATH PENALTY FOR KIDNAPPING

Ex. 21:16 And he that stealeth a man, and selleth him, or if he be found in his hand, he shall surely be put to death.

Deut. 24:7 If a man be found stealing any of his brethren of the children of Israel, and maketh merchandise of him, or selleth him; then that thief shall die; and thou shalt put evil away from among you.

AFTER TORAH

Mal. 3:8-10 Will a man rob God? Yet ye have robbed me. But ye say, Wherein have we robbed thee? In tithes and offerings. 9 Ye are cursed with a curse: for ye have robbed me, even this whole nation. 10 Bring ye all the tithes into the storehouse, that there may be meat in mine house, and prove me now herewith, saith יהוה of hosts, if I will not open you the windows of heaven, and pour you out a blessing, that there shall not be room enough to receive it.

APOSTLES

Rom. 2:21 (NKJV) You, therefore, who teach another, do you not teach yourself? You who preach that a man should not steal, do you steal?

2 Thess. 3:10 (NKJV) If anyone will not work, neither shall he eat.

Eph. 4:28 (NKJV) Let him who stole steal no longer, but rather let him labor, working with his hands what is good, that he may have something to give him who has need.

1Pet. 4:15 But let none of you suffer as a murderer, or as a thief....

18. NO FALSE WITNESS OR GOSSIP

Ex. 20:16 Thou shalt not bear false witness against thy neighbour.

Ex. 23:1 Thou shalt not raise (CJB: repeat TLV: spread) a false report: put not thine hand with the wicked to be an unrighteous witness.

Ex. 23:7a Keep thee far from a false matter;

Lev. 6:2-7 If a soul sin, and commit a trespass against יהוה, and lie unto his neighbour in that which was delivered him to keep, or in fellowship, or in a thing taken away by violence, or hath deceived his neighbour; 3 Or have found that which was lost, and lieth concerning it, and sweareth falsely; in any of all these that a man doeth, sinning therein: 4 Then it shall be, because he hath sinned, and is guilty, that he shall restore that which he took violently away, or the thing which he hath deceitfully gotten, or that which was delivered him to keep, or the lost thing which he found, 5 or whatever it was they swore falsely about. They must make restitution in full, add a fifth of the value to it and give it all to the owner on the day they present their guilt offering. 6 And as a penalty they must bring to the priest, that is, to יהוה, their guilt offering, a ram from the flock, one without defect and of the proper value. 7 In this way the priest will make atonement for them before יהוה, and they will be forgiven for any of the things they did that made them guilty." [also in Finding Lost Property and Borrowing]

Lev. 19:16 Thou shalt not go up and down as a **talebearer** among thy people: neither shalt thou stand against the blood of thy neighbour: I am יהוה.

Lev. 19:11b ...neither deal falsely, neither lie one to another.

Deut. 5:20 Neither shalt thou bear false witness against thy neighbour.

Deut. 19:16-21 If a false witness rise up against any man to testify against him that which is wrong; 17 Then both the men, between whom the controversy is, shall stand before יהוה, before the priests and the judges, which shall be in those days; 18 And the judges shall make diligent inquisition: and, behold, if the witness be a false witness, and hath testified falsely against his brother; 19 Then shall ye do unto him, as he had thought to have done unto his brother: so shalt thou put the evil away from among you. 20 And those which remain shall hear, and fear, and shall henceforth commit no more any such evil among you. 21 And thine eye shall not pity; but life shall go for life, eye for eye, tooth for tooth, hand for hand, foot for foot.

AFTER TORAH

Psalms 63:11b ....the mouth of them that speak lies shall be stopped.

Prov. 6:16,19 These six things doth יהוה hate: ... A false witness that speaketh lies, and he that soweth discord among brethren.

Prov. 19:5 A false witness shall not be unpunished, and he that speaketh lies shall not escape.

Prov. 12:19 The lip of truth shall be established **forever**: but a lying tongue is but for a moment.

Prov. 18:7 A fool's mouth is his destruction, and his lips are the snare of his soul.

Prov. 18:21 Death and life are in the power of the tongue....

Zech. 5:3,4 This is the curse that goeth forth over the face of the whole earth: ...it shall enter into the house of the thief, and into the house of him that sweareth falsely by My Name: and it shall remain in the midst of his house, and shall consume it with the timber thereof and the stones thereof.

YESHUA ישוע

Matt. 12:36-37 But I say unto you, That every idle word that men shall speak, they shall give account thereof in the day of judgment. 37 For by thy words thou shalt be justified, and by thy words thou shalt be condemned.

Matt. 15:11b ...that which cometh out of the mouth, this defileth a man.

John 8:31-32 Then said ישוע ... If ye continue in My Word, then are ye My disciples indeed; 32 And ye shall know the truth, and the truth shall make you free.

John 8:44 Ye are of your father the devil, and the lusts of your father ye will do. He was a murderer from the beginning, and abode not in the truth, because there is no truth in him. When he speaketh a lie, he speaketh of his own: for he is a liar, and the father of it.

APOSTLES

Acts 5:1-11 *[Anninias and Sapphira died because they lied about the sale of their land.]*

Eph. 4:25 Wherefore putting away lying, speak every man truth with his neighbour....

Eph. 4:15 But speaking the truth in love, may grow up into him [Messiah] in all things....

1 Pet. 3:10 (Alao Psalm 34:10-11) (CJB) Whoever wants to love life and see good days must keep his tongue from evil and his lips from speaking deceit....

Eph. 4:29 Let no corrupt communication proceed out of your mouth, but that which is good to the use of edifying, that it may minister grace unto the hearers.

James 3:2b, 6, 8-10 If any man offend not in word, the same is a perfect man, and able also to bridle the whole body. ... 6 And the tongue is a fire, a world of iniquity: so is the tongue among our members, that it defileth the whole body, and setteth on fire the course of nature; and it is set on fire of hell. ... 8 But the tongue can no man tame; it is an unruly evil, full of deadly poison. 9 Therewith bless we God, even the Father; and therewith curse we men, which are made after the similitude of God. 10 Out of the same mouth proceedeth blessing and cursing. My brethren, these things ought not so to be.

James 4:11 Speak not evil one of another....

Rev. 21:8b ...all liars, shall have their part in the lake which burneth with fire and brimstone....

Rev. 22:15 For without are dogs, and .. murderers, and ... whosoever loveth and maketh a lie.

19. VOWS, KEEP YOUR WORD

Lev. 5:4-6 Or if a soul swear, pronouncing with his lips to do evil, or to do good, whatsoever it be that a man shall pronounce with an oath, and it be hid from him; when he knoweth of it, then he shall be guilty in one of these. 5 And it shall be, when he shall be guilty in one of these things, that he shall confess that he hath sinned in that thing: 6 And he shall bring his [asham (shame, guilt)] offering unto יהוה for his sin which he hath sinned, a female from the flock, a lamb or a kid of the goats, for a sin offering; and the priest shall make an atonement for him concerning his sin. [also in Asham/Guilt/Shame offerings, p. 144, and Sinning in Ignorance, p. 210]

Lev. 27:2-8 Speak unto the children of Israel, and say unto them, When a man shall make a singular vow, the persons shall be for יהוה by thy estimation. 3 And thy estimation shall be of the male from twenty years old even unto sixty years old, even thy estimation shall be fifty shekels of silver, after the shekel of the sanctuary. 4 And if it be a female, then thy estimation shall be thirty shekels. 5 And if it be from five years old even unto twenty years old, then thy estimation shall be of the male twenty shekels, and for the female ten shekels. 6 And if it be from a month old even unto five years old, then thy estimation shall be of the male five shekels of silver, and for the female thy estimation shall be three shekels of silver. 7 And if it be from sixty years old and above; if it be a male, then thy estimation shall be fifteen shekels, and for the female ten shekels. 8 But if he be poorer than thy estimation, then he shall present himself before the priest, and the priest shall value him; according to his ability that vowed shall the priest value him.

Num. 30:2   If a man vow a vow unto יהוה, or swear an oath to bind his soul with a bond; he shall not break his word, he shall do according to all that proceedeth out of his mouth.

VOWS BY WOMEN: Num. 30:3-8 If a woman also vow a vow unto יהוה, and bind herself by a bond, being in her father's house in her youth; 4 And her father hear her vow, and her bond wherewith she hath bound her soul, and her father shall hold his peace at her: then all her vows shall stand, and every bond wherewith she hath bound her soul shall stand. 5 But if her father disallow her in the day that he heareth; not any of her vows, or of her bonds wherewith she hath bound her soul, shall stand: and יהוה shall forgive her, because her father disallowed her. 6 And if she had at all an husband, when she vowed, or uttered ought out of her lips, wherewith she bound her soul; 7 And her husband heard it, and held his peace at her in the day that he heard it: then her vows shall stand, and her bonds wherewith she bound her soul shall stand. 8 But if her husband disallowed her on the day that he heard it; then he shall make her vow which she vowed, and that which she uttered with her lips, wherewith she bound her soul, of none effect: and יהוה shall forgive her.

VOWS BY WIDOWS: Num. 30:9 But every vow of a widow, and of her that is divorced, wherewith they have bound their souls, shall stand against her.

VOWS BY WOMEN (cont.) Num. 30:10-12 And if she vowed in her husband's house, or bound her soul by a bond with an oath; 11 And her husband heard it, and held his peace at her, and disallowed her not: then all her vows shall stand, and every bond wherewith she bound her soul shall stand. 12 But if her husband hath utterly made them void on the day he heard them; then whatsoever proceeded out of her lips concerning her vows, or concerning the bond of her soul, shall not stand: her husband hath made them void; and יהוה shall forgive her.

VOWS BY WOMEN (cont.) Num. 30:13-16 Every vow, and every binding oath to afflict the soul, her husband may establish it, or her husband may make it void. 14 But if her husband altogether hold his peace at her from day to day; then he establisheth all her vows, or all her bonds, which are upon her: he confirmeth them, because he held his peace at her in the day that he heard them. 15 But if he shall any ways make them void after that he hath heard them; then he shall bear her iniquity. 16 These are the statutes, which יהוה commanded Moses, between a man and his wife, between the father and his daughter, being yet in her youth in her father's house.

Deut. 23:21 When thou shalt vow a vow unto יהוה thy God, thou shalt not slack to pay it: for יהוה thy God will surely require it of thee; and it would be sin in thee.

Deut. 23:22 But if thou shalt forbear to vow, it shall be no sin in thee.

Deut. 23:23 That which is gone out of thy lips thou shalt keep and perform; even a freewill offering, according as thou hast vowed unto יהוה thy God, which thou hast promised with thy mouth.

YESHUA ישוע and APOSTLES

Matt. 5:33-37 Again, ye have heard that it hath been said by them of old time, Thou shalt not forswear thyself, but **shalt perform unto the Lord thine oaths:** 34 But I say unto you, Swear not at all; neither by heaven; for it is God's throne: 35 Nor by the earth; for it is his footstool: neither by Jerusalem; for it is the city of the great King. 36 Neither shalt thou swear by thy head, because thou canst not make one hair white or black. 37 But let your communication be, Yea, yea; Nay, nay: for whatsoever is more than these cometh of evil.

James 5:12 But above all things, my brethren, swear not, neither by heaven, neither by the earth, neither by any other oath: but let your yea be yea; and your nay, nay; lest ye fall into condemnation.

THE TEN

20. THOU SHALT NOT COVET

This is one of the only commandments in the Torah that is about our thoughts rather than our actions.

Ex. 20:17 Thou shalt not covet thy neighbour's house, thou shalt not covet thy neighbour's wife, nor his manservant, nor his maidservant, nor his ox, nor his ass, nor any thing that is thy neighbour's.

Deut. 5:21 Neither shalt thou desire thy neighbour's wife, neither shalt thou covet thy neighbour's house, his field, or his manservant, or his maidservant, his ox, or his ass, or any thing that is thy neighbour's.

APOSTLES

Eph. 5:5-6 For this ye know, that no whoremonger, nor unclean person, nor <u>covetous man, who is an idolater,</u> hath any inheritance in the Kingdom of Messiah and of God. 6 Let no man deceive you with vain words: for because of these things cometh the wrath of God upon the children of disobedience.

Phil. 4:11-13 Not that I speak in respect of want: for I have learned, in whatsoever state I am, therewith to <u>be content</u>. 12 I know both how to be abased, and I know how to abound: every where and in all things I am instructed both to be full and to be hungry, both to abound and to suffer need. 13 I can do all things through Messiah which strengtheneth me.

Heb. 13:5 Let your conversation be <u>without covetousness</u>; and <u>be content</u> with such things as ye have: for he hath said, I will never leave thee, nor forsake thee.

21. NO ADULTERY

Sex is God's idea. *He created it! As the Inventor and Designer, He knows how it can best be enjoyed.*

Gen. 1:28 And God blessed them, and God said unto them, Be fruitful, and multiply....

Gen. 9:7 And you, be ye fruitful, and multiply; bring forth abundantly in the earth, and multiply therein.

Prov. 5:18b-19 ...rejoice with the wife of thy youth. 19 ...let her breasts satisfy thee at all times; and be thou ravished always with her love.

TORAH —*Sex outside of the beautiful way God designed it, ruins it.*

Ex. 20:14 Thou shalt not commit adultery.

Lev. 18 *The whole chapter is commandments against sexual sins, incest, etc.* [See: No Incest, p. 64.]

Lev. 18:20 Moreover thou shalt not lie carnally with thy neighbour's wife, to defile thyself with her.

Lev. 19:20-22 And whosoever lieth carnally with a woman, that is a bondmaid, betrothed to an husband, and not at all redeemed, nor freedom given her; she shall be scourged; they shall not be put to death, because she was not free. And he shall bring his [asham (shame, guilt)] offering unto יהוה, unto the door of the Tabernacle of the congregation, even a ram..... And the priest shall make an atonement for him with the ram of the [asham (shame, guilt)] offering before יהוה for his sin which he hath done: and the sin which he hath done shall be forgiven him.

Lev. 20:10 And the man that committeth adultery with another man's wife, even he that committeth adultery with his neighbour's wife, the adulterer and the adulteress shall surely be put to death.

Lev. 20:11-21 *Against all kinds of sexual sins, incest, etc.*

Deut. 5:18 Neither shalt thou commit adultery.

Deut. 22:22 If a man be found lying with a woman married to an husband, then they shall both of them die, both the man that lay with the woman, and the woman: so shalt thou put away evil from Israel.

Deut. 22:23-24 If a damsel that is a virgin be betrothed unto an husband, and a man find her in the city, and lie with her; 24 Then ye shall bring them both out unto the gate of that city, and ye shall stone them with stones that they die; the damsel, because she cried not, being in the city; and the man, because he hath humbled his neighbour's wife: so thou shalt put away evil from among you.

PROPHETS

Ezek.33:26 ...ye defile every one his neighbour's wife: and shall ye possess the land? *[Read on to see this is one of the reasons they were exiled.]*

Mal. 2:14,15 (CJB) ... ADONAI is witness between you and the wife of your youth that you have broken faith with her, though she is your companion, your wife by covenant. 15 ... Therefore, take heed to your spirit, and don't break faith with the wife of your youth.

YESHUA יֵשׁוּעַ

Matt. 5:27-30 Ye have heard that it was said by them of old time, Thou shalt not commit adultery: 28 But I say unto you, That whosoever looketh on a woman to lust after her hath committed adultery with her already in his heart. 29 And if thy right eye offend thee, pluck it out, and cast it from thee: for it is profitable for thee that one of thy members should perish, and not that thy whole body should be cast into hell. 30 And if thy right hand offend thee, cut it off, and cast it from thee: for it is profitable for thee that one of thy members should perish, and not that thy whole body should be cast into hell.

John 8:3-11 And the scribes and Pharisees brought unto him a woman taken in adultery; and when they had set her in the midst, 4 They say unto him, Master, this woman was taken in adultery, in the very act. 5 Now Moses in the Torah commanded us, that such should be stoned: but what sayest thou? 6 This they said, tempting him, that they might have to accuse him. But יֵשׁוּעַ stooped down, and with his finger wrote on the ground, as though he heard them not. 7 So when they continued asking him, he lifted up himself, and said unto them, He that is without sin among you, let him first cast a stone at her. 8 And again he stooped down, and wrote on the ground. 9 And they which heard it, being convicted by their own conscience, went out one by one, beginning at the eldest, even unto the last: and יֵשׁוּעַ was left alone, and the woman standing in the midst. 10 When יֵשׁוּעַ had lifted up himself, and saw none but the woman, he said unto her, Woman, where are those thine accusers? hath no man condemned thee? 11 She said, No man, Lord. And יֵשׁוּעַ said unto her, Neither do I condemn thee: go, and sin no more.

APOSTLES

Rom. 2:22a Thou that sayest a man should not commit adultery, dost thou commit adultery?

Again, God knows and tells us in the following several verses what will increase sexual enjoyment.

Eph. 5:21 Submit to one another.

Eph. 5:24 Wives submit to your husbands.

Eph. 5:25 (paraphrased) Husbands love your wives as Messiah loves the church. Give yourself up for her in order to set her apart for God. Feed her and take care of her.

Eph. 5:31 Leave your father and mother and cleave to your wife.

Eph. 5:33 Wife respect your husband.

I Pet. 1:14 As obedient children, not fashioning yourselves according to the former lusts in your ignorance:

Heb. 13:4 (TLV) Let marriage be held in honor among all and the marriage bed kept undefiled, for God will judge the sexually immoral and adulterers.

Rev. 2:22-23 (RSV) ...those who commit adultery with her I will throw into great tribulation, unless they repent.... 23 ...I am he who searches mind and heart, and I will give to each of you as your works deserve.

22. DIVORCE AND REMARRIAGE

Deut. 24:1 When a man hath taken a wife, and married her, and it come to pass that she find no favour in his eyes, because he hath found some uncleanness in her: then let him write her a bill of divorcement, and give it in her hand, and send her out of his house.

Deut. 24:2 And when she is departed out of his house, she may go and be another man's wife.

Deut. 24:3-4 And if the latter husband hate her, and write her a bill of divorcement, and giveth it in her hand, and sendeth her out of his house; or if the latter husband die, which took her to be his wife; 4 <u>Her former husband, which sent her away, may not take her again to be his wife, after that she is defiled; for that is abomination before</u> יהוה: and thou shalt not cause the land to sin, which יהוה thy God giveth thee for an inheritance. [also in Do not Defile the Land, p. 68]

AFTER TORAH

Isaiah 50:1-2 Thus saith יהוה, Where is the bill of your mother's <u>divorcement</u>, whom I have put away? Or which of my creditors is it to whom I have sold you? Behold, for your iniquities have ye sold yourselves, and for your transgressions is your mother put away. 2 Wherefore, when I came, was there no man? When I called, was there none to answer? Is my hand shortened at all, that it cannot redeem? Or have I no power to deliver?

יהוה sees idolatry as adultery against Him:

Jer. 3:1, 4 They say, If a man put away his wife, and she go from him, and become another man's, shall he return unto her again? Shall not that land be greatly polluted? But thou hast played the harlot with many lovers; yet return again to me, saith יהוה. ... Wilt thou not from this time cry unto me, My father, thou art the guide of my youth? [also in Defile not, p. 68]

Help us, Adonai, not to commit spiritual adultery:

Jer. 3:8-17 And I saw, when for all the causes whereby backsliding Israel committed adultery I had <u>put her away,</u> and given her a <u>bill of divorce</u>; yet her treacherous sister Judah feared not, but went and played the harlot also. 9 And it came to pass through the lightness of her whoredom, that she defiled the land, and committed adultery with stones and with stocks. ... 12 Go and proclaim these words toward the north, and say, Return, thou backsliding Israel, saith יהוה; and I will not cause mine anger to fall upon you: for I am merciful, saith יהוה, and I will not keep anger forever. 13 Only acknowledge thine iniquity, that thou hast transgressed against יהוה thy God.... 14 Turn, O backsliding children, saith יהוה; for I am married unto you: and I will take you ... and I will bring you to Zion: 15 And I will give you pastors according to mine heart, which shall feed you with knowledge and understanding. ... 17 At that time they shall call Jerusalem the throne of יהוה; and all the nations shall be gathered unto it, to the Name of יהוה, to Jerusalem: neither shall they walk any more after the imagination of their evil heart.

Mal. 2:16 (CJB) "For I hate divorce," says ADONAI the God of Isra'el,

YESHUA יֵשׁוּעַ

Matt. 5:31-32 (NKJV) "Furthermore it has been said, 'Whoever divorces his wife, let him give her a certificate of divorce.' 32 But I say to you that whoever divorces his wife for any reason except sexual immorality causes her to commit adultery; and whoever marries a woman who is divorced commits adultery."

Matt. 19:3-12 The Pharisees also came..., tempting him..., Is it lawful for a man to put away his wife for every cause? 4 And he answered and said unto them, Have ye not read, that he which made them at the beginning made them male and female, 5 And said, For this cause shall a man leave father and mother, and shall cleave to his wife: and they twain shall be one flesh? 6 Wherefore they are no more twain, but one flesh. What therefore God hath joined together, let not man put asunder. 7 They say unto him, Why did Moses then command to give a writing of divorcement, and to put her away? 8 He saith unto them, Moses because of the hardness of your hearts suffered you to put away your wives: but from the beginning it was not so. 9 And I say unto you, Whosoever shall put away his wife, except it be for fornication, and shall marry another, committeth adultery: and whoso marrieth her which is put away doth commit adultery. 10 His disciples say unto him, If the case of the man be so with his wife, it is not good to marry. 11 But he said unto them, All men cannot receive this saying, save they to whom it is given. 12 For there are some eunuchs, ... which have made themselves eunuchs for the kingdom of heaven's sake. He that is able to receive it, let him receive it.

Mark 10:2-12 *[the same as Matt. 19 above.]* ...Pharisees came ... tempting him. 3 And he answered ... 9 What therefore God hath joined together, let not man put asunder. 10 And in the house his disciples asked him again of the same matter. 11 And he saith unto them, Whosoever shall put away his wife, and marry another, committeth adultery against her. 12 And if a woman shall put away her husband, and be married to another, she committeth adultery.

Luke 16:18 Whosoever putteth away his wife, and marrieth another, committeth adultery: and whosoever marrieth her that is put away from her husband committeth adultery.

APOSTLES

I Cor. 7:10-16 And unto the married I command, yet not I, but the Lord, Let not the wife depart from her husband: 11 But and if she depart, let her remain unmarried, or be reconciled to her husband: and let not the husband put away his wife. 12 But to the rest speak I, not the Lord: If any brother hath a wife that believeth not, and she be pleased to dwell with him, let him not put her away. 13 And the woman which hath an husband that believeth not, and if he be pleased to dwell with her, let her not leave him. 14 For the unbelieving husband is sanctified by the wife, and the unbelieving wife is sanctified by the husband: else were your children unclean; but now are they holy. 15 But if the unbelieving depart, let him depart. A brother or a sister is not under bondage in such cases: but God hath called us to peace. 16 For what knowest thou, O wife, whether thou shalt save thy husband? Or how knowest thou, O man, whether thou shalt save thy wife?

23. JEALOUS HUSBAND

Num. 5:12-15 ... If any man's wife go aside, and commit a trespass against him, 13 And a man lie with her carnally, and it be hid from the eyes of her husband, and be kept close, and she be defiled, and there be no witness against her, neither she be taken with the manner; 14 And the spirit of jealousy come upon him, and he be jealous of his wife, and she be defiled: or if the spirit of jealousy come upon him, and he be jealous of his wife, and she be not defiled: 15 Then shall the man bring his wife unto the priest, and he shall bring her offering for her, the tenth part of an ephah of barley meal; he shall pour no oil upon it, nor put frankincense thereon; for it is an offering of jealousy, an offering of memorial, bringing iniquity to remembrance.

Num. 5:16-20 And the priest shall bring her near, and set her before יהוה: 17 The priest shall take <u>holy water</u> in an earthen vessel; and of the <u>dust that is in the floor of the Tabernacle</u> *(In Temple days, the floors would've been quite clean)* the priest shall take, and put it into the water: 18 And the priest shall set the woman before יהוה, and uncover the woman's head, and put the offering of memorial in her hands, which is the jealousy offering: and the priest shall have in his hand the bitter water that causeth the curse: 19 And the priest shall charge her by an oath, and say unto the woman, If no man have lain with thee, and if thou hast not gone aside to uncleanness with another instead of thy husband, be thou free from this bitter water that causeth the curse: 20 But if thou hast gone aside to another instead of thy husband, and if thou be defiled, and some man have lain with thee beside thine husband:

Num. 5:21-30 Then the priest shall charge the woman with an oath of cursing, and the priest shall say unto the woman, יהוה make thee a curse and an oath among thy people, when יהוה doth make thy thigh to rot, and thy belly to swell; 22 And this water that causeth the curse shall go into thy bowels, to make thy belly to swell, and thy thigh to rot: And the woman shall say, Amen, amen. 23 <u>And the priest shall write these curses in a book, and he shall blot them out with the bitter water</u>: 24 And he shall cause the woman to drink the bitter water that causeth the curse: and the water that causeth the curse shall enter into her, and become bitter. 25 Then the priest shall take the jealousy offering out of the woman's hand, and shall wave the offering before יהוה, and offer it upon the altar: 26 And the priest shall take an handful of the offering, even the memorial thereof, and burn it upon the altar, and afterward shall cause the woman to drink the water. 27 And when he hath made her to drink the water, then it shall come to pass, that, if she be defiled, and have done trespass against her husband, that the water that causeth the curse shall enter into her, and become bitter, and her belly shall swell, and her thigh shall rot: and the woman shall be a curse among her people. 28 And if the woman be not defiled, but be clean; then she shall be free, and shall conceive seed. 29 This is the law of jealousies, when a wife goeth aside to another instead of her husband, and is defiled; 30 Or when the spirit of jealousy cometh upon him, and he be jealous over his wife, and shall set the woman before יהוה, and the priest shall execute upon her all this law. 31 Then shall the man be guiltless from iniquity, and this woman shall bear her iniquity.

(There are husbands today who distrust their wives. They are suspicious of everything their wives do and in some cases treat them horribly. What can such wives do today to prove to their husbands that they are innocent? Nothing! This law brought vindication to those unfortunate women.)

24. BRIDE NOT A VIRGIN

Deut. 22:13-17 If any man take a wife, and go in unto her, and hate her, 14 And give occasions of speech against her, and bring up an evil name upon her, and say, I took this woman, and when I came to her, I found her not a maid: 15 Then shall the father of the damsel, and her mother, take and bring forth the tokens of the damsel's virginity unto the elders of the city in the gate: 16 And the damsel's father shall say unto the elders, I gave my daughter unto this man to wife, and he hateth her; 17 And, lo, he hath given occasions of speech against her, saying, I found not thy daughter a maid; and yet these are the tokens of my daughter's virginity. And they shall spread the cloth before the elders of the city.

(Cont.) 18 And the elders of that city shall take that man and chastise him; 19 And they shall amerce him in an hundred shekels of silver, and give them unto the father of the damsel, because he hath brought up an evil name upon a virgin of Israel: <u>and she shall be his wife; he may not put her away all his days.</u>

(Cont.) 20 But if this thing be true, and the tokens of virginity be not found for the damsel: 21 Then they shall bring out the damsel to the door of her father's house, and the men of her city shall stone her with stones that she die: because she hath wrought folly in Israel, to play the whore in her father's house: so shalt thou put evil away from among you.

25. NO RAPE

Ex. 22:16-17 And if a man entice a maid that is not betrothed, and lie with her, he shall surely endow her to be his wife. If her father utterly refuse to give her unto him, he shall pay money according to the dowry of virgins.

Deut. 22:23-24 If a damsel that is a virgin be betrothed unto an husband, and a man find her in the city, and lie with her; 24 Then ye shall bring them both out unto the gate of that city, and ye shall stone them with stones that they die; the damsel, because she cried not, being in the city; and the man, because he hath humbled his neighbour's wife: so thou shalt put away evil from among you.

Deut. 22:25-27 But if a man find a betrothed damsel in the field, and the man force her, and lie with her: then the man only that lay with her shall die: 26 But unto the damsel thou shalt do nothing; there is in the damsel no sin worthy of death: for as when a man riseth against his neighbour, and slayeth him, even so is this matter: 27 For he found her in the field, and the betrothed damsel cried, and there was none to save her.

Deut. 22:28-29 If a man find a damsel that is a virgin, which is not betrothed, and lay hold on her, and lie with her, and they be found; 29 Then the man that lay with her shall give unto the damsel's father fifty shekels of silver, and she shall be his wife; because he hath humbled her, <u>he may not put her away all his days</u>.

26. NO INCEST

Lev. 18:6 None of you shall approach to any that is near of kin to him, to uncover their nakedness: I am יהוה.

7 The nakedness of thy father,

or the nakedness of thy mother, shalt thou not uncover: she is thy mother; thou shalt not uncover her nakedness.

8 The nakedness of thy father's wife shalt thou not uncover: it is thy father's nakedness.

9 The nakedness of thy sister, the daughter of thy father, or daughter of thy mother, whether she be born at home, or born abroad, even their nakedness thou shalt not uncover.

10 The nakedness of thy son's daughter, or of thy daughter's daughter, even their nakedness thou shalt not uncover: for theirs is thine own nakedness.

11 The nakedness of thy father's wife's daughter, begotten of thy father, she is thy sister, thou shalt not uncover her nakedness.

12 Thou shalt not uncover the nakedness of thy father's sister: she is thy father's near kinswoman.

13 Thou shalt not uncover the nakedness of thy mother's sister: for she is thy mother's near kinswoman.

14 Thou shalt not uncover the nakedness of thy father's brother, thou shalt not approach to his wife: she is thine aunt.

15 Thou shalt not uncover the nakedness of thy daughter in law: she is thy son's wife; thou shalt not uncover her nakedness.

16 Thou shalt not uncover the nakedness of thy brother's wife: it is thy brother's nakedness.

17 Thou shalt not uncover the nakedness of a woman and her daughter,

17 (cont.) neither shalt thou take her son's daughter, or her daughter's daughter, to uncover her nakedness; for they are her near kinswomen: it is wickedness.

18 Neither shalt thou take a wife to her sister, to vex her, to uncover her nakedness, beside the other in her life time.

29 For whosoever shall commit any of these abominations, even the souls that commit them shall be cut off from among their people.

Lev. 20:11 And the man that lieth with his father's wife hath uncovered his father's nakedness: both of them shall surely be put to death; their blood shall be upon them.

Lev. 20:12 And if a man lie with his daughter in law, both of them shall surely be put to death: they have wrought confusion; their blood shall be upon them.

Lev. 20:14 And if a man take a wife and her mother, it is wickedness: they shall be burnt with fire, both he and they; that there be no wickedness among you.

Lev. 20:17 And if a man shall take his sister, his father's daughter, or his mother's daughter, and see her nakedness, and she see his nakedness; it is a wicked thing; and they shall be cut off in the sight of their people: he hath uncovered his sister's nakedness; he shall bear his iniquity.

Lev. 20:19-21 And thou shalt not uncover the nakedness of thy mother's sister, nor of thy father's sister: for he uncovereth his near kin: they shall bear their iniquity. 20 And if a man shall lie with his uncle's wife, he hath uncovered his uncle's nakedness: they shall bear their sin; they shall die childless. 21 And if a man shall take his brother's wife, it is an unclean thing: he hath uncovered his brother's nakedness; they shall be childless.

Deut. 22:30 A man shall not take his father's wife, nor discover his father's skirt.

Deut. 27:20 Cursed be he that lieth with his father's wife; because he uncovereth his father's skirt. And all the people shall say, Amen.

Deut. 27:22 Cursed be he that lieth with his sister, the daughter of his father, or the daughter of his mother. And all the people shall say, Amen.

Deut. 27:23 Cursed be he that lieth with his mother in law. And all the people shall say, Amen.

YESHUA יֵשׁוּעַ

Matt. 18:5-7 And whoso shall receive one such little child in My Name receiveth me. 6 But whoso shall offend one of these little ones which believe in Me, it were better for him that a millstone were hanged about his neck, and that he were drowned in the depth of the sea.

APOSTLES

I Cor. 5:1-5 It is reported commonly that there is fornication among you, and such fornication as is not so much as named among the Gentiles, that one should have his father's wife. 2 And ye are puffed up, and have not rather mourned, that he that hath done this deed might be taken away from among you. 3 For I verily, as absent in body, but present in spirit, have judged already, ... 4 In the Name of our Lord יֵשׁוּעַ Messiah, ... with the power of our Lord יֵשׁוּעַ Messiah, 5 To deliver such an one unto Satan for the destruction of the flesh, that the spirit may be saved in the day of the Lord יֵשׁוּעַ.

27. NO HOMOSEXUAL PRACTICE

Lev. 18:22 Thou shalt not lie with mankind, as with womankind: it is abomination.

Lev. 20:13 If a man also lie with mankind, as he lieth with a woman, both of them have committed an abomination: they shall surely be put to death; their blood shall be upon them.

Deut. 23:17 There shall be no whore of the daughters of Israel, nor a sodomite of the sons of Israel.

PROPHETS

Isaiah 55:3 ... neither let the eunuch say, Behold, I am a dry tree.

YESHUA יֵשׁוּעַ

Matt. 19:12 For there are some eunuchs, which were so born from their mother's womb: and there are some eunuchs, which were made eunuchs of men: and there be eunuchs, which have made themselves eunuchs for the kingdom of heaven's sake. He that is able to receive it, let him receive it. *["Eunuch" means one who is abstinent by choice or for physical reasons.]*

APOSTLES

Rom. 1:25- end Who changed the truth of God into a lie, and worshipped and served the creature more than the Creator, who is blessed **forever**. Amen. 26 For this cause God gave them up unto vile affections: for even their women did change the natural use into that which is against nature: 27 And likewise also the men, leaving the natural use of the woman, burned in their lust one toward another; men with men working that which is unseemly, and receiving in themselves that recompence of their error which was meet. 28 And even as they did not like to retain God in their knowledge, God gave them over to a reprobate mind, to do those things which are not convenient; 29 Being filled with all unrighteousness, fornication, wickedness, covetousness, maliciousness; full of envy, murder, debate, deceit, malignity; whisperers, 30 Backbiters, haters of God, despiteful, proud, boasters, inventors of evil things, disobedient to parents, 31 Without understanding, covenantbreakers, **without natural affection**, implacable, unmerciful: 32 Who knowing the judgment of God, that they which commit such things are worthy of death, not only do the same, but have pleasure in them that do them.

1 Cor 6:9-11a (NIV) Or do you not know that wrongdoers will not inherit the kingdom of God? Do not be deceived: Neither the sexually immoral nor idolaters nor adulterers nor men who have sex with men 10 nor thieves nor the greedy nor drunkards nor slanderers nor swindlers will inherit the kingdom of God. 11 And that is what some of you were.

28. NO CROSS DRESSING

Deut. 22:5 The woman shall not wear that which pertaineth unto a man, neither shall a man put on a woman's garment: for all that do so are abomination unto יהוה thy God.

29. DO NOT LIE WITH A BEAST

Ex. 22:19 Whosoever lieth with a beast shall surely be put to death.

Lev. 18:23-24a Neither shalt thou lie with any beast to defile thyself therewith: neither shall any woman stand before a beast to lie down thereto: it is confusion. 24 Defile not ye yourselves in any of these things:

Lev. 20:15-16 And if a man lie with a beast, he shall surely be put to death: and ye shall slay the beast. And if a woman approach unto any beast, and lie down thereto, thou shalt kill the woman, and the beast: they shall surely be put to death; their blood shall be upon them.

Deut. 27:21 Cursed be he that lieth with any manner of beast.

30. RESPECT MALE ANATOMY, NO MATTER WHAT

Deut. 25:11-12 When men strive together one with another, and the wife of the one draweth near for to deliver her husband out of the hand of him that smiteth him, and putteth forth her hand, and taketh him by the secrets: 12 Then thou shalt cut off her hand, thine eye shall not pity her.

31. NO PROSTITUTION

Deut. 23:17a There shall be no whore of the daughters of Israel,

Deut. 23:18 Thou shalt not bring the hire of a whore, or the price of a dog, into the house of יהוה thy God for any vow: for even both these are abomination unto יהוה thy God. [also in Who may/may not enter Temple, p. 153]

AFTER TORAH

Hos.4:14 I won't punish your daughters when they act like whores, or your daughters-in-law when they commit adultery; because the men are themselves going off with whores and sacrificing with prostitutes. Yes, a people without understanding will come to ruin.

Amos 2:7 ...and a man and his father will go in unto the same maid, to profane My Holy Name.

32. DEFILE NOT THE LAND

Lev. 18:24-28 Defile not ye yourselves in any of these things [*incest, sons thro fire, homosexual acts, lie with beasts, etc.*]: for in all these the nations are defiled which I cast out before you: 25 And the land is defiled: therefore I do visit the iniquity thereof upon it, and the land itself vomiteth out her inhabitants. 26 Ye shall therefore keep My statutes and My judgments, and shall not commit any of these abominations; neither any of your own nation, nor any stranger that sojourneth among you: 27 (For all these abominations have the men of the land done, which were before you, and the land is defiled;) 28 That the land spue not you out also, when ye defile it, as it spued out the nations that were before you.

Num. 35:33-34 So ye shall not pollute the land wherein ye are: for blood it defileth the land: and the land cannot be cleansed of the blood that is shed therein, but by the blood of him that shed it. 34 Defile not therefore the land which ye shall inhabit, wherein I dwell: for I יהוה dwell among the children of Israel.

Deut. 21:22-23 And if a man have committed a sin worthy of death, and he be to be put to death, and thou <u>hang him on a tree</u>: 23 His body shall not remain all night upon the tree, but thou shalt in any wise bury him that day; (for <u>he that is hanged is accursed of God</u>;) that thy land be not defiled... [also in No Kiling, p. 48, and Trees, p. 13] *[They obeyed this command for* ישוע*.]*

Deut. 24:1-4 When a man hath taken a wife, and married her, and ... write her a bill of divorcement, ... she may go and be another man's wife. 3 And if the latter husband ... write her a bill of divorcement, ... 4 <u>Her former husband, which sent her away, may not take her again to be his wife, after that she is defiled; for that is abomination before</u> יהוה: and <u>thou shalt not cause the land to sin</u>, which יהוה thy God giveth thee for an inheritance. [also in Divoice and Remarriage, p. 60]

UNSOLVED MURDER, CLEANSE THE LAND: **Deut. 21:1-9** If one be found slain ... lying in the field, and it be not known who hath slain him: 2 ... 3 And it shall be, that the city which is next unto the slain man, even the elders of that city shall take an heifer, which hath not been wrought with, and which hath not drawn in the yoke; 4 And the elders of that city shall bring down the heifer unto a rough valley, which is neither eared nor sown, and shall strike off the heifer's neck there in the valley: 5 And the priests ... shall come near; ... 6 And all the elders of that city, ... shall wash their hands over the heifer that is beheaded in the valley: 7 And they shall answer and say, Our hands have not shed this blood, neither have our eyes seen it. 8 Be merciful, O יהוה, unto thy people Israel, whom thou hast redeemed, and lay not innocent blood unto thy people of Israel's charge. And the blood shall be forgiven them. 9 So shalt thou put away the guilt of innocent blood from among you.... [also in No killing, p. 48]

AFTER TORAH

Psalm 106:38,40 And shed innocent blood, even the blood of their sons and of their daughters...: and the land was polluted with blood. ... Therefore was the wrath of יהוה kindled against His people.... [*How much more for our nation shedding the blood of the pre-born?*]

Jer. 3:1, 4 They say, If a man put away his wife, and she go from him, and become another man's, shall he return unto her again? Shall not that land be greatly polluted?

YESHUA יֵשׁוּעַ was hung on a tree

Matt 27:57-60 When the even was come, there came a rich man of Arimathaea, named Joseph, who also himself was יֵשׁוּעַ' disciple: 58 He went to Pilate, and begged the body of יֵשׁוּעַ. Then Pilate commanded the body to be delivered. 59 And when Joseph had taken the body, he wrapped it in a clean linen cloth, 60 And laid it in his own new tomb, which he had hewn out in the rock: and he rolled a great stone to the door of the sepulchre, and departed.

APOSTLES

Gal. 3:13-14 Messiah hath redeemed us from the curse of the Torah, being made a curse for us: for it is written, Cursed is every one that hangeth on a tree: 14 That the blessing of Abraham might come on the Gentiles through יֵשׁוּעַ Messiah; that we might receive the promise of the Spirit through faith. [also in Trees, p. 133]

33. ALTAR

Notice that this commandment was given right after the Ten Commandments

Ex. 20:24, 25-26 An altar of earth thou shalt make unto me, ... And if thou wilt make me an altar of stone, thou shalt not build it of hewn stone: for if thou lift up thy tool upon it, thou hast polluted it. Neither shalt thou go up by steps unto mine altar, that thy nakedness be not discovered thereon.

Ex. 20:24 and shalt sacrifice thereon thy burnt offerings,

Deut. 27:6 [crossing Jordan] Thou shalt build the altar of יהוה thy God of whole stones: and thou shalt offer burnt offerings thereon unto יהוה thy God:

APOSTLES

Rom. 12:1-2 I beseech you therefore, brethren, by the mercies of God, that ye present your bodies a living sacrifice, holy, acceptable unto God, which is your reasonable service. 2 And be not conformed to this world: but be ye transformed by the renewing of your mind, that ye may prove what is that good, and acceptable, and perfect, will of God.

34. PEACE/WELLBEING/SHELEM OFFERING

*("Shelem" is the root word of **Shalom**.) Notice that this commandment was first given right after God spoke the Ten Commandments from Mt. Sinai. Today Yeshua gives us this peace and sense of well-being.*

(Abbreviated here. See more in OFFERINGS p. 141-142)

Ex. 20:24 An altar of earth thou shalt make unto Me, and shalt sacrifice thereon thy burnt offerings, and thy peace offerings, thy sheep, and...oxen: in all places where I record My Name I will come unto thee, and I will bless thee.

Lev. 3 *The whole chapter. Here are key phrases:* 1 And if his oblation be a sacrifice of peace offering, ...of the herd; ...male or female, ...without blemish before יהוה. 2 And he shall lay his hand upon the head of his offering, and kill it at the door of the Tabernacle...: the priests shall sprinkle the blood upon the altar round about. 3 And he shall offer ...all the fat ...upon the inwards, 4 And ...the caul above the liver, with the kidneys, it shall he take away. 5 And Aaron's sons shall burn it on the altar ...a sweet savour unto יהוה. ...9... the whole [tail]...7... a sheep...12... a goat ....

Lev. 6:12 And ...the priest shall burn wood on it every morning, and lay the burnt offering...upon it; and ...burn thereon the fat of the peace offerings.

Lev. 7:29-33 ...He that offereth ...his peace offerings unto יהוה .... 30 His own hands shall bring the offerings of יהוה ..., the fat with the breast, ...for a wave offering before יהוה. 31 And the priest shall burn the fat...: but the breast shall be Aaron's and his sons'. 32 And the right shoulder ...for an heave offering ...of your peace offerings. 33 He among the sons of Aaron, that offereth the blood of the peace offerings, and the fat, shall have the right shoulder for his part.

Lev. 19:5-7 And ...peace offerings unto יהוה, ye shall offer it at your own will. 6 It shall be eaten the same day ye offer it, and on the morrow: and if ought remain until the third day, it shall be burnt in the fire. 7 And if it be eaten at all on the third day, it is abominable; it shall not be accepted....

Lev. 22:21 And whosoever offereth a sacrifice of peace offerings unto יהוה to accomplish his vow, ...in beeves or sheep, it shall be perfect to be accepted; there shall be no blemish therein.

NAZARITE OFFERING: Num. 6:14, 18 and one ram without blemish for peace offerings ... 18 And the Nazarite ... shall take the hair of the head of his separation, and put it in the fire which is under the sacrifice of the peace offerings. [See Nazarite Vow, p. 189.]

MOADIM: Num. 10:10 Also in the day of your gladness, and in your solemn days, and in the beginnings of your months, ye shall blow with the trumpets over ... our peace offerings. SHAVUOT: Lev. 23:19 ...and two lambs of the first year for a sacrifice of peace...

Deut. 27:7 [crossing Jordan] And thou shalt offer peace offerings, and shalt eat there, and rejoice before יהוה thy God. [also in Rejoice, p. 187]

YESHUA ישוע and APOSTLES

John 14:27 Peace I leave with you, my peace I give unto you: not as the world giveth, give I unto you. Let not your heart be troubled, neither let it be afraid.

Phil. 4:7 And the peace of God, which passeth all understanding, shall keep your hearts and minds through Messiah ישוע.

Col. 3:15 And let the peace of God rule in your hearts, to the which also ye are called in one body; and be ye thankful.

[See more in Covenant of Peace, p. 237]

35. GIVE SLAVES REST ON THE SABBATH

Exodus 20:10 and Deut. 5:14 (CJB) The seventh day is a Shabbat for ADONAI your God. On it, you are not to do any kind of work—not you, your son or your daughter, not your male or female slave, not your livestock, and not the foreigner staying with you inside the gates to your property.

This would most likely also include all the Sabbath days of all the Appointed Times—all seven of them, including the first and last days of Unleavened Bread and of Sukkot, which totals nine days. (See Deut. 16:11,14. Slaves are included in the celebrations.)—in addition to the weekly Sabbath days off!

Foreign slaves had to be circumcised to partake of Passover

Exodus 12:44, 48 (NRSV) ...but any slave who has been purchased may eat of it [Passover lamb] after he has been circumcised; ....

36. DON'T MISTREAT SLAVES

Ex. 21:20-21 And if a man smite his servant, or his maid, with a rod, and he die under his hand; he shall be surely punished. 21 Notwithstanding, if he continue a day or two, he shall not be punished: for he is his money. [verse 20 also in No killing, p. 47]

Ex. 21:26-27 And if a man smite the eye of his servant, or the eye of his maid, that it perish; he shall **let him go free** for his eye's sake. And if he smite out his manservant's tooth, or his maidservant's tooth; he shall **let him go free** for his tooth's sake.

37. OBTAINING SLAVES

Hebrew doesn't have a word that means exclusively "slave." It has עבד *eved H5650 (from the root word* avad, to work). *It means* slave, servant, bondman, worshipper *and is used many times to indicate "a servant of* יהוה*." There's also the word* שכיר *sah-kheer H7916 (from the root verb* sah-khar, to hire, to earn wages) hired, hireling, hired labor. *Hebrew has two words for* handmaid *or* maidservant *that are also used to mean* bondwoman *or* slave girl. *It does have* מס *H4522* mahs *that means* tax *or* **levy** *and can mean a tax in the form of* forced labor. *(I Kings 5:13 And king Solomon raised a* **levy** *out of all Israel; and the* **levy** *was thirty thousand men.) This might sound like slavery, but though the labor is forced, it doesn't mean it is unpaid. So possibly in Hebrew, a slave is like an employee whose boss provides everything, like food, housing, etc.*

Lev. 25:44-46 Both thy bondmen, and thy bondmaids, which thou shalt have, shall be of the heathen (Hebrew: goyim, CJB: nations) that are round about you; of them shall ye buy bondmen and bondmaids. 45 Moreover of the children of the strangers that do sojourn among you, of them shall ye buy, and of their families that are with you, which they begat in your land: and they shall be your possession. 46 And ye shall take them **as an inheritance for your children after you, to inherit them for a possession;** they shall be your bondmen **forever**: but over your brethren the children of Israel, ye shall not rule one over another with rigour. [also in Jubilee, p. 184]

The fact that these slaves were their possession and could be inherited by their children sounds barbaric. But remember slaves were possibly more like around the clock servants/employees whose pay instead of money is housing and all provisions, kind of like life time job and social security. They could leave anytime. A slave who ran away was free [See p. 74]. And think about this. The nations around them were lawless. Their leaders could've been cruel, terrorist rulers like Lenin, Stalin, Hitler, or even ISIS. (Some of Israel's own kings and queens, later, were wicked, but there was still law in the land.) So these foreign slaves could've come from bondage worse than that of the starving serfs of the Middle Ages. Being taken from that to a nation that had rules to treat slaves well might possibly have been a better life for them.

Deut. 20:10-18 When you draw near to a town to fight against it, offer it terms of peace. 11 If it accepts your terms of peace and surrenders to you, then all the people in it shall serve you at forced labor. (מַס H4522, see p. 71)

Did they ever take foreign slaves this way?

They took captives of people they weren't supposed to, who brought disease and wickedness with them.

Numbers 31:7, 9, 14, 15-16 They did battle against Midian, as יהוה had commanded Moses, and killed every male.... 9 The Israelites took the women of Midian and their little ones captive; .... 14 Moses became angry with the officers of the army .... 15 Moses said to them, "Have you allowed all the women to live? 16 These women here, on Balaam's advice, made the Israelites act treacherously against יהוה in the affair of Peor, so that the plague came among the congregation of יהוה....

They made slaves of the people they were supposed to destroy.

Joshua 17:12-13; See also Judges 1:27-28   the Manassites could not take possession of those towns; but the Canaanites continued to live in that land. But when the Israelites grew strong, they **put the Canaanites to forced labor,** but did not utterly drive them out....

Judges 1:29-34 And Ephraim did not drive out the Canaanites who lived in Gezer; but the Canaanites lived among them.... 30 Zebulun did not drive out the inhabitants of Kitron, or ... of Nahalol; **but the Canaanites lived among them, and became subject to forced labor.** ... 33 Naphtali did not drive out the inhabitants of Beth-shemesh, or ... Beth-anath, but lived among the Canaanites...; nevertheless the inhabitants of Beth-shemesh and of Beth-anath **became subject to forced labor for them.** ... 35 The Amorites continued to live in Har-heres, [and 2 more cities], but the hand of the house of Joseph rested heavily on them, and **they became subject to forced labor**.

King David did.

2 Samuel 8:2 He [David] also defeated the Moabites and, making them lie down on the ground, measured them off with a cord; he measured two lengths of cord for those who were to be put to death, and one length for those who were to be spared. And the Moabites became servants[H5650] to David and brought tribute.[H4503]

2 Samuel 8:6,14 Then David put garrisons among the Arameans of Damascus; and the Arameans became servants[H5650] to David and brought tribute. יהוה gave victory to David wherever he went. ... throughout all Edom he put garrisons, and all the Edomites became David's servants.[H5650] And יהוה gave victory to David wherever he went.

2 Samuel 10:19 When all the kings who were servants[H5650] of Hadadezer saw that they had been defeated by Israel, they made peace with Israel, and became subject[H5647] to them.

2 Samuel 12:31; 20:24 He brought out the people who were in it, and set them to work with saws and iron picks and iron axes, or sent them to the brickworks. Thus he did to all the cities of the Ammonites. ... Adoram was in charge of the forced labor;[H4522]

King Solomon made slaves of both Israelites and foreigners dwelling among them.

I Kings 5:13-16 (NRSV) King Solomon conscripted forced labor[H4522] out of all Israel; the levy numbered thirty thousand men. 14 He sent them to the Lebanon, ten thousand a month in shifts; they would be a month in the Lebanon and two months at home; Adoniram was in charge of the forced labor.[H4522] 15 Solomon also had seventy thousand laborers and eighty thousand stonecutters in the hill country, 16 besides Solomon's three thousand three hundred supervisors who were over the work, having charge of the people who did the work.

I Kings 9:15-21 (NRSV) This is the account of the forced labor[H4522] that King Solomon conscripted to build the house of the LORD and his own house, the Millo and the wall of Jerusalem, Hazor, Megiddo, Gezer ... 19 as well as all of Solomon's storage cities, the cities for his chariots, the cities for his cavalry, and whatever Solomon desired to build ... 20 All the people ... who were not of the people of Israel— 21 their descendants who were still left in the land, whom the Israelites were unable to destroy completely—these Solomon conscripted[H5647] for slave labor....

The people obviously did not like being forced to work for King Solomon.

I Kings 12:18 (NRSV) When King Rehoboam [Solomon's son] sent Adoram, who was taskmaster over the forced labor,[H4522] all Israel stoned him to death. King Rehoboam then hurriedly mounted his chariot to flee to Jerusalem.

King Asa also conscripted all the people.

I Kings 15:22 (NRSV) Then King Asa made a proclamation to all Judah, none was exempt: they carried away the stones of Ramah and its timber, with which Baasha had been building; with them King Asa built Geba of Benjamin and Mizpah.

38. SLAVES WHO ESCAPE ARE FREE

The following is very important. It further proves that slaves were more like around the clock servants. This law would have avoided a lot of the terror for the slaves in southern America:

Deut. 23:15-16 Thou shalt **not** deliver unto his master the servant **which is escaped** from his master unto thee: 16 He shall dwell with thee, even among you, in that place which he shall choose in one of thy gates, **where it liketh him best: thou shalt not oppress him**.

39. THE VALUE OF A SLAVE'S LIFE

We can't judge whether the slave's value was less than free people because we don't know at what price the average ransom would have been set in those days.

Ex. 21:29-32 (NRSV) If the ox has been accustomed to gore in the past, and its owner has been warned but has not restrained it, and it kills a man or a woman, <u>the ox shall be stoned, and its owner also shall be put to death</u>. 30 If a ransom is imposed on the owner, then the owner shall pay whatever is imposed for the redemption of the victim's life. 31 If it gores a boy or a girl, the owner shall be dealt with according to this same rule. 32 If the ox gores a male or female slave *[Hebrew slave, too? Not sure.]*, **the owner shall pay to the slaveowner thirty shekels of silver, and the ox shall be stoned.**

This of course, makes us think of Yeshua and it is very profound. Yeshua said He came "not to be served, but to serve" (Matt. 20:28; Mark 10:45). He emptied Himself taking the form of a slave (Phil 2:7). He proved this in many ways, but the final way was that He was betrayed for exactly the same price of a slave. The same retribution was "paid" (actually paid back) for His death as for the death of a slave required in the Torah! The silver was paid back in the Temple! (Matt. 27:3-5) It is as if, Judas, representing mankind, was paying God the restitution required so even this detail in the Torah would be fulfilled. The "beast" that did the killing, the devil, was known to kill and destroy many times before!

Keep in mind, though, that Yeshua was a slave to His Father, not the people. He did not obey what people told Him to do. He served people as unto the Father in obedience to Him only, as we also should do.

40. ISRAELITES CAN SELL THEMSELVES AS SLAVES

However, they can be redeemed and are not to be treated as slaves, but as hired servants.

Ex. 21:2-3 If thou buy an Hebrew servant, **six years he shall serve:** and **in the seventh he shall go out free** for nothing. If he came in by himself, he shall go out by himself: if he were married, then his wife shall go out with him. *[It doesn't mention children in this case.]*

Lev. 25:39-43 And if thy brother that dwelleth by thee be waxen poor, and be sold unto thee; **thou shalt not compel him to serve as a bondservant: 40 But as an hired servant,** and as a sojourner, he shall be with thee, and shall serve thee unto the year of Jubile[e]: 41 And then shall he depart from thee, both he and his children with him, and shall return unto his own family, and unto the possession of his fathers shall he return. 42 For they are my servants, which I brought forth out of the land of Egypt: **they shall not be sold as bondmen.** 43 **Thou shalt not rule over him with rigour** [NRSV: **harshness**]; but shalt fear thy God. [also in Poor, p. 97, and Jubilee, p. 184]

Lev. 25:47-55 And if a sojourner or stranger wax rich by thee, and thy brother that dwelleth by him wax poor, and sell himself unto the stranger or sojourner by thee, or to the stock of the stranger's family: 48 **After that he is sold he may be redeemed again**; one of his brethren may redeem him: 49 Either his uncle, or his uncle's son, may redeem him, or any that is nigh of kin unto him of his family may redeem him; or if he be able, he may redeem himself. 50 And he shall reckon with him that bought him from the year that he was sold to him unto the year of Jubile[e]: and the price of his sale shall be according unto the number of years, according to the time of an hired servant shall it be with him. ... 53 And **as a yearly hired servant shall he be with him:** and the other **shall not rule with rigour** [NRSV: **harshness**] over him in thy sight. 54 And if he be not redeemed in these years, then he shall go out in the year of Jubile[e], both he, and his children with him. 55 For unto me the children of Israel are servants; they are my servants whom I brought forth out of the land of Egypt: I am יהוה your God. [also in Poor, p. 97, and Jubilee, p. 184]

Lev. 26:13 I am יהוה your God, which brought you forth out of the land of Egypt, that ye should not be their bondmen; and I have broken the bands of your yoke, and made you go upright.

41. SEVERANCE PACKAGE FOR FREED HEBREW SLAVES

Deut. 15:12-15, 18 And if thy brother, an Hebrew man, or an Hebrew woman, be sold unto thee, and **serve thee six years;** then **in the seventh year thou shalt let him go free** from thee. 13 And when thou sendest him out free from thee, **thou shalt not let him go away empty:** 14 **Thou shalt furnish him liberally** out of thy flock, and out of thy floor, and out of thy winepress: of that wherewith יהוה thy God hath blessed thee thou shalt give unto him. And thou shalt remember that thou wast a bondman in the land of Egypt, and יהוה thy God redeemed thee: therefore I command thee this thing to day. ... 18 It shall not seem hard unto thee, when thou sendest him away free from thee; for he hath been worth a double hired servant to thee, in serving thee six years: and יהוה thy God shall bless thee in all that thou doest.

42. SLAVES PLEDGING FOR LIFE

Ex 21:5-6 And if the servant shall plainly say, I love my master, my wife, and my children; I will not go out free: Then his master shall bring him unto the judges; he shall also bring him to the door, or unto the door post; and his master shall bore his ear through with an aul; and he shall serve him **forever.**

Deut. 15:16-17 And it shall be, if he say unto thee, I will not go away from thee; because he loveth thee and thine house, because he is well with thee; Then thou shalt take an aul, and thrust it through his ear unto the door, and he shall be thy servant **forever**. And also unto thy maidservant thou shalt do likewise.

So, if a slave wants to keep his wife and family, he must submit to his master for life. It sounds barbaric, but this is God's rule and He is not barbaric, so we must not be looking at it right. The wife had to be a foreigner. If she were Hebrew, she would also be set free. So when he married this foreign slave, he would have known that she would never be free unless she ran away.. Also the master might be a benevolent man who treats his slaves/servants kindly and generously, providing and caring for them as kin. This is a wonderful analogy of us committing our lives to Yeshua as our Master, realizing that our family belongs to Him, and choosing to remain in His care, under His loving authority and protection in this harsh, dark world, rather than fending for ourselves all alone.

43. SLAVES WITH WIVES

Ex. 21:4 If his master have given him a wife, and she have born him sons or daughters; the wife and her children shall be her master's, and he shall go out by himself.

This does seem awful to our 21st century minds.(See above.) But the meaning for us today is that our children and spouses are not ours. They belong to our Master, Yeshua. We do not own them, so we should not be controlling or domineering over them.

44. SELLING DAUGHTER
(TO BE A WIFE, LIKE A REVERSE DOWRY)

Ex. 21:7-8, 10-11 And if a man sell his daughter to be a maidservant, she shall not go out as the menservants do. 8 If she please not her master, who hath betrothed her to himself, then shall he let her be redeemed: *[he cannot sell her]* to sell her unto a strange nation he shall have <u>no power</u>, seeing he hath dealt deceitfully with her. ... 10 If he take him another wife; her food, her raiment, and her duty of marriage, shall he not diminish. 11 And if he do not these three unto her, **then shall she go out free** without money *[without needing to be redeemed?]*. [verse 10 also in Second wife, p. 77]

45. FEMALE SLAVES
(SOMETIMES TAKEN TO BE WIVES)

Deut. 21:10-14 When thou goest forth to war against thine enemies, and יהוה thy God hath delivered them into thine hands, and thou hast taken them captive, 11 And seest among the captives a beautiful woman, and hast a desire unto her, that thou wouldest have her to thy wife; 12 Then thou shalt bring her home to thine house; and she shall shave her head, and pare her nails; 13 And she shall put the raiment of her captivity from off her, and shall remain in thine house, and bewail her father and her mother a full month: and after that thou shalt go in unto her, and be her husband, and she shall be thy wife. 14 And it shall be, if thou have no delight in her, then thou shalt let her go whither she will; but **thou shalt not sell her at all** for money, thou shalt not make merchandise of her, because thou hast humbled her.

46. SECOND WIFE (SOMETIMES A SLAVE)

Ex. 21:10 If he take him another wife; her food, her raiment, and her duty of marriage, shall he not diminish. [also in Selling daughter, p. 76]

Deut. 21:15-17 If a man have two wives, one beloved, and another hated, and they have born him children, both the beloved and the hated; and if the firstborn son be hers that was hated: 16 Then it shall be, when he maketh his sons to inherit that which he hath, that he may not make the son of the beloved firstborn before the son of the hated, which is indeed the firstborn: 17 But he shall acknowledge the son of the hated for the firstborn, by giving him a double portion of all that he hath: for he is the beginning of his strength; the right of the firstborn is his. [also in Firstborn son/children, p. 134]

APOSTLES: I Tim. 3:2,12 A bishop then must be blameless, **the husband of one wife,** ... 12 Let the deacons be the **husbands of one wife,** ruling their children and their own houses well.

YESHUA יֵשׁוּעַ and APOSTLES on SLAVERY

Yeshua told many parables about slaves and talked as if it was common to have slaves. But He told us we are to be like slaves to Him and we are not to "lord it over" others. Yeshua lets the indwelling of the Spirit gently teach us that enslaving others is not pleasing to Him.

[All Scripture in this section are NRSV unless marked}

Luke 17:7-10 Who among you would say to your slave who has just come in from plowing or tending sheep in the field, "Come here at once and take your place at the table'? 8 Would you not rather say to him, "Prepare supper for me, put on your apron and serve me while I eat and drink; later you may eat and drink'? 9 Do you thank the slave for doing what was commanded? 10 So you also, when you have done all that you were ordered to do, say, "We are worthless slaves; we have done only what we ought to have done!"

Matt. 20:25-28 But Jesus called them to him and said, "You know that the rulers of the Gentiles lord it over them, and their great ones are tyrants over them. 26 It will not be so among you; but whoever wishes to be great among you must be your servant, 27 and whoever wishes to be first among you must be your slave; 28 just as the Son of Man came not to be served but to serve, and to give his life a ransom for many."

Mark 10:42-45 (the same passage stated a tiny bit differently in verse 44) 44 and whoever wishes to be first among you must be slave of all.

SLAVERY

Rabbi Sha'ul (Paul) did what Yeshua said: I Cor. 9:19 For though I am free with respect to all, I have made myself a slave to all, so that I might win more of them.

Matt. 6:24 No one can serve two masters; for a slave will either hate the one and love the other, or be devoted to the one and despise the other. You cannot serve God and wealth.

Matt. 10:24-25 A disciple is not above the teacher, nor a slave above the master; it is enough for the disciple to be like the teacher, and the slave like the master. If they have called the master of the house Beelzebul, how much more will they malign those of his household!

In these two passages, Yeshua is implying that, as His slaves, beating those under us is wrong.

Luke 12:42,45-46 (also in Matt. 24:45-50) And the Lord said, "Who then is the faithful and prudent manager whom his master will put in charge of his slaves, to give them their allowance of food at the proper time? ... if that slave says to himself, 'My master is delayed in coming,' and if he begins to beat the other slaves, men and women, and to eat and drink and get drunk, 46 the master of that slave will come on a day when he does not expect him and at an hour that he does not know, and will cut him [off], and put him with the unfaithful.

There will be different levels of punishment for these disobedient slaves:

Luke 12:47-48 That slave who knew what his master wanted, but did not prepare himself or do what was wanted, will receive a severe beating. 48 But the one who did not know and did what deserved a beating will receive a light beating.

Reward for Yeshua's faithful slaves:

Luke 12:35-38 Be dressed for action and have your lamps lit; 36 be like those who are waiting for their master to return from the wedding banquet, so that they may open the door for him as soon as he comes and knocks. 37 Blessed are those slaves whom the master finds alert when he comes; truly I tell you, he will fasten his belt and have them sit down to eat, and he will come and serve them. 38 If he comes during the middle of the night, or near dawn, and finds them so, blessed are those slaves.

Matt. 24:46 Blessed is that slave whom his master will find at work when he arrives. 47 Truly I tell you, he will put that one in charge of all his possessions.

Luke 19:17 "Well done, good slave! Because you have been trustworthy in a very small thing, take charge of ten cities."

Matt. 25:21 His master said to him, "Well done, good and trustworthy slave; you have been trustworthy in a few things, I will put you in charge of many things; enter into the joy of your master."

John 8:34 Jesus answered them, "Very truly, I tell you, everyone who commits sin is a slave to sin.

APOSTLES

We can look at this as how to behave toward those over us and under us at work.

I Cor. 7:20-24 (RSV) Every one should remain in the state in which he was called. 21 Were you a slave when called? Never mind. But if you can gain your freedom, avail yourself of the opportunity. 22 For he who was called in the Lord as a slave is a freedman of the Lord. Likewise he who was free when called is a slave of Christ. 23 You were bought with a price; **do not become slaves of men**. 24 So, brethren, in whatever state each was called, there let him remain with God.

Galatians 3:26-28 For in Christ Jesus you are all children of God through faith. 27 As many of you as were baptized into Christ have clothed yourselves with Christ. 28 There is no longer Jew or Greek, there is no longer slave or free, there is no longer male and female; for all of you are one in Christ Jesus.

Gal. 5:13 For you were called to freedom, brothers and sisters; only do not use your freedom as an opportunity for self-indulgence, **but through love become slaves to one another.**

Eph. 6:5 Slaves obey your masters. Work willingly as unto the Lord. 6 not only while being watched, and in order to please them, but as slaves of Christ, doing the will of God from the heart. 7 Render service with enthusiasm, as to the Lord and not to men and women, 8 knowing that whatever good we do, we will receive the same again from the Lord, whether we are slaves or free.

Eph. 6:9 And, masters, do the same to them. Stop threatening them, for you know that both of you have the same Master in heaven, and with him there is no partiality.

Col. 3:11 In that renewal there is no longer Greek and Jew, circumcised and uncircumcised, barbarian, Scythian, slave and free; but Christ is all and in all!

Col. 3:22-25 Slaves, obey your earthly masters in everything, not only while being watched and in order to please them, but wholeheartedly, fearing the Lord. 23 Whatever your task, put yourselves into it, as done for the Lord and not for your masters, 24 since you know that from the Lord you will receive the inheritance as your reward; you serve the Lord Christ. 25 For the wrongdoer will be paid back for whatever wrong has been done, and there is no partiality.

Col. 4:1 Masters, treat your slaves justly and fairly, for you know that you also have a Master in heaven.

1 Timothy 6:1-2 Let all who are under the yoke of slavery regard their masters as worthy of all honor, so that the Name of God and the teaching may not be blasphemed. Those who have believing masters must not be disrespectful to them on the ground that they are members of the church; rather they must serve them all the more, since those who benefit by their service are believers and beloved. Teach and urge these duties.

Philemon verses15-16 Perhaps this is the reason he was separated from you for a while, so that you might have him back **forever**, 16 no longer as a slave but more than a slave, a beloved brother—especially to me but how much more to you, both in the flesh and in the Lord.

1 Pet. 2:18-21 (NASB) Servants, be submissive to your masters with all respect, not only to those who are good and gentle, but also to those who are unreasonable. 19 For this finds favor, if for the sake of conscience toward God a person bears up under sorrows when suffering unjustly. 20 For what credit is there if, when you sin and are harshly treated, you endure it with patience? But if when you do what is right and suffer for it you patiently endure it, this finds favor with God. 21 For you have been called for this purpose, since Christ also suffered for you, leaving you an example for you to follow in His steps....

Slave traders are categorized with murderers, etc.

I Timothy 1:9-10 This means understanding that the law is laid down not for the innocent but for the lawless and disobedient, for the godless and sinful, for the unholy and profane, for those who kill their father or mother, for murderers, 10 fornicators, sodomites, **slave traders,** liars, perjurers, and whatever else is contrary to the sound teaching.

YESHUA ישוע brings LIBERTY!

ישוע *sets us free! He releases us from our horrible, burdensome captivity and bondage to sin. He has conquered the kingdom of darkness that has enslaved us and treated us cruelly and inhumanely. He then takes us as His captives and treats us as His treasures as valuable as precious stones. [The Hebrew root of captive* שׁוִי *"sh'vi" is* שָׁבוּ *"shavu" (according to Strong's) which means a precious stone (in the high priest's breastplate).] Submitting to Him and being His slave is FREEDOM!! He is a gentle, loving, caring, nurturing, serving Master. His yoke is easy and His burden is light! In His slavery, there is rest!*

Matt. 11:28-30 Come to me, all you that are weary and are carrying heavy burdens, and I will give you rest. 29 Take my yoke upon you, and learn from me; for I am gentle and humble in heart, and you will find rest for your souls. 30 For my yoke is easy, and my burden is light.

Yeshua is a tender loving, caring father, intimate friend, mentoring teacher, protecting and providing King, and benevolent, gentle Master to us. He is all that and much more all rolled up in one.

May we be thoroughly cleansed and purified, then anointed with the oil of liberty to become cohen (priests) and kings for our King of Kings in His Kingdom!

May we become שַׁמָּשׁ *shamash (servants/ministers) to Him—the kind of servants and ministers that shine brilliantly from His brightness in us, brighter than the* שֶׁמֶשׁ *shemesh (sun), that we may bless Him and make Him smile as on a beautiful sunny day. And may we, like the shamash candle of the Hanukkah candles, help light His fire in others all over the world.*

47. DON'T INJURE PEOPLE, EYE FOR EYE

Ex. 21:18-19 And if men strive together, and one smite another with a stone, or with his fist, and he die not, but keepeth his bed: If he rise again, and walk abroad upon his staff, then shall he that smote him be quit: only he shall pay for the loss of his time, and shall cause him to be thoroughly healed.

Lev. 24:19-20 And if a man cause a blemish in his neighbour; as he hath done, so shall it be done to him; 20 Breach for breach, eye for eye, tooth for tooth: as he hath caused a blemish in a man, so shall it be done to him again.

Deut. 19:21 And thine eye shall not pity; but life shall go for life, eye for eye, tooth for tooth, hand for hand, foot for foot.

Deut. 27:24 Cursed be he that smiteth his neighbour secretly. And all the people shall say, Amen.

YESHUA יֵשׁוּעַ and APOSTLES

Matt. 5:38-39 Ye have heard that it hath been said, An eye for an eye, and a tooth for a tooth: 39 But I say unto you, That ye resist not evil: but whosoever shall smite thee on thy right cheek, turn to him the other also.

Luke 6:28-29 Bless them that curse you, and pray for them which despitefully use you. 29 And unto him that smiteth thee on the one cheek offer also the other; ....

Acts 23:3b Will you ... in violation of the Torah order me to be struck?"

I Pet. 3:9 (TLV) Do not repay evil for evil or insult for insult, but give a blessing instead ... so that you might inherit a blessing

48. DON'T INJURE AN UNBORN CHILD, LIFE FOR LIFE

Ex. 21:22-25 (TLV) "If men [NIV: people] fight, and hit a pregnant woman so that her child is born early, yet no harm follows, the one who hit her is to be strictly fined, according to what the woman's husband demands of him. He must pay as the judges determine. 23 But if any harm follows, then you are to penalize life for life, 24 eye for an eye, tooth for a tooth, hand for hand, foot for foot, 25 burn for burn, wound for wound, blow for blow.

Some have used this passage to support abortion. But the Hebrew doesn't say "miscarriage" as some versions say or imply. It says "and the child comes out." וְיָצְאוּ יְלָדֶיהָ It doesn't say "dies" either at all. It is saying as above that if they injure her so that the child is born, but there is no harm to the child, then the offender just has to pay for causing the premature birth. But if there is injury or fatality of the baby or mother then life for life, etc.

49. KEEP YOUR PROPERTY AND HOUSE SAFE FOR PEOPLE

Deut. 22:8 When thou buildest a new house, then thou shalt make a battlement [parapet] for thy roof, that thou bring not blood upon thine house, if any man fall from thence.

50. ANIMAL HURTING OR KILLING A PERSON

Ex. 21:28, 30-31 If an ox gore a man or a woman, that they die: then the ox shall be surely stoned, and his flesh shall not be eaten; but the owner of the ox shall be quit. ... If there be laid on him a sum of money, then he shall give for the ransom of his life whatsoever is laid upon him. Whether he have gored a son, or have gored a daughter, according to this judgment shall it be done unto him.

Ex. 21:29 But if the ox were wont to push with his horn in time past, and it hath been testified to his owner, and he hath not kept him in, but that he hath killed a man or a woman; the ox shall be stoned, and his owner also shall be put to death.

Ex. 21:32 If the ox shall push a manservant or a maidservant; he shall give unto their master thirty shekels of silver, and the ox shall be stoned.

51. BE KIND TO ANIMALS

Ex. 21:33-34 And if a man shall open a pit, or if a man shall dig a pit, and not cover it, and an ox or an ass fall therein; The owner of the pit shall make it good, and give money unto the owner of them; and the dead beast shall be his.

Ex. 21:35 And if one man's ox hurt another's, that he die; then they shall sell the live ox, and divide the money of it; and the dead ox also they shall divide.

Ex. 21:36 Or if it be known that the ox hath used to push in time past, and his owner hath not kept him in; he shall surely pay ox for ox; and the dead shall be his own.

Ex. 23:4-5 If thou meet thine enemy's ox or his ass going astray, thou shalt surely bring it back to him again. If thou see the ass of him that hateth thee lying under his burden, and wouldest forbear to help him, thou shalt surely help with him. [also in How to treat your Enemy]

Lev. 24:18 And he that killeth a beast shall make it good; beast for beast. ... 21 And he that killeth a beast, he shall restore it....

Deut. 22:4 Thou shalt not see thy brother's ass or his ox fall down by the way, and hide thyself from them: thou shalt surely help him to lift them up again.

Deut. 25:4 **Thou shalt not muzzle the ox when he treadeth out the corn** *[grain]*.

GIVE WORKING ANIMALS REST ON THE SABBATH: Deut. 5:14 and Ex. 20:10 But the seventh day is the Sabbath of יהוה thy God: in it thou shalt not do any work, thou ... nor thine ox, nor thine ass [donkey], nor any of thy cattle....

YESHUA יֵשׁוּעַ

Matt 12:11 He said to them, "Suppose one of you has only one sheep and it falls into a pit on the Sabbath; will you not lay hold of it and lift it out?

Luke 13:15 But the Lord answered him and said, "You hypocrites! Does not each of you on the Sabbath untie his ox or his donkey from the manger, and lead it away to give it water?

John 10:11-14 I am the good shepherd: the good shepherd giveth His life for the sheep. 12 But he that is an hireling, and not the shepherd, whose own the sheep are not, seeth the wolf coming, and leaveth the sheep, and fleeth: and the wolf catcheth them, and scattereth the sheep. 13 The hireling fleeth, because he is an hireling, and careth not for the sheep. 14 I am the good shepherd, and know My sheep, and am known of Mine.

APOSTLES

1 Cor. 9:7-10, 14-15 Who goeth a warfare any time at his own charges? who planteth a vineyard, and eateth not of the fruit thereof? or who feedeth a flock, and eateth not of the milk of the flock? 8 Say I these things as a man? or saith not the Torah the same also? 9 For it is written in the Torah of Moses, **Thou shalt not muzzle the mouth of the ox that treadeth out the corn** *[grain]*. Doth God take care *[only]* for oxen? 10 Or saith he it altogether for our sakes? For our sakes, no doubt, this is written: that he that ploweth should plow in hope; and that he that thresheth in hope should be partaker of his hope. ... 14 Even so hath the Lord ordained that they which preach the Gospel should live of the Gospel. 15 But I have used none of these things: neither have I written these things, that it should be so done unto me: for it were better for me to die, than that any man should make my glorying void. [Verse 14 also in Wages p. 97; Rules for Priests and Levites p. 221.]

I Tim. 5:17-18 Let the elders that rule well be counted worthy of double honour, especially they who labour in the word and doctrine. 18 For the scripture saith, **Thou shalt not muzzle the ox that treadeth out the corn** *[grain]*. And, The labourer is worthy of his reward.

52. PREVENT EXTINCTION

Deut. 22:6-7 If a bird's nest chance to be before thee in the way in any tree, or on the ground, whether they be young ones, or eggs, and the dam sitting upon the young, or upon the eggs, thou shalt not take the dam with the young: 7 But thou shalt in any wise let the dam go, and take the young to thee; that it may be well with thee, and that thou mayest prolong thy days. *(So birds do not go extinct! So we always have the beauty of birds and their songs!)* [also in That it May Go Well, p. 257]

53. DON'T DESTROY PROPERTY

Ex. 22:5 If a man shall cause a field or vineyard to be eaten, and shall put in his beast, and shall feed in another man's field; of the best of his own field, and of the best of his own vineyard, shall he make restitution.

Ex. 22:6 If fire break out, and catch in thorns, so that the stacks of corn, or the standing corn, or the field, be consumed therewith; he that kindled the fire shall surely make restitution.

Ex. 22:9 For all manner of trespass, whether it be for ox, for ass, for sheep, for raiment, or for any manner of lost thing, which another challengeth to be his, the cause of both parties shall come before the judges; and whom the judges shall condemn, he shall pay double unto his neighbour.

Deut. 23:25 When thou comest into the standing corn of thy neighbour, then thou mayest pluck the ears with thine hand; but thou shalt not move a sickle unto thy neighbour's standing corn. [also in Eating from Neighbor's Land, p. 96]

54. DON'T MOVE LANDMARKS

Deut. 27:17 Cursed be he that removeth his neighbour's landmark.

AFTER TORAH:

Prov.22:28 Remove not the ancient landmark, which thy fathers have set.

Prov. 23:10 Remove not the old landmark....

55. BORROWING AND STORING OTHER'S THINGS

Ex. 22:7-8 If a man shall deliver unto his neighbour money or stuff to keep, and it be stolen out of the man's house; if the thief be found, let him pay double. 8 If the thief be not found, then the master of the house shall be brought unto the judges, to see whether he have put his hand unto his neighbour's goods.

Ex. 22:10-13 If a man deliver unto his neighbour an ass, or an ox, or a sheep, or any beast, to keep; and it die, or be hurt, or driven away, no man seeing it: 11 Then shall an oath of יהוה be between them both, that he hath not put his hand unto his neighbour's goods; and the owner of it shall accept thereof, and he shall not make it good. 12 And if it be stolen from him, he shall make restitution unto the owner thereof. 13 If it be torn in pieces, then let him bring it for witness, and he shall not make good that which was torn....

Ex. 22:14-15 (NRSV) When someone borrows an animal from another and it is injured or dies, the owner not being present, full restitution shall be made. 15 If the owner was present, there shall be no restitution; if it was hired, only the hiring fee is due.

RESPECT PROPERTY

84

Lev. 6:4-5 ...<u>or that which was delivered him to keep,</u> or the lost thing which he found, 5 or whatever it was they swore falsely about. They must make restitution in full, add a fifth of the value to it and give it all to the owner on the day they present their guilt offering. [also in No False Witness, p. 53, and in Finding Lost, p. 85]

AFTER TORAH

I Kings 6:5-7 But as one was felling a beam, the axe head fell into the water: and he cried, and said, Alas, master! for it was borrowed. 6 And the man of God [Elisha] said, Where fell it? And he shewed him the place. And he cut down a stick, and cast it in thither; and the iron did swim. 7 Therefore said he, Take it up to thee. And he put out his hand, and took it.

Psalms 37:21 The wicked borrows and does not repay, But the righteous shows mercy and gives.

YESHUA יֵשׁוּעַ and APOSTLES

Matt. 5:42 Give to him that asketh thee, and from him that would borrow of thee turn not thou away. [also in Lending, p. 126]

Rom. 13:8 Owe no man any thing, but to love one another: for he that loveth another hath fulfilled the Torah.

[For, lending, see Lending Money, p. 125-126]

56. FINDING LOST PROPERTY (FINDERS ARE NOT KEEPERS)

Ex. 23:4-5 If thou meet thine enemy's ox or his ass going astray, thou shalt surely bring it back to him again. [also in How to Treat your Enemy, p. 90]

Lev. 6:3-5 Or have <u>found that which was lost, and lieth</u> concerning it....: 4 Then it shall be, because he hath sinned, and is guilty, that he shall restore that which he ... hath deceitfully gotten, or that which was delivered him to keep, o<u>r the lost thing which he found,</u> 5 or whatever it was they swore falsely about. They must make restitution in full, add a fifth of the value to it and give it all to the owner on the day they present their guilt offering. [also in No False Witness, p. 53, and Borrowing, p. 84]

Deut. 22:1-3 Thou shalt not see thy brother's ox or his sheep go astray, and hide thyself from them: thou shalt in any case bring them again unto thy brother. 2 And if thy brother be not nigh unto thee, or if thou know him not, then thou shalt bring it unto thine own house, and it shall be with thee until thy brother seek after it, and thou shalt restore it to him again. 3 In like manner shalt thou do with his ass; and so shalt thou do with his raiment; and with all lost thing of thy brother's, which he hath lost, and thou hast found, shalt thou do likewise: thou mayest not hide thyself.

57. BE KIND TO STRANGERS AND FOREIGNERS
(HOW TO TREAT THEM)

Ex. 22:21 Thou shalt **neither vex a stranger, nor oppress him**: for ye were strangers in the land of Egypt.

Ex. 23:9 Also **thou shalt not oppress a stranger:** for ye know the heart of a stranger, seeing ye were strangers in the land of Egypt.

Lev. 19:33-34 And if a stranger sojourn with thee in your land, **ye shall not vex him.** 34 But the stranger that dwelleth with you **shall be unto you as one born among you**, and **thou shalt love him as thyself;** for ye were strangers in the land of Egypt: I am יהוה your God.

Lev. 24:16 ...: as well the stranger, as he that is born in the land, when he blasphemeth the Name of יהוה, shall be put to death.

Lev. 25:35-38 And if thy brother be waxen poor, and fallen in decay with thee; then thou shalt relieve him: yea, **though he be a stranger, or a sojourner;** that he may live with thee. 36 Take thou no usury of him, or increase: but fear thy God; that thy brother may live with thee. 37 Thou shalt not give him thy money upon usury, nor lend him thy victuals for increase. 38 I am יהוה your God, which brought you forth out of the land of Egypt,...

Num. 1:51b and 3:10b and the stranger that cometh nigh *[the Tabernacle]* shall be put to death. [also in Tabernacle, p. 150]

Deut. 10:19 **Love ye therefore the stranger:** for ye were strangers in the land of Egypt.

Deut. 24:14 Thou shalt not oppress an hired servant that is poor and needy, whether he be of thy brethren, or of thy **strangers** that are in thy land within thy gates: [also in Wages, p. 97, and Poor, p. 100]

Deut. 24:17a Thou **shalt not pervert the judgment of the stranger,** nor of the fatherless; [also in Orphans p. 88, and Unbiased Justice, p. 118]

PSALMS, PROPHETS, YESHUA ישוע, and APOSTLES

Psalm 146:9 יהוה preserveth the **strangers;**

Jer. 7:6-7 If ye oppress not the **stranger,** ... Then will I cause you to dwell in this place... **forever**....

Matt. 25:34-36 Come, ye blessed of my Father, inherit the kingdom prepared for you...: For ... I was a **stranger,** and ye took me in: naked, and ye clothed me....

Acts 10:28 (TLV) *[Peter said,]* "You yourselves know that it is not permitted for a Jewish man to associate with a non-Jew or to visit him. *[But see above, the Torah commands to love the stranger. God correctd Peter.]* Yet God has shown me that I should call no one unholy or unclean."

Heb. 13:2-3 (NRSV) Do not neglect to show hospitality to **strangers,** for by doing that some have entertained angels without knowing it. 3 Remember those who are in prison, as though you were in prison with them; those who are being tortured, as though you yourselves were being tortured. [also in Love thy neighbor, p. 95]

58. ONE TORAH FOR YOU AND THE STRANGER

Exodus 12:44, 48-49 [Passover] But every man's servant that is bought for money, when thou hast circumcised him, then shall he eat thereof. ... 48 And when a stranger shall sojourn with thee, and will keep the Passover to יהוה, let all his males be circumcised, and then let him come near and keep it; and **he shall be as one that is born in the land:** for no uncircumcised person shall eat thereof. 49 **One Torah shall be to him that is homeborn, and unto the stranger** that sojourneth among you. [also in Passover, p. 161 and Circumcision, p. 192]

Lev. 18:26 Ye shall therefore keep My statutes and My judgments, and shall not commit any of these abominations *[secual sins is what's listed in Lev. 18]*; neither any of your own nation, nor any **stranger that sojourneth among you:**

Lev. 24:22 Ye shall have **one manner of law** *[mishpat: judgment]*, **as well for the stranger, as for one of your own country:** for I am יהוה your God. *[The verses before this are about blasphemy, murder, eye for eye, injuing an animal, etc.]*

Num. 9:14 And if a **stranger shall sojourn among you,** and will keep the passover ... ye shall have **one ordinance, both for the stranger, and for him that was born in the land.**

Num. 15:13-16 All that are born of the country shall do these things after this manner, in offering an offering made by fire, of a sweet savour unto יהוה. 14 And if a stranger sojourn with you, or whosoever be among you in your generations, and will offer an offering made by fire, of a sweet savour unto יהוה; as ye do, so he shall do. 15 **One ordinance shall be both for you of the congregation, and also for the stranger that sojourneth with you,** an ordinance **forever** in your generations: as ye are, so shall the stranger be before יהוה. 16 **One Torah and one manner shall be for you, and for the stranger** that sojourneth with you.

Num. 15:29-30 **Ye shall have one Torah** for him that sinneth through ignorance, both for him that is **born among the children of Israel, and for the stranger that sojourneth among them**. 30 But the soul that doeth ought presumptuously, **whether he be born in the land, or a stranger,** the same reproacheth יהוה; and that soul shall be cut off from among his people.

Num. 35:15 These six cities shall be a refuge, **both for the children of Israel, and for the stranger,** and for **the sojourner among them**: that every one that killeth any person unawares may flee thither.

AFTER TORAH

Isaiah 56:6-7 Also **the sons of the stranger, that join themselves to** יהוה, to serve Him, and to love the Name of יהוה, to be His servants, **every one that keepeth the Sabbath** from polluting it, and **taketh hold of My Covenant;** Even them will I bring to My holy mountain, and make them joyful in My house of prayer: their burnt offerings and their sacrifices shall be accepted upon Mine altar; for Mine house shall be called an house of prayer for all people.

59. BE KIND TO WIDOWS AND ORPHANS

Ex. 22:22-24 Ye shall not afflict any widow, or fatherless child. If thou afflict them in any wise, and they cry at all unto me, I will surely hear their cry; And my wrath shall wax hot, and I will kill you with the sword; and your wives shall be widows, and your children fatherless.

[The following are also in other appropriate sections about the poor and lending money, etc.]

Deut. 14:28-29 At the end of three years thou shalt bring forth all the tithe of thine increase the same year, and shalt lay it up within thy gates: And ... the stranger, and the fatherless, and the widow, which are within thy gates, shall come, and shall eat and be satisfied; that יהוה thy God may bless thee in all the work of thine hand which thou doest.

Deut. 16:11 (Feast of Weeks) ... And thou shalt rejoice before יהוה thy God, thou, and thy son, and thy daughter, and thy manservant, and thy maidservant, and the Levite that is within thy gates, and the stranger, and the fatherless, and the widow, that are among you, in the place which יהוה thy God hath chosen to place His Name there. ...

Deut. 16:14 (Feast of Tabernacles) And thou shalt rejoice in thy feast, thou, and thy son, and thy daughter, and thy manservant, and thy maidservant, and the Levite, the stranger, and the fatherless, and the widow, that are within thy gates.

Deut. 24:17 Thou shalt not pervert the judgment of the stranger, nor of the fatherless; nor take a widow's raiment to pledge: [first part also in Unbiased Justice, p. 118]

Deut. 26:12 When thou hast made an end of tithing all the tithes of thine increase the third year, which is the year of tithing, and hast given it unto the Levite, the stranger, the fatherless, and the widow, that they may eat within thy gates, and be filled;

Deut. 27:19 Cursed be he that perverteth the judgment of the stranger, fatherless, and widow.

AFTER TORAH

Psalm 82:3 Defend the poor and fatherless: do justice to the afflicted and needy.

Psalm 146:9 יהוה preserveth the strangers; He relieveth the fatherless and widow:

Prov. 23:10-11 Remove not the old landmark; and enter not into the fields of the fatherless: For their Redeemer is mighty; He shall plead their cause with thee.

Isaiah 1:17 Learn to do well; ... relieve the oppressed, judge the fatherless, plead for the widow.

Jer. 7:6-7 If ye oppress not the stranger, the fatherless, and the widow, ... Then will I cause you to dwell in this place, in the Land that I gave to your fathers, **forever and ever.**

Jer. 22:3,5 ... and do no wrong ... to the stranger, the fatherless, nor the widow.... 5 ...if ye will not hear these words, I swear by Myself, saith יהוה, that this house shall become a desolation.

Zech. 7:10 And oppress not the widow, nor the fatherless, the stranger, nor the poor;

YESHUA יֵשׁוּעַ

Matt. 23:14 Woe unto you, scribes and Pharisees, hypocrites! for ye devour widows' houses.... (He also says this in Mark 12:40 and Luke 20:47)

Luke 6:38 Give, and it shall be given unto you; good measure, pressed down, and shaken together, and running over....

Luke 14:13-14 ... when thou makest a feast, call the poor, the maimed, the lame, the blind:

APOSTLES

In Acts 6:1-7 *[Men were chosen to take care of the widows, in obedience to this law.]*

I Tim 5:3, 8 Honour widows that are widows indeed. (The whole chapter is about widows.) Verse 8 But if any provide not for his own, and specially for those of his own house, he hath denied the faith, and is worse than an infidel. [also in Poor, p. 101]

2 Cor. 9:7 Every man according as he purposeth in his heart, so let him give; not grudgingly, or of necessity: for God loveth a cheerful giver.

Eph. 4:28 Share with those in need.

James 1:27 Pure religion and undefiled before God and the Father is this, To visit the fatherless and widows in their affliction, and to keep himself unspotted from the world.

James 2:15-16 If a brother or sister be naked, and destitute of daily food, 16 And one of you say unto them, Depart in peace, be ye warmed and filled; notwithstanding ye give them not those things which are needful to the body; what doth it profit? [also in Poor, p. 101]

60. BE KIND TO THE DEAF AND BLIND

Lev. 19:14 Thou shalt not curse the deaf, nor put a stumblingblock before the blind, but shalt fear thy God: I am יהוה.

Deut. 27:18 Cursed be he that maketh the blind to wander out of the way.

Luke 14:13-14 ... when thou makest a feast, call the poor, the **maimed,** the **lame,** the **blind:**

61. RISE BEFORE THE ELDERLY

Leviticus 19:32 Rise in the presence of the aged, show respect for the elderly and revere your God. I am יהוה.

I Tim. 5:1 Rebuke not an elder, but intreat him as a father.

62. HOW TO TREAT YOUR ENEMY

Ex. 23:4-5 If thou meet thine enemy's ox or his ass going astray, thou shalt surely bring it back to him again. 5 If thou see the ass of him that hateth thee lying under his burden, and wouldest forbear to help him, thou shalt surely help with him. [also in Lost Property, p. 85]

Lev. 19:18 Thou shalt not avenge, nor bear any grudge.... [also in No revenge, next page]

AFTER TORAH

Prov. 16:7 When a man's ways please יהוה, He maketh even his enemies to be at peace with him.

YESHUA ישוע

Matt. 5:43-47 Ye have heard that it hath been said, Thou shalt love thy neighbour, and hate thine enemy." 44 But I say unto you, **Love your enemies, bless them that curse you,** do good to them that hate you, and pray for them which despitefully use you, and persecute you; 45 That ye may be the children of your Father which is in Heaven: for he maketh his sun to rise on the evil and on the good, and sendeth rain on the just and on the unjust. 46 For if ye love them which love you, what reward have ye? do not even the publicans the same? 47 And if ye salute your brethren only, what do ye more than others? do not even the publicans so?

Luke 6:27-36 But I say unto you which hear, **Love your enemies, do good to them which hate you,** 28 Bless them that curse you, and pray for them which despitefully use you. 29 And unto him that smiteth thee on the one cheek offer also the other; and him that taketh away thy cloke forbid not to take thy coat also. 30 Give to every man that asketh of thee; and of him that taketh away thy goods ask them not again. 31 And **as ye would that men should do to you, do ye also to them likewise.** 32 For if ye love them which love you, what thank have ye? for sinners also love those that love them. 33 And if ye do good to them which do good to you, what thank have ye? for sinners also do even the same. ... 35 But **love ye your enemies, and do good, and lend, hoping for nothing again;** and your reward shall be great, and ye shall be the children of the Highest: for he is kind unto the unthankful and to the evil. 36 Be ye therefore merciful, as your Father also is merciful.

APOSTLES

Rom. 12:19-21 Dearly beloved, avenge not yourselves, but rather give place unto [*God's*] wrath: for it is written, Vengeance is Mine; I will repay, saith יהוה. 20 Therefore if thine enemy hunger, feed him; if he thirst, give him drink: for in so doing thou shalt heap coals of fire on his head. 21 Be not overcome of evil, but overcome evil with good.

Heb. 10:30 For we know Him that hath said, Vengeance belongeth unto Me, I will recompense, saith יהוה. And again, The Lord shall judge his people.

63. NO REVENGE, NO GRUDGE

Lev. 19:18 Thou shalt **not avenge, nor bear any grudge** against the children of thy people, but thou shalt love thy neighbour as thyself: I am יהוה. [*But for murder? See No killing p.47-48.*]

Num. 31:1-3 And יהוה spake unto Moses, saying, 2 Avenge the children of Israel of the Midianites: afterward shalt thou be gathered unto thy people. 3 And Moses spake unto the people, saying, Arm some of yourselves unto the war, and let them go against the Midianites, and avenge יהוה of Midian.

Deut. 32:35,41,43 To Me belongeth vengeance, and recompence; their foot shall slide in due time: for the day of their calamity is at hand, and the things that shall come upon them make haste. ... 41 ...I will render vengeance to mine enemies.... 43 Rejoice, O ye nations, with His people: for He will avenge the blood of his servants, and will render vengeance to His adversaries,

PROPHETS

Zech. 8:17 And let none of you imagine evil in your hearts against his neighbour; and love no false oath: for all these are things that I hate, saith יהוה.

YESHUA ישוע

Matt. 6:14-15 For if ye forgive men their trespasses, your heavenly Father will also forgive you: But if ye forgive not men their trespasses, neither will your Father forgive your trespasses

Matt. 18:34-35 And his lord was wroth, and delivered him to the tormentors, till he should pay all that was due unto him. 35 So likewise shall my heavenly Father do also unto you, if ye from your hearts forgive not every one his brother their trespasses.

Mark 11:25-26 And when ye stand praying, forgive, if ye have ought against any: that your Father also which is in heaven may forgive you your trespasses. But if ye do not forgive, neither will your Father which is in heaven forgive your trespasses.

Luke 6:29 And unto him that smiteth thee on the one cheek offer also the other; and him that taketh away thy cloke forbid not to take thy coat also.

Matt. 5:38-41 Ye have heard that it hath been said, An eye for an eye, and a tooth for a tooth: 39 But I say unto you, That ye resist not evil: but whosoever shall smite thee on thy right cheek, turn to him the other also. 40 And if any man will sue thee at the law, and take away thy coat, let him have thy cloke also. 41 And whosoever shall compel thee to go a mile, go with him twain.

Luke 6:37 Judge not, and ye shall not be judged: condemn not, and ye shall not be condemned: forgive, and ye shall be forgiven:

Luke 17:3-4 Take heed to yourselves: If thy brother trespass against thee, rebuke him; and if he repent, forgive him. And if he trespass against thee seven times in a day, and seven times in a day turn again to thee, saying, I repent; thou shalt forgive him.

Luke 23:34 Then said ישוע, Father, forgive them; for they know not what they do.

APOSTLES

Rom. 12:19 Dearly beloved, avenge not yourselves, but rather give place unto [*God's*]wrath: for it is written, Vengeance is mine; I will repay, saith יהוה. (See Deut. 32:35-41)

Eph. 4:32 And be ye kind one to another, tenderhearted, forgiving one another, even as God for Messiah's sake hath forgiven you.

Heb. 12:14-15 Follow peace with all men, and holiness, without which no man shall see the Lord: 15 Looking diligently lest any man fail of the grace of God; lest any **root of bitterness** springing up trouble you, and thereby many be defiled;

I Pet. 3:9 (TLV) Do not repay evil for evil or insult for insult, but give a blessing instead ... so that you might inherit a blessing.

64. MAKE RESTITUTION

Ex. 22:1 If a man shall steal an ox, or a sheep, and kill it, or sell it; **he shall restore five oxen for an ox, and four sheep for a sheep**.

Ex. 22:4 If the theft be certainly found in his hand alive, whether it be ox, or ass, or sheep; **he shall restore double.**

Ex. 22:5-6 If a man shall cause a field or vineyard to be eaten, and shall put in his beast, and shall feed in another man's field; of the best of his own field, and of the best of his own vineyard, **shall he make restitution**. 6 If fire break out, ... he that kindled the fire shall surely make restitution.

Ex. 22:7-8,12 If a man shall deliver unto his neighbour money or stuff to keep, and it be stolen out of the man's house; if the thief be found, **let him pay double.** If the thief be not found, then the master of the house shall be brought unto the judges, to see whether he have put his hand unto his neighbour's goods. ... 12 And if it be stolen from him, he shall **make restitution** unto the owner thereof.

Ex. 22:9 For all manner of trespass, whether it be for ox, for ass, for sheep, for raiment, or for any manner of lost thing, which another challengeth to be his, the cause of both parties shall come before the judges; and whom the judges shall condemn, he **shall pay double** unto his neighbour.

Ex. 21:29-32 (NRSV) If the ox has been accustomed to gore in the past, and its owner has been warned but has not restrained it, and it kills a man or a woman, the ox shall be stoned, and its owner also shall be put to death. 30 If a ransom is imposed on the owner, then the owner shall pay whatever is imposed for the redemption of the victim's life. 31 If it gores a boy or a girl.... 32 If ... a slave, the owner shall pay.... [also in Animals, p. 82, Value of a Slave, p. 74]

Ex. 22:2-3 If a thief be found breaking up [*in?*] ... he should **make full Restitution;** if he have nothing, then he shall be sold for his theft. [also in Thou shalt not steal, p. 52]

Lev. 6:4b-7 ...he shall restore that which he took violently away, or the thing which he hath deceitfully gotten, or that which was delivered him to keep, or the lost thing which he found, 5 or whatever it was they swore falsely about. They must **make restitution in full, add a fifth of the value to it** and give it all to the owner on the day they present their guilt offering. 6 ... a ram from the flock, one without defect and of the proper value. 7 In this way the priest will make atonement for them before יהוה.... [also in False Witness, p. 124, Lost, p. 85, and Borrowing, p. 84]

Lev. 22:10, 13b-14 (NIV) " 'No one outside a priest's family may eat the sacred offering, nor may the guest of a priest or his hired worker eat it. ... No unauthorized person, however, may eat it. 14 " 'Anyone who eats a sacred offering by mistake **must make restitution to the priest** for the offering **and add a fifth of the value to it.** [also in Priests, p. 220, and What Can't Eat, p. 127]

Num. 5:6-8 Speak unto the children of Israel, When a man or woman shall commit any sin that men commit, to do a trespass against יהוה, and that person be guilty; 7 Then they shall confess their sin which they have done: and **he shall recompense his trespass** with the principal thereof, **and add unto it the fifth part thereof, and give it unto him against whom he hath trespassed.** 8 But if the man have no kinsman to recompense the trespass unto, let the trespass be recompensed unto יהוה, even to the priest; beside the ram of the atonement, whereby an atonement shall be made for him.

YESHUA

Luke 19:8-9a And Zacchaeus stood, and said unto the Lord; Behold, Lord, the half of my goods I give to the poor; and if I have taken any thing from any man by false accusation, I restore him fourfold. 9 And Jesus said unto him, This day is salvation come to this house,

65. LOVE YOUR NEIGHBOR

Lev. 19:17-18 Thou shalt not hate thy brother in thine heart: thou shalt in any wise rebuke thy neighbor, and not suffer [carry] sin upon him.18 Thou shalt not avenge, nor bear any grudge against the children of thy people, but **thou shalt love thy neighbor as thyself:** I am יהוה. [verse 17 also in Must Testify p. 124, verse 18 in No Grudge p. 91]

Lev 19:34a But the stranger that dwelleth with you shall be unto you as one born among you, and **thou shalt love him as thyself**.... [also in Stranger, p. 86]

Deu 10:19a Love ye therefore the stranger.... [also in Stranger, p. 86]

AFTER TORAH:

Prov. 10:12 Hatred stirreth up strifes: but love covereth all sins.

YESHUA ישוע

Matt. 22:39 (also Mk. 12:31) And the second is like unto it, **Thou shalt love thy neighbour as thyself.**

Matt. 5:23-24 Therefore if thou bring thy gift to the altar, and there rememberest that thy brother hath ought against thee; 24 Leave there thy gift ... first be reconciled to thy brother, and then come and offer thy gift.

Matt 7:12-16 Therefore all things whatsoever ye would that men should do to you, do ye even so to them: for **this is the Torah** and the prophets. 13 Enter ye in at the strait gate: for wide is the gate, and broad is the way, that leadeth to destruction, and many there be which go in threat: 14 Because strait is the gate, and narrow is the way, which leadeth unto life, and few there be that find it.

Luke 7:47b ... to whom little is forgiven, the same loveth little.

Luke 6:31-33 And as ye would that men should do to you, do ye also to them likewise. 32 For if ye love them which love you, what thank have ye? for sinners also love those that love them. 33 And if ye do good to them which do good to you, what thank have ye? for sinners also do even the same. [also in Enemies, p. 90]

Luke 10:29 But he, willing to justify himself, said unto ישוע, And who is my neighbour? *[And ישוע proceeded to tell the parable of the Good Samaritan.]* ... 36 Which now of these three, thinkest thou, was neighbour unto him that fell among the thieves?

John 13:34-35 A new commandment I give unto you, That ye love one another; as I have loved you, that ye also love one another. 35 By this shall all men know that ye are My disciples, if ye have love one to another.

John 15:12 This is My commandment, That ye love one another, as I have loved you. 13 Greater love hath no man than this, that a man lay down his life for his friends.

Rom. 12:9 (NIV) Let love be without hypocrisy.

Rom. 12:10 Be kindly affectioned one to another with brotherly love; in honour preferring one another.

Rom. 13:8-10 Owe no man any thing, but to love one another: for he that loveth another hath fulfilled the Torah. 9 For this, Thou shalt not commit adultery, Thou shalt not kill, Thou shalt not steal, Thou shalt not bear false witness, Thou shalt not covet; and if there be any other commandment, it is briefly comprehended in this saying, namely, **Thou shalt love thy neighbour as thyself**. 10 Love worketh no ill to his neighbour: therefore love is the fulfilling of the Torah.

I Cor. 13:2-8 (TLV) [If I] have not love, I am nothing. 3 If I give away all that I own ... so I might boast but have not love, I gain nothing. 4 Love is patient, love is kind, it does not envy, it does not brag, it is not puffed up, 5 it does not behave inappropriately, it does not seek its own way, it is not provoked, it keeps no account of wrong, 6 it does not rejoice over injustice but rejoices in the truth; 7 it bears all things, it believes all things, it hopes all things, it endures all things. 8 Love never fails....

1 Cor. 14:1 (NASB) Pursue love....

Gal. 5:14 **For all the Torah is fulfilled in one word, even in this; Thou shalt love thy neighbour as thyself.**

Eph. 4:2-3 With all lowliness and meekness, with longsuffering, forbearing one another in love; Endeavouring to keep the unity of the Spirit in the bond of peace.

Eph. 4:15 (NRSV) ... Speak the truth in love.

Eph. 4:29,31-32 Let no corrupt communication proceed out of your mouth, but that which is good to the use of edifying, that it may minister grace unto the hearers. ... Let all bitterness, and wrath, and anger, and clamour, and evil speaking, be put away from you, with all malice: And be ye kind one to another, tenderhearted, forgiving one another, even as God for Messiah's sake hath forgiven you.

Eph. 5:2,19,21 Walk in love.... (CJB) 19 Sing psalms, hymns and spiritual songs to each other.... 21 Submit to one another in fear of the Messiah.

Col. 3:14 (NRSV) Above all, clothe yourselves with love, which binds everything together in perfect harmony.

1 Thess. 4:9 But as touching brotherly love ye need not that I write unto you: for ye yourselves are taught of God to love one another.

1 Tim. 6:11 (NRSV) ...**pursue** righteousness, godliness, faith, **love**, endurance, gentleness.

2 Tim. 2:22-26 (NRSV) Shun youthful passions and **pursue** righteousness, faith, **love**,

Heb. 13:1-3 Let mutual love continue. 2 Do not neglect to show hospitality to strangers, for by doing that some have entertained angels without knowing it. 3 Remember those who are in prison, as though you were in prison with them; those who are being tortured, as though you yourselves were being tortured. [also in Strangers, p. 86]

I Pet. 1:22 Seeing ye have purified your souls in obeying the truth through the Spirit unto unfeigned love of the brethren, see that ye love one another with a pure heart fervently

I Pet. 4:8-10 (ASV) ...above all things being fervent in your love among yourselves; for love covereth a multitude of sins: 9 using hospitality one to another without murmuring: 10 ...as each hath received a gift, ministering it among yourselves, as good stewards of the manifold grace of God;

1 John 2:10-11 (NASB) The one who loves his brother abides in the Light and there is no cause for stumbling in him. 11 But the one who hates his brother is in the darkness and walks in the darkness, and does not know where he is going because the darkness has blinded his eyes.

I John 3:17 But whoso hath this world's good, and seeth his brother have need, and shutteth up his bowels of compassion from him, how dwelleth the love of God in him?

1John 3:14 We know that we have passed from death unto life, because we love the brethren. He that loveth not his brother abideth in death.

1 John 4:7-10 Beloved, let us love one another: for love is of God; and every one that loveth is born of God, and knoweth God. 8 He that loveth not knoweth not God; for God is love. 9 In this was manifested the love of God toward us, because that God sent his only begotten Son into the world, that we might live through Him. 10 Herein is love, not that we loved God, but that He loved us, and sent His Son to be the propitiation for our sins.

1 John 4:11-16 Beloved, if God so loved us, we ought also to love one another. 12 No man hath seen God at any time. If we love one another, God dwelleth in us, and His love is perfected in us. ... 16 ...God is love; and he that dwelleth in love dwelleth in God, and God in him. ...

1 John 4:18-19 There is no fear in love; but perfect love casteth out fear.... He that feareth is not made perfect in love. 19 We love Him, because He first loved us.

1 John 4:20-21 If a man say, I love God, and hateth his brother, he is a liar: for he that loveth not his brother whom he hath seen, how can he love God whom he hath not seen? 21 And this commandment have we from Him, That he who loveth God love his brother also. [also in Love יהוה, p. 240]

2 John 1:5-6 And now I beseech thee, ... not as though I wrote a new commandment unto thee, but that which we had from the beginning, that we love one another. 6 And this is love, that we walk after His commandments. This is the commandment, that, as ye have heard from the beginning, ye should walk in it.

66. WAGES FOR SERVANTS/EMPLOYEES

Lev 19:13 Do not hold back the wages of a hired man overnight.

Deut. 24:14-15 Thou shalt not oppress an hired servant that is poor and needy, whether he be of thy brethren, or of thy strangers that are in thy land within thy gates: At his day thou shalt give him his hire, neither shall the sun go down upon it; for he is poor, and setteth his heart upon it: lest he cry against thee unto יהוה, and it be sin unto thee. [also in Strangers, p. 86, and Poor, p. 100]

AFTER TORAH

Jer. 22:13 Woe unto him that buildeth his house by unrighteousness, and his chambers by wrong; that useth his neighbour's service without wages, and giveth him not for his work;

YESHUA ישוע and APOSTLES

Matt. 10:7-10 And as ye go, preach, saying, The kingdom of heaven is at hand. 8 Heal the sick, cleanse the lepers, raise the dead, cast out devils: freely ye have received, freely give. 9 Provide neither gold, nor silver, nor brass in your purses, 10 Nor scrip for your journey, neither two coats, neither shoes, nor yet staves: **for the workman is worthy of his meat** [NKJV: food].

Luke 3:14 ... Be content with your wages.

Luke 10:7-9 And in the same house remain, eating and drinking such things as they give: **for the labourer is worthy of his hire.** Go not from house to house. 8 And into whatsoever city ye enter, and they receive you, eat such things as are set before you: 9 And heal the sick that are therein, and say unto them, The kingdom of God is come nigh unto you.

I Cor. 9:13-14 Do ye not know that they which minister about holy things live of the things of the Temple? and they which wait at the altar are partakers with the altar? 14 Even so hath יהוה ordained that they which preach the Gospel should live of the Gospel. [also in Animals p. 83; Levites, p. 221]

I Tim. 5:17-18 Let the elders that rule well be counted worthy of double honour, especially they who labour in the word and doctrine. 18 For the Scripture saith, Thou shalt not muzzle the ox that treadeth out the corn. And [CJB: in other words], **The labourer is worthy of his reward**.

67. LEAVING GLEANINGS FOR POOR

Lev. 19:9-10 And when ye reap the harvest of your land, thou shalt not wholly reap the corners of thy field, neither shalt thou gather the gleanings of thy harvest. And thou shalt not glean thy vineyard, neither shalt thou gather every grape of thy vineyard; thou shalt leave them for the poor and stranger: I am יהוה your God.

Lev. 23:22 And when ye reap the harvest of your land, thou shalt not make clean riddance of the corners of thy field when thou reapest, neither shalt thou gather any gleaning of thy harvest: thou shalt leave them unto the poor, and to the stranger: I am יהוה your God.

Deut. 24:19 When thou cuttest down thine harvest in thy field, and hast forgot a sheaf in the field, thou shalt not go again to fetch it: it shall be for the stranger, for the fatherless, and for the widow: that יהוה thy God may bless thee in all the work of thine hands.

Deut. 24:20 When thou beatest thine olive tree, thou shalt not go over the boughs again: it shall be for the stranger, for the fatherless, and for the widow.

Deut. 24:21-22 When thou gatherest the grapes of thy vineyard, thou shalt not glean it afterward: it shall be for the stranger, for the fatherless, and for the widow. 22 And thou shalt remember that thou wast a bondman in the land of Egypt: therefore I command thee to do this thing.

AFTER TORAH

Matt. 12:1 At that time ישוע went on the Sabbath day through the corn; and his disciples were an hungred, and began to pluck the ears of corn, and to eat.

68. EATING FROM NEIGHBOR'S LAND

Deut. 23:24 When thou comest into thy neighbour's vineyard, then thou mayest eat grapes thy fill at thine own pleasure; but thou shalt not put any in thy vessel.

Deut. 23:25 When thou comest into the standing corn of thy neighbour, then thou mayest pluck the ears with thine hand; but thou shalt not move a sickle unto thy neighbour's standing corn. [also in Don't Destroy Property, p. 84]

AFTER TORAH

Matt. 12:1 At that time ישוע went on the Sabbath day through the corn; and his disciples were an hungred, and began to pluck the ears of corn, and to eat.

THE POOR

69. TAKING CARE OF THE POOR (AND LEVITES)

Lev. 25:25-28 If thy brother be waxen poor, and hath sold away some of his possession, and if any of his kin come to redeem it, then shall he redeem that which his brother sold. 26 And if the man have none to redeem it, and himself be able to redeem it; 27 Then let him count the years of the sale thereof, and restore the overplus unto the man to whom he sold it; that he may return unto his possession. 28 But if he be not able to restore it to him, then that which is sold shall remain in the hand of him that hath bought it until the year of Jubile: and in the Jubile it shall go out, and he shall return unto his possession. [also in Jubilee, p. 184]

Lev. 25:35-37 And if thy brother be waxen poor, and fallen in decay with thee; then thou shalt relieve him: yea, though he be a stranger, or a sojourner; that he may live with thee. 36 Take thou no usury of him, or increase: but fear thy God; that thy brother may live with thee. 37 Thou shalt not give him thy money upon usury, nor lend him thy victuals for increase. [also in Jubilee, p. 184 and in Lending money, p. 125]

Lev. 25:39-41 And if thy brother that dwelleth by thee be waxen poor, and be sold unto thee; thou shalt not compel him to serve as a bondservant: 40 But as an hired servant, and as a sojourner, he shall be with thee, and shall serve thee unto the year of Jubile: 41 And then shall he depart from thee, both he and his children with him.... [See more in Slaves. p. 74, Jubilee, p. 184]

Lev. 25:47-50,54 And if a sojourner or stranger wax rich by thee, and thy brother that dwelleth by him wax poor, and sell himself unto the stranger or sojourner by thee, or to the stock of the stranger's family: 48 After that he is sold he may be redeemed again; one of his brethren may redeem him: 49 Either his uncle, or his uncle's son, may redeem him, or any that is nigh of kin unto him of his family may redeem him; or if he be able, he may redeem himself. 50 And he shall reckon with him that bought him from the year that he was sold to him unto the year of Jubile: and the price of his sale shall be according unto the number of years, according to the time of an hired servant shall it be with him. ... 54 And if he be not redeemed in these years, then he shall go out in the year of Jubile, both he, and his children with him. [also in Slaves, p. 75, and Jubilee, p. 184]

Deut. 15:7-8 If there be among you a poor man of one of thy brethren within any of thy gates in thy land which יהוה thy God giveth thee, thou shalt not harden thine heart, nor shut thine hand from thy poor brother: 8 But thou shalt open thine hand wide unto him, and shalt surely lend him sufficient for his need, in that which he wanteth. [cont. in Shmitah Release, p. 156]

Deut. 15:10-11 Thou shalt surely give him, and thine heart shall not be grieved when thou givest unto him: because that for this thing יהוה thy God shall bless thee in all thy works, and in all that thou puttest thine hand unto. For the poor shall never cease out of the land: therefore I command thee, saying, Thou shalt open thine hand wide unto thy brother, to thy poor, and to thy needy, in thy land.

Deut. 24:14 Thou shalt not oppress an hired servant that is poor and needy, whether he be of thy brethren, or of thy strangers that are in thy land within thy gates: [also in Strangers, p. 86]

Deut. 26:12-15 When thou hast made an end of tithing all the tithes of thine increase the third year, which is the year of tithing, and hast given it unto the Levite, the stranger, the fatherless, and the widow, that they may eat within thy gates, and be filled; 13 Then thou shalt say before יהוה thy God, I have brought away the hallowed things out of mine house, and also have given them unto the Levite, and unto the stranger, to the fatherless, and to the widow, according to all thy commandments: ... 15 Look down from thy holy habitation, from heaven, and bless thy people Israel.... [See more in Tithe, p. 196.]

AFTER TORAH

Prov. 19:17 (TLV) One who is kind to the poor lends to ADONAI, and ADONAI will reward him for his good deed.

Isaiah 58:6-11 Is not this the fast that I choose: to loose the bonds of injustice, to undo the thongs of the yoke, to let the oppressed go free, and to break every yoke? 7 Is it not to **share your bread with the hungry, and bring the homeless poor into your house; when you see the naked, to cover them,** and not to hide yourself from your own kin? 8 Then your light shall break forth like the dawn, and your healing shall spring up quickly; your vindicator shall go before you, the glory of the Lord shall be your rear guard. 9 Then you shall call, and the Lord will answer; you shall cry for help, and he will say, Here I am. If you remove the yoke from among you, the pointing of the finger, the speaking of evil, 10 **if you offer your food to the hungry and satisfy the needs of the afflicted,** then your light shall rise in the darkness and your gloom be like the noonday. 11 The Lord will guide you continually, and satisfy your needs in parched places, and make your bones strong; and you shall be like a watered garden, like a spring of water, whose waters never fail.

Jer. 22:15-16 Shalt thou reign, because thou closest thyself in cedar? did not thy father eat and drink, and do judgment and justice, and then it was well with him? 16 He judged **the cause of the poor and needy; then it was well with him**: was not this to know me? saith יהוה.

Ezek. 16:49-50 Behold, this was the iniquity of thy sister Sodom, pride, fulness of bread, and abundance of idleness was in her and in her daughters, **neither did she strengthen the hand of the poor and needy.** 50 And they were haughty, and committed abomination before me: therefore I took them away....

YESHUA ישוע

Matt. 25:34-36 Come, ye blessed of my Father, inherit the kingdom prepared for you from the foundation of the world: For I was an hungred, and ye gave me meat: I was thirsty, and ye gave me drink: I was a stranger, and ye took me in: Naked, and ye clothed me: I was sick, and ye visited me: I was in prison, and ye came unto me.

THE POOR

Matt. 19:21 (and Mark 10:21 and Luke 18:22) ישוע said unto him, If thou wilt be perfect, go and sell that thou hast, and **give to the poor,** and thou shalt have treasure in heaven: and come and follow me.

Mark 14:7 (and Matt. 26:11 and John 12:8) For ye have the poor with you always, and whensoever ye will ye may do them good: but Me ye have not always.

Luke 14:12-14 ... When thou makest a dinner or a supper, call not thy friends, nor thy brethren, neither thy kinsmen, nor thy rich neighbours; lest they also bid thee again, and a recompence be made thee. 13 But when thou makest a feast, call the poor, the maimed, the lame, the blind: 14 And thou shalt be blessed; for they cannot recompense thee: for thou shalt be recompensed at the resurrection of the just. [parts also in Stranger, p. 86, and Blind, p. 89]

Luke 14:33 So likewise, whosoever he be of you that forsaketh not all that he hath, he cannot be my disciple.

John 13:29 For some of them thought, because Judas had the bag, that ישוע had said unto him ... that he should give something to the poor.

APOSTLES:

Acts 10:1-4 There was a certain man in Caesarea called Cornelius, a centurion of the ... Italian band, 2 A devout man, and one that feared God with all his house, which gave much alms to the people, and prayed to God alway. 3 He saw in a vision ... an angel of God ... saying unto him, Cornelius. 4 ... Thy prayers and thine alms are come up for a memorial before God.

I Cor. 13:3 And though I bestow all my goods to feed the poor, and though I give my body to be burned, and have not charity, it profiteth me nothing.

Gal. 2:10 Only they would that we should remember the poor; the same which I also was forward to do.

I Tim. 5:8,16 If any one does not provide for his relatives, and especially for his own family, he has disowned the faith and is worse than an unbeliever (RSV). ... 16 If any man or woman that believeth have widows, let them relieve them, and let not the church be charged; that it may relieve them that are widows indeed (SNB). {verse 8 also in Widows and Orphans, p. 89]

James 2:15-16 If a brother or sister be naked, and destitute of daily food, 16 And one of you say unto them, Depart in peace, be ye warmed and filled; notwithstanding ye give them not those things which are needful to the body; what doth it profit? [also in Orphans, p. 89]

1 John 3:17 But whoso hath this world's good, and seeth his brother have need, and shutteth up his bowels of compassion from him, how dwelleth the love of God in him?

70. DON'T MENTION THE NAMES OF OTHER GODS

Exodus 23:13 And in all things that I have said unto you be circumspect: and **make no mention** of the name of other gods, neither let it be heard out of thy mouth. [also in No other gods, p. 31]

71. DESTROY THE NAMES OF OTHER GODS

Deut. 12:2,3 Ye shall utterly destroy all the places, wherein the nations which ye shall possess served their gods, ... and ye shall hew down the graven images of their gods, and **destroy the names** of them out of that place.

Zech. 13:2 And it shall come to pass in that day, saith יהוה of hosts, that I will cut off the names of the idols out of the land, and they shall no more be remembered: and also I will cause the prophets and the unclean spirit to pass out of the land.

72. DON'T INQUIRE OR IMITATE OTHER WORSHIP

Deut. 12:29-31 When יהוה thy God shall cut off the nations from before thee, whither thou goest to possess them, and thou succeedest them, and dwellest in their land; 30 Take heed to thyself that thou be not snared by following them, after that they be destroyed from before thee; and that thou **enquire not after their gods**, saying, How did these nations serve their gods? even so will I do likewise. 31 Thou shalt not do so unto יהוה thy God: for every abomination to יהוה, which he hateth, have they done unto their gods; for even their sons and their daughters they have burnt in the fire to their gods.

Deut 18:9 When thou art come into the land which יהוה thy God giveth thee, thou shalt not learn to do after the abominations of those nations.

AFTER TORAH

Jer. 10:1-2 Hear ye the Word which יהוה speaketh unto you, O house of Israel: 2 Thus saith יהוה, **Learn not the way of the heathen**, and be not dismayed at the signs of heaven; for the heathen are dismayed at them. 3 For the customs of the people are vain: ...

Rev. 2:24-25 But to the rest of you in Thyatira, who do not hold this [Jezebel's] teaching, **who have not learned what some call "the deep things of satan,"** to you I say, I do not lay on you any other burden; 25 only hold fast to what you have until I come.

73. DON'T DO WHAT HEATHEN NATIONS DO/DID

Lev. 18:3 After the doings of the land of Egypt, wherein ye dwelt, shall ye not do: and after the doings of the land of Canaan, whither I bring you, shall ye not do: neither shall ye walk in their ordinances.

Lev. 20:23-25 And ye shall not walk in the manners of the nation, which I cast out before you: for they committed all these things, and therefore I abhorred them. 24 But I have said unto you, Ye shall inherit their land, and I will give it unto you to possess it, a land that floweth with milk and honey: I am יהוה your God, **which have separated you from other people.**

AFTER TORAH

Psalm 106:35-36,40 But were mingled among the heathen, and learned their works. 36 And they served their idols: ... [*sacrificed their children*] ... 40 Therefore was the wrath of יהוה kindled against his people, insomuch that he abhorred his own inheritance.

Isaiah 8:9-13 (NRSV) Band together, you peoples, and be dismayed; listen, all you <u>far countries</u>; gird yourselves and be dismayed! .... 11 For the Lord spoke thus to me while his hand was strong upon me, and warned me **not to walk in the way of this people,** saying: 12 Do not call conspiracy all that this people calls conspiracy, and do not fear what it fears, or be in dread. 13 But the Lord of hosts, him you shall regard as holy; let him be your fear, and let him be your dread.

Isaiah 52:11 Depart ye, depart ye, go ye out from thence, touch no unclean thing; go ye out of the midst of her; be ye clean, that bear the vessels of יהוה. [also in Don't Touch, p. 201]

Jer. 10:1-6 Hear ye the Word which יהוה speaketh unto you, O house of Israel: 2 Thus saith יהוה, **Learn not the way of the heathen,** and be not dismayed at the signs of heaven; for the heathen are dismayed at them. 3 For the customs of the people are vain....

APOSTLES

2 Cor. 6:17 Wherefore come out from among them, and **be ye separate,** saith the Lord.

Eph. 4:17-20 This I say therefore, and testify in the Lord, that ye henceforth **walk not as other Gentiles walk, in the vanity of their mind,** 18 Having the understanding darkened, being alienated from the life of God through the ignorance that is in them, because of the blindness of their heart: 19 Who being past feeling have given themselves over unto lasciviousness, to work all uncleanness with greediness. 20 But ye have not so learned Messiah; ....

Eph. 5:11-13 And have no fellowship with the unfruitful works of darkness, but rather reprove them. 12 **For it is a shame even to speak of those things which are done of them in secret.** 13 But all things that are reproved are made manifest by the light: for whatsoever doth make manifest is light.

74. DO NOT OFFER CHILDREN TO OTHER GODS OR MAKE THEM PASS THROUGH FIRE.

Lev. 18:21 And thou shalt not let any of thy seed pass through the fire to Molech, neither shalt thou profane the Name of thy God: I am יהוה. [also in Name in Vain, p. 40]

Lev. 20:2-5 Again, thou shalt say to the children of Israel, Whosoever he be of the children of Israel, or of the strangers that sojourn in Israel, that giveth any of his seed unto Molech; he shall surely be put to death: the people of the land shall stone him with stones. 3 And I will set my face against that man, and will cut him off from among his people; because he hath given of his seed unto Molech, to defile my sanctuary, and to profane my holy Name. 4 And if the people of the land do any ways hide their eyes from the man, when he giveth of his seed unto Molech, and kill him not: 5 Then I will set my face against that man, and against his family, and will cut him off, and all that go a whoring after him, to commit whoredom with Molech, from among their people.

Deut. 12:31 Thou shalt not do so unto יהוה thy God: for every abomination to יהוה, which he hateth, have they done unto their gods; for even their sons and their daughters they have burnt in the fire to their gods.

Deut 18:10 There shall not be found among you any one that maketh his son or his daughter to pass through the fire....

AFTER TORAH

Psalm 106:38,40 And shed innocent blood, even the blood of their sons and of their daughters, whom they sacrificed unto the idols of Canaan: and the land was polluted with blood. ... Therefore was the wrath of יהוה kindled ... he abhorred his own inheritance.

Jer. 19:5 They have built also the high places of Baal, to burn their sons with fire *for* burnt offerings unto Baal, which I commanded not, nor spake *it*, neither came *it* into my **mind**....

Jer. 32:35 And they built the high places of Baal, which *are* in the valley of the son of Hinnom, to cause their sons and their daughters to pass through *the fire* unto Molech; which I commanded them not, neither came it into my **mind**, that they should do this abomination....

YESHUA ישוע

Matt. 18:6-9 But whoso shall offend one of these little ones which believe in me, it were better for him that a millstone were hanged about his neck, and that he were drowned in the depth of the sea. 7 ... woe to that man by whom the offence cometh! ... 8 ... it is better for thee to enter into life halt or maimed, rather than having two hands or two feet to be cast into **everlasting** fire. 9 ... it is better for thee to enter into life with one eye, rather than having two eyes to be cast into hell fire.

Matt. 18:10 Take heed that ye despise not one of these little ones; for I say unto you, That in heaven their angels do always behold the face of my Father which is in heaven.

Matt. 18:14 Even so it is not the will of your Father which is in heaven, that one of these little ones should perish.

75. NO SORCERY, WITCHCRAFT, CUTTING, TATTOOS, ETC.

Ex. 22:18 Thou shalt not suffer a witch to live.

Lev. 19:26b, 28 ...neither shall ye use enchantment, nor observe times (ASV: augury; CJB fortune telling). ... Ye shall **not make any cuttings in your flesh** for the dead, nor print (RSV: **tattoo) any marks upon you**: I am יהוה.

Lev. 20:6 And the soul that turneth after such as have familiar spirits, and after wizards, to go a whoring after them, I will even set my face against that soul, and will cut him off from among his people.

Lev. 20:27 A man also or woman that hath a familiar spirit, or that is a wizard, shall surely be put to death: they shall stone them with stones: their blood shall be upon them.

Deut. 18:10-14 There shall not be found among you any one ... that useth divination, or an observer of times, or an enchanter, or a witch, 11 or a charmer, or a consulter with familiar spirits, or a wizard, or a necromancer. 12 For all that do these things are an abomination unto יהוה: and because of these abominations יהוה thy God doth drive them out from before thee. 13 Thou shalt be perfect with יהוה thy God. 14 For these nations, which thou shalt possess, hearkened unto observers of times (AS: augury; RSV: soothsayers), and unto diviners: but as for thee, יהוה thy God hath not suffered thee so to do.

Deut. 14:1-2 Ye are the children of יהוה your God: **ye shall not cut yourselves**, nor make any baldness between your eyes for the dead. For thou art an holy people unto יהוה thy God, and יהוה hath chosen thee to be a peculiar people unto himself, above all the nations that are upon the earth.

AFTER TORAH, YESHUA ישוע and APOSTLES

I Sam. 15:23 For rebellion is as the sin of witchcraft....

Luke 10:19 Behold, I give unto you power [NRSV: authority] to tread on serpents and scorpions, and over all the power of the enemy....

Mark 16:17 And these signs shall follow them that believe; In My Name shall they cast out devils....

Acts 19:17-20 And ... all the Jews and Greeks also dwelling at Ephesus; and fear fell on them all, and the Name of the Lord ישוע was magnified. 18 And many that believed came, and confessed, and shewed their deeds. 19 Many of them also which used curious arts [NIV: sorcery] brought their books together, and burned them before all men: and they counted the price of them, and found it fifty thousand pieces of silver. 20 So mightily grew the word of God and prevailed.

Acts 16:16 And it came to pass, as we went to prayer, a certain damsel possessed with a spirit of divination met us, which brought her masters much gain by soothsaying: ... 18 And this did she many days. But Paul, being grieved, turned and said to the spirit, I command thee in the Name of ישוע Messiah to come out of her. And he came out the same hour.

Gal 5:19-21 ... **witchcraft;** ... they which do such things shall not inherit the kingdom of God.

76. PUT FALSE PROPHETS, ETC., TO DEATH

Deut. 13:1-5 If there arise among you a prophet, or a dreamer of dreams, and giveth thee a sign or a wonder, And the sign or the wonder come to pass, whereof he spake unto thee, saying, Let us go after other gods, which thou hast not known, and let us serve them; Thou shalt not hearken unto the words of that prophet, or that dreamer of dreams: for יהוה your God proveth you, to know whether ye love יהוה your God with all your heart and with all your soul. Ye shall walk after יהוה your God, and ... cleave unto Him. And that prophet, or that dreamer of dreams, shall be put to death; because he hath spoken to turn you away from יהוה your God, ... to thrust thee out of the way which יהוה thy God commanded thee to walk in. So shalt thou put the evil away from the midst of thee. [See also Ezek. 14:7-10, p. 37.]

Deut. 18:20-22 But the prophet, which shall presume to speak a word in My Name, which I have not commanded him to speak, or that shall speak in the name of other gods, even that prophet shall die. 21 And if thou say in thine heart, How shall we know the word which יהוה hath not spoken? 22 When a prophet speaketh in the Name of יהוה, if the thing follow not, nor come to pass, that is the thing which יהוה hath not spoken, but the prophet hath spoken it presumptuously: thou shalt not be afraid of him.

AFTER TORAH

Jer. 23:9,11-12 Mine heart within me is broken because of the prophets; all my bones shake; ... 11 For both prophet and priest are profane; yea, in My House *[the Temple]* have I found their wickedness, saith יהוה. 12 Wherefore their way shall be unto them as slippery ways in the darkness: they shall be driven on, and fall therein: for I will bring evil upon them, even the year of their visitation, saith יהוה.

Jer. 23:13-15 And I have seen folly in the prophets of Samaria; they prophesied in Baal, and caused my people Israel to err [NRSV: led my people Israel astray]. 14 I have seen also in the prophets of Jerusalem an horrible thing: they commit adultery, and walk in lies: they strengthen also the hands of evildoers, that none doth return from his wickedness: they are all of them unto me as Sodom, and the inhabitants thereof as Gomorrah. 15 Therefore thus saith יהוה of hosts concerning the prophets; Behold, I will feed them with wormwood, and make them drink the water of gall [NRSV: give them poisoned water to drink]: for from the prophets of Jerusalem is profaneness gone forth into all the land.

Jer. 23:16-17 (NASB) Thus says the LORD of hosts, "Do not listen to the words of the prophets who are prophesying to you. They are leading you into futility; They speak a vision of their own imagination, Not from the mouth of the LORD. 17 They keep saying to those who despise Me, ... 'You will have peace '; And as for everyone who walks in the stubbornness of his own heart, They say, 'Calamity will not come upon you.'"

Jer. 23:21-22 I have not sent these prophets, yet they ran: I have not spoken to them, yet they prophesied 22 But if they had stood in My counsel, and had caused My people to hear My words, then they should have turned them from their evil way, and from the evil of their doings.

Jer.23:25-27,31-32,39-40 I have heard what the prophets said, that prophesy lies in My Name, saying, I have dreamed, I have dreamed. 26 How long shall this be in the heart of the prophets that prophesy lies? yea, they are prophets of the deceit of their own heart; 27 Which think to cause My people to forget My Name by their dreams which they tell every man to his neighbour.... 31 Behold, I am against the prophets, saith יהוה, that use their tongues, and say, He saith. 32 Behold, I am against them that prophesy false dreams, saith יהוה, and do tell them, and cause My people to err by their lies, and by their lightness; yet I sent them not, nor commanded them.... 39 Therefore, behold, I, even I, will utterly forget you, and I will forsake you, and the city that I gave you and your fathers, and cast you out of My presence: 40 And I will bring an **everlasting** reproach upon you, and a **perpetual** shame, which shall not be forgotten.

Jer. 28:1-4 ... *[false prophet]* Hananiah the son of Azur the prophet, ... spake ... in the house of יהוה, in the presence of the priests and of all the people, saying, 2 Thus speaketh יהוה of hosts, the God of Israel, saying, I have broken the yoke of the king of Babylon. 3 Within two full years will I bring again into this place all the vessels of יהוה's house, that Nebuchadnezzar king of Babylon took away from this place.... 4 And I will bring again to this place ... king of Judah, with all the captives of Judah, that went into Babylon, saith יהוה: for I will break the yoke of the king of Babylon.

Jer. 28:5-9 Then the prophet Jeremiah said unto the *[false]* prophet Hananiah in the presence of the priests, and in the presence of all the people that stood in the house of יהוה, ... 8 The prophets that have been before me and before thee of old prophesied both against many countries, and against great kingdoms, of war, and of evil, and of pestilence. 9 The prophet which prophesieth of peace, when the word of the prophet shall come to pass, then shall the prophet be known, that יהוה hath truly sent him.

Jer. 28:15-17 Then said the prophet Jeremiah unto Hananiah the prophet, Hear now, Hananiah; יהוה hath not sent thee; but thou makest this people to trust in a lie. 16 Therefore thus saith יהוה; Behold, I will cast thee from off the face of the earth: this year thou shalt die, because thou hast taught rebellion against יהוה. 17 So Hananiah the prophet died the same year in the seventh month.

Ezek. 13:3-6,8-10 ... Woe unto the foolish prophets, that follow their own spirit, and have seen nothing! 4 O Israel, thy prophets ... 5 ...have not gone up into the gaps, neither made up *[repaired]* the hedge for the house of Israel to stand in the battle in the day of יהוה. 6 They have seen vanity and lying divination... and יהוה hath not sent them: ... 8 Therefore thus saith Adonai יהוה; Because ye have spoken vanity, and seen lies, therefore, behold, I am against you, saith יהוה. 9 And Mine hand shall be upon [TLV: against] the prophets that see vanity, and that divine lies: they shall not be in the assembly of My people, ... neither shall they enter into the land of Israel; and ye shall know that I am Adonai יהוה. 10 Because, even because they have seduced My people, saying, Peace; and there was no peace....

Ezek. 13:17-18,22-23 Likewise, thou son of man, set thy face against the daughters of thy people, which prophesy out of their own heart; and prophesy thou against them, 18 And say, Thus saith Adonai יהוה; ... 22 Because with lies ye have made the heart of the righteous sad, whom I have not made sad; and strengthened the hands of the wicked, that he should not return from his wicked way, by promising him life: 23 Therefore ye shall see no more vanity, nor divine divinations: for I will deliver My people out of your hand: and ye shall know that I am יהוה.

Zech. 13:4-5 (ASV) And it shall come to pass in that day, that the prophets shall be ashamed every one of his vision, when he prophesieth; ...to deceive: 5 but he shall say, I am no prophet, I am a tiller of the ground....

YESHUA ישוע

Matt. 7:15 Beware of false prophets, which come to you in sheep's clothing, but inwardly they are ravening wolves.

Matt. 7:22-23 Many will say to Me in that day, Lord, Lord, have we not prophesied in Thy Name? and in Thy Name have cast out devils? and in Thy Name done many wonderful works? 23 And then will I profess unto them, I never knew you: depart from Me, ye that work iniquity.

Matt. 10:41 He that receiveth a prophet in the name of a prophet shall receive a prophet's reward....

Matt. 11:9 and Luke 7:26 But what went ye out for to see? A prophet? yea, I say unto you, and more than a prophet.

Matt. 13:57 And they were offended in Him. But ישוע said unto them, A prophet is not without honour, save in his own country, and in his own house. Mark 6:4 But ישוע said unto them, A prophet is not without honour, but in his own country, and among his own kin, and in his own house. John 4:44 For ישוע Himself testified, that a prophet hath no honour in his own country.

Matt. 24:11,24 (and Mark 13:22) And many false prophets shall rise, and shall deceive many. ... 24 For there shall arise false messiahs, and false prophets, and shall shew great signs and wonders; insomuch that, if it were possible, they shall deceive the very elect.

Matt. 24:15 and Mark 13:14 When ye therefore shall see the abomination of desolation, spoken of by Daniel the prophet....

Luke 4: 17-21 And there was delivered unto Him the book of the prophet Esaias [Isaiah]. And when He had opened the book, he found the place where it was written, 18 The Spirit of יהוה is upon me, ... 20 And He closed the book, and He gave it again to the minister, and sat down. And the eyes of all them that were in the synagogue were fastened on Him. 21 And He began to say unto them, This day is this Scripture fulfilled in your ears.

Luke 6:26 Woe unto you, when all men shall speak well of you! for so did their fathers to the false prophets.

Luke 9:56 For **the Son of man is not come to destroy men's lives, but to save them.**

Luke 11:29 … This is an evil generation: they seek a sign; and there shall no sign be given it, but the sign of Jonas [Jonah] the prophet.

Luke 13:33 …for it cannot be that a prophet perish out of Jerusalem.

Luke 24:25-27 Then He [Yeshua] said unto them, O fools, and slow of heart to **believe all that the prophets have spoken**: 26 Ought not Messiah to have suffered these things, and to enter into His glory? 27 And beginning at Moses and all the prophets, He expounded unto them in all the Scriptures the things concerning Himself.

APOSTLES about FALSE PROPHETS

Acts 20:28-31 Take heed…. 29 For I know this, that after my departing shall grievous wolves enter in among you, not sparing the flock. 30 Also of your own selves shall men arise, speaking perverse things, to draw away disciples after them. 31 Therefore watch, and remember….

Acts 13:6-11 And when they had gone through the isle unto Paphos, they found a certain sorcerer, a false prophet, a Jew, whose name was Barjesus: … 8 …withstood them, seeking to turn away the deputy from the faith. 9 Then Saul, (who also is called Paul,) filled with the Holy Spirit, set his eyes on him, 10 And said, O full of all subtilty and all mischief, thou child of the devil, thou enemy of all righteousness, wilt thou not cease to pervert the right ways of the Lord? 11 And now, behold, the hand of the Lord is upon thee, and thou shalt be blind, not seeing the sun for a season. And immediately there fell on him a mist and a darkness; and he went about seeking some to lead him by the hand.

2 Pet. 2:1 But there were false prophets also among the people, even as there shall be false teachers among you, who privily shall bring in damnable heresies, even denying the Lord that bought them, and bring upon themselves swift destruction.

1 John 4:1 Beloved, **believe not every spirit, but try the spirits whether they are of God:** because many false prophets are gone out into the world.

Jude 1:4 (NRSV) For certain intruders have stolen in among you … who pervert the grace of our God into licentiousness and deny our only Master and Lord, Jesus Christ.

Rev. 19:20 And the beast was taken, and with him the false prophet that wrought miracles before him, with which he deceived them that had received the mark of the beast, and them that worshipped his image. These both were cast alive into a lake of fire burning with brimstone.

Rev. 22:18-19 For I testify unto every man that heareth the words of the prophecy of this book, If any man shall add unto these things, God shall add unto him the plagues that are written in this book: 19 And if any man shall take away from the words of the book of this prophecy, God shall take away his part out of the book of life, and out of the holy city, and from the things which are written in this book.

APOSTLES about GOOD, TRUE PROPHESYING

Acts 2:16-18 But this is that which was spoken by the prophet Joel; 17 And it shall come to pass in the last days, saith God, I will pour out of My Spirit upon all flesh: and your sons and your daughters shall prophesy, and your young men shall see visions, and your old men shall dream dreams: 18 And on My servants and on My handmaidens I will pour out in those days of My Spirit; and they shall prophesy:

Acts 21:9,10b And the same man had four daughters, virgins, which did prophesy. 10 ...there came down from Judaea a certain prophet, named Agabus.

Rom. 12:6 Having then gifts differing according to the grace that is given to us, whether prophecy, let us prophesy according to the proportion of faith;

1 Cor. 13:2 And though I have the gift of prophecy, and understand all mysteries, and all knowledge; and though I have all faith, so that I could remove mountains, and have not charity, I am nothing.

1 Cor. 13:9 For we know in part, and we prophesy in part.

1 Cor. 14:3 ...he that prophesieth speaketh unto men to edification, and exhortation, and comfort.

1 Cor. 14:5 I would that ye all spake with tongues, but rather that ye prophesied: for greater is he that prophesieth than he that speaketh with tongues, except he interpret, that the church may receive edifying.

1 Cor. 14:24-25 But if all prophesy, and there come in one that believeth not, or one unlearned, he is convinced of all, he is judged of all: 25 And thus are the secrets of his heart made manifest; and so falling down on his face he will worship God, and report that God is in you of a truth. *[Is not this the most important purpose of prophecy?!!]*

1 Cor. 14:29-31 Let the prophets speak two or three, and **let the other judge.** 30 If any thing be revealed to another that sitteth by, let the first hold his peace. 31 For ye may all prophesy one by one, that all may learn, and all may be comforted. *[Learning and being comforted sounds more like teaching and ministering than it does what we tend to think of as prophesy these days.]*

1 Cor. 14:32 And **the spirits of the prophets are subject to the prophets.**

1 Thess. 5:20 Despise not prophesyings.

1 Tim. 4:14 Neglect not the gift that is in thee, which was given thee by prophecy....

2 Pet. 1:20-21 Knowing this first, that no prophecy of the Scripture is of any private interpretation. 21 For the prophecy came not in old time by the will of man: but holy men of God spake as they were moved by the Holy Spirit.

Rev. 10:11 And he said unto me, Thou must prophesy again before many peoples, and nations, and tongues, and kings.

Rev. 11:3 And I will give power unto my two witnesses, and they shall prophesy....

Rev. 19:10 ... I am thy fellowservant, and of thy brethren that have the testimony of ישוע: worship God: for the testimony of ישוע is the spirit of prophecy.

77. PUT PEOPLE TO DEATH WHO ENTICE TO SERVE OTHER GODS

Deut. 13:6-11 If thy brother, the son of thy mother, or thy son, or thy daughter, or the wife of thy bosom, or thy friend, which is as thine own soul, entice thee secretly, saying, Let us go and serve other gods, which thou hast not known, thou, nor thy fathers; 7 Namely, of the gods of the people which are round about you, nigh unto thee, or far off from thee, from the one end of the earth even unto the other end of the earth; 8 Thou shalt not consent unto him, nor hearken unto him; neither shall thine eye pity him, neither shalt thou spare, neither shalt thou conceal him: 9 But thou shalt surely kill him; thine hand shall be first upon him to put him to death, and afterwards the hand of all the people. 10 And thou shalt stone him with stones, that he die; because he hath sought to thrust thee away from יהוה thy God, which brought thee out of the land of Egypt, from the house of bondage. 11 And all Israel shall hear, and fear, and shall do no more any such wickedness as this is among you. [also in No other gods, p. 31]

AFTER TORAH

Zech. 5:4 I will bring it *[the flying scroll}* forth, saith יהוה of hosts, and it shall enter into the house of the thief, and into the house of him that sweareth falsely by My Name: and it shall remain in the midst of his house, and shall consume it [both] the timber ... and the stones....

Micah 7:6 For the son dishonoureth the father, the daughter riseth up against her mother, the daughter in law against her mother in law; a man's enemies are the men of his own house.

YESHUA ישוע and APOSTLES

Matt. 10:34-38 Think not that I am come to send peace on earth: I came not to send peace, but a sword. 35 For I am come to set a man at variance against his father, and the daughter against her mother, and the daughter in law against her mother in law. 36 And a man's foes shall be they of his own household. 37 He that loveth father or mother more than Me is not worthy of Me: and he that loveth son or daughter more than Me is not worthy of Me. 38 And he that taketh not his cross, and followeth after Me, is not worthy of Me.

Luke 9:56 For **the Son of man is not come to destroy men's lives, but to save them.**

Luke 10:19 Behold, I give unto you **power** to tread on serpents and scorpions, and **over all the power of the enemy**....

Mark 16:17 And these signs shall follow them that believe; In My Name shall they cast out devils....

2 Cor. 10:3-5 For ... we do not war after the flesh: 4 (For the weapons of our warfare are not carnal, but mighty through God to the pulling down of strong holds;) 5 Casting down imaginations, and every high thing that exalteth itself against the knowledge of God, and bringing into captivity every thought to the obedience of Messiah;

78. PUT WHOLE CITY TO DEATH IF TURNS TO OTHER GODS

[Yes, this law seems horrible! But see the turn around in the New Covenant. Hallelujah!]

Deut. 13:12-17 If thou shalt hear say in one of thy cities, which יהוה thy God hath given thee to dwell there, saying, 13 Certain men, the children of Belial, are gone out from among you, and have withdrawn the inhabitants of their city, saying, Let us go and serve other gods, which ye have not known; 14 Then shalt thou enquire, and make search, and ask diligently; and, behold, if it be truth, and the thing certain, that such abomination is wrought among you; 15 Thou shalt surely smite the inhabitants of that city with the edge of the sword, destroying it utterly, and all that is therein, and the cattle thereof, with the edge of the sword. 16 And thou shalt gather all the spoil of it into the midst of the street thereof, and shalt burn with fire the city, and all the spoil thereof every whit, for יהוה thy God: and it shall be an heap **forever**; it shall not be built again. 17 And there shall cleave nought of the cursed thing to thine hand: that יהוה may turn from the fierceness of his anger, and shew thee mercy, and have compassion upon thee, and multiply thee.... [also in No other gods, p. 32]

YESHUA ישוע

Matt. 11:21-24 & Luke 10:13-15 Woe unto thee, Chorazin! woe unto thee, Bethsaida! for if the mighty works, which were done in you, had been done in Tyre and Sidon, they would have repented long ago in sackcloth and ashes. 22 ... It shall be more tolerable for Tyre and Sidon at the day of judgment, than for you. 23 And thou, Capernaum, ... shalt be brought down to hell: for if the mighty works ... done in thee, had been done in Sodom, it would have remained until this day. 24 But ... it shall be more tolerable for the land of Sodom in the day of judgment, than for thee.

Luke 9:51-56 ...when the time was come that he should be received up, he steadfastly set his face to go to Jerusalem, 52 And sent messengers ... *[who]* entered into a village of the Samaritans, to make ready for him. 53 And they did not receive him, because his face was as though he would go to Jerusalem. 54 And when his disciples James and John saw this, they said, Lord, wilt thou that we command fire to come down from heaven, and consume them, even as [Elijah] did? [2 Kings 1:11-15] 55 But he turned, and rebuked them, and said, Ye know not what manner of spirit ye are of. 56 For **the Son of man is not come to destroy men's lives, but to save them**. And they went to another village.

Luke 10:10-12 But into whatsoever city ye enter, and they receive you not, go your ways out into the streets of the same, and say, 11 Even the very dust of your city, which cleaveth on us, we do wipe off against you: notwithstanding be ye sure of this, that the kingdom of God is come nigh unto you. 12 But I say unto you, that it shall be more tolerable in that day for Sodom, than for that city.

APOSTLES

Let's be like Paul whose witness turned whole idolatrous cities to ישוע: Ephesus, Corinth, Phillipi, etc.

Acts 19:23-27 ... there arose no small stir about that Way. 24 For a certain man named Demetrius, a silversmith, which made silver shrines for Diana, brought no small gain unto the craftsmen; 25 Whom he called together with the workmen of like occupation, and said, Sirs, ye know that by this craft we have our wealth. 26 Moreover ye see and hear, that **not alone at Ephesus,**

but almost throughout all Asia, this Paul hath persuaded and turned away much people, saying that they be no gods, which are made with hands: 27 So that not only this our craft is in danger to be set at nought; but also that the temple of the great goddess Diana should be despised, and her magnificence should be destroyed, whom all Asia and the world worshippeth.

79. DESTROY HEATHEN NATIONS IN CANAAN (AND AMELEK), MAKE NO COVENANT WITH THEM

[Yes, this law seems horrible! See on the next page in Psalms why God gave it.]

Ex. 23:31-33 And I will set thy bounds from the Red sea even unto the sea of the Philistines, and from the desert unto the river: for I will deliver the inhabitants of the land into your hand; and thou shalt drive them out before thee. 32 Thou shalt make no covenant with them, nor with their gods. 33 They shall not dwell in thy land, lest they make thee sin against me: for if thou serve their gods, it will surely be a snare unto thee.

Num. 33:51-53 Speak unto the children of Israel, and say unto them, When ye are passed over Jordan into the land of Canaan; 52 Then ye shall drive out all the inhabitants of the land from before you, and destroy all their pictures, and destroy all their molten images, and quite pluck down all their high places: 53 And ye shall dispossess the inhabitants of the land, and dwell therein: for I have given you the land to possess it. [also in No idols, p. 35]

Num. 33:55-56 But if ye will not drive out the inhabitants of the land from before you; then it shall come to pass, that those which ye let remain of them shall be pricks in your eyes, and thorns in your sides, and shall vex you in the land wherein ye dwell. 56 Moreover it shall come to pass, that I shall do unto you, as I thought to do unto them.

Deut. 7:2-4 And when יהוה thy God shall deliver them before thee; thou shalt smite them, and utterly destroy them; thou shalt make no covenant with them, nor shew mercy unto them: Neither shalt thou make marriages with them; thy daughter thou shalt not give unto his son, nor his daughter shalt thou take unto thy son. For they will turn away thy son from following me, that they may serve other gods: so will the anger of יהוה be kindled against you, and destroy thee suddenly.

Deut. 7:16-24 And thou shalt consume all the people which יהוה thy God shall deliver thee; thine eye shall have no pity upon them: neither shalt thou serve their gods; for that will be a snare unto thee. 17 If thou shalt say in thine heart, These nations are more than I; how can I dispossess them? 18 Thou shalt not be afraid of them: but shalt well remember what יהוה thy God did unto Pharaoh, and unto all Egypt; ... [also in No other gods, p. 31]

Deut. 9:1-3 Hear, O Israel: Thou art to pass over Jordan this day, to go in to possess nations greater and mightier than thyself, cities great and fenced up to heaven, 2 A people great and tall, the children of the Anakims, whom thou knowest, and of whom thou hast heard say, Who can stand before the children of Anak! 3 Understand therefore this day, that יהוה

thy God is he which goeth over before thee; as a consuming fire he shall destroy them, and he shall bring them down before thy face: so shalt thou drive them out, and destroy them quickly, as יהוה hath said unto thee.

Deut. 25:17-19 Remember what Amalek did unto thee by the way, when ye were come forth out of Egypt; 18 How he met thee by the way, and smote the hindmost of thee, even all that were feeble behind thee, when thou wast faint and weary; and he feared not God. 19 Therefore it shall be, when יהוה thy God hath given thee rest from all thine enemies round about, in the land which יהוה thy God giveth thee for an inheritance to possess it, that thou shalt blot out the remembrance of Amalek from under heaven; thou shalt not forget it.

AFTER TORAH

Judges 2:2-4 And ye shall make no league with the inhabitants of this land; ye shall throw down their altars: but ye have not obeyed my voice: why have ye done this? 3 Wherefore I also said, I will not drive them out from before you; but they shall be as thorns in your sides, and their gods shall be a snare unto you. 4 And ... the people lifted up their voice, and wept.

I Sam. 15:2-3, 5, 20-23 Thus saith יהוה of hosts, I remember that which Amalek did to Israel, how he laid wait for him in the way, when he came up from Egypt. Now go and smite Amalek, and utterly destroy all that they have, and spare them not; but slay both man and woman, infant and suckling, ox and sheep, camel and ass. ... 5 And Saul came to a city of Amalek, and laid wait in the valley. ... 20 And Saul said unto Samuel, Yea, I have obeyed the voice of יהוה, and have gone the way which יהוה sent me, and have brought Agag the king of Amalek, and have utterly destroyed the Amalekites. 21 But the people took of the spoil, sheep and oxen, the chief of the things which should have been utterly destroyed, to sacrifice unto יהוה thy God in Gilgal. 22 And Samuel said, Hath יהוה as great delight in burnt offerings and sacrifices, as in obeying the voice of יהוה? Behold, to obey is better than sacrifice, and to hearken than the fat of rams. 23 For rebellion is as the sin of witchcraft, and stubbornness is as iniquity and idolatry. Because thou hast rejected the word of יהוה, he hath also rejected thee from being king.

I Sam. 28:18 Because thou obeyedst not the voice of יהוה, nor executedst his fierce wrath upon Amalek, therefore hath יהוה done this thing unto thee this day.

[Here's why God gave this very hard to swallow ruling:]

Psalm 106:34-40 They did not destroy the nations, concerning whom יהוה commanded them: 35 But were mingled among the heathen, and learned their works. 36 And they served their idols: which were a snare unto them. 37 Yea, they sacrificed their sons and their daughters unto devils, 38 And shed innocent blood, even the blood of their sons and of their daughters, whom they sacrificed unto the idols of Canaan: and the land was polluted with blood. 39 Thus were they defiled with their own works, and went a whoring with their own inventions.

114

40 Therefore was the wrath of יהוה kindled against his people, insomuch that he abhorred his own inheritance. *[And our nation is following the custom of killing pre-born children!!]*

[Let all the following verses comfort you. There is forgiveness and deliverance for all now from even the worst sins because of Yeshua ישוע sacrificing His own Blood.]

Ezek. 18:32 (NIV) For **I take no pleasure in the death of anyone**, declares the Sovereign LORD. Repent and live!

YESHUA ישוע

John 3:14-21 And as Moses lifted up the serpent in the wilderness, even so must the Son of man be lifted up: 15 That **whosoever believeth in Him should not perish,** but have eternal life. 16 For God so loved the world, that He gave His only begotten Son, that whosoever believeth in Him should not perish, but have **everlasting** Life. 17 **For God sent not His Son into the world to condemn the world; but that the world through Him might be saved.** 18 He that believeth on Him is not condemned: but he that believeth not is condemned already, because he hath not believed in the Name of the only begotten Son of God. 19 And this is the condemnation, that Light is come into the world, and men loved darkness rather than Light, because their deeds were evil. 20 For every one that doeth evil hateth the Light, neither cometh to the Light, lest his deeds should be reproved. 21 But he that doeth truth cometh to the Light, that his deeds may be made manifest, that they are wrought in God.

Mark 16:15 **Go ye into all the world,** and **preach the Gospel** to every creature.

Matt. 28:19-20 **Go ye** therefore, and **teach all nations,** baptizing them in the Name of the Father, and of the Son, and of the Holy Spirit: 20 Teaching them to observe all things whatsoever I have commanded you: and, lo, I am with you alway, even unto the end of the world. Amen.

APOSTLES

I Tim. 2:1-6 I exhort therefore, that, first of all, supplications, prayers, intercessions, and giving of thanks, be made for all men; 2 For kings, and for all that are in authority; that we may lead a quiet and peaceable life in all godliness and honesty. 3 For this is good and acceptable in the sight of God our Saviour; 4 **Who will have all men to be saved, and to come unto the knowledge of the truth.** 5 For there is one God, and one mediator between God and men, the man **Messiah** ישוע; 6 **Who gave Himself a ransom for all,** to be testified in due time.

2 Pet. 3:9 The Lord is not slack concerning his promise, as some men count slackness; but is longsuffering to us-ward, **not willing that any should perish, but that all should come to repentance.**

[Starting with the Apostles, missionaries over the centuries and still today are leading whole nations away from idols and heathen practices to know and love and worship the One True God.]

Num. 1:2-4 Take ye the sum of all the congregation of the children of Israel, after their families, by the house of their fathers, with the number of their names, every male by their polls; 3 From twenty years old and upward, <u>all that are able to go forth to war</u> in Israel: thou and Aaron shall number them by their armies. 4 And with you there shall be a man of every tribe; every one head of the house of his fathers. [also in Census, p. 213]

Num.1:47-49 But the Levites after the tribe of their fathers were not numbered among them. 48 For יהוה had spoken unto Moses, saying, 49 Only thou shalt not number the tribe of Levi, neither take the sum of them among the children of Israel: [also in Census, p. 213]

Num. 10:9 And if ye go to war in your land against the enemy that oppresseth you, then ye shall blow an alarm with the trumpets; and ye shall be remembered before יהוה your God, and ye shall be saved from your enemies. [also in Silver Trumpets, p. 216]

Num. 26:1-2 And it came to pass after the plague, that יהוה spake unto Moses and unto Eleazar the son of Aaron the priest, saying, 2 Take the sum of all the congregation of the children of Israel, from twenty years old and upward, throughout their fathers' house, all <u>that are able to go to war</u> in Israel.

Num. 31:25-31 (NIV) The LORD said to Moses, 26 "You and Eleazar the priest and the family heads of the community are to count all the people and animals that were captured. 27 Divide the spoils equally between the soldiers who took part in the battle and the rest of the community. 28 From the soldiers who fought in the battle, set apart as tribute for the LORD one out of every five hundred, whether people, cattle, donkeys or sheep. 29 Take this tribute from their half share and give it to Eleazar the priest as the LORD's part. 30 From the Israelites' half, select one out of every fifty, whether people, cattle, donkeys, sheep or other animals. Give them to the Levites, who are responsible for the care of the LORD's Tabernacle." 31 So Moses and Eleazar the priest did as the LORD commanded Moses.

Deut. 20:1-4 When thou goest out to battle against thine enemies, and seest horses, and chariots, and a people more than thou, be not afraid of them: for יהוה thy God is with thee, which brought thee up out of the land of Egypt. 2 And it shall be, when ye are come nigh unto the battle, that the priest shall approach and speak unto the people, 3 And shall say unto them, Hear, O Israel, ye approach this day unto battle against your enemies: let not your hearts faint, fear not, and do not tremble, neither be ye terrified because of them; 4 For יהוה your God is he that goeth with you, to fight for you against your enemies, to save you.

Deut. 20:10-15 When thou comest nigh unto a city to fight against it, then proclaim **shalom** unto it. 11 And it shall be, if it make thee answer of peace, and open unto thee, then it shall be, that all the people that is found therein shall be tributaries unto thee, and they shall serve thee. 12 And if it will make no peace with thee, but will make war against thee, then thou

shalt besiege it: 13 And when יהוה thy God hath delivered it into thine hands, thou shalt smite every male thereof with the edge of the sword: 14 But the women, and the little ones, and the cattle, and all that is in the city, even all the spoil thereof, shalt thou take unto thyself; and thou shalt eat the spoil of thine enemies, which יהוה thy God hath given thee. 15 Thus shalt thou do unto all the cities which are very far off from thee,

> YESHUA: Matt. 10:12-13 And when ye come into an house, salute it. And if the house be worthy, let your peace come upon it: but if it be not worthy, let your peace return to you.

> Luke 10:5-6 And into whatsoever house ye enter, first say, Peace be to this house. And if the son of peace be there, your peace shall rest upon it: if not, it shall turn to you again.

Deut. 23:9 (NKJV) When the army goes out against your enemies, then keep yourself from every wicked thing.

WHAT SOLDIERS MAY STAY HOME FROM WAR:

Deut. 20:5-8 And the officers shall speak unto the people, saying, What man is there that hath **built a new house**, and hath not dedicated it? let him go and return to his house, lest he die in the battle, and another man dedicate it. 6 And what man is he that hath **planted a vineyard**, and hath not yet eaten of it? let him also go and return unto his house, lest he die in the battle, and another man eat of it. 7 And what man is there that hath **betrothed a wife,** and hath not taken her? let him go and return unto his house, lest he die in the battle, and another man take her. 8 And the officers shall speak further unto the people, and they shall say, What man is there that is **fearful and fainthearted**? let him go and return unto his house, lest his brethren's heart faint as well as his heart.

Deut. 24:5 When a man hath taken a **new wife**, he shall not go out to war, neither shall he be charged with any business: but he shall be free at home one year, and shall cheer up his wife which he hath taken.

YESHUA ישוע

Luke 14:16-24 Then said he unto him, A certain man made a great supper, and bade many: 17 And sent his servant at supper time to say to them that were bidden, Come; for all things are now ready. 18 And they all with one consent began to make excuse. The first said unto him, I have **bought a piece of ground**, and I must needs go and see it: I pray thee have me excused. 19 And another said, I have **bought five yoke of oxen**, and I go to prove them: I pray thee have me excused. 20 And another said, I have **married a wife,** and therefore I cannot come. 21 So that servant came, and shewed his lord these things. Then the master of the house being angry said to his servant, Go out quickly into the streets and lanes of the city, and bring in hither the poor, and the maimed, and the halt, and the blind. 22 And the servant said, Lord, it is done as thou hast commanded, and yet there is room. 23 And the lord said unto the servant, Go out into the highways and hedges, and compel them to come in, that my house may be filled. 24 For I say unto you, That none of those men which were bidden shall taste of my supper.

81. UNBIASED JUSTICE

Ex. 23:2-3 Thou shalt not follow a multitude to do evil; neither shalt thou speak in a cause to decline after many to wrest judgment: Neither shalt thou countenance a poor man in his cause. (TLV: "Do not follow a crowd to do evil. Nor are you to testify in a case, to follow a crowd and pervert justice. 3 On the other hand, nor should you takes sides with a poor man in his case.)

Ex. 23:6 Thou shalt not wrest the judgment of thy poor in his cause. (CJB: Do not deny anyone justice in his lawsuit simply because he is poor.)

Ex. 23:7 Keep thee far from a false matter; and the innocent and righteous slay thou not: for I will not justify the wicked.

Lev. 19:15 Ye shall do no unrighteousness in judgment: thou shalt not respect the person of the poor, nor honour the person of the mighty: but in righteousness shalt thou judge thy neighbour.

Deut. 1:16-17 And I charged your judges at that time, saying, Hear the causes between your brethren, and judge righteously between every man and his brother, and the stranger that is with him. 17 Ye shall not respect persons in judgment; but ye shall hear the small as well as the great; ye shall not be afraid of the face of man; for the judgment is God's: and the cause that is too hard for you, bring it unto me, and I will hear it.

Deut 16:18-20 Judges and officers shalt thou make thee in all thy gates, which יהוה thy God giveth thee, throughout thy tribes: and they shall judge the people with just judgment. 19 Thou shalt not wrest (NRSV: distort) judgment; thou shalt not respect persons, neither take a gift: for a gift doth blind the eyes of the wise, and pervert the words of the righteous. 20 That which is altogether just shalt thou follow (NRSV: Justice, and only justice, you shall pursue), that thou mayest live, and inherit the land which יהוה thy God giveth thee.

Deut. 24:17a, 18 Thou shalt not pervert the judgment of the stranger, nor of the fatherless; ... 18 But thou shalt remember that thou wast a bondman in Egypt, and יהוה thy God redeemed thee thence: therefore I command thee to do this thing. [also in Strangers, p. 86, and Widows and Orphans, p. 88]

Deut. 25:1 If there be a controversy between men, and they come unto judgment, that the judges may judge them; then they shall justify the righteous, and condemn the wicked.

Deut. 27:19 Cursed be he that perverteth the judgment of the stranger, fatherless, and widow. [[also in Strangers, p. 86, and Widows and Orphans, p. 88]

AFTER TORAH

Isaiah 1:17 Learn to do well; ... relieve the oppressed, judge the fatherless, plead for the widow.

Psalm 82:3 Defend the poor and fatherless: do justice to the afflicted and needy.

Prov. 18:5 (NRSV) It is not right to be partial to the guilty, or to subvert the innocent in judgment.

82. TAKE NO BRIBE / GIFT

Ex. 23:8 And thou shalt take no gift [bribe]: for the gift blindeth the wise, and perverteth the words of the righteous. (TLV: Take no bribe, for a bribe blinds those who have sight, and perverts the words of the righteous.)

Deut. 16:19 Thou shalt not wrest judgment; thou shalt not respect persons, neither take a gift: for a gift doth blind the eyes of the wise, and pervert the words of the righteous.

Deut. 27:25 Cursed be he that taketh reward to slay an innocent person. And all the people shall say, Amen.

AFTER TORAH

Prov. 17:23 (NKJV) A wicked man accepts a bribe behind the back To pervert the ways of justice.

Prov. 21:14 A gift in secret pacifieth anger: and a reward in the bosom strong wrath.

JUDAS BRIBED TO BETRAY ישוע

Matt. 26:14-16 Then one of the twelve, called Judas Iscariot, went unto the chief priests, 15 And said unto them, What will ye give me, and I will deliver Him unto you? And they covenanted with him for thirty pieces of silver. 16 And from that time he sought opportunity to betray Him.

Mark 14:10-11 And Judas Iscariot, one of the twelve, went unto the chief priests, to betray Him unto them. 11 And when they heard it, they were glad, and promised to give him money.

83. MUST DO WHAT TOP PRIEST-LEVITE JUDGES SAY

Deut. 17:8-13 If there arise a matter too hard for thee in judgment, between blood and blood, between plea and plea, and between stroke and stroke, being matters of controversy within thy gates: then shalt thou arise, and get thee up into the place which יהוה thy God shall choose; 9 And thou shalt come unto the **priests the Levites,** and unto the judge that shall be in those days, and enquire; and they shall shew thee the sentence of judgment: 10 And thou shalt do according to the sentence, which they of that place which יהוה shall choose shall shew thee; and thou shalt observe to do according to all that they inform thee: 11 According to the sentence of the law which they shall teach thee, and according to the judgment which they shall tell thee, thou shalt do: thou shalt not decline from the sentence which they shall shew thee, to the right hand, nor to the left. 12 **And the man that will do presumptuously, and will not hearken unto the priest that standeth to minister there before** יהוה **thy God, or unto the judge, even that man shall die:** and thou shalt put away the evil from Israel. 13 And all the people shall hear, and fear, and do no more presumptuously.

84. NO MORE THAN 40 LASHES/STRIPES AND IN FRONT OF JUDGE

Deut. 25:1-3 If there be a controversy between men, and they come unto judgment, that the judges may judge them; then they shall justify the righteous, and condemn the wicked. 2 And it shall be, if the wicked man be worthy to be beaten, that the judge shall cause him to lie down, and to be beaten before his face, according to his fault, by a certain number. 3 **Forty stripes** he may give him, and not exceed: lest, if he should exceed, and beat him above these with many **stripes**, then thy brother should seem vile unto thee.

JEREMIAH FLOGGED

Jer. 20:1-2 (CJB) Now when the cohen (priest) Pash'chur son of Immer, chief official in the house of ADONAI, heard Yirmeyahu (Jeremiah) prophesying these things, 2 he had him **flogged** and put him in the stocks at the Upper Binyamin Gate of the house of ADONAI.

YESHUA ישוע PREDICTING FLOGGING

OF HIMSELF: Matt. 20:18-19 (NRSV) "See, we are going up to Jerusalem, and the Son of Man will be handed over to the chief priests and scribes, and they will condemn Him to death; 19 then they will hand Him over to the Gentiles to be mocked and **flogged** and crucified; and on the third day He will be raised."

Luke 18:33 (NRSV) After they have **flogged** Him, they will kill Him, and on the third day He will rise again."

OF BELIEVERS: Matt. 10:17 (CJB) 17 Be on guard, for there will be people who will hand you over to the local Sanhedrins and **flog** you in their synagogues.

YESHUA ישוע FLOGGED

Isaiah 53:5 But He was wounded for our transgressions, He was bruised for our iniquities: the chastisement of our peace was upon Him; and **with His stripes we are healed**.

Mark 15:15 (NRSV) So Pilate, wishing to satisfy the crowd, released Barabbas for them; and after **flogging** Jesus, he handed him over to be crucified.

Luke 23:13-16,22 (NRSV) Pilate then called together the chief priests, the leaders, and the people, 14 and said to them, "You brought me this man as one who was perverting the people; and here I have examined him in your presence and have not found this man guilty of any of your charges against him 15 Neither has Herod, for he sent him back to us. Indeed, he has done nothing to deserve death. 16 I will therefore **have him flogged** and release him." ... A third time He said to them, "Why, what evil has he done? I have found in him no ground for the sentence of death; I will therefore **have him flogged** and then release him."

John 19:1 (NRSV) Then Pilate took Jesus and had him **flogged**.

I Peter 2:24 Who His own self bare our sins in His own Body on the tree, that we, being dead to sins, should live unto righteousness: by whose **stripes** ye were healed.

APOSTLES FLOGGED

Acts 16:20-23 (CJB) Bringing them to the judges, they said, "These men (Paul and Silas)] are causing a lot of trouble in our city.... 21 ...advocating customs that are against the law for us to accept or practice, since we are Romans." 22 The mob joined in the attack against them, and the judges tore their clothes off them and ordered that they be **flogged**. 23 After giving them a **severe beating**, they threw them in prison, charging the jailer to guard them securely.

Acts 22:25 (CJB) But as they were stretching him out with thongs to be **flogged**, Sha'ul (Paul) said to the captain standing by, "Is it legal for you to **whip** a man who is a Roman citizen...[w/ no] trial?"

2 Corinthians 11:24 Of the Jews five times received I **forty stripes** save one.

DEATH PENALTY, A LIST   *(Page numbers are for this book.)*

Notice "must make careful inquiry first." Deterrent to crime? Maybe. There's very little record of it ever being followed. Yeshua took this death penalty, this curse of the law, upon Himself and won forgiveness for us (p. 259).

WORSHIPPING IDOLS "**utterly destroyed**" Ex. 22:20; "**Make careful inquiry first.**" Stoned. Deut. 17:2-7 (p. 31, 32)

BLASPHEMING THE NAME OF THE LORD **Stoned** by whole congregation. Lev. 24:14-16 (p. 40, 86)

BREAKING THE SABBATH **Stoned** Ex 31:14,15; Ex 35:2; Nu. 15:36 (p.42)

MAGIC (a witch, NRSV: female sorcerer) "Thou shall not suffer a witch to live" Ex. 22:18 (p. 105)

WITCHCRAFT (medium or wizard). **Stoned** Lev. 20:27 Don't practice any such things. Deut. 18:9-14 (p. 105).

GIVING CHILDREN TO MOLECH (false god). **Stoned** Lev. 20:2 (p. 104)

CLOSING YOUR EYES TO OTHERS DOING THIS "I (God) will **cut him off**" Lev. 20:4 (p. 104)

STRANGERS COMING NEAR THE TEMPLE **Put to death** Num 1:51; 3:10; 3:38; Num 18:7 (p.86, 150)

HITTING OR CURSING YOUR PARENTS, **Put to death** Ex. 21:15,17 (p.46)

BEING A REBELLIOUS, GLUTTONOUS, DRUNKARD SON. **Stone** Deut 21:18-21 (p. 195)

MURDER It says "**put to death**" six times!!! Ex. 21:21; Lev. 24:17; Num 35:16-18, 21, 30-31 (p. 47-48, 123) But not for murdering a slave if he doesn't die until 1-2 days later. Ex. 21:20-21 (p. 71)

IF YOUR OX KILLS if was known to gore. Ox stoned, owner **put to death**. Ex. 21:28-29, 32 (p. 74, 82, 92)

KIDNAPPING an Israelite, **put to death** Ex. 21:16 (p. 52)

NOT OBEYING THE COURT VERDICT of a priest. "That man **shall die**." Deut. 17:8-13 (p. 119)

FALSE WITNESS, give the punishment of the crime he accused, "**life for life,** eye for eye..." Deut. 19:15-21 (p. 53)

LEADING OTHERS TO FALSE GODS: (Even with visions...signs...omens that come to pass!) "**Put to death**. Show no pity... your hand shall be the first ...to execute them." Deut. 13:1-11 (p. 32, 106)
    Whole towns that go after other gods. **Put to the sword**. Deut 13:12-17 (Destroy everything, incl. animals. Burn all the spoil in its public square.) (p. 32, 112)

FALSE PROPHET who what he says does not come to pass. "He **shall die**." Deut 18:20-22 (p. 106)

REBEL AND DISOBEY Joshua's commands. Josh 1:18

ADULTERY, **both put to death** Lev. 20:10; Deut. 22:22. Only scourged if the woman is a slave. Lev. 19:20 (p. 58)

BRIDE NOT A VIRGIN when she marries. **Stoned** Deut. 22:20-21 (p. 63)

PRIEST'S DAUGHTER PROSTITUTE: **Burned** Lev. 21:9 (p. 221) (Her father can't mourn her death. p. 222)

RAPING A VIRGIN ENGAGED: **Stoned.** If not engaged, must marry & never divorce her. Deut. 22:23, 28-29 (p. 63)

NOT SCREAMING WHEN RAPED in the city, if you are a virgin engaged. **Both stoned**. Deut. 22:23, 25 (p. 63)

BESTIALITY, by either a man or a woman. **Put to death.** Lev. 20: 15-16 (.p. 67)

MAN LYING WITH A MAN **Put to death.** *(Maybe not for women??!)* Lev. 20:13 (p. 66)

MARRYING BOTH A MOTHER AND DAUGHTER All three are to be **burned**. Lev. 20:14 (p. 65)

LYING WITH DAUGHTER-IN-LAW or FATHER'S WIFE, **both put to death.** Lev. 20:12 (p. 64-65)

INCEST Lev. 18. Incest with sister, daughter-in-law, granddaughter, aunt, daughter or granddaughter of woman you have sex with, sister-in-law, any near of kin (Lev. 18:6), any kinsmen's wife. Daughter: "Don't uncover the nakedness of a woman and her daughter." Lev. 20:17 *This includes his own daughter!* "**cut off from their people**." Lev. 18:29 (p. 64)

85. CHILDREN NOT PUNISHED FOR PARENTS' SINS AND VICE VERSA

Deut. 24:16 The fathers shall not be put to death for the children, neither shall the children be put to death for the fathers: every man shall be put to death for his own sin.

Mercy to a thousand generations, but iniquity to third and fourth generation:

> Ex. 34:7 Keeping mercy for thousands, forgiving iniquity and transgression and sin, and that will by no means clear the guilty; visiting the iniquity of the fathers upon the children, and upon the children's children, unto the third and to the fourth generation.

> Deut. 7:9-10 Know therefore that יהוה thy God, He is God, the faithful God, which keepeth covenant and mercy with them that love Him and keep His commandments to a thousand generations; 10 And repayeth them that hate Him to their face, to destroy them: He will not be slack to him that hateth Him, He will repay him to his face.

AFTER TORAH

2 Kings 14:5-6 (also 2 Chron 25:3-4) And it came to pass, as soon as the kingdom was confirmed in his hand [King Amaziah son of King Joash], that he slew his servants which had slain the king his father. 6 But the children of the murderers he slew not: according unto that which is written in the book of the Torah of Moses, wherein יהוה commanded, saying, The fathers shall not be put to death for the children, nor the children be put to death for the fathers; but every man shall be put to death for his own sin.

Jer. 31:30 But every one shall die for his own iniquity: every man that eateth the sour grape, his teeth shall be set on edge.

Ezek. 18:1-4, 19-20 The Word of יהוה came unto me again, saying, 2 What mean ye, that ye use this proverb concerning the land of Israel, saying, The fathers have eaten sour grapes, and the children's teeth are set on edge? 3 As I live, saith יהוה, ye shall not have occasion any more to use this proverb in Israel. 4 Behold, all souls are mine; as the soul of the father, so also the soul of the son is mine: the soul that sinneth, it shall die. ... 19 Yet say ye, Why? doth not the son bear the iniquity of the father? When the son hath done that which is lawful and right, and hath kept all My statutes, and hath done them, he shall surely live. 20 The soul that sinneth, it shall die. The son shall not bear the iniquity of the father, neither shall the father bear the iniquity of the son: the righteousness of the righteous shall be upon him, and the wickedness of the wicked shall be upon him.

86. TWO OR THREE WITNESSES

Num. 35:30 Whoso killeth any person, the murderer shall be put to death by the mouth of witnesses: but one witness shall not testify against any person to cause him to die. [also in No killing, p. 48]

Deut. 17:6-7 At the mouth of two witnesses, or three witnesses, shall he that is worthy of death be put to death; but at the mouth of one witness he shall not be put to death. 7 The hands of the witnesses shall be first upon him to put him to death, and afterward the hands of all the people. So thou shalt put the evil away from among you.

Deut. 19:15 One witness shall not rise up against a man for any iniquity, or for any sin, in any sin that he sinneth: at the mouth of two witnesses, or at the mouth of three witnesses, shall the matter be established.

AFTER TORAH

Prov. 18:17 He that is first in his own cause seemeth just; but his neighbour cometh and searcheth him. NRSV: 17 The one who first states a case seems right, until the other comes and cross-examines.

YESHUA ישוע

Matt. 18:16 But if he will not hear thee, then take with thee one or two more, that in the mouth of two or three witnesses every word may be established.

John 8:17-18 It is also written in your Torah, that the testimony of two men is true. 18 I am one that bear witness of Myself, and the Father that sent Me beareth witness of Me.

Mark. 14:55-62 55 And the chief priests and all the council sought for witness against ישוע .... 56 For many bare false witness against Him, but their witness agreed not together. 57 And there arose certain ... against Him, saying, 58 We heard Him say, I will destroy this Temple that is made with hands, and within three days I will build another made without hands. 59 But neither so did their witness agree together. ... 61 ... Again the high priest asked Him ..., Art thou the Messiah, the Son of the Blessed? 62 And ישוע said, I am: and ye shall see the Son of man sitting on the right hand of power, and coming in the clouds of heaven. 63 Then the high priest rent his clothes, and saith, What need we any further witnesses?

APOSTLES

Acts 2:32 This ישוע hath God raised up, whereof we all are witnesses.

2 Cor. 13:1b (RSV) Any charge must be sustained by the evidence of two or three witnesses.

I Tim. 5:19 Against an elder receive not an accusation, but before two or three witnesses.

Heb. 10:28 He that despised Moses' Torah died without mercy under two or three witnesses:

Rev. 11:3 And I will give power unto my two witnesses, and they shall prophesy a thousand two hundred and threescore days, clothed in sackcloth.

123

87. MUST TESTIFY IF YOU ARE A WITNESS

Lev. 5:1, 5-6 And if a soul sin, and hear the voice of swearing, and is a witness, whether he hath seen or known of it; **if he do not utter it, then he shall bear his iniquity**. ... 5 And it shall be, when he shall be guilty in one of these things, that he shall confess that he hath sinned in that thing: 6 And he shall bring his [asham (shame, guilt)] offering unto יהוה for his sin which he hath sinned....

Lev. 5:1, 5-6 (same as above, but in TLV) If a soul sins—after hearing a charge of an oath, and he is a witness whether he has seen or otherwise known—**if he fails to report it, then he will bear his guilt.** ... 6 Then he is to bring his [asham (shame, guilt)] offering to Adonai for his sin that he committed: a female from the flock, a lamb or a goat, as a sin offering. ....

Lev. 19:17 (TLV) You are not to hate your brother in your heart. Instead, you are to firmly rebuke your neighbor, and **not bear sin because of him**. *(We are not to ignore sin!)* [also in Love neighbor, p. 94]

Deut. 13:6,8 If thy brother, ... or thy son, or thy daughter, or the wife of thy bosom, or thy friend, ... entice thee **secretly**, saying, Let us go and serve other gods ... 8 Thou shalt not consent unto him, nor hearken unto him; neither shall thine eye pity him, **neither shalt thou spare, neither shalt thou conceal him**.... [also in No other gods, p. 32]

Deut. 13:12-15 If thou shalt hear say in one of thy cities....13 Certain men ... are gone out from among you, and have withdrawn the inhabitants of their city, saying, Let us go and serve other gods.... 14 Then shalt thou inquire, and make search, and ask diligently; and, behold, if it be truth, and the thing certain, that such abomination is wrought among you; 15 Thou shalt surely smite the inhabitants of that city.... [also in No other gods, p. 32]

Deut. 17:2- If there be found among you, within any of thy gates ... man or woman, that hath ... 3 And hath gone and served other gods, ... 4 And it be told thee, and thou hast heard of it, and inquired diligently, and, behold, it be true.... 5 Then shalt thou bring forth that man or that woman.... [also in No other gods, p. 32]

AFTER TORAH

Isaiah 43:10-12 Ye are My witnesses, saith יהוה, and My servant whom I have chosen: that ye may know and believe Me, and understand that I am He: before Me there was no God formed, neither shall there be after Me. 11 I, even I, am יהוה; and beside Me there is no saviour. 12 I have declared, and have saved, and I have shewed, when there was no strange god among you: therefore ye are My witnesses, saith יהוה, that I am God.

YESHUA ישוע and APOSTLES

Acts 1:8 But ye shall receive power, after that the Holy Spirit is come upon you: and ye shall be witnesses unto Me both in Jerusalem, and in all Judaea, and in Samaria, and unto the uttermost part of the earth.

88. HONEST BUSINESS PRACTICES

Lev. 19:35 Ye shall do no unrighteousness in judgment, in meteyard, in weight, or in measure. 36 Just balances, just weights, a just ephah, and a just hin, shall ye have: I am יהוה your God, which brought you out of the land of Egypt.

Deut. 25:13-16 Thou shalt not have in thy bag divers weights, a great and a small. 14 Thou shalt not have in thine house divers measures, a great and a small. 15 But thou shalt have a perfect and just weight, a perfect and just measure shalt thou have: that thy days may be lengthened in the land which יהוה thy God giveth thee. 16 For all that do such things, and all that do unrighteously, are an abomination unto יהוה thy God.

YESHUA ישוע

Matt. 7:2 For with what judgment ye judge, ye shall be judged: and with what measure ye mete, it shall be measured to you again.

Mark 4:24 And he said unto them, Take heed what ye hear: with what measure ye mete, it shall be measured to you: and unto you that hear shall more be given.

Luke 6:38 Give, and it shall be given unto you; good measure, pressed down, and shaken together, and running over, shall men give into your bosom. For with the same measure that ye mete withal it shall be measured to you again.

89. LENDING MONEY

Ex. 22:25 If thou lend money to any of my people that is poor by thee, thou shalt not be to him as an usurer, neither shalt thou lay upon him usury.

Ex. 22:26-27 If thou at all take thy neighbour's raiment to pledge, thou shalt deliver it unto him by that the sun goeth down: 27 For that is his covering only, it is his raiment for his skin: wherein shall he sleep? and it shall come to pass, when he crieth unto me, that I will hear; for I am gracious.

Lev. 25:17 Ye shall not therefore oppress one another; but thou shalt fear thy God: for I am יהוה your God.

Lev. 25:35-38 And if thy brother be waxen poor, and fallen in decay with thee; then thou shalt relieve him: yea, though he be a stranger, or a sojourner; that he may live with thee. 36 Take thou no usury of him, or increase: but fear thy God; that thy brother may live with thee. 37 Thou shalt not give him thy money upon usury, nor lend him thy victuals for increase. 38 I am יהוה your God, which brought you forth out of the land of Egypt, to give you the land of Canaan, and to be your God. [also in Jubilee, p. 183, Poor, p. 99, and Stranger, p. 86]

Deut. 23:19-20 Thou shalt not lend upon usury to thy brother; usury of money, usury of victuals, usury of any thing that is lent upon usury: 20 Unto a stranger thou mayest lend upon usury; but unto thy brother thou shalt not lend upon usury: that יהוה thy God may bless thee in all that thou settest thine hand to in the land whither thou goest to possess it.

Deut. 24:6 No man shall take the nether or the upper millstone to pledge: for he taketh a man's life to pledge.

Deut. 24:10-11 When thou dost lend thy brother any thing, thou shalt not go into his house to fetch his pledge. 11 Thou shalt stand abroad, and the man to whom thou dost lend shall bring out the pledge abroad unto thee.

Deut. 24:12 And if the man be poor, thou shalt not sleep with his pledge:

Deut. 24:13 In any case thou shalt deliver him the pledge again when the sun goeth down, that he may sleep in his own raiment, and bless thee: and it shall be righteousness unto thee before יהוה thy God.

Deut. 24:17b nor of the fatherless; nor take a widow's raiment to pledge: [also in Widows p. 88]

Deut. 15:5-6 Only if thou carefully hearken unto the voice of יהוה thy God, to observe to do all these commandments which I command thee this day. 6 For יהוה thy God blesseth thee, as he promised thee: and thou shalt lend unto many nations, but thou shalt not borrow; and thou shalt reign over many nations, but they shall not reign over thee. [also in Keep All, p. 21]

YESHUA ישוע

Matt. 5:42 Give to him that asketh thee, and from him that would borrow of thee turn not thou away. [also in Borrowing, p. 84]

Luke 6:34-35 And if ye lend to them of whom ye hope to receive, what thank have ye? for sinners also lend to sinners, to receive as much again. 35 But love ye your enemies, and do good, and lend, hoping for nothing again; and your reward shall be great, and ye shall be the children of the Highest: for he is kind unto the unthankful and to the evil. [also in Enemy, p. 90]

[For borrowing, see page 84.]

Ex. 21:28 If an ox gore a man or a woman, that they die: then the ox shall be surely stoned, and his flesh shall not be eaten; [also in animals hurting people, p. 82]

Ex. 22:31 neither shall ye eat any flesh that is torn of beasts in the field; ye shall cast it to the dogs.

Lev. Chapter 11 *clean and unclean animals*

Lev. 19:5-7 And if ye offer a sacrifice of peace offerings unto יהוה, ... eaten the same day ... (or) the morrow: ... if it be eaten at all on the third day, it is abominable; it shall not be accepted....

Lev. 20:24-26 But I have said unto you, Ye shall inherit their land, and I will give it unto you to possess it, a land that floweth with milk and honey: I am יהוה your God, which have separated you from other people. 25 Ye shall therefore put difference between clean beasts and unclean, and between unclean fowls and clean: and ye shall not make your souls abominable by beast, or by fowl, or by any manner of living thing that creepeth on the ground, which I have separated from you as unclean. 26 And ye shall be holy unto me: for I יהוה am holy, and have severed you from other people, that ye should be mine.

Lev. 22:10, 13b-14 (NIV) " 'No one outside a priest's family may eat the sacred offering, nor may the guest of a priest or his hired worker eat it. ... No unauthorized person, however, may eat it. 14 " 'Anyone who eats a sacred offering by mistake must make restitution to the priest for the offering and add a fifth of the value to it. [also in Restitution, p. 93, and Priests, p. 220]

Lev. 22:29-30 And when ye will offer a sacrifice of thanksgiving unto יהוה, offer it at your own will. 30 On the same day it shall be eaten up; ye shall leave none of it until the morrow: I am יהוה. [also in Offerings, p. 142]

Deut. 12:15 Notwithstanding thou mayest kill and eat flesh in all thy gates, whatsoever thy soul lusteth after, according to the blessing of יהוה thy God which he hath given thee: the unclean and the clean may eat thereof, as of the roebuck, and as of the hart.

Deut. 12:17-18 Thou mayest not eat **within thy gates** the tithe of thy corn, or of thy wine, or of thy oil, or the firstlings of thy herds or of thy flock, nor any of thy vows which thou vowest, nor thy freewill offerings, or heave offering of thine hand: 18 But thou **must eat them before** יהוה thy God in the place which יהוה thy God shall choose,

Deut. 12:25 Thou shalt not eat it [blood]; that it may go well with thee, and with thy children after thee, when thou shalt do that which is right in the sight of יהוה.

Deut. 14:3, 7-8 Thou shalt not eat any abominable thing. ... 7 Nevertheless these ye shall not eat of them that chew the cud, or of them that divide the cloven hoof; as the camel, and the hare, and the coney: for they chew the cud, but divide not the hoof; therefore they are unclean unto you. 8 And the swine, because it divideth the hoof, yet cheweth not the cud, it is unclean unto you: ye shall not eat of their flesh, **nor touch their dead carcase**.

Deut. 14:9-21 *[Further explains which animals can and cannot be eaten.]*

Deut. 14:21a Ye shall not eat of any thing that dieth of itself: thou shalt give it unto the stranger that is in thy gates, that he may eat it; or thou mayest sell it unto an alien: for thou art an holy people unto יהוה thy God.

YESHUA ישוע

NOTICE THAT THE TOPIC HERE IS EATING WITHOUT WASHING HANDS, NOT ABOUT EATING UNCLEAN ANIMALS: Matt. 15:1-2, 10-11, 16-20 Then came to ישוע scribes and Pharisees, which were of Jerusalem, saying, 2 Why do thy disciples transgress the tradition of the elders? for they wash not their hands when they eat bread. ... 10 And he called the multitude, and said unto them, Hear, and understand: 11 Not that which goeth into the mouth defileth a man; but that which cometh out of the mouth, this defileth a man. ... 16 And ישוע said, Are ye also yet without understanding? 17 Do not ye yet understand, that whatsoever entereth in at the mouth goeth into the belly, and is cast out into the draught? 18 But those things which proceed out of the mouth come forth from the heart; and they defile the man. 19 For out of the heart proceed evil thoughts, murders, adulteries, fornications, thefts, false witness, blasphemies: 20 These are the things which defile a man: **but to eat with unwashen hands defileth not a man.**

Mark 7:14-16 And when he had called all the people unto him, he said unto them, Hearken unto me every one of you, and understand: 15 T**here is nothing from without a man, that entering into him can defile him: but the things which come out of him, those are they that defile the man.** 16 If any man have ears to hear, let him hear. [also in Wash, p. 208]

APOSTLES

Acts 10:11-17 And saw heaven opened, and a certain vessel descending unto him, as it had been a great sheet knit at the four corners, and let down to the earth: 12 Wherein were all manner of fourfooted beasts of the earth, and wild beasts, and creeping things, and fowls of the air. 13 And there came a voice to him, Rise, Peter; kill, and eat. 14 But Peter said, Not so, Lord; for I have never eaten any thing that is common or unclean. 15 And the voice spake unto him again the second time, What God hath cleansed, that call not thou common. 16 This was done thrice: and the vessel was received up again into heaven. 17 Now while Peter doubted in himself what this vision which he had seen should mean....

Acts 10:19 While Peter thought on the vision, the Spirit said unto him, Behold, three men seek thee. 20 Arise therefore, and get thee down, and go with them, doubting nothing: for I have sent them.

Acts 11:2,12 And when Peter was come up to Jerusalem, they that were of the circumcision contended with him, 3 Saying, Thou wentest in to men uncircumcised, and didst eat with them. {He tells them the whole vision} ... 12 And the Spirit bade me go with them, nothing doubting.

Acts 15:7-9 Peter rose up, and said unto them, Men and brethren, ye know how that a good while ago God made choice among us, that the Gentiles by my mouth should hear the word of the Gospel, and believe. 8 And God, which knoweth the hearts, bare them witness, giving them the Holy Spirit, even as he did unto us; 9 And put no difference between us and them, purifying their hearts by faith.

Gal. 2:11-16 But when Peter was come to Antioch, I withstood him to the face, because he was to be blamed. 12 For before that certain came from James, he did eat with the Gentiles: but when they were come, he withdrew and separated himself, fearing them which were of the circumcision. 13 And the other Jews dissembled likewise with him; insomuch that Barnabas also was carried away with their dissimulation. 14 But when I saw that they walked not uprightly according to the truth of the Gospel, I said unto Peter before them all, If thou, being a Jew, livest after the manner of Gentiles, and not as do the Jews, why compellest thou the Gentiles to live as do the Jews? 15 We who are Jews by nature, and not sinners of the Gentiles, 16 Knowing that a man is not justified by the works of the law, but by the faith of יׁשוע Messiah, even we have believed in יׁשוע Messiah, that we might be justified by the faith of Messiah, and not by the works of the law: for by the works of the law shall no flesh be justified.

Rom. 14:2-4 For one believeth that he may eat all things: another, who is weak, eateth herbs. 3 Let not him that eateth despise him that eateth not; and let not him which eateth not judge him that eateth: for God hath received him. 4 Who art thou that judgest another man's servant? to his own master he standeth or falleth. Yea, he shall be holden up: for God is able to make him stand.

Rom 14:14-15, 20 I know, and am persuaded by the Lord יׁשוע, that there is nothing unclean of itself: but to him that esteemeth any thing to be unclean, to him it is unclean. 15 But if thy brother be grieved with thy meat, now walkest thou not charitably. Destroy not him with thy meat, for whom Messiah died. ... 20 For meat destroy not the work of God.

Rom. 14:17 For the kingdom of God is not meat and drink; but righteousness, and peace, and joy in the Holy Spirit.

Rom. 14:21-23 It is good neither to eat flesh, nor to drink wine, nor any thing whereby thy brother stumbleth, or is offended, or is made weak. 22 Hast thou faith? have it to thyself before God. Happy is he that condemneth not himself in that thing which he alloweth. 23 And he that doubteth is damned if he eat, because he eateth not of faith: for whatsoever is not of faith is sin.

I Tim. 4:3-5 Forbidding to marry, and commanding to abstain from meats, which God hath created to be received with thanksgiving of them which believe and know the truth. 4 For every creature of God is good, and nothing to be refused, if it be received with thanksgiving: 5 For it is sanctified by the word of God and prayer.

91. CAN'T EAT KID IN MOTHER'S MILK

Ex. 23:19b Thou shalt not seethe a kid in his mother's milk.

Ex. 34:26b Thou shalt not seethe a kid in his mother's milk.

Deut. 14:21b for thou art an holy people unto יהוה thy God. Thou shalt not seethe a kid in his mother's milk.

Lev. 22:28 And whether it be cow or ewe, ye shall not kill it and her young both in one day.

92. DON'T EAT FAT OR BLOOD

Gen. 9:4 But flesh with the life thereof, which is the blood thereof, shall ye not eat.

Lev. 3:17 It shall be a **perpetual statute** for your generations **throughout all your dwellings**, that ye eat **neither fat nor blood**.

Lev. 7:23-25 Speak unto the children of Israel, saying, Ye shall eat **no manner of fat, of ox, or of sheep, or of goat.** 24 And the fat of the beast that dieth of itself, and the fat of that which is torn with beasts, may be used in any other use: but ye shall in no wise eat of it. 25 For whosoever eateth the fat of the beast, of which men offer an offering made by fire unto יהוה, even the soul that eateth it shall be cut off from his people.

Lev. 7:26 Moreover ye shall eat **no manner of blood, whether it be of fowl or of beast,** in any of your dwellings.

Lev. 17:10-14 And whatsoever man there be of the house of Israel, or of the strangers that sojourn among you, that eateth any manner of blood; I will even set my face against that soul that eateth blood, and will cut him off from among his people. 11 **For the life of the flesh is in the blood:** and I have given it to you upon the altar to make an atonement for your souls: for it is the blood that maketh an atonement for the soul. 12 Therefore I said unto the children of Israel, No soul of you shall eat blood, neither shall any stranger that sojourneth among you eat blood. 13 And whatsoever man there be of the children of Israel, or of the strangers that sojourn among you, which hunteth and catcheth any beast or fowl that may be eaten; he shall even pour out the blood thereof, and cover it with dust. 14 **For it is the life of all flesh; the blood of it is for the life thereof:** therefore I said unto the children of Israel, Ye shall eat the blood of no manner of flesh: for the life of all flesh is the blood thereof: whosoever eateth it shall be cut off.

Lev. 19:26 Ye shall not eat any thing with the blood:

Deut. 12:16 Only ye shall not eat the blood; ye shall pour it upon the earth as water.

Deut. 12:23-25 Only be sure that thou eat not the blood: **for the blood is the life;** and thou mayest not eat the life with the flesh. 24 Thou shalt not eat it; thou shalt pour it upon the earth as water. 25 Thou shalt not eat it; that it may go well with thee, and with thy children after thee, when thou shalt do that which is right in the sight of יהוה. [also in That it may go well, p. 257]

Deut. 15:23 Only thou shalt not eat the blood thereof; thou shalt pour it upon the ground as water.

PROPHETS

Ezek. 33:25 (CJB) ... You eat [flesh] with the blood, you raise your eyes to your idols, and you shed blood — and you still expect to possess the land? *[Read on to see these are some of the reasons they were exiled.]*

YESHUA ישוע

John 6:53 Then ישוע said unto them, Verily, verily, I say unto you, Except ye eat the flesh of the Son of Man, and drink His Blood, ye have no life in you.

APOSTLES

Acts 15:19-21, 28-29 Wherefore my sentence is, that we trouble not them, which from among the Gentiles are turned to God: 20 But that we write unto them, that they abstain from pollutions of idols, and from fornication, and **from things strangled, and from blood.** 21 For Moses of old time hath in every city them that preach him, being read in the synagogues every Sabbath day. ... 28 For it seemed good to the Holy Spirit, and to us, to lay upon you no greater burden than these necessary things; 29 That ye abstain from **meats offered to idols, and from blood, and from things strangled,** and from fornication: from which if ye keep yourselves, ye shall do well. Fare ye well.

Food sacrificed to idols would've also been strangled or improperly slaughtered:

I Cor. 8:1, 8-13 Now as touching things offered unto idols.... But meat commendeth us not to God: for neither, if we eat, are we the better; neither, if we eat not, are we the worse. 9 But take heed lest by any means this liberty of yours become a stumblingblock to them that are weak. 10 For if any man see thee which hast knowledge sit at meat in the idol's temple, shall not the conscience of him which is weak be emboldened to eat those things which are offered to idols; 11 And through thy knowledge shall the weak brother perish, for whom Messiah died? 12 But when ye sin so against the brethren, and wound their weak conscience, ye sin against Messiah. 13 Wherefore, if meat make my brother to offend, I will eat no flesh while the world standeth, lest I make my brother to offend.

I Cor. 10:20-33 But I say, that the things which the Gentiles sacrifice, they sacrifice to devils, and not to God: and I would not that ye should have fellowship with devils. 21 Ye cannot drink

FOOD

the cup of the Lord, and the cup of devils: ye cannot be partakers of the Lord's table, and of the table of devils. 22 Do we provoke the Lord to jealousy? are we stronger than he? 23 All things are lawful for me, but all things are not expedient: all things are lawful for me, but all things edify not. 24 Let no man seek his own, but every man another's wealth. 25 Whatsoever is sold in the shambles, that eat, asking no question for conscience sake: 26 For the earth is the Lord's, and the fulness thereof. 27 If any of them that believe not bid you to a feast, and ye be disposed to go; whatsoever is set before you, eat, asking no question for conscience sake. 28 But if any man say unto you, This is offered in sacrifice unto idols, eat not for his sake that shewed it, and for conscience sake: for the earth is the Lord's, and the fulness thereof: 29 Conscience, I say, not thine own, but of the other: for why is my liberty judged of another man's conscience? 30 For if I by grace be a partaker, why am I evil spoken of for that for which I give thanks? 31 Whether therefore ye eat, or drink, or whatsoever ye do, do all to the glory of God. 32 Give none offence, neither to the Jews, nor to the Gentiles, nor to the church of God: 33 Even as I please all men in all things, not seeking mine own profit, but the profit of many, that they may be saved.

Rev. 2:20 Notwithstanding I have a few things against thee, because thou sufferest that woman Jezebel, which calleth herself a prophetess, to teach and to seduce my servants to commit fornication, and to eat things sacrificed unto idols.

93. FRUIT TREES, TREES

Lev. 19:23-25 And when ye shall come into the land, and shall have planted all manner of trees for food, then ye shall count the fruit thereof as uncircumcised: three years shall it be as uncircumcised unto you: it shall not be eaten of. 24 But in the fourth year all the fruit thereof shall be holy to praise יהוה withal. 25 And in the fifth year shall ye eat of the fruit thereof, that it may yield unto you the increase thereof: I am יהוה your God.

Deut. 16:21 Thou shalt not plant thee a grove of any trees near unto the altar of יהוה thy God, which thou shalt make thee. [also in No idols, p. 36]

Deut. 20:19-20 When thou shalt besiege a city a long time, in making war against it to take it, thou shalt not destroy the trees thereof by forcing an axe against them: for thou mayest eat of them, and thou shalt not cut them down (for the tree of the field is man's life) to employ them in the siege: 20 Only the trees which thou knowest that they be not trees for meat, thou shalt destroy and cut them down; and thou shalt build bulwarks against the city that maketh war with thee, until it be subdued.

Deut. 21:22-23 And if a man have committed a sin worthy of death, and he be to be put to death, and thou hang him on a tree: 23 His body shall not remain all night upon the tree, but thou shalt in any wise bury him that day; (for he that is hanged is accursed of God;) that thy land be not defiled, which יהוה thy God giveth thee for an inheritance. [also in No killing, p. 48, and Defile Not Land, p. 68]

YESHUA ישוע AND APOSTLES

Luke 13:6-9 A certain man had a fig tree planted in his vineyard; ... Behold, these three years I come seeking fruit on this fig tree, and find none: cut it down; why cumbereth it the ground? 8 And he answering said unto him, Lord, let it alone this year also, till I shall dig about it, and dung it: 9 And if it bear fruit, well: and if not, then after that thou shalt cut it down.

Gal. 3:13 Messiah hath redeemed us from the curse of the Torah, being made a curse for us: for it is written, Cursed is every one that hangeth on a tree: [also in Defile not the land, p. 68 and in Punishment, p. 234]

94. NO MIXING KINDS

Lev. 19:19 Thou shalt not let thy cattle gender with a diverse kind: thou shalt not sow thy field with mingled seed: neither shall a garment mingled of linen and woollen come upon thee.

Deut. 22:9 Thou shalt not sow thy vineyard with divers seeds: lest the fruit of thy seed which thou hast sown, and the fruit of thy vineyard, be defiled.

Deut. 22:10 Thou shalt not plow with an ox and an ass together.

Deut. 22:11 Thou shalt not wear a garment of divers sorts, as of woollen and linen together.

95. FIRSTBORN SONS/CHILDREN

Ex. 13:1-2,11-15 And יהוה spake unto Moses, saying, 2 Sanctify unto me all the firstborn, whatsoever openeth the womb among the children of Israel, both of man and of beast: it is mine. ... 11 And it shall be when יהוה shall bring thee into the land of the Canaanites, as he sware unto thee and to thy fathers, and shall give it thee, 12 That thou shalt set apart unto יהוה all that openeth the matrix, ... all the firstborn of man among thy children shalt thou redeem. 14 And it shall be when thy son asketh thee in time to come, saying, What is this? that thou shalt say unto him, By strength of hand יהוה brought us out from Egypt, from the house of bondage: 15 And it came to pass, when Pharaoh would hardly let us go, that יהוה slew all the firstborn in the land of Egypt, both the firstborn of man, and the firstborn of beast: therefore I sacrifice to יהוה all that openeth the matrix, being males; but all the firstborn of My children I redeem.

Ex. 22:29b the firstborn of thy sons shalt thou give unto Me.

Num. 3:12-13 And I, behold, I have taken the Levites from among the children of Israel instead of all the firstborn that openeth the matrix among the children of Israel: therefore the Levites shall be Mine; 13 Because all the firstborn are Mine; for on the day that I smote all the firstborn in the land of Egypt I hallowed unto Me all the firstborn in Israel, both man and beast: Mine shall they be: I am יהוה.

Num. 3:15,39 Number the children of Levi after the house of their fathers, by their families: every male from a month old and upward shalt thou number them. ... 39 All that were numbered of the Levites, which Moses and Aaron numbered at the commandment of יהוה, throughout their families, all the males from a month old and upward, were twenty and two thousand.

Num. 3:40-50 And יהוה said unto Moses, Number all the firstborn of the males of the children of Israel from a month old and upward, and take the number of their names. 41 And thou shalt take the Levites for Me (I am יהוה) instead of all the firstborn among the children of Israel; and the cattle of the Levites instead of all the firstlings among the cattle of the children of Israel. ... 45 Take the Levites instead of all the firstborn among the children of Israel, and the cattle of the Levites instead of their cattle; and the Levites shall be Mine: I am יהוה. 46 And for those that are to be redeemed of the two hundred and threescore and thirteen of the firstborn of the children of Israel, which are more than the Levites; 47 Thou shalt even take five shekels apiece by the poll, after the shekel of the sanctuary shalt thou take them: (the shekel is twenty gerahs:) 48 And thou shalt give the money, wherewith the odd number of them is to be redeemed, unto Aaron and to his sons. 49 And Moses took the redemption money of them that were over and above them that were redeemed by the Levites: 50 Of the firstborn of the children of Israel took he the money; a thousand three hundred and threescore and five shekels, after the shekel of the sanctuary....

Num. 8:16-18 For they are wholly given unto Me from among the children of Israel; instead of such as open every womb, even instead of the firstborn of all the children of Israel, have I taken them unto Me. 17 For all the firstborn of the children of Israel are Mine, both man and beast: on the day that I smote every firstborn in the land of Egypt I sanctified them for Myself. 18 And I have taken the Levites for all the firstborn of the children of Israel. 19 And I have given the Levites as a gift to Aaron and to his sons from among the children of Israel, to do the service of the children of Israel in the Tabernacle of the congregation, and to make an atonement for the children of Israel: that there be no plague among the children of Israel, when the children of Israel come nigh unto the Sanctuary.

Num. 18:1,14-18 And יהוה said unto Aaron... Every thing devoted in Israel shall be thine. 15 Every thing that openeth the matrix in all flesh, which they bring unto יהוה, whether it be of men or beasts, shall be thine: nevertheless the firstborn of man shalt thou surely redeem, and the firstling of unclean beasts shalt thou redeem. 16 ... 17 But the firstling of a cow, or the firstling of a sheep, or the firstling of a goat, thou shalt not redeem; they are holy: thou shalt sprinkle their blood upon the altar, and shalt burn their fat for an offering made by fire, for a sweet savour unto the יהוה. 18 And the flesh of them shall be thine, as the wave breast and as the right shoulder are thine.

Deut. 21:15-17 If a man have two wives, one beloved, and another hated, and they have born him children, both the beloved and the hated; and if the firstborn son be hers that was hated: 16 Then it shall be, when he maketh his sons to inherit that which he hath, that he may not make the son of the beloved firstborn before the son of the hated, which is indeed the firstborn: 17 But he shall acknowledge the son of the hated for the firstborn, by giving him a double portion of all that he hath: for he is the beginning of his strength; the right of the firstborn is his.   [also in Second wife, p. 77]

APOSTLES

Rom. 8:29 For whom He did foreknow, He also did predestinate to be conformed to the image of His Son, that He might be the **firstborn** among many brethren.

Col. 1:13-16a Who hath delivered us from the power of darkness, and hath translated us into the Kingdom of His dear Son: 14 In whom we have redemption through His Blood, even the forgiveness of sins: 15 Who is the image of the invisible God, the **firstborn** of every creature: For by Him were all things created....

96. REDEEMING FIRSTBORN

Ex. 34:20 But the firstling of an ass thou shalt redeem with a lamb: and if thou redeem him not, then shalt thou break his neck. All the firstborn of thy sons thou shalt redeem. And none shall appear before Me empty.

Num. 18:15-16 Every thing that openeth the matrix in all flesh, which they bring unto יהוה, whether it be of men or beasts, shall be thine: nevertheless the firstborn of man shalt thou surely redeem, and the firstling of unclean beasts shalt thou redeem. 16 And those that are to be redeemed from a month old shalt thou redeem, according to thine estimation, for the money of five shekels, after the shekel of the sanctuary, which is twenty gerahs.

97. FIRSTBORN ANIMALS

Ex. 22:30 Likewise shalt thou do with [the firstborn of] thine oxen, and with thy sheep: seven days it shall be with his dam; on the eighth day thou shalt give it me.

Ex. 34:19 All that openeth the matrix is Mine; and every firstling among thy cattle, whether ox or sheep, that is male.

Num. 3:12b ... I hallowed unto Me all the firstborn in Israel, both man and beast: Mine shall they be: I am יהוה.

Deut. 15:19-23 All the firstling males that come of thy herd and of thy flock thou shalt sanctify unto יהוה thy God: thou shalt do no work with the firstling of thy bullock, nor shear the firstling of thy sheep. Thou shalt eat it before יהוה thy God year by year in the place which יהוה shall choose, thou and thy household. And if there be any blemish therein, as if it be lame, or blind, or have any ill blemish, thou shalt not sacrifice it unto יהוה thy God. Thou shalt eat it within thy gates: the unclean and the clean person shall eat it alike, as the roebuck, and as the hart. Only thou shalt not eat the blood thereof; thou shalt pour it upon the ground as water. [also in Eat, p. 188, and verse 23 also in Don't Eat Fat or Blood, p. 130]

Lev. 27:26-27 Only the firstling of the beasts, which should be יהוה's firstling, no man shall sanctify it; whether it be ox, or sheep: it is יהוה's. 27 And if it be of an unclean beast, then he shall redeem it according to thine estimation, and shall add a fifth part of it thereto: or if it be not redeemed, then it shall be sold according to thy estimation.

98. FIRSTFRUIT OFFERING

See also FirstFruit/Resurrection, p. 168 and Shavuot, p. 175

Ex. 22:29a Thou shalt not delay to offer the first of thy ripe fruits....

Ex. 23:19 The first of the firstfruits of thy land thou shalt bring into the house of יהוה thy God.

Ex. 34:26 The first of the firstfruits of thy land thou shalt bring unto the house of יהוה thy God.

Lev. 2:12-16 As for the **oblation** of the firstfruits, ye shall offer them unto יהוה: but they shall not be burnt on the altar for a sweet savour. ... 14 And if thou offer a meat [grain] offering of thy firstfruits unto יהוה, thou shalt offer for the meat offering of thy firstfruits green ears of corn [grain: wheat or barley] dried by the fire, even corn beaten out of full ears. 15 And thou shalt **put oil upon it, and lay frankincense** thereon: it is a meat offering. 16 And the priest shall burn the memorial of it, part of the beaten corn thereof, and part of the oil thereof, with all the frankincense thereof: it is an offering made by fire unto יהוה.

Num. 15:18-20 Speak unto the children of Israel, and say unto them, When ye come into the land whither I bring you, 19 Then it shall be, that, when ye eat of the bread of the land, ye shall offer up an heave offering unto יהוה. 20 Ye shall offer up a cake of the first of your dough for an heave offering: as ye do the heave offering of the threshingfloor, so shall ye heave it. 21 Of the first of your dough ye shall give unto יהוה an heave offering in your generations.

Deut. 26:1-10 And it shall be, when thou art come in unto the land which יהוה thy God giveth thee for an inheritance, and possessest it, and dwellest therein; 2 That thou shalt take of the first of all the fruit of the earth, which thou shalt bring of thy land that יהוה thy God giveth thee, and shalt put it in a basket, and shalt go unto the place which יהוה thy God shall choose to place His Name there. 3 And thou shalt go unto the priest that shall be in those days, and say unto him, I profess this day unto יהוה thy God, that I am come unto the country which יהוה sware unto our fathers for to give us. 4 And the priest shall take the basket out of thine hand, and set it down before the altar of יהוה thy God. 5 And thou shalt speak and say before יהוה thy God, A Syrian ready to perish was my father, and he went down into Egypt, and sojourned there with a few, and became there a nation, great, mighty, and populous: ... 8 And יהוה brought us forth out of Egypt with a mighty hand, and with an outstretched arm, and with great terribleness, and with signs, and with wonders: 9 And He hath brought us into this place, and hath given us this land, even a land that floweth with milk and honey. 10 And now, behold, I have brought the firstfruits of the land, which Thou, O יהוה, hast given me. And thou shalt set it before יהוה thy God, and worship before יהוה thy God: [Parts also in Worship in the Place He chooses, p. 154, Firstfruit/Resurrection, p. 168, Shavuot, p. 175, and Rejoice, p. 187]

99. DEDICATING THINGS TO יהוה

Lev. 27:14-15 And when a man shall sanctify his house to be holy unto יהוה, then the priest shall estimate it, whether it be good or bad: as the priest shall estimate it, so shall it stand. 15 And if he that sanctified it will redeem his house, then he shall add the fifth part of the money of thy estimation unto it, and it shall be his.

Lev. 27:16-21,25 And if a man shall sanctify unto יהוה some part of a field of his possession, then thy estimation shall be according to the seed thereof: an homer of barley seed shall be valued at fifty shekels of silver. 17 If he sanctify his field from the year of Jubile, according to thy estimation it shall stand. 18 But if he sanctify his field after the Jubile, then the priest shall reckon unto him the money according to the years that remain, even unto the year of the Jubile, and it shall be abated from thy estimation. 19 And if he that sanctified the field will in any wise redeem it, then he shall add the fifth part of the money of thy estimation unto it, and it shall be assured to him. 20 And if he will not redeem the field, or if he have sold the field to another man, it shall not be redeemed any more. 21 But the field, when it goeth out in the Jubile, shall be holy unto יהוה, as a field devoted; the possession thereof shall be the priest's. ... 25 And all thy estimations shall be according to the shekel of the sanctuary: twenty gerahs shall be the shekel. [also in Jubilee, p. 183]

Lev. 27:28-29 Notwithstanding no devoted thing, that a man shall devote [or vow] unto יהוה of all that he hath, both of man and beast, and of the field of his possession, shall be sold or redeemed: every devoted thing is most holy unto יהוה. 29 None devoted, which shall be devoted of men, shall be redeemed; but shall surely be put to death. (*What????!! Perhaps the following two translations will clarify. For no one sentenced to death can freedom be bought.*)

CJB: 28-29 However, nothing consecrated unconditionally which a person may consecrate to ADONAI out of all he owns—person, animal or field he possesses—is to be sold or redeemed; because everything consecrated unconditionally is especially holy to ADONAI. 29 No person who has been sentenced to die, and thus unconditionally consecrated, can be redeemed; he must be put to death.

TLV: 28-29 "Nevertheless, no devoted thing which a man sets apart from all that he has for ADONAI, whether man or animal, or from the field of his possession, may be sold or redeemed. Every devoted thing is most holy to Adonai. 29 "No one who may be set apart from men for destruction is to be ransomed. He is surely to be put to death.

100. ALTAR OFFERINGS AND SACRIFICES

NO LEAVEN: Ex. 23:18 Thou shalt not offer the blood of my sacrifice with leavened bread; neither shall the fat of my sacrifice remain until the morning. *[Except the Shavuot <u>wave</u> offering includes two <u>leavened</u> loaves. See page 170]*

Ex. 34:25a Thou shalt not offer the blood of my sacrifice with leaven....

BURNT OFFERING: Lev. 1:3-17 If his offering be a burnt sacrifice of the **herd,** let him offer a **male without blemish**: he shall offer it of his own voluntary will at the door of the Tabernacle of the congregation before יהוה. 4 And **he shall put his hand upon the head of the burnt offering**; and it shall be accepted for him to make atonement for him. 5 And **he shall kill the bullock** before יהוה: and the priests, Aaron's sons, shall bring the blood, and sprinkle the blood round about upon the altar that is by the door of the Tabernacle of the congregation. 6 And he shall flay the burnt offering, and cut it into his pieces. 7 And the sons of Aaron the priest shall put fire upon the altar, and lay the wood in order upon the fire: 8 And the priests, Aaron's sons, shall lay the parts, the head, and the fat, in order upon the wood that is on the fire which is upon the altar: 9 But <u>his inwards and his legs shall he wash in water</u>: and **the priest shall burn all on the altar,** to be a burnt sacrifice, an offering made by fire, of a sweet savour unto יהוה. 10 And if his offering be of the **flocks**, namely, of the **sheep, or of the goats,** for a burnt sacrifice; he shall bring it a **male without blemish**. 11 And he shall kill it on the side of the altar northward before יהוה: and the priests, Aaron's sons, shall sprinkle his blood round about upon the altar. ... 14 And if the burnt sacrifice for his offering to יהוה be of **fowls**, then he shall bring his offering of **turtledoves, or of young pigeons**. 15 And the priest shall bring it unto the altar, and wring off his head, and burn it on the altar; and the blood thereof shall be wrung out at the side of the altar: 16 And he shall pluck away his crop with his feathers, and cast it beside the altar on the east part, by the place of the ashes: 17 And he shall cleave it with the wings thereof, but shall not divide it asunder: and the priest shall burn it upon the altar, upon the wood that is upon the fire: it is a burnt sacrifice, an offering made by fire, of a sweet savour unto יהוה.

Lev. 7:8 And the priest that offereth any man's burnt offering, even the priest shall have to himself the skin of the burnt offering which he hath offered.

Lev. 9:23-24 And Moses and Aaron went into the Tabernacle of the congregation, and came out, and blessed the people: and the glory of יהוה appeared unto all the people. 24 And there came a fire out from before יהוה, and consumed upon the altar the **burnt offering** and the fat: which when all the people saw, they shouted, and fell on their faces.

APOSTLES

Rom. 12:1 I beseech you therefore, brethren, by the mercies of God, that ye **present your bodies a living sacrifice**, **holy, acceptable unto God**, which is your reasonable service [worship].

GRAIN OFFERING, NO LEAVEN: Lev. 2:1-11 And when any will offer a **meat [grain] offering** unto יהוה, his offering shall be of fine flour; and he shall **pour oil upon it,** and put **frankincense** thereon: 2 And he shall bring it to Aaron's sons the priests: and he shall take thereout his handful of the flour thereof, and of the oil thereof, with all the frankincense thereof; and the priest shall burn the memorial of it upon the altar, to be an offering made by fire, of a sweet savour unto יהוה: 3 And the remnant of the meat [grain] offering shall be Aaron's and his sons': it is a thing most holy of the offerings of יהוה made by fire. 4 And if thou bring an oblation of a meat [grain] offering **baken in the oven,** it shall be **unleavened cakes of fine flour mingled with oil, or unleavened wafers anointed with oil.** 5 And if thy oblation be a meat offering **baken in a pan,** it shall be of fine flour unleavened, mingled with oil. ... 11 No meat offering, which ye shall bring unto יהוה, shall be made with leaven: for ye shall burn **no leaven, nor any honey, in any offering** of יהוה made by fire.

Lev. 6:14-17, 22-23 And this is the law of the **meat [grain] offering:** the sons of Aaron shall offer it before יהוה, before the altar. 15 And he shall take of it his handful, of the flour of the meat offering, and of the oil thereof, and all the frankincense which is upon the meat offering, and shall burn it upon the altar for a sweet savour, even the memorial of it, unto יהוה. 16 And the remainder thereof shall Aaron and his sons eat: with unleavened bread shall it be eaten in the holy place; in the court of the Tabernacle of the congregation they shall eat it. 17 It shall not be baken with leaven. ... 22 And the priest of his sons that is anointed in his stead shall offer it: it is a **statute forever** unto יהוה, it shall be wholly burnt. 23 For every meat offering **for the priest** shall be wholly burnt: it shall not be eaten.

Lev. 7:9-10 And all the meat offering that is baken in the oven, and all that is dressed in the fryingpan, and in the pan, shall be the priest's that offereth it. 10 And every meat offering, mingled with oil, and dry, shall all the sons of Aaron have, one as much as another.

OFFERINGS MUST BE ACCOMPANIED WITH GRAIN AND DRINK/WINE OFFERINGS: Num. 15:2-9 Speak unto the children of Israel, and say unto them, When ye be come into the land of your habitations, which I give unto you, 3 And will make an offering by fire unto יהוה, a burnt offering, or a sacrifice in performing a vow, or in a freewill offering, or in your solemn feasts, to make a sweet savour unto יהוה, of the **herd, or** of the **flock:** 4 Then shall he that offereth his offering unto יהוה bring a **meat [grain] offering** of a **tenth deal of flour** mingled with the fourth part of an hin of **oil.** 5 And the fourth part of an **hin of wine** for a drink offering shalt thou prepare with the burnt offering or sacrifice, for one lamb. 6 Or **for a ram,** thou shalt prepare for a **meat [grain] offering two tenth** deals **of flour** mingled with the third part of an hin of oil. ... 8 And when thou preparest a **bullock** for a burnt offering, or for a sacrifice in performing a vow, or peace offerings unto יהוה: 9 Then shall he bring with a bullock a **meat [grain] offering of three tenth** deals of **flour** mingled with half an hin of oil.

DRINK/WINE OFFERING: Num. 15:7-14 And for a drink offering thou shalt offer the **third part of an hin of wine,** for a sweet savour unto יהוה. ... 10 And thou shalt bring for a drink offering **half an hin of wine,** for an offering made by fire, of a sweet savour unto יהוה. 11 Thus shall it be done for one bullock, or for one ram, or for a lamb, or a kid. 12 According to the number that ye shall prepare....14 And if a stranger sojourn with you ... will offer an offering made by fire, of a sweet savour unto יהוה; as ye do, so he shall do.

MUST OFFER SALT: Lev. 2:13 And every oblation of thy meat offering shalt thou season with salt; neither shalt thou suffer the salt of the covenant of thy God to be lacking from thy meat offering: with all thine offerings thou shalt offer salt.

YESHUA: Matt. 5:12-13 Rejoice, and be exceeding glad: for great is your reward in heaven: for so persecuted they the prophets which were before you. 13 **Ye are the salt of the earth:** but if the salt have lost his savour, wherewith shall it be salted? it is thenceforth good for nothing, but to be cast out, and to be trodden under foot of men.

PEACE/WELLBEING/SHELEM (root word of SHALOM) OFFERING: Lev. 3:1-6 And if his oblation be a sacrifice of peace offering, if he offer it of the **herd;** whether it be a **male or female,** he shall offer it **without blemish** before יהוה. 2 And **he shall lay his hand upon the head of his offering, and kill it** at the door of the Tabernacle of the congregation: and Aaron's sons the priests shall sprinkle the blood upon the altar round about. 3 And he shall offer of the sacrifice of the peace offering an offering made by fire unto יהוה; the fat that covereth the inwards, and all the fat that is upon the inwards, 4 And the two kidneys, and the fat that is on them, which is by the flanks, and the caul above the liver, with the kidneys, it shall he take away. 5 And Aaron's sons shall burn it on the altar ... it is ... a sweet savour unto יהוה. 6 And if his offering for a sacrifice of peace offering unto יהוה be of the **flock; male or female,** he shall offer it **without blemish.** [also in Peace Offering, p. 70]

Lev. 7:28-34 And יהוה spake unto Moses, saying, 29 Speak unto the children of Israel, saying, He that offereth the sacrifice of his **peace offerings** unto יהוה shall bring his oblation unto יהוה of the sacrifice of his peace offerings. 30 **His own hands shall bring the offerings** of יהוה made by fire, the fat with the breast, it shall he bring, that the breast may be waved for a wave offering before יהוה. 31 And the priest shall burn the fat upon the altar: but the breast shall be Aaron's and his sons'. 32 And the right shoulder shall ye give unto the priest for an heave offering of the sacrifices of your peace offerings. 33 He among the sons of Aaron, that offereth the blood of the **peace offerings**, and the fat, shall have the right shoulder for his part. 34 For the wave breast and the heave shoulder have I ... given them unto Aaron the priest and unto his sons by a **statute forever** from among the children of Israel.

Lev. 22:21 And whosoever offereth a sacrifice of peace offerings unto יהוה to accomplish his vow, or a freewill offering in beeves or sheep, it shall be perfect to be accepted; there shall be no blemish therein.

PEACE/SHALOM OFFERING FOR THANKSGIVING: Lev. 7:11-21 And this is the law of the sacrifice of peace offerings.... If he offer it for a **thanksgiving,** then he shall offer with the **sacrifice of thanksgiving** unleavened cakes mingled with oil, and unleavened wafers anointed with oil, and cakes mingled with oil, of fine flour, fried. 13 Besides the cakes, he shall offer for his offering leavened bread with the **sacrifice of thanksgiving of his peace offerings.** 14 And of it he shall offer **one out of the whole** oblation for an heave offering unto יהוה, and it **shall be the priest's** that sprinkleth the blood of the peace offerings. 15 And the flesh of the sacrifice of his **peace offerings for thanksgiving shall be eaten the same day** that it is offered; he shall not leave any of it until the morning. 16 But if the sacrifice of his offering be a vow, or a **voluntary offering,** it shall be eaten the same day that he offereth his sacrifice: and on the morrow also the remainder of it shall be eaten: 17 But the remainder of the flesh of the sacrifice on the third day shall be burnt with fire. 18 And if any of the flesh of the sacrifice of his **peace offerings** be eaten at all on the third day, it shall not be accepted, neither shall it be imputed unto him that offereth it: it shall be an abomination, and the soul that eateth of it shall bear his iniquity. 19 **And the flesh that toucheth any unclean thing shall not be eaten; it shall be burnt with fire**: and as for the flesh, all that be clean shall eat thereof. 20 But the soul that eateth of the flesh of the sacrifice of **peace offerings,** that pertain unto יהוה, having his uncleanness upon him, even that soul shall be cut off from his people. 21 Moreover the soul that shall touch any unclean thing, as the uncleanness of man, or any unclean beast, or any abominable unclean thing, and eat of the flesh of the sacrifice of **peace offerings,** which pertain unto יהוה, even that soul shall be cut off from his people.

Lev. 22:29-30 And when ye will offer a **sacrifice of thanksgiving** unto יהוה, offer it at your own will. 30 On the same day it shall be eaten up; ye shall leave none of it until the morrow: I am יהוה. [also in What can't eat, p. 127]

SIN OFFERING: Lev. 6:25-29 ... This is the law of the sin offering: In the place where the burnt offering is killed shall the sin offering be killed before יהוה: it is most holy. 26 **The priest that offereth it for sin shall eat it:** in the holy place shall it be eaten, in the court of the Tabernacle of the congregation. 27 **Whatsoever shall touch the flesh thereof shall be holy:** and when there is sprinkled of the blood thereof upon any garment, thou shalt wash that whereon it was sprinkled in the holy place. 28 But the earthen vessel wherein it is sodden shall be broken: and if it be sodden in a brasen pot, it shall be both scoured, and rinsed in water. 29 **All the males among the priests shall eat thereof:** it is most holy.

SIN OFFERING FOR A PRIEST: Lev. 4:1-12 And יהוה spake unto Moses, saying, 2 Speak unto the children of Israel, saying, If a soul shall sin **through ignorance** against any of the commandments of יהוה concerning things which ought not to be done, and shall do against any of them: 3 **If the priest that is anointed do sin** according to the sin of the people; then let him bring for his sin, which he hath sinned, **a young bullock without blemish** unto יהוה for a sin offering. 4 And he shall bring the bullock unto the door of the **Tabernacle** of the congregation before יהוה; and **shall lay his hand upon the bullock's head, and**

kill the bullock before יהוה. 5 ... 6 And the priest shall dip his finger in the blood, and sprinkle of the blood **seven times before יהוה, before the veil of the sanctuary.** 7 And the priest shall put **some of the blood upon the horns of the altar of sweet incense** before יהוה, which is in the Tabernacle...; and shall pour all the blood of the bullock at the bottom of the altar of the burnt offering.... 8 And he shall take off from it all the fat of the bullock for the sin offering; the fat that covereth the inwards, and all the fat that is upon the inwards, 9 And the two kidneys, and the fat that is upon them, which is by the flanks, and the caul above the liver, with the kidneys, it shall he take away, 10 As it was taken off from the bullock of the sacrifice of peace offerings: and the priest shall burn them upon the altar of the burnt offering. 11 **And the skin of the bullock, and all his flesh, with his head, and with his legs, and his inwards, and his dung,** 12 Even **the whole bullock shall he carry forth without the camp unto a clean place, where the ashes are poured out, and burn him on the wood with fire:** where the ashes are poured out shall he be burnt.

SIN OFFERING FOR THE WHOLE CONGREGATION: Lev. 4:13-21 And if the whole congregation of Israel **sin through ignorance**, and the thing be hid from the eyes of the assembly, and they have done somewhat against any of the commandments of יהוה concerning things which should not be done, and are guilty; 14 When the sin, which they have sinned against it, is known, then the congregation shall offer **a young bullock** for the sin, and bring him before the Tabernacle of the congregation. 15 And the **elders of the congregation shall lay their hands upon the head of the bullock** before יהוה: and the bullock shall be killed before יהוה. 16 And the priest that is anointed shall bring of the bullock's blood to the **Tabernacle** of the congregation: 17 And the priest shall dip his finger in some of the blood, and s**prinkle it seven times before יהוה, even before the veil**. 18 And he shall put some of the blood upon the horns of the altar which is before יהוה, ... and shall pour out all the blood at the bottom of the altar of the burnt offering, which is at the door of the **Tabernacle** of the congregation. 19 And he shall take all his fat from him, and burn it upon the altar. 20 ... and the priest shall make an atonement for them, and it shall be forgiven them. 21 **And he shall carry forth the bullock without the camp, and burn him** as he burned the first bullock: it is a sin offering for the congregation.

Num. 15:24-26 Then it shall be, if ought be **committed by ignorance** without the knowledge of the congregation, that **all the congregation** shall offer one young bullock for a burnt offering, for a sweet savour unto יהוה, with his meat offering, and his drink offering, according to the manner, and one kid of the goats for a sin offering. 25 And the priest shall make an atonement for all the congregation of the children of Israel, and it shall be forgiven them; for it is **ignorance**: ... 26 **And it shall be forgiven** all the congregation of the children of Israel, and the stranger that sojourneth among them; seeing all the people were in **ignorance**.

SIN OFFERING FOR A RULER: Lev. 4:22-26 When a ruler hath sinned, and done somewhat **through ignorance** against any of the commandments of יהוה his God concerning things which should not be done, and is guilty; 23 Or if his sin, wherein he hath sinned, come to his knowledge; he shall bring his offering, **a kid of the goats, a male without blemish:** 24 And **he shall lay his hand upon the head of the goat, and kill it** in the place where they kill the burnt offering before יהוה: it is a sin offering. 25 And the priest shall take of the blood of the sin offering with his finger, and put it upon the horns of the altar of burnt offering, and shall pour out his blood at the bottom of the altar of burnt offering. 26 And he shall burn all his fat upon the altar, as the fat of the sacrifice of peace offerings: and the priest shall make an atonement for him as concerning his sin, and **it shall be forgiven him.**

SIN OFFERING FOR A COMMON PERSON: Lev. 4:27-35 And if any one of the common people sin **through ignorance,** while he doeth somewhat against any of the commandments of יהוה concerning things which ought not to be done, and be guilty; 28 Or if his sin, which he hath sinned, come to his knowledge: then he shall bring his offering, **a kid of the goats, a female without blemish,** for his sin.... 29 And he shall **lay his hand upon the head of the sin offering, and slay the sin offering** in the place of the burnt offering. 30 And the priest shall take of the blood thereof with his finger, and put it upon the horns of the altar of burnt offering, and shall pour out all the blood thereof at the bottom of the altar. 31 And he shall take away all the fat thereof, ... and the priest shall burn it upon the altar for a sweet savour unto יהוה; and the priest shall make an atonement for him, **and it shall be forgiven him.** 32 And if he bring a **lamb for a sin offering**, he shall bring it **a female without blemish**. 33 And **he shall lay his hand upon the head of the sin offering, and slay it**.... 35 ...and the priest shall make an atonement for his sin ... **and it shall be forgiven him.**

Num. 15:27-29 And if **any soul sin through ignorance,** then he shall bring **a she goat** of the first year for a sin offering. 28 And the priest shall make an atonement for the soul that sinneth ignorantly, when he sinneth by ignorance before יהוה, to make an atonement for him; and it shall be forgiven him. 29 Ye shall have one Torah for him that **sinneth through ignorance,** both for him that is born among the children of Israel, and for the stranger ... among them.

ASHAM/GUILT/SHAME OFFERING: Lev. 5:1-11 And if a soul **sin**, and hear the voice of swearing, and is a witness, whether he hath seen or known of it; if he do not utter it, then he shall bear his iniquity. 2 Or if a soul touch any unclean thing, whether it be a carcase of an unclean beast, or a carcase of unclean cattle, or the carcase of unclean creeping things, and if it be hidden from him; he also shall be unclean, and guilty. 3 Or if he touch the uncleanness of man, whatsoever uncleanness it be that a man shall be defiled withal, and it be hid from him; when he knoweth of it, then he shall be guilty. 4 Or if a soul swear, pronouncing with his lips to do evil, or to do good, whatsoever it be that a man shall pronounce with an oath, and it be hid from him; when he knoweth of it, then he shall be guilty in one of these. 5 And it shall be, when **he shall be guilty** in one of these things, that he shall confess that he hath sinned in that thing: 6 And he shall bring his **[asham] offering** unto יהוה for his sin which he hath sinned, **a female from the flock,** a lamb or a kid of the goats, for a sin offering; and the priest shall make an atonement for him concerning his sin. 7 And if he be not able to bring a lamb, then he shall bring for his **[asham]**, which he hath committed, two turtledoves, or two young pigeons, unto יהוה; one **for a sin offering, and the other for a burnt offering.**... 11 But if he be not able to bring two turtledoves, or two young pigeons, then he ... shall bring ... the **tenth part of an ephah of fine flour** for a sin offering; he shall put no oil upon it, neither shall he put any frankincense thereon: **for it is a sin offering.**...

Lev. 7:1-6 Likewise this is the law of the **[asham] offering**: it is most holy. 2 In the place where they kill the burnt offering shall they kill the **[asham] offering**: and the blood thereof shall he sprinkle round about upon the altar. 3 And he shall offer of it all the fat thereof; the rump, and the fat that covereth the inwards, 4 And the two kidneys, and the fat that is on them,... and the caul that is above the liver, with the kidneys, it shall he take away: 5 And the priest shall burn them upon the altar for an offering made by fire unto יהוה: it is a **[asham] offering**. 6 Every male among the priests shall eat thereof: ... in the holy place: it is most holy.

Lev. 5:15-16 **If a soul commit a ... sin through ignorance,** in the holy things of יהוה; then he shall bring for his **[asham]** unto יהוה a ram without blemish out of the flocks, with thy estimation by shekels of silver, after the shekel of the sanctuary, for a **[asham] offering**: 16 And he shall make amends for the harm that he hath done in the holy thing, and shall add the fifth part thereto, and give it unto the priest: ... and it shall be forgiven him.

Lev. 5:17-19 And if a soul sin, and commit any of these things which are forbidden to be done by the commandments of יהוה; **though he wist it not,** yet is he guilty, and shall bear his iniquity. 18 And he shall bring a ram without blemish out of the flock, with thy estimation, for a **[asham] offering**, unto the priest: and the priest shall make an atonement for him concerning his ignorance wherein he erred and wist it not, and it shall be forgiven him. 19 It is a **[asham] offering**: he hath certainly **[committed asham]** against יהוה.

SACRIFICED ANIMAL MUST BE KILLED AT THE TEMPLE: Lev. 17:3-5 What man soever there be of the house of Israel, that killeth an ox, or lamb, or goat, in the camp, or that killeth it out of the camp, 4 **And bringeth it not** unto the **door of the Tabernacle** of the congregation, to offer an offering unto יהוה before the Tabernacle of יהוה; blood shall be imputed unto that man; he hath shed blood; and that man shall be cut off from among his people: 5 To the end that the children of Israel may bring their sacrifices, which they offer in the open field, even that they may bring them unto יהוה, unto the **door of the Tabernacle** of the congregation, unto the priest, and offer them for peace offerings unto יהוה.

Lev. 17:8-9 And thou shalt say unto them, Whatsoever man there be of the house of Israel, or of the strangers which sojourn among you, that offereth a burnt offering or sacrifice, 9 And bringeth it **not** unto the **door of the Tabernacle** of the congregation, to offer it unto יהוה; even that man shall be cut off from among his people.

OFFER ONLY TO GOD: Lev. 17:7 And they shall no more offer their sacrifices unto devils, after whom they have gone a whoring. This shall be a **statute forever** unto them.....

ANYONE WHO TOUCHES GRAIN, SIN, OR [ASHAM] OFFERINGS SHALL BE **HOLY**: Lev. 6:17-18,27 It [grain offering] shall not be baken with leaven. ...it is **most holy,** as is the **sin offering**, and as the [asham] **offering**. 18 All the males among the children of Aaron shall eat of it. It shall be a **statute forever** in your generations concerning the **offerings** of יהוה made by fire: **every one that toucheth them shall be holy.** ... 27 **Whatsoever shall touch the flesh thereof shall be holy.** BUT **NOT** FOR PEACE OFFERINGS: Lev. 7:18-19 ...the flesh... of his peace offerings... 19 **And the flesh that toucheth any unclean thing shall not be eaten; it shall be burnt with fire**: *(See also Hag. 2:12.)*

MOADIM OFFERINGS: Num. 28:2 Command the children of Israel, and say unto them, My offering, and My bread for My sacrifices made by fire, for a sweet savour unto Me, shall ye observe to offer unto Me in their due season [Moadim]. ... Num.29:39 These things [offerings] ye shall do unto יהוה in your set Feasts, beside your vows, and your freewill offerings, for your burnt offerings, ... and for your peace offerings. *[Numbers chapter 28-29 gives all the offerings for all the Appointed Times. (See the other Moadim laws, p. 158-182)]*

DAILY OFFERINGS: Num. 28:3b-8 ... This is the offering made by fire which ye shall offer unto יהוה; two lambs of the first year without spot **day by day**, for a continual burnt offering. 4 The one lamb shalt thou **offer in the morning**, and the other lamb shalt thou offer at even; 5 And a tenth part of an ephah of flour for a meat offering, mingled with the fourth part of an hin of beaten oil. 6 It is a continual burnt offering, which was ordained in mount Sinai for a sweet savour, a sacrifice made by fire unto יהוה. 7 And the drink offering thereof shall be the fourth part of an hin for the one lamb: in the holy place shalt thou cause the strong wine to be poured unto יהוה for a drink offering. 8 And the other lamb shalt thou **offer at evening:** as the meat offering of the morning, and as the drink offering thereof, thou shalt offer it, a sacrifice made by fire, of a sweet savour unto יהוה.

SABBATH OFFERINGS: Num. 28:9-10 And on the Sabbath day two lambs of the first year without spot, and two tenth deals of flour for a meat offering, mingled with oil, and the drink offering thereof: 10 This is the burnt offering of every Sabbath, beside the continual(daily) burnt offering, and [its] drink offering.

NEW MOON OFFERINGS: Num. 28:11-15 And in the beginnings of your months ye shall offer a burnt offering unto יהוה; two young bullocks, and one ram, seven lambs of the first year without spot; 12 And three tenth deals of flour for a meat offering, mingled with oil, for one bullock; and two tenth deals of flour for a meat offering, mingled with oil, for one ram; 13 And a several tenth deal of flour mingled with oil for a meat offering unto one lamb; for a burnt offering of a sweet savour, a sacrifice made by fire unto יהוה. 14 And their drink offerings shall be half an hin of wine unto a bullock, and the third part of an hin unto a ram, and a fourth part of an hin unto a lamb: this is the burnt offering of every month throughout the months of the year. 15 And one kid of the goats for a sin offering unto יהוה shall be offered, beside the continual (daily) burnt offering, and [its] drink offering.

PESAKH/PASSOVER TEMPLE OFFERINGS *(done by the priests for the whole nation, not the individual family offerings. See p. 161-162 for that.)*: Num. 28:16 And in the fourteenth day of the first month is the Passover of יהוה. ... 19 But ye shall offer a sacrifice made by fire for a burnt offering unto יהוה; two young bullocks, and one ram, and seven lambs of the first year: they shall be unto you without blemish: 20 And their [grain] offering shall be of flour mingled with oil: three tenth deals shall ye offer for a bullock, and two tenth deals for a ram; 21 A several tenth deal shalt thou offer for every lamb, throughout the seven lambs: 22 And one goat for a sin offering, to make an atonement for you. 23 Ye shall offer these beside the burnt offering in the morning, which is for a continual burnt offering. 24 After this manner ye shall offer daily, throughout the seven days, the [grain] of the sacrifice made by fire, of a sweet savour unto יהוה: it shall be offered beside the continual (daily) burnt offering, and [its] drink offering.

SHAVUOT/PENTECOST OFFERINGS: Num. 28:26-31 Also in the day of the firstfruits ... 27 ... ye shall offer the burnt offering for a sweet savour unto יהוה; two young bullocks, one ram, seven lambs of the first year; 28 And their [grain] offering of flour mingled with oil, three tenth deals unto one bullock, two tenth deals unto one ram, 29 A several tenth deal unto one lamb, throughout the seven lambs; 30 And one kid of the goats, to make an atonement for you. 31 Ye shall offer them beside the continual (daily) burnt offering....

ROSH HASHANAH/YOM TERUAH/FEAST OF TRUMPETS OFFERINGS: 1 And in the seventh month, on the first day of the month ... 2 And ye shall offer a burnt offering for a sweet savour unto יהוה; one young bullock, one ram, and seven lambs of the first year without blemish: 3 And their [grain] offering shall be of flour mingled with oil, three tenth deals for a bullock, and two tenth deals for a ram, 4 And one tenth deal for one lamb, throughout the seven lambs: 5 And one kid of the goats for a sin offering, to make an atonement for you: 6 Beside *(in addition to)* the burnt offering of the month (New Moon) ....

YOM KIPPUR/DAY OF ATONEMENT OFFERINGS: Num. 29: 7-11 And ... on the tenth day of this seventh month... 8 ... ye shall offer a burnt offering unto יהוה for a sweet savour; one young bullock, one ram, and seven lambs of the first year; they shall be unto you without blemish: 9 And their [grain] offering shall be of flour mingled with oil, three tenth deals to a bullock, and two tenth deals to one ram, 10 A several tenth deal for one lamb, throughout the seven lambs: 11 One kid of the goats for a sin offering; beside the sin offering of atonement, and the continual burnt offering, and the [grain] offering of it, and their drink offerings.

SUKKOT/FEAST OF TABERNACLE OFFERINGS: Num. 29:12-38 And on the fifteenth day of the seventh month ... 13 ...[**first day**] ye shall offer a burnt offering, a sacrifice made by fire, of a sweet savour unto יהוה; thirteen young bullocks, two rams, and fourteen lambs of the first year; they shall be without blemish: 14 And their [grain] offering shall be of flour mingled with oil, three tenth deals [per] bullock..., two tenth deals to each ram ..., 15 And a several tenth deal to each lamb ...: 16 And one kid of the goats for a sin offering; beside the [daily] burnt offering.... 17 And on the **second day** ye shall offer twelve young bullocks, two rams, fourteen lambs of the first year without spot: 18 And their [grain] offering and their drink offerings ...: 19 And one kid of the goats for a sin offering..... 20 And on the **third day** eleven bullocks, two rams, fourteen lambs...; 21 And their [grain] offering and their drink offerings...: 22 And one goat for a sin offering.... 23 And on the **fourth day** ten bullocks, two rams, and fourteen lambs ...: 24 ... 25 And one kid of the goats for a sin offering.... 26 And on the **fifth day** nine bullocks, two rams, and fourteen lambs ...: 27 ... 28 And one goat for a sin offering.... 29 And on the **sixth day** eight bullocks, two rams, and fourteen lambs ... 30 ... 31 And one goat for a sin offering.... 32 And on the **seventh day** seven bullocks, two rams, and fourteen lambs ... 33 ... 34 And one goat for a sin offering.... 35 On the **eighth day** ye shall have a solemn assembly: ye shall do no servile work therein: 36 But ye shall offer...: one bullock, one ram, seven lambs... 37 ...: 38 And one goat for a sin offering; beside the continual (daily) burnt offering.....

AFTER TORAH and APOSTLES

Psalm 141:2 Let my prayer be set forth before thee as incense; and the lifting up of my hands as the evening sacrifice.

Psalm 69: 30 I will praise the Name of God with a song, and will magnify Him with thanksgiving. 31 This also shall please יהוה better than an ox or bullock that hath horns and hoofs.

Rom. 12:1 I beseech you therefore, brethren, by the mercies of God, that ye **present your bodies a living sacrifice**, holy, acceptable unto God, which is your reasonable service [worship].

Heb. 13:15 By Him [Yeshua] therefore let us offer the sacrifice of praise to God continually, that is, the fruit of our lips giving thanks to His Name. 16 But to do good and to communicate [NRSV: share what you have] forget not: for with such sacrifices God is well pleased.

YESHUA FULFILLED ALL SACRIFICES: Heb. 10:10-12,14 By the which will we are sanctified **through the offering of the body** of ישוע Messiah once for all. 11 And every priest standeth daily ministering and offering oftentimes the same sacrifices, which can never take away sins: 12 But this Man, after He had offered **one sacrifice for sins forever**, sat down on the right hand of God.... 14 For **by one offering** He hath **perfected forever** them that are sanctified.

101. THE FIRE ON THE ALTAR MUST NEVER GO OUT

Lev. 6:12-13 And the fire upon the altar shall be burning in it; it shall not be put out: and the priest shall burn wood on it every morning, and lay the burnt offering in order upon it; and he shall burn thereon the fat of the peace offerings. 13 The fire shall ever be burning upon the altar; it shall never go out.

102. SACRIFICIAL ANIMALS MUST BE W/O BLEMISH

Lev. 22:17-25 And יהוה spake unto Moses, saying, 18 ... Whatsoever he be of the house of Israel, or of the strangers in Israel, that **will offer his oblation for all his vows, and for all his freewill offerings**, which they will offer unto יהוה for a burnt offering; 19 Ye shall offer at your own will **a male without blemish, of the beeves, of the sheep, or of the goats.** 20 But whatsoever hath a blemish, that shall ye not offer: for it shall not be acceptable for you. 21 ... **it shall be perfect** to be accepted; there shall be no blemish therein. 22 Blind, or broken, or maimed, or having a wen, or scurvy, or scabbed, ye shall not offer these unto יהוה, nor make an offering by fire of them upon the altar unto יהוה. 23 Either a bullock or a lamb that hath any thing superfluous or lacking in his parts, that mayest thou offer for a freewill offering; but for a vow it shall not be accepted. 24 Ye shall not offer unto יהוה that which is bruised, or crushed, or broken, or cut; neither shall ye make any offering thereof in your land. 25 Neither from a stranger's hand shall ye offer the bread of your God of any of these; because their corruption is in them, and blemishes be in them: they shall not be accepted for you.

Lev. 27:9-10 And if it be a beast, whereof men bring an offering unto יהוה, all that any man giveth of such unto יהוה **shall be holy.** 10 He shall not alter it, nor change it, a good for a bad, or a bad for a good: and if he shall at all change beast for beast, then it and the exchange thereof shall be holy.

Deut. 17:1 Thou shalt not sacrifice unto יהוה thy God any bullock, or sheep, wherein is blemish, or any evil favouredness: for that is an abomination unto יהוה thy God.

APOSTLES

Rom. 12:1 I beseech you therefore, brethren, by the mercies of God, that ye present your bodies a living sacrifice, **holy, acceptable unto God**, which is your reasonable service [worship].

103. SACRIFICIAL ANIMALS MUST BE 8 DAYS OLD

Lev. 22:26-28 And יהוה spake unto Moses, saying, 27 When a bullock, or a sheep, or a goat, is brought forth, then it shall be seven days under the dam [the mother]; and from the eighth day and thenceforth it shall be accepted for an offering made by fire unto יהוה. 28 And whether it be cow or ewe, ye shall not kill it and her young both in one day.

104. PASSOVER LAMBS MUST BE 1 YEAR OLD

Ex. 12:3-5a ... In the tenth day of this month they shall **take to them every man a lamb,** according to the house of their fathers, a lamb for an house: ... 5 **Your lamb shall be without blemish, a male of the first year....**

LAVER/WASH HANDS AND FEET: Ex. 30:18-21 Thou shalt also make a laver of brass, and his foot also of brass, to wash withal: and thou shalt put it between the Tabernacle of the congregation and the altar, and thou shalt put water therein. 19 For Aaron and his sons shall wash their hands and their feet thereat: 20 When they go into the Tabernacle of the congregation, they shall wash with water, that they die not; or when they come near to the altar to minister, to burn offering made by fire unto יהוה: 21 So they shall wash their hands and their feet, that they die not: and it shall be a **statute forever** to them, even to him and to his seed **throughout their generations**. [also in wash, p. 207, verse 21 in Priests, p. 222]

OIL FOR THE MENORAH: Lev. 24:2-4 Command the children of Israel, that they bring unto thee pure oil olive beaten for the light, to cause the lamps to burn continually. 3 Without the veil of the testimony, in the Tabernacle of the congregation, shall Aaron order it from the evening unto the morning before יהוה continually: it shall be a **statute forever** in your generations. 4 He shall order the lamps upon the pure candlestick before יהוה continually.

Num. 8:2 Speak unto Aaron, and say unto him, When thou lightest the lamps, the seven lamps shall give light over against the candlestick.

TWELVE LOAVES: Lev. 24:5-9 And thou shalt take fine flour, and bake twelve cakes thereof: two tenth deals shall be in one cake. 6 And thou shalt set them in two rows, six on a row, upon the pure table before יהוה. 7 And thou shalt put pure frankincense upon each row, that it may be on the bread for a memorial, even an offering made by fire unto יהוה. 8 Every Sabbath he shall set it in order before יהוה continually, being taken from the children of Israel by an **everlasting Covenant**. 9 And it shall be Aaron's and his sons'; and they shall eat it in the holy place: for it is most holy unto him of the offerings of יהוה....

LEVITES IN CHARGE OF THE VESSELS: Num. 1:50-53 But thou shalt appoint the Levites over the Tabernacle of testimony, and over all the vessels thereof, and over all things that belong to it: they shall bear the Tabernacle, and all the vessels thereof; and they shall minister unto it, and shall encamp round about the Tabernacle. 51 And when the Tabernacle setteth forward, the Levites shall take it down: and when the Tabernacle is to be pitched, the Levites shall set it up: and the stranger that cometh nigh shall be put to death. 52 And the children of Israel shall pitch their tents, every man by his own camp, and every man by his own standard, throughout their hosts. 53 But the Levites shall pitch round about the Tabernacle of testimony, that there be no wrath upon the congregation of the children of Israel: and the Levites shall keep the charge of the Tabernacle of testimony.

CAMP AROUND THE TABERNACLE: Num 2:1-2 And יהוה spake unto Moses and unto Aaron, saying, 2 Every man of the children of Israel shall pitch by his own standard, with the ensign of their father's house: far off about the Tabernacle of the congregation shall they pitch....

CAMP AROUND THE TABERNACLE (cont.): Num. 2:17 Then the Tabernacle of the congregation shall set forward with the camp of the Levites in the midst of the camp: as they encamp, so shall they set forward, every man in his place by their standards. *[Read the whole passage for the full instructions.]*

WORK ASSIGNMENTS OF THE LEVITE FAMILIES

Num. 4:2-4 Take the sum of the sons of Kohath from among the sons of Levi, after their families, by the house of their fathers, 3 From thirty years old and upward even until fifty years old, all that enter into the host, to do the work in the Tabernacle of the congregation. 4 This shall be the service of the sons of Kohath in the Tabernacle of the congregation, about the most holy things:

Num. 4:5-7 And when the camp setteth forward, Aaron shall come, and his sons, and they shall take down the covering veil, and cover the ark of testimony with it: 6 And shall put thereon the covering of badgers' skins, and shall spread over it a cloth wholly of blue, and shall put in the staves thereof. 7 And upon the table of shewbread they shall spread a cloth of blue, and put thereon the dishes, and the spoons, and the bowls, and covers to cover withal: and the continual bread shall be thereon: ... (on and on...)

Num. 3:22-25a Take also the sum of the sons of Gershon, throughout the houses of their fathers, by their families; 23 From thirty years old and upward until fifty years old shalt thou number them; all that enter in to perform the service, to do the work in the Tabernacle of the congregation. 24 This is the service of the families of the Gershonites, to serve, and for burdens: 25 And they shall bear the curtains...

TEMPLE "TAX"

Ex. 30:11-16 And יהוה spake unto Moses, saying, 12 When thou takest the sum of the children of Israel after their number, then shall they give every man a ransom for his soul unto יהוה, when thou numberest them; that there be no plague among them, when thou numberest them. 13 This they shall give, every one that passeth among them that are numbered, half a shekel after the shekel of the sanctuary: (a shekel is twenty gerahs:) an half shekel shall be the offering of יהוה. 14 Every one that passeth among them that are numbered, from twenty years old and above, shall give an offering unto יהוה. 15 The rich shall not give more, and the poor shall not give less than half a shekel, when they give an offering unto יהוה, to make an atonement for your souls. 16 And thou shalt take the atonement money of the children of Israel, and shalt appoint it for the service of the Tabernacle of the congregation; that it may be a memorial unto the children of Israel before יהוה, to make an atonement for your souls. [first part also in Take a Census, p. 213]

2 Chron. 13:10-11 (NRSV) But as for us, ... We have priests ministering to the LORD who are descendants of Aaron, and Levites for their service. 11 They ... set out the rows of bread on the table of pure gold, and care for the golden lampstand so that its lamps may burn every evening;

YESHUA יֵשׁוּעַ

Matt. 17:24-27 (CJB) When they came to K'far-Nachum, the collectors of the half-shekel came to Kefa and said, "Doesn't your rabbi pay the Temple tax?" 25 "Of course he does," said Kefa. When he arrived home, Yeshua spoke first. "Shim`on, what's your opinion? The kings of the earth—from whom do they collect duties and taxes? From their sons or from others?" 26 "From others," he answered. "Then," said Yeshua, "The sons are exempt. 27 But to avoid offending them—go to the lake, throw out a line, and take the first fish you catch. Open its mouth, and you will find a shekel. Take it and give it to them for me and for you."

AFTER TORAH

2 Chron. 13:10-11 (NRSV) But as for us, the Lord is our God, and we have not abandoned him. We have priests ministering to the Lord who are descendants of Aaron, and Levites for their service. 11 They offer to the Lord every morning and every evening burnt offerings and fragrant incense, set out the rows of bread on the table of pure gold, and care for the golden lampstand so that its lamps may burn every evening;

RULES FOR BUILDING THE TABERNACLE and FOR MAKING the FURNISHINGS and the PRIESTLY VESTMENTS and for ORDAINING THE PRIESTS are in Exodus chapters 25-31.

106. WHO/WHAT MAY AND MAY NOT ENTER THE TEMPLE

Deut. 23:1 He that is wounded in the stones, or hath his privy member cut off, shall not enter into the congregation of יהוה. [Acts 8:26 ...behold, a man of Ethiopia, an eunuch of great authority under Candace queen of the Ethiopians... had come to Jerusalem for to worship....]

Deut. 23:2 A bastard shall not enter into the congregation of יהוה; even to his tenth generation shall he not enter into the congregation of יהוה. [*BlueletterBible.org*: bastard: child of incest, illegitimate child, Jewish-Gentile mixed child. *This Hebrew word is found only twice in the Bible, here and in Zech. 9:6 "And a bastard shall dwell in Ashdod."*]

Deut. 23:3-6 An **Ammonite** or **Moabite** shall not enter into the congregation of יהוה; even to their tenth generation shall they not enter into the congregation of יהוה **forever**: 4 Because they met you not with bread and with water in the way, when ye came forth out of Egypt; and because they hired against thee Balaam the son of Beor of Pethor of Mesopotamia, to curse thee. 5 Nevertheless יהוה thy God would not hearken unto Balaam; but יהוה thy God turned the curse into a blessing unto thee, because יהוה thy God loved thee. 6 Thou shalt not seek their peace nor their prosperity all thy days **forever**.

Deut. 23:7-8 Thou shalt not abhor an Edomite; for he is thy brother: thou shalt not abhor an Egyptian; because thou wast a stranger in his land. 8 The children that are begotten of them shall enter into the congregation of יהוה in their third generation.

Deut. 23:18 Thou shalt not bring the hire of a whore, or the price of a dog [male prostitute], into the house of יהוה thy And their children spake half in the speech of Ashdod, and could not speak in the Jews' language, God for any vow: for even both these are abomination unto יהוה thy God. [also in No Prostitution, p. 67]

AFTER TORAH

Ruth 1:4 And they took them wives of the women of **Moab**; the name of the one was Orpah, and the name of the other **Ruth**.... *[Ruth became the great grandmother of King David (Ruth 4:21-22).]*

Neh. 13:23 In those days also saw I Jews that had married wives of Ashdod, of **Ammon**, and of **Moab**.... 24 And I contended with them....

Matt. 27:3-8 Then Judas, which had betrayed Him, when he saw that He was condemned, repented himself, and brought again the thirty pieces of silver to the chief priests and elders, 4 Saying, I have sinned in that I have betrayed the innocent blood. And they said, What is that to us? see thou to that. 5 And he cast down the pieces of silver in the Temple, and departed, and went and hanged himself. 6 And the chief priests took the silver pieces, and said, **It is not lawful for to put them into the treasury, because it is the price of blood**. 7 And they took counsel, and bought with them the potter's field, to bury strangers in. 8 Wherefore that field was called, The field of blood, unto this day.

Through Yeshua's Blood, we may all enter, and we are His Temple.

YESHUA ישוע

Matt. 12:6 But I say unto you, That in this place is One greater than the Temple.

APOSTLES

1 Cor. 3:16-17 Know ye not that ye are the Temple of God, and that the Spirit of God dwelleth in you? 17 If any man defile the Temple of God, him shall God destroy; for the Temple of God is holy, which Temple ye are.

1 Cor. 6:19-20 What? know ye not that your body is the Temple of the Holy Spirit which is in you, which ye have of God, and ye are not your own? 20 For ye are bought with a price: therefore glorify God in your body, and in your spirit, which are God's.

107. WORSHIP GOD ONLY IN THE PLACE HE CHOOSES

Deut. 12:5-7 But unto the place which יהוה your God shall choose out of all your tribes to put His Name there, ... thither thou shalt come: 6 And thither ye shall bring your burnt offerings, .. sacrifices, ... tithes, and heave offerings, ... vows, and your freewill offerings, and the firstlings of your herds and ...flocks: 7 And there ye shall eat before יהוה your God, and ye shall rejoice ..., ye and your households, wherein יהוה thy God hath blessed thee.

Deut. 12:11 Then there shall be a place which יהוה your God shall choose to cause His Name to dwell there; thither shall ye bring all that I command you; your burnt offerings, and your sacrifices, your tithes, and the heave offering ..., and ... vows which ye vow unto יהוה:

Deut. 12:13-26 Take heed to thyself that thou offer not thy burnt offerings in every place that thou seest: 14 But in the place which יהוה shall choose in one of thy tribes, there thou shalt offer thy burnt offerings.... 17 Thou mayest not eat within thy gates the tithe of thy corn [grain], ... wine, ... oil, or the firstlings of thy herds or ...flock, nor ... vows ... nor thy freewill offerings, or heave offering 18 But thou must eat them before יהוה thy God in the place which יהוה thy God shall choose, ... 26 ...thy holy things which thou hast, and thy vows, thou shalt take, and go unto the place which יהוה shall choose:

Deut. 16:6-14 But at the place which יהוה thy God shall choose to place His Name in, there thou shalt sacrifice the **Passover**... And thou shalt roast and eat it in the place which יהוה thy God shall choose: and thou shalt turn in the morning, and go unto thy tents. ...10, 11c And thou shalt keep the **Feast of Weeks** ... in the place which יהוה thy God hath chosen to place His Name there. ... 13 Thou shalt observe the **Feast of Tabernacles** ... 14 Seven days shalt thou keep a solemn Feast unto יהוה thy God in the place which יהוה shall choose

Deut. 26:2 That thou shalt take of the **first** of all the **fruit** of the earth, which thou shalt bring of thy land that יהוה thy God giveth thee, and shalt put it in a basket, and shalt go unto the place which יהוה thy God shall choose to place His Name there.

Deut. 31:11 When all Israel is come to appear before יהוה thy God in the place which He shall choose, thou shalt read this Torah before all Israel in their hearing.

ALSO FOR HIGH COURT DECISIONS: Deut. 17:8-9 If there arise a matter too hard for thee in judgment, ... being matters of controversy within thy gates: then shalt thou arise, and get thee up into **the place which יהוה thy God shall choose;** 9 And thou shalt come unto the priests the Levites, and unto the judge ... and inquire; and they shall shew thee the sentence of judgment: ...

YESHUA ישוע

John 4:19-24 The woman saith unto Him, Sir, I perceive that thou art a prophet. 20 Our fathers worshipped in this mountain; and ye say, that in Jerusalem is the place where men ought to worship. 21 ישוע saith unto her, Woman, believe Me, the hour cometh, when ye shall neither in this mountain, nor yet at Jerusalem, worship the Father. 22 Ye worship ye know not what: we know what we worship: for salvation is of the Jews. 23 But the hour cometh, and now is, when the true worshippers shall worship the Father in spirit and in truth: for the Father seeketh such to worship Him.

108. SHMITAH YEAR, LET LAND REST

Ex. 23:10-11 And six years thou shalt sow thy land, and shalt gather in the fruits thereof: 11 But the **seventh year** thou shalt let it rest and lie still; that the poor of thy people may eat: and what they leave the beasts of the field shall eat. In like manner thou shalt deal with thy vineyard, and with thy oliveyard.

Lev. 25 whole chapter, following are parts of it: Lev. 25:1-7 And יהוה spake unto Moses in mount Sinai, saying, 2 Speak unto the children of Israel..., When ye come into the land which I give you, then shall the land keep a Sabbath unto יהוה. 3 Six years thou shalt sow thy field, and six years thou shalt prune thy vineyard, and gather in the fruit thereof; 4 But in the **seventh year** shall be a Sabbath of rest unto the land, a Sabbath for יהוה: thou shalt neither sow thy field, nor prune thy vineyard. 5 That which groweth of its own accord of thy harvest thou shalt not reap, neither gather the grapes of thy vine undressed: for it is a year of rest unto the land. 6 And the Sabbath of the land shall be meat for you; for thee, and for thy servant, and for thy maid, and for thy hired servant, and for thy stranger that sojourneth with thee, 7 And for thy cattle, and for the beast that are in thy land, shall all the increase thereof be meat.

Lev. 26:14-16, 32-35 But if ye will not hearken unto Me, and will not do all these commandments; 15 ...but that ye break My Covenant: 16 I also will do this unto you; I will even appoint over you terror, consumption, and the burning ague, that shall consume the eyes, and cause sorrow of heart: and ye shall sow your seed in vain, for your enemies shall eat it. ... 32 And I will bring the land into desolation: and your enemies which dwell therein shall be astonished at it. 33 And I will scatter you among the heathen, and will draw out a sword after you: and your land shall be desolate, and your cities waste. 34 **Then shall the land enjoy her Sabbaths, as long as it lieth desolate, and ye be in your enemies' land;** even then shall the land rest, and enjoy her Sabbaths. 35 As long as it lieth desolate it shall rest; because it did not rest in your Sabbaths, when ye dwelt upon it. [all of Lev. 25 is in Punishment for Disobedience, p. 229]

Lev. 26:43 The land also shall be left of them, and shall enjoy her Sabbaths, while she lieth desolate without them: and they shall accept of the punishment of their iniquity: because, even because they despised my judgments, and because their soul abhorred my statutes.

AFTER TORAH

2 Chron. 36:17-19, 21 Therefore he brought upon them the king of the Chaldees, who slew their young men with the sword in the house of their sanctuary, and had no compassion upon young man or maiden, old man, or him that stooped for age: he gave them all into his hand. 18 And all the vessels of the house of God, great and small, and the treasures of the house of יהוה , and the treasures of the king, and of his princes; all these he brought to Babylon. 19 And they burnt the house of God, and brake down the wall of Jerusalem, and burnt all the palaces thereof with fire, and destroyed all the goodly vessels thereof. ... 21 To fulfil the Word of יהוה by the mouth of Jeremiah, **until the land had enjoyed her Sabbaths**: for as long as she lay desolate she kept Sabbath, to fulfil threescore and ten years.

109. SHMITAH YEAR, RELEASE ALL DEBT

Deut 15:1-3 At the end of every **seven years** thou shalt make a **Release**. 2 And this is the manner of the release: Every creditor that lendeth ought unto his neighbour shall release it; he shall not exact it of his neighbour, or of his brother; because it is called יהוה's release. 3 Of a foreigner thou mayest exact it again: but that which is thine with thy brother thine hand shall release;

Deut. 15:9 Beware that there be not a thought in thy wicked heart, saying, The **seventh year,** the **Year of Release**, is at hand; and thine eye be evil against thy poor brother, and thou givest him nought; and he cry unto יהוה against thee, and it be sin unto thee.

Deut. 15:12 And if thy brother, an Hebrew man, or an Hebrew woman, be sold unto thee, and serve thee six years; then in the **seventh year** thou shalt let him go free from thee. [Cont. in Severance for freed Hebrew slaves, p. 75]

YESHUA ישוע and APOSTLES

Matt. 6:12,14 And forgive us our debts, as we forgive our debtors. ... 14 For if ye forgive men their trespasses, your heavenly Father will also forgive you: *(See more on forgiveness on p. 264)*

Col. 2:13b-14 (NIV) ... He forgave us all our sins, 14 having canceled the charge of our legal indebtedness, which stood against us and condemned us; He has taken it away, nailing it to the Cross.

110. SHMITAH YEAR, READ THE TORAH TO ALL

Deut. 31:10-13 And Moses commanded them, saying, At the end of every **seven years**, in the solemnity of the **Year of Release**, in the Feast of Tabernacles [Sukkot], 11 When all Israel is come to appear before יהוה thy God in the place which He shall choose, thou shalt read this Torah before all Israel in their hearing. 12 Gather the people together, men, and women, **and children**, and thy stranger that is within thy gates, that they may hear, and that they may learn, and fear יהוה your God, and observe to do all the Words of this Torah: 13 And **that their children,** which have not known any thing, may hear, and learn to fear יהוה your God.... [also in Keep All, p. 22, Sukkot, p. 180, and Teach Your Children, p. 194]

AFTER TORAH

Nehemiah 8:1-9 And all the people gathered themselves together as one man.... 2 And Ezra the priest brought the Torah before the congregation both of men and women, and all that could hear with understanding, upon the first day of the seventh month. *[Their first reading of Torah in exile. They read it at the commanded time also. See 8:18 (next)}* 3 And he read therein ... from the morning until midday.... 8 So they read in the book in the Torah of God distinctly, and gave the sense, and caused them to understand the reading. ... 9 And Nehemiah ... and Ezra ... and the Levites that taught the people, said..., This day is holy unto יהוה your God; mourn not, nor weep. For all the people wept, when they heard the words of the Torah. ... 10 ... for the joy of יהוה is your strength. [also in Rosh Hashanah, p. 176]

Neh. 8:18 Also **day by day, from the first day unto the last day, he read in the book of the Torah of God.** And they kept the **Feast seven days;** and on the **eighth day** was a solemn assembly. *[This was at the commanded time: Sukkot.]* [also in Sukkot, p. 181]

111. THREE TIMES A YEAR MALES GO TO JERUSALEM

Ex. 23:14-17 Three times thou shalt keep a feast unto me in the year. 15 Thou shalt keep the **Feast of Unleavened Bread:** ... 16 And the **Feast of Harvest** [Shavuot], the **firstfruits** of thy labours, ... and the **Feast of Ingathering** [Sukkot], *which is* in the end of the year [Sukkot].... 17 **Three times in the year** all thy males shall appear before the Lord [Adon] יהוה.

Ex. 34:23 **Thrice in the year** shall all your men children appear before the Lord [Adon] יהוה....

Deut. 16:16 **Three times in a year** shall all thy males appear before יהוה thy God in the place which He shall choose; in the **Feast of Unleavened Bread,** and in the **Feast of Weeks,** and in the **Feast of Tabernacles:**

YESHUA ישוע and Apostle Paul

John 5:1 After this there was a Feast of the Jews; and ישוע went up to Jerusalem.

John 7:2, 10, 14 Now the Jews' **Feast of Tabernacles** was at hand. ... 10 But when His brethren were gone up, then went he also up unto the Feast, not openly, but as it were in secret. ... 14 Now about the midst of the Feast ישוע went up into the Temple, and taught.

Acts 18:19-21 ... reasoned with the Jews. 20 When they desired him to tarry longer ... 21 But bade them farewell, saying, I must by all means keep this Feast that cometh in Jerusalem....

Acts 20:16 For Paul had determined to sail by Ephesus, because he would not spend the time in Asia: for he hasted, if it were possible for him, to be at Jerusalem the **Day of Pentecost.**

112. DON'T COME TO יהוה EMPTY HANDED

Ex. 23:15b ...and none shall appear before Me empty

Ex. 34:20c And none shall appear before Me empty.

Deut. 12:26 Only thy holy things which thou hast, and thy vows, thou shalt take, and go unto the place which יהוה shall choose:

Deut. 16:16b and they shall not appear before יהוה empty: Every man shall give as he is able, according to the blessing of יהוה thy God which He hath given thee.

YESHUA ישוע

Matt. 19:21 (and Mark 10:21 and Luke 18:22) ...go and sell that thou hast, and give to the poor, and thou shalt have treasure in heaven: and come and follow Me.

Luke 14:33 So likewise, whosoever he be of you that forsaketh not all that he hath, he cannot be My disciple.

113. MOADIM/APPOINTED TIMES/FEASTS

Lev. 23:1-2,4 And יהוה spake unto Moses, saying, 2 Speak unto the children of Israel, and say unto them, Concerning the Feasts of יהוה, which ye shall proclaim to be holy convocations, even these are My Feasts. ... 4 These are the feasts of יהוה, even holy convocations, which ye shall proclaim in their seasons.

114. ROSH KHODESH/NEW MOON

Num. 10:10 Also in the day of your gladness, and in your solemn days, and **in the beginnings of your months**, ye shall blow with the [two silver] trumpets over your burnt offerings, and over the sacrifices of your peace offerings; that they may be to you for a memorial before your God: I am יהוה your God.

Num. 28:11-15 And in the beginnings of your months ye shall offer a burnt offering unto יהוה; two young bullocks, and one ram, seven lambs.... [See New Moon offerings p. 146]

AFTER TORAH

Psalm 81:3-4 Blow up the trumpet (shofar) in the **New Moon**, in the time appointed, on our solemn feast day. 4 For this was a statute for Israel, and a law of the God of Jacob.

Isaiah 66:23 And it shall come to pass, that from one **New Moon** to another, and from one Sabbath to another, shall all flesh come to worship before Me, saith יהוה.

Ezekiel 46:1,6 Thus saith Adonai יהוה; The gate of the inner court that looketh toward the east shall be shut the six working days; but on the Sabbath it shall be opened, and in the day of the **New Moon** it shall be opened. ... 6 And in the day of the **New Moon** it shall be a young bullock without blemish, and six lambs, and a ram: they shall be without blemish.

Amos 8:4-5 Hear this, O ye that swallow up the needy, even to make the poor of the land to fail, 5 Saying, When will the **New Moon** be gone, that we may sell corn? and the Sabbath...?

THINGS THAT HAPPENED ON THE NEW MOON

Gen. 8:5,13 And the waters decreased continually until the tenth month: in the tenth month, on the **first day of the month**, were the tops of the mountains seen. ... 13 And it came to pass in the six hundredth and first year, in the first month, the **first day of the month**, the waters were dried up from off the earth: and Noah removed the covering of the ark, and looked, and, behold, the face of the ground was dry.

Ex. 40:2,17 On the **first day of the first month** shalt thou set up the Tabernacle of the tent of the congregation. ... 17 And it came to pass in the first month in the second year, on **the first day of the month**, that the Tabernacle was reared up.

Num. 1:1-3,18 And יהוה spake unto Moses in the wilderness of Sinai, in the Tabernacle of the congregation, on the **first day of the second month**, in the second year after they were come out of the land of Egypt, saying, 2 Take ye the sum of all the congregation of the children of Israel, after their families, by the house of their fathers, with the number of their names, every male by their polls; 3 From twenty years old and upward, all that are able to go forth to war in Israel: thou and Aaron shall number them by their armies. … 18 And they assembled all the congregation together **on the first day of the second month**....

Num. 33:38 And Aaron the priest went up into mount Hor at the commandment of יהוה, and died there, in the fortieth year after the children of Israel were come out of the land of Egypt, in the **first day of the fifth month.**

Deut. 1:3 And it came to pass in the fortieth year, in the eleventh month, on the **first day of the month**, that Moses spake unto the children of Israel, according unto all that יהוה had given him in commandment unto them;

Deut. 29:17 And it came to pass in the seven and twentieth year, in the first month, in **the first day of the month**, the word of יהוה came unto me, saying,

I Sam. 20:5, 18 And David said unto Jonathan, Behold, to morrow is the **New Moon**, and I should not fail to sit with the king at meat: but let me go, that I may hide myself in the field unto the third day at even. … 18 Then Jonathan said to David, To morrow is the **New Moon**: H2320 and thou shalt be missed, because thy seat will be empty.

I Kings 4:23 And he said, Wherefore wilt thou go to him to day? it is neither **New Moon**, nor Sabbath. And she said, It shall be well.

I Chron. 23:31 And to offer all burnt sacrifices unto יהוה in the sabbaths, in the **New Moons**, and on the set Feasts, by number, according to the order commanded unto them, continually before יהוה:

II Chron. 2:4 Behold, I build an house to the Name of יהוה my God, to dedicate it to him, and to burn before Him sweet incense, and for the continual shewbread, and for the burnt offerings morning and evening, on the sabbaths, and on the **New Moons**, and on the solemn Feasts of יהוה our God. This is an **ordinance forever** to Israel.

II Chron. 8:13 Even after a certain rate every day, offering according to the commandment of Moses, on the Sabbaths, and on the **New Moons**, and on the solemn Feasts....

II Chron. 29:17 Now they began on **the first day of the first month** to sanctify, and on the eighth day of the month came they to the porch of יהוה: so they sanctified the house of יהוה in eight days; and in the sixteenth day of the first month they made an end.

II Chron. 31:3 He (King Hezekiah) appointed also the king's portion of his substance for the burnt offerings, to wit, for the morning and evening burnt offerings, and the burnt offerings for the Sabbaths, and for the **New Moons**, and for the set Feasts, as it is written in the law of יהוה.

Ezra 3:3-5 And they set the altar upon his bases; for fear was upon them because of the people of those countries: and they offered burnt offerings thereon unto יהוה , even burnt offerings morning and evening. ... 5 And afterward offered the continual burnt offering, both of the **New Moons**, and of all the set Feasts of יהוה that were consecrated....

Ezra 7:9   For upon **the first day of the first month** began he to go up from Babylon, and on **the first day of the fifth month** came he to Jerusalem, according to the good hand of his God upon him.

Neh. 10:33 For the shewbread, and for the continual meat offering, and for the continual burnt offering, of the Sabbaths, of the **New Moons**, for the set Feasts, and for the holy things, and for the sin offerings to make an atonement for Israel, and for all the work of the house of our God.

Ezek. 26:1 And it came to pass in the eleventh year, in the **first day of the month**, that the word of יהוה came unto me, saying,

Ezekiel 31:1 And it came to pass in the eleventh year, in the third month, in **the first day of the month**, that the Word of יהוה came unto me, saying, …

Ezekiel 32:1 And it came to pass in the twelfth year, in the twelfth month, in **the first day of the month**, that the Word of יהוה came unto me, saying, …

Ezekiel 45:18 Thus saith Adonai יהוה; In the first month, in **the first day of the month**, thou shalt take a young bullock without blemish, and cleanse the sanctuary:

Ezekiel 46:3 Likewise the people of the land shall worship at the door of this gate before יהוה in the Sabbaths and in the **New Moons**....

Hag. 1:1 In the second year of Darius the king, in the sixth month, in **the first day of the month**, came the Word of יהוה by Haggai the prophet unto Zerubbabel the son of Shealtiel, governor of Judah, and to Joshua the son of Josedech, the high priest, saying...

APOSTLES

Col. 2:16-17 (NRSV) Therefore do not let anyone condemn you in matters of food and drink or of observing festivals, **New Moons,** or Sabbaths. 17 These are only a shadow of what is to come, but the substance belongs to Christ. *[So Torah gives us a glimpse of what is to come!]*

115. PESAKH/PASSOVER (SEE ALSO FEAST OF UNLEAVENED BREAD)

Ex. 12 *whole chapter. Following is part of it:* Ex. 12:1-14 And יהוה spake ... saying, 2 This month shall be ... the first month of the year to you. 3 ... In the tenth day of this month they shall **take to them every man a lamb,** according to the house of their fathers, **a lamb for an house:** 4 And if the household be too little for the lamb, let him and his neighbour next unto his house take it according to the number of the souls; every man according to his eating shall make your count for the lamb. 5 **Your lamb shall be without blemish, a male of the first year:** ye shall take it out from the sheep, or from the goats: 6 And ye shall keep it up until the fourteenth day of the same month: and the whole assembly of the congregation of Israel shall kill it in the evening. 7 **And they shall take of the blood, and strike it on the two side posts and on the upper door post of the houses, wherein they shall eat it.** 8 And they shall **eat the flesh in that night, roast with fire, and unleavened bread; and with bitter herbs they shall eat it.** 9 Eat not of it raw, nor sodden at all with water, but roast with fire; his head with his legs.... 10 And ye shall let nothing of it remain until the morning; and that which remaineth of it until the morning ye shall burn with fire. 11 And thus shall ye **eat it; with your loins girded, your shoes on your feet, and your staff in your hand; and ye shall eat it in haste: it is** יהוה**'s Passover.** 12 For I will pass through the land of Egypt this night, and will smite all the firstborn in the land of Egypt, both man and beast; and against all the gods of Egypt I will execute judgment: I am יהוה. 13 And ... **when I see the blood, I will pass over you,** and the plague shall not be upon you.... 14 And this day ... ye shall keep it a feast to יהוה **throughout your generations;** ye shall keep it a feast by **an ordinance forever.** ... 24 ... an **ordinance** to thee and to thy sons **forever.** 25 And ... when ye be come to the land ... ye shall keep this service. 26 And ... **when your children shall say** unto you, What mean ye by this service? *[Four Question tradition]* 27 That ye shall say, It is the sacrifice of יהוה's **passover**, who passed over the houses of the children of Israel in Egypt, when he smote the Egyptians, and delivered our houses.

Exodus 12:44, 48 (NRSV) ...but any slave who has been purchased may eat of it after he has been circumcised; ... 48 If an alien who resides with you wants to celebrate the Passover to the LORD, all his males shall be circumcised; then he may draw near to celebrate it; **he shall be regarded as a native of the land.** But **no uncircumcised person shall eat of it;** [also in Slavery, p. 71, One Law, p. 87, and Circumcision, p. 192]

Ex. 34:25b neither shall the sacrifice of the Feast of the Passover be left unto the morning.

Lev. 23:5-8 In the fourteenth day of the first month at even is יהוה's Passover. *[Cont. in Unleavened Bread p. 162]*

Num. 9:1-3 And יהוה spake unto Moses in the wilderness of Sinai, in the first month of the second year after they were come out of the land of Egypt, saying, 2 Let the children of Israel also keep the Passover at His appointed season [Moad]. 3 In the fourteenth day of this month, at even, ye shall keep it in His appointed season [Moad]: according to all the rites of it, and according to all the ceremonies thereof, shall ye keep it.

Num. 9:10-13 Speak unto the children of Israel, saying, **If any man** of you or of your posterity shall **be unclean by reason of a dead body,** or be in a journey afar off, yet he shall keep the Passover unto יהוה. 11 The fourteenth day of **the second month** at even **they shall keep it**, and eat it with unleavened bread and bitter herbs. 12 They shall leave none of it unto the morning, nor break any bone of it: according to all the ordinances of the Passover they shall keep it. 13 **But the man that is clean**, and is not in a journey, **and forbeareth** *[fails]* **to keep the Passover, even the same soul shall be cut off** from among his people: because he brought not the offering of יהוה in His appointed season [Moad], that man shall bear his sin.

Num. 9:14 And if a stranger shall sojourn among you, and will keep the Passover unto יהוה; according to the ordinance of the Passover, and according to the manner thereof, so shall he do: ye shall have one ordinance, both for the stranger, and for him that was born in the land.

Num. 28:16 And in the fourteenth day of the first month is the Passover of יהוה. 17 And in the fifteenth day of this month is the feast: seven days shall unleavened bread be eaten. 18 In the first day shall be an **holy convocation**; ye shall do no manner of servile work therein:

Deut. 16:1-2, 4-7 Observe the month of Abib, and keep the Passover unto יהוה thy God: for in the month of Abib יהוה thy God brought thee forth out of Egypt by night. 2 Thou shalt therefore sacrifice the Passover unto יהוה thy God, of the flock and the herd, in the place which יהוה shall choose to place His Name there. ... 4 ...neither shall there any thing of the flesh, which thou sacrificedst the first day at even, remain all night until the morning. 5 Thou mayest **not sacrifice the Passover within any of thy gates**, which יהוה thy God giveth thee: 6 But at the place which יהוה thy God shall choose to place His Name in, there thou shalt sacrifice the Passover at even, at the going down of the sun, at the season that thou camest forth out of Egypt. 7 And thou shalt roast and eat it in the place which יהוה thy God shall choose: and thou shalt turn in the morning, and go unto thy tents.

116. MATZAH/FEAST OF UNLEAVENED BREAD

Ex. 23:15a Thou shalt keep the **Feast of Unleavened Bread**: (thou shalt eat unleavened bread seven days, as I commanded thee, in the time appointed of the month Abib; for in it thou camest out from Egypt).

Ex. 34:18 **The Feast of Unleavened Bread** shalt thou keep. Seven days thou shalt eat unleavened bread, as I commanded thee, in the time of the month Abib [Aviv]: for in the month Abib [Aviv] thou camest out from Egypt.

Lev. 23:5-8 In the fourteenth day of the first month at even is יהוה's Passover. 6 And on the fifteenth day of the same month is the **Feast of Unleavened Bread** unto יהוה: seven days ye must eat unleavened bread. 7 In the **first day** ye shall have an **holy convocation**: ye shall do no servile work therein. 8 But ye shall offer an offering made by fire unto יהוה seven days: in the **seventh day is an holy convocation**: ye shall do no servile work therein.

Num. 28:17 And in the fifteenth day of this month is the feast: seven days shall unleavened bread be eaten.

Deut. 16:3-4a, 8 Thou shalt eat no leavened bread with it; seven days shalt thou eat unleavened bread therewith, even the <u>bread of affliction</u>; for thou camest forth out of the land of Egypt in haste: that thou mayest remember the day ... all the days of thy life. And there shall be no leavened bread seen with thee in all thy coast **seven days**; ... 8 **Six days thou shalt eat unleavened bread**: and on the **seventh day shall be a solemn assembly** to יהוה thy God: thou shalt do no work therein.

AFTER TORAH

PASSOVER was a foreshadowing and foretelling of the greatest event in history. It is mentioned many more times in Scripture than any of the other Moadim [Feasts].

Josh 5:10-11 And the children of Israel encamped in Gilgal, and kept the **Passover** on the fourteenth day of the month at even in the plains of Jericho. 11 And they did eat of the old corn of the land on the morrow after the **Passover**, unleavened cakes, and parched corn in the selfsame day.

2 Chron. 29:17; 30:1-20 Now they began on the first day of the first month to sanctify [the Temple], and on the eighth day of the month came they to the porch of יהוה: so they sanctified the house of יהוה in eight days; and in the sixteenth day of the first month they made an end. ... 30:1 And **Hezekiah** sent to all Israel and Judah, and wrote letters also to Ephraim and Manasseh, that they should come to the house of יהוה at Jerusalem, to keep the **Passover** unto יהוה God of Israel. 2 For the king had taken counsel, and his princes, and all the congregation in Jerusalem, to keep the **Passover** in the second month. 3 For they could not keep it at that [correct] time, because the priests had not sanctified themselves sufficiently, neither had the people gathered themselves together to Jerusalem. 4 And the thing pleased the king and all the congregation. 5 So they established a decree to make proclamation throughout all Israel, from Beersheba even to Dan, that they should come to keep the **Passover** unto יהוה God of Israel at Jerusalem: for they had not done it of a long time in such sort as it was written. 6 So the posts went with the letters from the king and his princes throughout all Israel and Judah, and according to the commandment of the king, saying, Ye children of Israel, turn again unto יהוה God of Abraham, Isaac, and Israel, and he will return to the remnant of you, that are escaped out of the hand of the kings of Assyria. ... 10 So the posts passed from city to city through the country of Ephraim and Manasseh even unto Zebulun: but they laughed them to scorn, and mocked them. 11 Nevertheless divers of Asher and Manasseh and of Zebulun humbled themselves, and came to Jerusalem. 12 Also in Judah the hand of God was to give them one heart to do the commandment of the king and of the princes, by the word of יהוה. 13 And there assembled at Jerusalem much people to keep the **Feast of Unleavened Bread** in the **second month**, a very great congregation. ... 15 Then they killed the **Passover** on the fourteenth day

of the second month: and the priests and the Levites were ashamed, and sanctified themselves, and brought in the burnt offerings into the house of יהוה. ... 17 For there were many in the congregation that were not sanctified: therefore the Levites had the charge of the killing of the **Passover**s for every one that was not clean, to sanctify them unto יהוה. 18 For a multitude of the people, even many of Ephraim, and Manasseh, Issachar, and Zebulun, had not cleansed themselves, yet did they eat the **Passover** otherwise than it was written. But Hezekiah prayed for them, saying, The good LORD pardon every one 19 that prepareth his heart to seek God, יהוה God of his fathers, though he be not cleansed according to the purification of the sanctuary. 20 And יהוה hearkened to Hezekiah, and healed the people.

2 Chron. 35:1-19 Moreover Josiah kept a **Passover** unto יהוה in Jerusalem: and they killed the **Passover** on the **fourteenth day of the first month**. 2 And he set the priests in their charges, and encouraged them to the service of the house of יהוה, 3 And said unto the Levites that taught all Israel, which were holy unto יהוה, ... prepare yourselves ... And stand in the holy place according to the divisions of the families of the fathers of your brethren ... 6 So kill the **Passover**, and sanctify yourselves, and prepare your brethren, that they may do according to the word of יהוה by the hand of Moses. 7 And **Josiah** gave to the people, of the flock, lambs and kids, all for the **Passover** offerings, for all that were present, to the number of thirty thousand, and three thousand bullocks: these were of the king's substance. ... 10 So the service was prepared, and the priests stood in their place, and the Levites in their courses, according to the king's commandment. 11 And they killed the **Passover**, and the priests sprinkled the blood from their hands, and the Levites flayed them. ... 13 And they roasted the **Passover** with fire according to the ordinance: but the other holy offerings sod they in pots, and in caldrons, and in pans, and divided them speedily among all the people. ... 15 And the singers the sons of Asaph were in their place, ... 17 And the children of Israel that were present kept the **Passover** at that time, and the Feast of Unleavened Bread seven days. 18 And there was no **Passover** like to that kept in Israel from the days of Samuel the prophet; neither did all the kings of Israel keep such a **Passover** as Josiah kept, and the priests, and the Levites, and all Judah and Israel that were present, and the inhabitants of Jerusalem. 19 In the eighteenth year of the reign of Josiah was this **Passover** kept. *[He would've been age 26.]*

2 Kings 23:21-22 And the **king [Josiah]** commanded all the people, saying, Keep the **Passover** unto יהוה your God, as it is written in the book of this covenant. Surely there was not holden such a **Passover** from the days of the judges that judged Israel, nor in all the days of the kings of Israel, nor of the kings of Judah;

Ezek. 45:21 In the first month, in the fourteenth day of the month, ye shall have the **Passover**, a feast of seven days; unleavened bread shall be eaten.

Ezra 6:19-20-22 And the children of the captivity kept the **Passover** upon the **fourteenth day of the first month**. 20 For the priests and the Levites were purified together, all of them were pure, and killed the **Passover** for all the children of the captivity, and for their brethren the priests, and for themselves. 21 And the children of Israel, which were come again out of captivity, and all such as had separated themselves unto them from the filthiness of the heathen of the land, to seek יהוה God of Israel, did eat, 22 And kept the **Feast of Unleavened Bread** seven days with joy: for יהוה had made them joyful....

Luke 2:41 Now His parents went to Jerusalem every year at the **Feast of the Passover**.

John 2:13, 23 And the Jews' **Passover** was at hand, and Jesus went up to Jerusalem, ... 23 Now when he was in Jerusalem at the **Passover**, in the Feast day, many believed in His Name, when they saw the miracles which He did.

John 6:4 And the **Passover**, a Feast of the Jews, was nigh.

John 11:55 And the Jews' **Passover** was nigh at hand: and many went out of the country up to Jerusalem before the **Passover**, to purify themselves.

John 12:1 Then Jesus six days before the **Passover** came to Bethany [which is near the Temple], where Lazarus was which had been dead, whom He raised from the dead.

Acts 12:3-4 And because he saw it pleased the Jews, he proceeded further to take Peter also. (Then were the **Days of Unleavened Bread**.) 4 ...intending after **Passover** [Greek: *pascha*, pronounced *paskha*, from Hebrew *Pesakh* (Passover)] to bring him forth to the people.

Acts 20:6 And we sailed away from Philippi after the days of **Unleavened Bread**,

PASSOVER AND UNLEAVENED BREAD FULFILLED

Matt. 26:17-29 Now the first day of the **Feast of Unleavened Bread** the disciples came to ישוע, saying unto him, Where wilt Thou that we prepare for Thee to eat the **Passover**? 18 And He said, Go into the city to such a man, and say unto him, The Master saith, My time is at hand; I will keep the **Passover** at thy house with My disciples. 19 And the disciples did as ישוע had appointed them; and they made ready the **Passover**. 20 Now when the even was come, He sat down with the twelve. 21 And as they did eat, He said, Verily I say unto you, that one of you shall betray me. 22 And they were exceeding sorrowful, and began every one of them to say unto Him, Lord, is it I? 23 And He answered and said, He that dippeth his hand with Me in the dish, the same shall betray Me. ... 26 And as they were eating, ישוע took bread, and blessed it, and brake it, and gave it to the disciples, and said, Take, eat; this is My Body. 27 And He took the cup, and gave thanks, and gave it to them, saying, Drink ye all of it; 28 For this is My Blood of the New Covenant, which is shed for many for the remission of sins. 29 But I say unto you, I will not drink henceforth of this fruit of the vine, until that day when I drink it new with you in My Father's Kingdom.

Mark 14:12-25 And the first day of unleavened bread, when they killed the **Passover**, His disciples said unto Him, Where wilt thou that we go and prepare that thou mayest eat the **Passover**? 13 And He sendeth forth two of His disciples, and saith unto them, Go ye into the city, and there shall meet you a man bearing a pitcher of water: follow him. 14 And wheresoever he shall go in, say ye to the goodman of the house, The Master saith, Where is the guestchamber, where I shall eat the **Passover** with My disciples? 15 And he will shew you a large upper room furnished and prepared: there make ready for us. 16 And His disciples went forth, and came into the city, and found as He had said unto them: and they made ready the **Passover**. 17 And in the evening He cometh with the twelve. 18 And as they sat and did eat, ישוע said, Verily I say unto you, One of you which eateth with Me shall betray Me. 19 And they began to be sorrowful, and to say unto Him one by one, Is it I? and another said, Is it I? 20 And He answered and said unto them, It is one of the twelve, that dippeth with Me in the dish. .... 22 And as they did eat, ישוע took bread, and blessed, and brake it, and gave to them, and said, Take, eat: this is My Body. 23 And He took the cup, and when He had given thanks, He gave it to them: and they all drank of it. 24 And He said unto them, This is My Blood of the New Covenant, which is shed for many. 25 Verily I say unto you, I will drink no more of the fruit of the vine, until that day that I drink it new in the Kingdom of God.

Luke 22:14-23 And when the hour was come, He sat down, and the twelve apostles with Him. 15 And He said unto them, With desire I have desired to eat this **Passover** with you before I suffer: 16 For I say unto you, I will not any more eat thereof, until it be fulfilled in the Kingdom of God. 17 And He took the cup, and gave thanks, and said, Take this, and divide it among yourselves: 18 For I say unto you, I will not drink of the fruit of the vine, until the Kingdom of God shall come. 19 And He took bread, and gave thanks, and brake it, and gave unto them, saying, This is My Body which is given for you: this do in remembrance of Me. 20 Likewise also the cup after supper, saying, This cup is the New Covenant in My Blood, which is shed for you. 21 But, behold, the hand of him that betrayeth Me is with Me on the table. 22 And truly the Son of Man goeth, as it was determined: but woe unto that man by whom He is betrayed! 23 And they began to enquire among themselves, which of them it was that should do this thing.

John 13:1-11, 21-28, 30 Now before the feast of the **Passover**, when ישוע knew that His hour was come that He should depart out of this world unto the Father, having loved His own which were in the world, He loved them unto the end. 2 And supper being ended, the devil having now put into the heart of Judas Iscariot, Simon's son, to betray Him; 3 ישוע knowing that the Father had given all things into His hands, and that He was come from God, and went to God; 4 He riseth from supper, and laid aside His garments; and took a towel, and girded Himself. 5 After that He poureth water into a bason, and began to wash the disciples' feet, and to wipe them with the towel wherewith He was girded. 6 Then cometh He to Simon Peter: and Peter saith unto Him, Lord, dost thou wash my feet? 7 ישוע answered and said unto him, What I do thou knowest not now; but thou shalt know hereafter. 8 Peter saith unto Him, Thou shalt never wash my feet. ישוע answered him, If I wash thee not, thou hast no part with Me. 9 Simon Peter saith unto Him, Lord, not my feet only, but also my hands and my head. 10 ישוע saith to him, He that is washed needeth not save to wash his feet, but is clean every whit: and ye are clean, but not all. 11 For He knew who should betray Him;

therefore said He, Ye are not all clean. ... 21 When ישוע had thus said, He was troubled in spirit, and testified, and said, Verily, verily, I say unto you, that one of you shall betray Me. 22 Then the disciples looked one on another, doubting of whom He spake. 23 Now there was leaning on ישוע' bosom one of His disciples, whom ישוע loved. 24 Simon Peter therefore beckoned to him, that he should ask who it should be of whom He spake. 25 He then lying on ישוע' breast saith unto Him, Lord, who is it? 26 ישוע answered, He it is, to whom I shall give a sop, when I have dipped it. And when He had dipped the sop, He gave it to Judas Iscariot, the son of Simon. 27 And after the sop Satan entered into him. Then said ישוע unto him, That thou doest, do quickly. 28 Now no man at the table knew for what intent He spake this unto him. ... 30 He then having received the sop went immediately out: and it was night.

I Cor. 5:6-8   Your glorying is not good. Know ye not that a little leaven leaveneth the whole lump? 7 Purge out therefore the old leaven, that ye may be a new lump, as ye are unleavened. For even Messiah our **Passover** is sacrificed for us: 8 **Therefore let us keep the feast,** not with old leaven, neither with the leaven of malice and wickedness; but with the unleavened bread of sincerity and truth.

I Cor. 10:16-17   The cup of blessing which we bless, is it not the communion of the Blood of Messiah? The bread which we break, is it not the communion of the Body of Messiah? 17 For we being many are one bread, and one Body: for we are all partakers of that one bread.

I Cor. 11:23-29   For I have received of the Lord that which also I delivered unto you, That the Lord ישוע the same night in which He was betrayed took bread: 24 And when He had given thanks, He brake it, and said, Take, eat: this is My Body, which is broken for you: this do in remembrance of Me. 25 After the same manner also He took the cup, when He had supped, saying, This cup is the New Covenant in My Blood: this do ye, as oft as ye drink it, in remembrance of Me. 26 For as often as ye eat this bread, and drink this cup, ye do shew the Lord's death till He come. 27 Wherefore whosoever shall eat this bread, and drink this cup of the Lord, unworthily, shall be guilty of the Body and Blood of the Lord. 28 But let a man examine himself, and so let him eat of that bread, and drink of that cup. 29 For he that eateth and drinketh unworthily, eateth and drinketh damnation to himself, not discerning the Lord's Body. 30 For this cause many are weak and sickly among you, and many sleep.

Read the accounts of His crucifixion:
   Matthew chapters 26 and 27
   Mark chapters 14 and 15
   Luke chapters 22 and 23
   John chapters 18 and 19

117. FEAST OF FIRSTFRUITS/RESURRECTION DAY

See also FirstFruit Offering, p. 137

Lev. 23:9-14 And יהוה spake unto Moses, saying, 10 Speak unto the children of Israel, and say unto them, When ye be come into the land which I give unto you, and shall reap the harvest thereof, then ye shall bring a sheaf of the **firstfruits** of your harvest unto the priest: 11 And he shall wave the sheaf before יהוה, to be accepted for you: **on the morrow after the Sabbath** the priest shall wave it. 12 And ye shall offer that day when ye wave the sheaf an he lamb without blemish of the first year for a burnt offering unto יהוה. 13 And the meat offering thereof shall be two tenth deals of fine flour mingled with oil, an offering made by fire unto יהוה for a sweet savour: and the drink offering thereof shall be of wine, the fourth part of an hin. 14 And ye shall eat neither bread, nor parched corn, nor green ears, until the selfsame day that ye have brought an offering unto your God: it shall be a **statute forever throughout your generations in all your dwellings**.

Deut. 26:2-5, 10-11 ...thou shalt take of the **first** of all the **fruit** of the earth, which thou shalt bring of thy land that יהוה thy God giveth thee, and shalt **put it in a basket**, and shalt go unto the place which יהוה thy God shall choose to place His Name there. 3 And thou shalt go unto the priest that shall be in those days, and say unto him, I profess this day unto יהוה thy God, that I am come unto the country which יהוה sware unto our fathers for to give us. 4 And the priest shall take the basket out of thine hand, and set it down before the altar of יהוה thy God. 5 And thou shalt speak and say before יהוה thy God, A Syrian ready to perish was my father, and he went down into Egypt, ... 10 And now, behold, I have brought the **firstfruits** of the land, which thou, O יהוה, hast given me. And thou shalt set it before יהוה thy God, and worship before יהוה thy God: 11 And thou shalt **rejoice** in every good thing which יהוה thy God hath given unto thee, and unto thine house, thou, and the Levite, and the stranger that is among you. [part also in Rejoice, p. 186]

FULFILLED

ישוע rose from the dead on this Moad/Feast Day. Following are the Scriptures about His resurrection in chronological order, including the repetitions. We are including all the Scriptures because this is the most important event in all the history of mankind. [The few Words of ישוע are in bold.]

Matt 28:1-7 In the end of the Sabbath, as it began to dawn toward the first day of the week, came Mary Magdalene and the other Mary to see the sepulchre. 2 And, behold, there was a great earthquake: for the angel of the Lord descended from heaven, and came and rolled back the stone from the door, and sat upon it. 3 His countenance was like lightning, and his raiment white as snow: 4 And for fear of him the keepers did shake, and became as dead men. 5 And the angel answered and said unto the women, Fear not ye: for I know that ye seek ישוע, which was crucified. 6 He is not here: for He is risen, as He said. Come, see the place where the Lord lay. 7 And go quickly, and tell His disciples that He is risen from the dead; and, behold, He goeth before you into Galilee; there shall ye see Him: lo, I have told you.

Luke 24:1-8 Now upon the first day of the week, very early in the morning, they came unto the sepulchre, bringing the spices which they had prepared, and certain others with them. 2 And they found the stone rolled away from the sepulchre. 3 And they entered in, and found not the body of the Lord יֵשׁוּעַ. 4 And it came to pass, as they were much perplexed thereabout, behold, two men stood by them in shining garments: 5 And as they were afraid, and bowed down their faces to the earth, they said unto them, Why seek ye the living among the dead? 6 He is not here, but is risen: remember how He spake unto you when He was yet in Galilee, 7 Saying, The Son of man must be delivered into the hands of sinful men, and be crucified, and the third day rise again. 8 And they remembered His words,

Matt. 28:8-10 And they departed quickly from the sepulchre with fear and great joy; and did run to bring His disciples word. 9 And as they went to tell His disciples, behold, יֵשׁוּעַ met them, saying, **All hail.** And they came and held Him by the feet, and worshipped Him. 10 Then יֵשׁוּעַ said to them, "Do not be afraid. Go and tell My brothers to go to Galilee; there they will see Me."

Luke 24:9-11 And returned from the sepulchre, and told all these things unto the eleven, and to all the rest. 10 It was Mary Magdalene, and Joanna, and Mary the mother of James, and other women that were with them, which told these things unto the apostles. 11 And their words seemed to them as idle tales, and they believed them not.

John 20:1-2 The first day of the week cometh Mary Magdalene early, when it was yet dark, unto the sepulchre, and seeth the stone taken away from the sepulchre. 2 Then she runneth, and cometh to Simon Peter, and to the other disciple, whom יֵשׁוּעַ loved, and saith unto them, They have taken away the Lord out of the sepulchre, and we know not where they have laid Him.

Luke 24:12 Then arose Peter, and ran unto the sepulchre; and stooping down, he beheld the linen clothes laid by themselves, and departed, wondering in himself at that which was come to pass.

John 20:3-10 Peter therefore went forth, and that other disciple, and came to the sepulchre. 4 So they ran both together: and the other disciple did outrun Peter, and came first to the sepulchre. 5 And he stooping down, and looking in, saw the linen clothes lying; yet went he not in. 6 Then cometh Simon Peter following him, and went into the sepulchre, and seeth the linen clothes lie, 7 And the napkin, that was about His head, not lying with the linen clothes, but wrapped together in a place by itself. 8 Then went in also that other disciple, which came first to the sepulchre, and he saw, and believed. 9 For as yet they knew not the Scripture, that He must rise again from the dead. 10 Then the disciples went away again unto their own home.

John 20:11-17 But Mary stood without at the sepulchre weeping: and as she wept, she stooped down, and looked into the sepulchre, 12 And seeth two angels in white sitting, the one at the head, and the other at the feet, where the body of יֵשׁוּעַ had lain. 13 And they say unto her, Woman, why weepest thou? She saith unto them, Because they have taken away my Lord, and I know not where they have laid Him. 14 And when she had thus said, she turned herself back, and saw ישוע standing, and knew not that it was ישוע. 15 ישוע saith unto her, **Woman, why weepest thou? whom seekest thou?** She, supposing Him to be the gardener, saith unto Him, Sir, if thou have borne Him hence, tell me where thou hast laid Him, and I will take Him away. 16 ישוע saith unto her, **Mary.** She turned herself, and saith unto Him, Rabboni; which is to say, Master. 17 ישוע saith unto her, **Touch Me not; for I am not yet ascended to My Father: but go to My brethren, and say unto them, I ascend unto My Father, and your Father; and to My God, and your God.**

[The account of this unsurpassing event continues on page 167.]

APOSTLES

I Cor. 15:20-27   But now is Messiah risen from the dead, and become the **firstfruits** of them that slept. 21 For since by man came death, by man came also the resurrection of the dead. 22 For as in Adam all die, even so in Messiah shall all be made alive. 23 But every man in his own order: Messiah the **firstfruits**; afterward they that are Messiah's at His coming. 24 Then cometh the end, when He shall have delivered up the Kingdom to God, even the Father; when He shall have put down all rule and all authority and power. 25 For He must reign, till He hath put all enemies under his feet. 26 The last enemy that shall be destroyed is death. 27 For He hath put all things under His feet.

James 1:18   Of His own will begat He us with the Word of truth, that we should be a kind of **firstfruits** of His creatures.

Rev. 14:1-5   And I looked, and, lo, a Lamb stood on the mount Zion, and with Him an hundred forty and four thousand, having His Father's Name written in their foreheads. 2 And I heard a voice from heaven, as the voice of many waters, and as the voice of a great thunder: and I heard the voice of harpers harping with their harps: 3 And they sung as it were a new song before the throne, and before the four beasts, and the elders: and no man could learn that song but the hundred and forty and four thousand, which were redeemed from the earth. 4 These are they which were not defiled with women; for they are virgins. These are they which follow the Lamb whithersoever He goeth. These were **redeemed** from among men, **being the firstfruits unto God and to the Lamb.** 5 And in their mouth was found no guile: for they are without fault before the throne of God.

118. COUNTING OF THE OMAR/SEVEN WEEKS

Lev. 23:15-16 And ye shall **count** unto you from the morrow after the Sabbath, from the day that ye brought the sheaf of the wave offering; **seven Sabbaths** shall be complete: 16 Even unto the morrow after the seventh Sabbath shall ye **number fifty days;** and ye shall offer a new meat [grain] offering unto יהוה.

All events in the very first fifty days after the very first Passover:

PROTECTED BY THE PILLAR OF CLOUD AND FIRE Ex. 13:21 And יהוה went before them by day in a pillar of a cloud, to lead them the way; and by night in a pillar of fire, to give them light; to go by day and night:

Ex. 14:19-20 And the angel of God, which went before the camp of Israel, removed and went behind them; and the pillar of the cloud went from before their face, and stood behind them: 20 And it came between the camp of the Egyptians and the camp of Israel; and it was a cloud and darkness to them, but it gave light by night to these: so that the one came not near the other all the night.

CROSSED THE RED SEA Ex. 14:21-22

EGYPTIAN ARMY DESTROYED Ex. 14:23-29

SINGING AND DANCING Ex. 15:1; 20-21 Then sang Moses and the children of Israel this song unto יהוה, and spake, saying, I will sing unto יהוה, for He hath triumphed gloriously: the horse and his rider hath He thrown into the sea. ... 20 And Miriam the prophetess, the sister of Aaron, took a timbrel in her hand; and all the women went out after her with timbrels and with dances. 21 And Miriam answered them, Sing ye to יהוה, for He hath triumphed gloriously; the horse and his rider hath He thrown into the sea.

BITTER WATER MADE SWEET Ex. 15:23-25 And when they came to Marah, they could not drink of the waters of Marah, for they were bitter: therefore the name of it was called Marah. 24 And the people murmured against Moses, saying, What shall we drink? 25 And he cried unto יהוה; and יהוה shewed him a tree, which when he had cast into the waters, the waters were made sweet:

QUAIL Ex. 16:13a;   MANNA Ex. 16:13b-15

WATER FROM THE ROCK Ex. 17:5-6

AMELIKITES DEFEATED Ex. 17:11-13

JETHRO CAME Ex. 18

THREE DAYS OF PREPARATION BEFORE MT. SINAI Ex. 19:10-11 ... And יהוה said unto Moses, Go unto the people, and sanctify them to day and to morrow, and let them wash their clothes, 11 And be ready against the third day: for the third day יהוה will come down in the sight of all the people upon mount Sinai.

What יֵשׁוּעַ said and did during those fifty days (in chronological order)

[His Words are in **bold**.]

Matt. 28:9-10 **All hail ... 10 ...Be not afraid: go tell My brothers that they go into Galilee, and there shall they see Me.**

Luke 24:13-27 And, behold, two of them went that same day to a village called Emmaus, which was from Jerusalem about threescore furlongs. 14 And they talked together of all these things which had happened. 15 And it came to pass, that, while they communed together and reasoned, יֵשׁוּעַ Himself drew near, and went with them. 16 But their eyes were holden that they should not know Him. 17 And He said unto them, **What manner of communications are these that ye have one to another, as ye walk, and are sad?** 18 And the one of them, whose name was Cleopas, answering said unto Him, Art thou only a stranger in Jerusalem, and hast not known the things which are come to pass there in these days? 19 And He said unto them, **What things?** And they said unto Him, Concerning יֵשׁוּעַ of Nazareth, which was a prophet mighty in deed and word before God and all the people: 20 And how the chief priests and our rulers delivered Him to be condemned to death, and have crucified Him. 21 But we trusted that it had been He which should have redeemed Israel: and beside all this, to day is the third day since these things were done. 22 Yea, and certain women also of our company made us astonished, which were early at the sepulchre; 23 And when they found not His body, they came, saying, that they had also seen a vision of angels, which said that He was alive. 24 And certain of them which were with us went to the sepulchre, and found it even so as the women had said: but Him they saw not. 25 Then He said unto them, **O fools, and slow of heart to believe all that the prophets have spoken: 26 Ought not Messiah to have suffered these things, and to enter into His glory?** 27 And beginning at Moses and all the prophets, He expounded unto them in all the Scriptures the things concerning Himself.

(cont.) Luke 24:28-35 And they drew nigh unto the village, whither they went: and He made as though He would have gone further. 29 But they constrained Him, saying, Abide with us: for it is toward evening, and the day is far spent. And He went in to tarry with them. 30 And it came to pass, as He sat at meat with them, He took bread, and blessed it, and brake, and gave to them. 31 And their eyes were opened, and they knew Him; and He vanished out of their sight. 32 And they said one to another, Did not our heart burn within us, while He talked with us by the way, and while He opened to us the Scriptures? 33 And they rose up the same hour, and returned to Jerusalem, and found the eleven gathered together, and them that were with them, 34 Saying, The Lord is risen indeed, and hath appeared to Simon. 35 And they told what things were done in the way, and how He was known of them in breaking of bread.

(cont.) Luke 24:36-43 And as they thus spoke, Himself stood in the midst of them, and says unto them, **Peace be unto you.** 37 But they were terrified and affrighted, and supposed that they had seen a spirit. 38 And He said unto them, **Why are ye troubled? and why do thoughts arise in your hearts? 39 Behold My hands and My feet, that it is I Myself: handle Me,**

and see; for a spirit has not flesh and bones, as ye see Me have. 40 And when He had thus spoken, He shewed them His hands and His feet. 41 And while they yet believed not for joy, and wondered, He said unto them, **Have ye here any meat?** 42 And they gave Him a piece of a broiled fish, and of an honeycomb. 43 And He took it, and did eat before them.

John 20:19-23 ... came and stood in the midst, and says unto them, **Peace be unto you.** 20 And when He had so said, He shewed unto them His hands and His side. Then were the disciples glad, when they saw the Lord. 21 Then said to them again, **Peace be unto you: as My Father has sent me, even so send I you.** 22 And when He had said this, He breathed on them, and says unto them, **Receive ye the Holy Spirit: 23 Whose soever sins ye remit, they are remitted unto them; and whose soever sins ye retain, they are retained.**

John 20:26-30 And after eight days again His disciples were within, and Thomas with them: then came ישוע, the doors being shut, and stood in the midst, and said, **Peace be unto you.** 27 Then saith He to Thomas, **reach hither thy finger, and behold My hands; and reach hither thy hand, and thrust it into My side: and be not faithless, but believing.** 28 And Thomas answered and said unto Him, My Lord and my God. 29 ישוע saith unto him, **Thomas, because you have seen Me, you have believed: blessed are they that have not seen, and yet have believed.** 30 And many other signs truly did ישוע in the presence of His disciples, which are not written in this book:

John 21:3-6, 9-14 Simon Peter saith unto them, I go a fishing. They say unto him, We also go with thee. They went forth, and entered into a ship immediately; and that night they caught nothing. 4 But when the morning was now come, ישוע stood on the shore: but the disciples knew not that it was ישוע. 5 Then ישוע saith unto them, **Children, have ye any meat?** They answered Him, No. 6 And He said unto them, **Cast the net on the right side of the ship, and ye shall find.** They cast therefore, and now they were not able to draw it for the multitude of fishes. ... 9 As soon then as they were come to land, they saw a fire of coals there, and fish laid thereon, and bread. 10 ישוע saith unto them, **Bring of the fish which ye have now caught.** 11 Simon Peter went up, and drew the net to land full of great fishes, an hundred and fifty and three: and for all there were so many, yet was not the net broken. 12 ישוע saith unto them, **Come and dine.** And none of the disciples durst ask Him, Who art thou? knowing that it was the Lord. 13 ישוע then cometh, and taketh bread, and giveth them, and fish likewise. 14 This is now the third time that ישוע shewed Himself to His disciples, after that He was risen from the dead.

John 21:15-22 So when they had dined, ישוע saith to Simon Peter, **Simon, son of Jonas, lovest thou Me more than these? ... Feed My lambs.** 16 ... **Simon, son of Jonas, lovest thou Me? ... Feed My sheep.** 17 He saith unto him the third time, **Simon, son of Jonas, lovest thou Me? ....** says unto him, **Feed My sheep. 18 Verily, verily, I say unto you, When thou wast young, you girdedst thyself, and walkedst whither thou wouldest: but when thou shalt be old, thou shalt stretch forth thy hands, and another shall gird thee, and carry thee** whither thou wouldest not. 19 ... Follow Me. ... 22 saith unto him, **If I will that he tarry till I come, what is that to thee? Follow thou Me.**

Matt. 28:18-20 **All power is given unto Me in heaven and in earth. 19 Go ye therefore, and teach all nations, baptizing them in the Name of the Father, and of the Son, and of the Holy Spirit: 20 Teaching them to observe all things whatsoever I have commanded you: and, lo, I am with you alway, even unto the end of the world. Amen.**

Mark 16:15-18 And He said unto them, **Go ye into all the world, and preach the Gospel to every creature. 16 He that believes and is baptized shall be saved; but he that believes not shall be damned. 17 And these signs shall follow them that believe; In My Name shall they cast out devils; they shall speak with new tongues; 18 They shall take up serpents; and if they drink any deadly thing, it shall not hurt them; they shall lay hands on the sick, and they shall recover.**

Acts 1:4-11 And, being assembled together with them, commanded them that they should not depart from Jerusalem, but **wait for the promise of the Father, which**, says He, **ye have heard of Me. 5 For John truly baptized with water; but ye shall be baptized with the Holy Spirit not many days hence.** 6 ... 7 And He said unto them, **It is not for you to know the times or the seasons, which the Father has put in his own power. 8 But ye shall receive power, after that the Holy Spirit is come upon you: and ye shall be witnesses unto Me both in Jerusalem, and in all Judaea, and in Samaria, and unto the uttermost part of the earth.** 9 And when He had spoken these things, while they beheld, He was taken up; and a cloud received Him out of their sight. 10 And while they looked steadfastly toward heaven as He went up, behold, two men stood by them in white apparel; 11 Which also said, Ye men of Galilee, why stand ye gazing up into heaven? this same ישוע, which is taken up from you into Heaven, shall so come in like manner as ye have seen Him go into Heaven.

Luke 24:44-51 And He said unto them, **These are the words which I spoke unto you, while I was yet with you, that all things must be fulfilled, which were written in the Torah of Moses, and in the prophets, and in the psalms, concerning me.** 45 Then opened He their understanding, that they might understand the Scriptures, 46 And said unto them, **Thus it is written, and thus it behooved Messiah to suffer, and to rise from the dead the third day: 47 And that repentance and remission of sins should be preached in His Name among all nations, beginning at Jerusalem. 48 And ye are witnesses of these things. 49 And, behold, I send the promise of My Father upon you: but tarry ye in the city of Jerusalem, until ye be endued with power from on high.** 50 And He led them out as far as to Bethany, and He lifted up His hands, and blessed them. 51 And it came to pass, while He blessed them, He was parted from them, and carried up into Heaven.

119. SHAVUOT/FEAST OF WEEKS/PENTECOST

See also FirstFruit Offering, p. 137

JEWISH LEADERS SAY THAT GOD CAME TO MT SINAI ON SHAVUOT Ex. 19:1 In the third month, when the children of Israel were gone forth out of the land of Egypt, the same day came they into the wilderness of Sinai.

Ex. 34:22a And thou shalt observe the **Feast of Weeks**, of the **firstfruits of wheat harvest**....

Lev. 23:15-21 And ye shall count unto you from the morrow after the Sabbath, from the day that ye brought the sheaf of the wave offering; seven Sabbaths shall be complete: 16 Even unto the morrow after the seventh Sabbath shall ye number fifty days; and ye shall offer a new meat offering unto יהוה. 17 Ye shall bring out of your habitations **two wave loaves** of two tenth deals: they shall be of fine flour; **they shall be baken with leaven**; they are the **firstfruits** unto יהוה. 18 And ye shall offer with the bread seven lambs without blemish of the first year, and one young bullock, and two rams: they shall be for a burnt offering unto יהוה, ... 19 Then ye shall sacrifice one kid of the goats for a sin offering, and two lambs of the first year for a sacrifice of peace offerings. 20 And **the priest shall wave them with the bread of the firstfruits for a wave offering** before יהוה, with the two lambs: they shall be holy to יהוה for the priest. 21 And ye shall proclaim on the selfsame day, that it may be an **holy convocation unto you**: ye shall do no servile work therein: it shall be a **statute forever in all your dwellings throughout your generations**.

Num. 28:26-27, 30 Also in the day of the firstfruits, when ye bring a new meat offering unto יהוה, after your weeks be out, ye shall have an **holy convocation**; ye shall do **no servile work**: 27 But ye shall offer the burnt offering for a sweet savour unto יהוה; two young bullocks, one ram, seven lambs of the first year; ... 30 And one kid of the goats....

Deut. 16:9-12 Seven weeks shalt thou number unto thee: begin to number the seven weeks from such time as thou beginnest to put the sickle to the corn *[barley?]*. 10 And thou shalt keep the **Feast of Weeks** unto יהוה thy God with a tribute of a freewill offering of thine hand, which thou shalt give unto יהוה thy God, according as יהוה thy God hath blessed thee: 11 **And thou shalt rejoice before** יהוה **thy God,** thou, and thy son, and thy daughter, and thy manservant, and thy maidservant, and the Levite that is within thy gates, and the stranger, and the fatherless, and the widow, that are among you, in the place which יהוה thy God hath chosen to place His Name there. 12 And thou shalt remember that thou wast a bondman in Egypt: and thou shalt observe and do these statutes. [also in Rejoice, p. 186]

Deut. 26:1-10 ... thou shalt take of the **first** of all the **fruit** of the earth, which thou shalt bring of thy land that יהוה thy God giveth thee, and shalt **put it in a basket,** and shalt go unto the place which יהוה thy God shall choose to place His Name there. 3 And thou shalt go unto the priest ... and say unto him, I profess this day unto יהוה thy God, that I am come unto the country which יהוה sware unto our fathers for to give us. 4 And the priest shall take the basket out of thine hand, and set it down before the altar of יהוה thy God. 5 And thou shalt speak and say before יהוה thy God, A Syrian ready to perish was my father... 10 And now, behold, I have brought the firstfruits of the land, which Thou, O יהוה, hast given me. And thou shalt set it before יהוה thy God, and worship before יהוה thy God: [also in Firstfruit offering p. 137, Worship in the Place He chooses, p. 154, Firstfruit/Resurrection, p. 168, and Rejoice ,p. 187]

FULFILLED:

Acts 2:1-4 And when the day of **Pentecost** [Shavuot] was fully come, they were all with one accord in one place. 2 And suddenly there came a sound from heaven as of a rushing mighty wind, and it filled all the house where they were sitting. 3 And there appeared unto them cloven tongues like as of fire, and it sat upon each of them. 4 And they were all filled with the Holy Spirit, and began to speak with other tongues, as the Spirit gave them utterance.

Rom. 8:23 And not only they, but ourselves also, which have the **firstfruits** of the Spirit, even we ourselves groan within ourselves, waiting for the adoption, to wit, the redemption of our body.

120. YOM TERUAH/ROSH HASHANAH/FEAST OF TRUMPETS

Lev. 23:23-25 And יהוה spake unto Moses, saying, 24 Speak unto the children of Israel, saying, In the **seventh month, in the first day of the month,** shall ye have a **Sabbath,** a memorial of **blowing of trumpets** [H8643 Teruah which means "blowing the shofar and shouting for joy"], an holy convocation. 25 Ye shall do no servile work therein: but ye shall offer an offering made by fire unto יהוה.

Num. 29:1 And in the **seventh month, on the first day of the month**, ye shall have an **holy convocation**; ye shall do no servile work: it is a **day of blowing the trumpets** [H8643 Teruah תרועה which means "blowing the shofar and shouting for joy"] unto you.

AFTER TORAH

Ezra 3:1 And when the **seventh month was come,** and the children of Israel were in the cities, the people gathered themselves together as one man to Jerusalem.

Neh.7:73b - 8:1-6 ...and when the **seventh month came,** the children of Israel were in their cities. 8:1 And all the people gathered themselves together as one man into the street that was before the water gate; and they spake unto Ezra the scribe to bring the book of the Torah of Moses, which יהוה had commanded to Israel. 2 And Ezra the priest brought the Torah before the congregation both of men and women, and all that could hear with understanding, **upon the first day of the seventh month.** 3 And he read therein before the street that was before the water gate from the morning until midday, before the men and the women, and those that could understand; and the ears of all the people were attentive unto the book of the Torah. 4 And Ezra the scribe stood upon a pulpit of wood, which they had made... 5 And Ezra opened the book in the sight of all the people; (for he was above all the people;) and ...all the people stood up: 6 And Ezra blessed יהוה, the great God. And all the people answered, Amen, Amen, with lifting up their hands: and they bowed their heads, and worshipped יהוה with their faces to the ground.

(cont.) Neh. 8:7-9 ... and the Levites, caused the people to understand the Torah: and the people stood in their place. 8 So they read in the book in the Torah of God distinctly, and gave the sense, and caused them to understand the reading. 9 And Nehemiah, ...the Tirshatha *[governor]*, and Ezra the priest the scribe, and the Levites that taught the people, said unto all the people, **This day is holy** unto יהוה your God; mourn not, nor weep. For all the people wept, when they heard the words of the Torah. [Neh. 81-9 also in Shmitah: Read Torah to all, p. 156]

(cont.) Neh. 8:10-13 Then he said unto them, Go your way, eat the fat, and drink the sweet, and send portions unto them for whom nothing is prepared: for **this day is holy unto our יהוה:** neither be ye sorry; **for the joy of יהוה is your strength**. 11 So the Levites stilled all the people, saying, Hold your peace, **for the day is holy;** neither be ye grieved. 12 And all the people went their way to eat, and to drink, and to send portions, and to make great mirth, because they had understood the words that were declared unto them. 13 And on the second day were gathered together the chief of the fathers of all the people, the priests, and the Levites, unto Ezra the scribe, even to understand the words of the Torah.

TERUAH (תרועה *H8643)*: Joshua 6:5,20 ...all the people shall shout with a **great shout** *[H8643 Teruah תרועה]*; and the (Jericho) wall ...shall fall.... 20 ...and the people shouted with a **great shout** *[Teruah תרועה]*, that the wall fell....

I Sam. 4:5 And when the Ark of the Covenant of יהוה came into the camp, all Israel shouted with a **great shout** *[Teruah תרועה]*, so that the earth rang again.

Ezra 3:11b,13b ...And all the people shouted with a **great shout** *[Teruah תרועה]*, when they praised יהוה, because the foundation of the house of יהוה was laid. ... 13 ...and the noise was heard afar off.

Psalm 33:3 Sing unto him a new song; play skilfully with a **loud noise** *[Teruah תרועה]*.

Psalm 47:5 God is gone up with a **shout** *[Teruah תרועה]*, יהוה with the sound of a **trumpet**.

Psalm 89:15 Blessed is the people that know the **joyful sound** *[Teruah תרועה* (NRSV: Feastal shout)]*: they shall walk, O יהוה, in the light of Thy countenance.

TO BE FULFILLED:

Matt. 24:30-31 And then shall appear the sign of the Son of man in heaven: and then shall all the tribes of the earth mourn, and they shall see the Son of man coming in the clouds of heaven with power and great glory. 31 And He shall send His angels **with a great sound of a trumpet,** and they shall gather together His elect from the four winds, from one end of heaven to the other.

I Thess. 4:16 For the Lord Himself shall descend from heaven with a shout, with the voice of the archangel, and **with the trump of God**: and the dead in Messiah shall rise first: 17 Then we which are alive and remain shall be caught up together with them in the clouds, to meet the Lord in the air: and so shall we ever be with the Lord. 18 Wherefore comfort one another with these words.

Rev. 8:6 And the seven angels which had the **seven trumpets** prepared themselves to sound.

121. YOM KIPPUR / DAY OF ATONEMENT

Lev. 16 *the whole chapter. Here are a few portions.* 16:1-2, 31 after the death of the two sons of Aaron.... 2 ... יהוה said unto Moses, Speak unto Aaron thy brother, that he come not at all times into the Holy Place within the veil before the Mercy Seat, which is upon the Ark; **that he die not:** for I will appear in the cloud upon the Mercy Seat. ... 31 It shall be a **Sabbath of rest** unto you, and ye shall **afflict your souls,** by a **statute forever.**

WEAR WHITE LINEN Lev. 16:4 He shall put on the **holy linen coat,** and he shall have the linen breeches upon his flesh, and shall be girded with a linen girdle, and with the **linen mitre** shall he be attired: these are holy garments; therefore shall he **wash his flesh in water,** and so put them on.

Lev. 16:11-14 And Aaron shall bring the bullock of the **sin offering, which is for himself,** and shall make **an atonement for himself, and for his house....** *FIRST TIME BEHIND CURTAIN:* 12 And he shall take a censer full of **burning coals of fire from off the altar** before יהוה, and his **hands full of sweet incense** beaten small, and bring it within the veil: 13 And he shall put the incense upon the fire before יהוה, that the **cloud of the incense** may cover the Mercy Seat that is upon the testimony, **that he die not:** *SECOND TIME BEHIND CURTAIN:* 14 And he shall take of the blood of the bullock, and sprinkle it with his finger upon the Mercy Seat eastward ... seven times.

TWO GOATS: Lev. 16:7-10, 15-16, 21-22 And he shall take the **two goats,** and present them before יהוה at the door of the Tabernacle of the congregation. 8 And Aaron shall **cast lots upon the two goats; one lot for יהוה, and the other lot for the scapegoat.** 9 And Aaron shall bring the goat upon which יהוה's lot fell, and offer him for a sin offering. 10 But the goat, on which the lot fell to be the scapegoat, shall be presented alive before יהוה, to make an atonement with him, and to let him go for a scapegoat into the wilderness. ... *THIRD TIME BEHIND CURTAIN:* 15 Then shall he kill the goat of the sin offering, that is for the people, and bring his blood within the veil, and do with that blood as he did with the blood of the bullock.... 16 ...because of the uncleanness of the children of Israel, and because of their transgressions in all their sins: ... 21 And Aaron shall l**ay both his hands upon the head of the live goat, and confess over him all the <u>iniquities</u> of the children of Israel,** and all their <u>transgressions</u> in all their <u>sins</u>, putting them upon the head of the goat, and shall send him away by the hand of a fit man into the wilderness: 22 And the goat shall bear upon him all their iniquities unto a land not inhabited: and he shall let go the goat in the wilderness.

Lev. 16:23-24, 33 And Aaron ... **shall put off the linen garments,** which he put on when he went into the Holy Place, and shall leave them there: 24 And he shall **wash his flesh with water** in the holy place, and put on his garments, and come forth, and offer his burnt offering, and the burnt offering of the people, and make an **atonement for himself,** and for **the people.** ... 33 And he shall make an atonement for the **holy sanctuary,** ... for the **Tabernacle** ... and for the **altar,** ... for the **priests....**

Lev. 6:30 And no sin offering, whereof any of the blood is brought into the Tabernacle of the congregation to reconcile withal **in the holy place,** shall be eaten: it shall be burnt in the fire.

Lev. 23:26-32 And יהוה spake unto Moses, saying, 27 Also on the **tenth day of this seventh month** there shall be a **Day of Atonement**: it shall be an **holy convocation** unto you; and ye shall **afflict your souls**, and offer an offering made by fire unto יהוה. 28 And ye shall **do no work** in that same day: for it is a **Day of Atonement**, to make an atonement for you before יהוה your God. 29 For whatsoever soul it be that shall not be afflicted in that same day, he shall be cut off from among his people. 30 And whatsoever soul it be that doeth any work in that same day, the same soul will I destroy from among his people. 31 Ye shall do no manner of work: it shall be a **statute forever throughout your generations in all your dwellings**. 32 It shall be unto you a **Sabbath of rest**, and ye shall **afflict your souls**: in the ninth day of the month at even[ing], from even[ing] unto even[ing], shall ye celebrate your **Sabbath**.

Num. 29:7 And ye shall have on the tenth day of this seventh month an **holy convocation**; and ye shall **afflict your souls**: ye shall **not do any work** therein:

APOSTLES

Acts 27:9 ...sailing was now dangerous, because the **fast** was now already past....

Heb. 9:6-7 Now ... the priests went always into the first Tabernacle, accomplishing the service of God. 7 But into the second went the High Priest alone once every year, not without blood, which he offered for himself, and for the errors of the people:

Heb. 9:11-12 But Messiah being come an High Priest of good things to come, by a greater and more perfect Tabernacle, not made with hands, that is to say, not of this building; 12 Neither by the blood of goats and calves, **but by His own Blood He entered in once into the Holy Place,** having obtained **eternal Redemption** for us.

Heb. 9:13-15 For if the blood of bulls and of goats, and the ashes of an heifer sprinkling the unclean, sanctifieth to the purifying of the flesh: 14 How much more shall the **Blood of Messiah**, who through the eternal Spirit offered Himself without spot to God, purge your conscience from dead works to serve the living God? 15 And for this cause He is the mediator of the New Covenant, that by means of death, for the Redemption of the transgressions that were under the first Covenant, they which are called might receive the promise of eternal inheritance.

Heb. 9:24-28 For Messiah is not entered into the Holy Places made with hands, which are the figures of the true; **but into Heaven itself,** now to appear in the presence of God for us: 25 Nor yet that He should offer Himself often, as the High Priest entereth into the Holy Place every year with blood of others; 26 For then must He often have suffered since the foundation of the world: but now once in the end of the world hath He appeared to put away sin by the sacrifice of Himself.

122. SUKKOT/FEAST OF TABERNACLES

Ex. 23:16b and the **Feast of Ingathering**, which is in the end of the year, when thou hast gathered in thy labours out of the field.

Ex. 34:22b and the **Feast of Ingathering** at the year's end.

Lev. 23:33-38 And יהוה spake unto Moses, saying, 34 Speak unto the children of Israel, saying, **The fifteenth day of this seventh month** shall be the **Feast of Tabernacles** for seven days unto יהוה. 35 **On the first day shall be an holy convocation: ye shall do no servile work therein.** 36 Seven days ye shall offer an offering made by fire unto יהוה: **on the eighth day shall be an holy convocation** unto you; and ye shall offer an offering made by fire unto יהוה: it is a solemn assembly; and **ye shall do no servile work therein** 37 These are the feasts of יהוה, which ye shall proclaim to be holy convocations, to offer an offering made by fire unto יהוה, a burnt offering, and a meat offering, a sacrifice, and drink offerings, every thing upon his day: 38 Beside the Sabbaths of יהוה, and beside your gifts, and beside all your vows, and beside all your freewill offerings, which ye give unto יהוה.

Lev. 23:39-43 Also in the fifteenth day of the seventh month, when ye have gathered in the fruit of the land, ye shall keep a feast unto יהוה seven days: **on the first day shall be a Sabbath, and on the eighth day shall be a Sabbath.** 40 **And ye shall take you on the first day the boughs of goodly trees, branches of palm trees, and the boughs of thick trees, and willows of the brook**; and **ye shall rejoice before** יהוה **your God seven days.** 41 And ye shall keep it a feast unto יהוה seven days in the year. **It shall be a statute forever in your generations:** ye shall celebrate it in the seventh month. 42 Ye shall **dwell in booths seven days;** all that are Israelites born shall dwell in booths: 43 That your generations may know that I made the children of Israel to dwell in booths, when I brought them out of the land of Egypt: I am יהוה your God.

Num. 29:12 And on the fifteenth day of the seventh month ye shall have an **holy convocation**; ye shall do **no servile work**, and ye shall keep a feast unto יהוה **seven days**:

Deut. 16:13-15 Thou shalt observe **the Feast of Tabernacles seven days,** after that thou hast gathered in thy corn *[grain]* and thy wine: 14 And thou shalt **rejoice** in thy feast, thou, and thy son, and thy daughter, and thy manservant, and thy maidservant, and the Levite, the stranger, and the fatherless, and the widow, that are within thy gates. 15 Seven days shalt thou keep a **solemn Feast** unto יהוה thy God in the place which יהוה shall choose: because יהוה thy God shall bless thee in all thine increase, and in all the works of thine hands, therefore thou shalt surely **rejoice**. [also in Rejoice, p. 186]

Deut. 31:10-13 And Moses commanded them, saying, At the end of every seven years, in the solemnity of the Year of Release [Shmitah], in the **Feast of Tabernacles** [Sukkot], 11 When all Israel is come to appear before יהוה thy God in the place which He shall choose, thou shalt read this Torah before all Israel in their hearing. 12 Gather the people together, men, and women, and children, and thy stranger that is within thy gates, that they may hear, and that they may learn, and fear יהוה your God, and observe to <u>do all the Words of this Torah</u>: 13 And **that their children,** <u>which have not known any thing, may hear, and learn to fear</u> יהוה <u>your God,</u>.... [also in Keep All, p. 22, Shmitah, p. 156, and in Teach Your Children, p. 194]

AFTER TORAH

DEDICATING THE TEMPLE: 2 Chron. 5:3; 7:1, 8-9 ...Israel assembled themselves unto the king in the **Feast** which was in the **seventh month**. ... 7:1 Now when Solomon had made an end of praying, the fire came down from heaven, and consumed the burnt offering and the sacrifices; and the glory of יהוה filled the house. 8 ...Solomon kept the **Feast seven days**, and all Israel with him.... 9 And in the **eighth day** they made a solemn assembly....

Neh. 8:14-18 And they found written in the Torah which יהוה had commanded by Moses, that the children of Israel should **dwell in booths** in the **Feast of the seventh month**: 15 And that they should publish and proclaim in all their cities, and in Jerusalem, saying, Go forth unto the mount, and fetch olive branches, and pine branches, and myrtle branches, and palm branches, and branches of thick trees, to make **booths**, as it is written. 16 So the people went forth, and brought them, and made themselves booths, every one upon the roof of his house, and in their courts, and in the courts of the house of God, and in the street of the water gate, and in the street of the gate of Ephraim. 17 And all ... that were come again out of the captivity made **booths**, and sat under the **booths**: for since the days of Jeshua the son of Nun unto that day had not the children of Israel done so. And there was very great gladness. 18 Also **day by day, from the first day unto the last day, he read in the book of the Torah of God.** And they kept the **Feast seven days;** and on the **eighth day** was a solemn assembly.... [verse 18 also in Shmitah, Read Torah to all, p. 157]

Ezra 3:4 They kept also the **Feast of Tabernacles**, as it is written, and offered the daily burnt offerings by number, according to the custom, as the duty of every day required;

Neh. 9:1 Now in the twenty and fourth day of this month [two days after Sukkot] the children of Israel were assembled with fasting, and with sackclothes, and earth upon them.

Zech. 14:16-19 And it shall come to pass, that every one that is left of all the nations which came against Jerusalem shall even go up from year to year to worship the King, יהוה of hosts, and to keep the **Feast of Tabernacles**. 17 And it shall be, that whoso will not come up..., even upon them shall be no rain. 18 And ... there shall be the plague, wherewith יהוה will smite the heathen that come not up to keep the **Feast of Tabernacles**. 19 This shall be the punishment ... of all nations that come not up to keep the **Feast of Tabernacles**.

SUKKOT LAST DAY/GREAT DAY/HOSHIANA RABBAH

By Yeshua's time, the last day of Sukkot had come to be known as the Great Day and Hoshiana Rabbah (Great Hosanna) because of the culmination of the daily festive Water Drawing Ceremony. According to the Talmud, Sukkah 51a, it was a huge, joyous, seven day celebration. "One who did not see the Celebration of the Place of the Drawing of the Water never saw celebration in his days. ... There were golden candelabra atop poles there in the courtyard. ... And the light from the candelabra was so bright that there was not a courtyard in Jerusalem that was not illuminated from the light of the Place of the Drawing of the Water." Men would dance with flaming torches, Levite musicians would sing the fifteen Psalms of Ascent (120-134). "Two priests stood at the Upper Gate." They blew their trumpets "when the rooster crowed at dawn, ... when they who would draw the water reached the tenth stair ... to indicate that the time to draw water from the Siloam pool had arrived, [and] when they reached the Women's Courtyard with the basins of water in their hands...." On the eighth day, the priests led a procession with the water seven times around the altar before the water was poured out. They thanked ADONAI for the rain of the past year and prayed for rain for the next year. They sang Isaiah 12:2-3 and sang Hoshiana (Hosanna) (save now) (Psalm 18:25). They also asked the Lord when Ezekiel 47 would be fulfilled. Yeshua interrupted this beautiful ceremony to declare and reveal Himself (John 7:37 below).

Isaiah 12:2-3 Behold, God is ישועתי (yeshuati - my salvation); I will trust, and not be afraid: for יה יהוה is my strength and my song; He also is become my ישועה (yeshuah-salvation). Therefore with joy shall ye draw water out of the wells of ישועה (salvation). (Yes, they were singing "wells of Yeshuah"!!)

Psalm 18:25 O יהוה: save now (Hoshia na), I beseech thee, O יהוה, I beseech thee, send now prosperity.

YESHUA ישוע

John 7:2, 10, 14 Now the Jews' **Feast of Tabernacles** was at hand. ... 10 But when his brethren were gone up, then went He also up unto the Feast, not openly, but as it were in secret. ... 14 Now about the midst of the Feast ישוע went up into the Temple, and taught.

John 7:37-40 In the last day, that **great day of the Feast**, ישוע stood and cried, saying, If any man thirst, let him come unto Me, and drink. 38 He that believeth on Me, as the Scripture hath said, out of his belly shall flow rivers of living water. 39 (But this spake He of the Spirit, which they that believe on Him should receive: for the Holy Spirit was not yet given; because that ישוע was not yet glorified.) 40 Many of the people therefore, when they heard this saying, said, Of a truth this is the Prophet.

Matt. 17:4 Then answered Peter, and said unto ישוע, Lord, it is good for us to be here: if thou wilt, let us make here three **tabernacles**; one for thee, and one for Moses, and one for Elias.

John 12:13 [They] took branches of palm trees, and went forth to meet Him, and cried, Hosanna (Hoshiana): Blessed is the King of Israel that cometh in the Name of יהוה. [Mark 11:8 ...and others cut down branches off the trees, and strawed them in the way.] *[Why on Passover? Some say they were welcoming Him as king, which was normally done on Sukkot. But also ישוע is יהוה Himself come to <u>tabernacle</u> with man.]*

APOSTLES

Rev. 7:9-10 After this I beheld, and, lo, a great multitude, which no man could number, of all nations, and kindreds, and people, and tongues, stood before the throne, and before the Lamb, clothed with white robes, and palms *[branches]* in their hands; 10 And cried with a loud voice, saying, Salvation to our God which sitteth upon the throne, and unto the Lamb.

123. YOVEL/JUBILEE

(The KJV spells it Jubile which with the "J" then being pronounced like a "Y", it was closer to the Hebrew which is pronounced Yo-vel. Even so "Jubilee" does have a very nice ring to it.)

(For Sabbatical year, see Shmitah Year, pages 153-154.)

Lev. 25-27 *whole chapters. Following are portions.* Lev. 25:8-10a And thou shalt **number seven Sabbaths of years** unto thee, **seven times seven years;** and the space of the seven Sabbaths of years shall be unto thee **forty and nine years.** 9 Then shalt thou cause **the trumpet of the Jubile to sound on the tenth day of the seventh month, in the <u>Day of Atonement</u>** shall ye make the trumpet sound throughout all your land. 10 **And ye shall hallow the fiftieth year, and proclaim liberty throughout all the land unto all the inhabitants thereof: it shall be a Jubile unto you;**

NO PLANTING OR HARVESTING: Lev. 25:11-12 A **Jubile** shall that fiftieth year be unto you: ye shall not sow, neither reap that which groweth of itself in it, nor gather the grapes in it of thy vine undressed. 12 For it is the **Jubile**; it shall be holy unto you: ye shall eat the increase thereof out of the field.

SIXTH YEAR BOUNTY: Lev. 25:20-22 And if ye shall say, What shall we eat the **seventh year**? behold, we shall not sow, nor gather in our increase: 21 Then I will command My blessing upon you in the sixth year, and it shall bring forth fruit for three years. 22 And ye shall sow the eighth year, and eat yet of old fruit until the ninth year; until her fruits come in ye shall eat of the old store.

RETURN ALL PROPERTY TO ORIGINAL OWNERS: Lev. 25:10b, 13-16, 23-24 ...and ye shall return every man unto his possession, and ye shall return every man unto his family. ... 13 In the year of this **Jubile** ye shall return every man unto his possession. 14 And if thou sell ought unto thy neighbour, or buyest ought of thy neighbour's hand, y**e shall not oppress one another:** 15 According to the number of years after the **Jubile** thou shalt buy of thy neighbour, and according unto the number of years of the fruits he shall sell unto thee: 16 According to the multitude of years thou shalt increase the price thereof, and according to the fewness of years thou shalt diminish the price of it: for according to the number of the years of the fruits doth he sell unto thee. 17 Ye shall not therefore oppress one another ... 23 **The land shall not be sold forever**: for the land is mine; for ye are strangers and sojourners with me. 24 And in all the land of your possession ye shall grant a redemption for the land.

RETURN POSSESSIONS: Lev. 25:25-28 If thy brother be waxen poor, and hath sold away *some* of his possession, and if any of his kin come to redeem it, then shall he redeem that which his brother sold. 26 And if the man have none to redeem it, and himself be able to redeem it; 27 Then let him count the years of the sale thereof, and restore the overplus unto the man to whom he sold it; that he may return unto his possession. 28 **But if he be not able to restore it** to him, then that which is sold shall remain in the hand of him that hath bought it until the year of **Jubile**: and in the **Jubile** it shall go out, and he shall return unto his possession.

DO NOT RETURN CITY HOUSES: Lev. 25:29-30 And if a man sell a dwelling house in a walled city, then he may redeem it within a whole year after it is sold; within a full year may he redeem it. 30 And if it be not redeemed within the space of a full year, then the house that is in the walled city shall be **established forever** to him that bought it **throughout his generations**: it shall not go out in the **Jubile**.

RETURN VILLAGE HOUSES: Lev. 25:31-34 But the houses of the villages which have no wall round about them shall be counted as the fields of the country: they may be redeemed, and they shall go out in the **Jubile**. 32 Notwithstanding the cities of the Levites, and the houses of the cities of their possession, may the Levites redeem at any time. 33 And if a man purchase of the Levites, then the house that was sold, and the city of his possession, shall go out in the year of **Jubile**: for the houses of the cities of the Levites are their possession among the children of Israel. 34 But the field of the suburbs of their cities may not be sold; for it is their **perpetual possession**. [also in Rules for Priests and Levites, p. 223]

SET HEBREW SLAVES FREE: Lev. 25:39-50,55 And if thy brother that dwelleth by thee be waxen poor, and be sold unto thee; thou shalt not compel him to serve as a bondservant: 40 But as an hired servant, and as a sojourner, he shall be with thee, and shall serve thee unto the year of **Jubile**: 41 And then shall he depart from thee, both he and his children with him, and shall return unto his own family, and unto the possession of his fathers shall he return. ... 47 And if a sojourner or stranger wax rich by thee, and thy brother that dwelleth by him wax poor, and sell himself unto the stranger or sojourner by thee, or to the stock of the stranger's family: ... 49 ... any that is nigh of kin unto him of his family may redeem him; or if he be able, he may redeem himself. 50 And he shall reckon with him that bought him from the year that he was sold to him unto the year of **Jubile**: ... 54 And if he be not redeemed in these years, then he shall go out in the year of **Jubile**, both he, and his children with him. 55 For unto me the children of Israel are servants; they are my servants whom I brought forth out of the land of Egypt: I am יהוה your God.

RETURN FIELDS DEDICATED TO THE LORD: Lev. 27:16-24 And if a man shall sanctify unto יהוה some part of a field of his possession, then thy estimation shall be according to the seed thereof: an homer of barley seed shall be valued at fifty shekels of silver. 17 If he sanctify his field from the year of **Jubile**, according to thy estimation it shall stand. 18 But if he sanctify his field after the **Jubile**, then the priest shall reckon unto him the money according to the years that remain, even unto the year of the **Jubile**, ... 24 In the year of the **Jubile** the field shall return unto him of whom it was bought, even to him to whom the possession of the land did belong. [also in Dedicating things to יהוה]

AFTER TORAH

Isaiah 61:1-2 The Spirit of Adonia יהוה is upon me; because יהוה hath anointed me to preach good tidings unto the meek; He hath sent me to bind up the brokenhearted, to proclaim liberty to the captives, and the opening of the prison to them that are bound; 2 To proclaim **the acceptable year of** יהוה, and the day of vengeance of our God; to comfort all that mourn;

YESHUA ישוע

Luke 4:16-21 And He came to Nazareth, where He had been brought up: and, as His custom was, He went into the synagogue on the Sabbath day, and stood up for to read. 17 And there was delivered unto Him the book of the prophet Esaias [Isaiah]. And when He had opened the book, He found the place where it was written, 18 *The Spirit of the Lord is upon me, because He hath anointed me to preach the Gospel to the poor; He hath sent me to heal the brokenhearted, to preach deliverance to the captives, and recovering of sight to the blind, to set at liberty them that are bruised,* 19 ***To preach the acceptable year of*** יהוה [NIV: year of the LORD's favor]. 20 And He closed the book, and He gave it again to the minister, and sat down. And the eyes of all them that were in the synagogue were fastened on Him. 21 And He began to say unto them, This day is this Scripture fulfilled in your ears.

124. REJOICE!!!

SUKKOT: Lev. 23:40 And ye shall take you on the first day the boughs of goodly trees, branches of palm trees, and the boughs of thick trees, and willows of the brook; and ye shall **rejoice** before יהוה your God seven days.

IN THE PLACE HE CHOOSES [THE TEMPLE] ANYTIME: Deut. 12:7, 11-12, 18 And there ye shall eat [in the Temple] before יהוה your God, and ye shall **rejoice** in all that ye put your hand unto, ye and your households, wherein יהוה thy God hath blessed thee. ... 11 Then there shall be a place which יהוה your God shall choose to cause His Name to dwell there; thither shall ye bring all that I command you; your burnt offerings, and your sacrifices, your tithes, and the heave offering of your hand, and all your choice vows which ye vow unto יהוה: 12 And ye shall **rejoice** before יהוה your God, ye, and your sons, and your daughters, and your menservants, and your maidservants, and the Levite that is within your gates; forasmuch as he hath no part nor inheritance with you. ... 18 But thou must eat them before יהוה thy God in the place which יהוה thy God shall choose, thou, and thy son, and thy daughter, and thy manservant, and thy maidservant, and the Levite that *is* within thy gates: and thou shalt **rejoice** before יהוה thy God in all that thou puttest thine hands unto. [also in Place He shall choose, p. 154]

Deut. 14:23-26 And thou shalt eat before יהוה thy God, in the place which He shall choose to place His Name there, the tithe of thy corn, of thy wine, and of thine oil, and the firstlings of thy herds and of thy flocks; ... 24 And if the way be too long for thee, so that thou art not able to carry it; or if the place be too far from thee, which יהוה thy God shall choose to set His Name there, ... 25 Then shalt thou turn it into money, and bind up the money in thine hand, and shalt go unto the place which יהוה thy God shall choose: 26 And thou shalt bestow that money for whatsoever thy soul lusteth after, for oxen, or for sheep, or for wine, or for strong drink, or for whatsoever thy soul desireth: and thou shalt eat there before יהוה thy God, and thou shalt **rejoice**, thou, and thine household. [also in Tithe, p. 196]

SHAVUOT: Deut. 16:11 And thou shalt **rejoice** before יהוה thy God, thou, and thy son, and thy daughter, and thy manservant, and thy maidservant, and the Levite that is within thy gates, and the stranger, and the fatherless, and the widow, that are among you, in the place which יהוה thy God hath chosen to place His Name there. [also in Widows and Orphans, p. 88]

SUKKOT: Deut. 16:14-15 And thou shalt **rejoice** in thy feast, thou, and thy son, and thy daughter, and thy manservant, and thy maidservant, and the Levite, the stranger, and the fatherless, and the widow, that are within thy gates. 15 Seven days shalt thou keep a solemn feast unto יהוה thy God in the place which יהוה shall choose: because יהוה thy God shall bless thee in all thine increase, and in all the works of thine hands, therefore thou shalt surely **rejoice**. [verse 14 also in Widows and Orphans, p. 88]

BRINGING FIRSTFRUITS TO THE TEMPLE: Deut. 26:10-11 And now, behold, I have brought the firstfruits of the land, which thou, O יהוה, hast given me. And thou shalt set it before יהוה thy God, and worship before יהוה thy God: 11 And thou shalt **rejoice** in every good thing which יהוה thy God hath given unto thee, and unto thine house, thou, and the Levite, and the stranger that is among you. [also in Feast of Firstfruits, p. 168]

CROSSING JORDAN: Deut. 27:7 And thou shalt offer peace offerings, and shalt eat there, and **rejoice** before יהוה thy God. [also in peace offering, p. 70]

ALL TIMES: Deut. 28:47 Because thou servedst not יהוה thy God with **joyfulness**, and with **gladness** of heart, for the abundance of all things; 48 Therefore shalt thou serve thine enemies which יהוה shall send against thee, in hunger, and in thirst, and in nakedness, and in want of all things: ... [also in Obey, p. 26]

END TIMES: Deut. 32:43 **Rejoice**, O ye nations, *with* His people: for He will avenge the blood of his servants, and will render vengeance to His adversaries, and will be merciful unto His land, *and* to His people.

YESHUA ישוע

John 15:11 These things have I spoken unto you, that My **joy** might remain in you, and that your **joy** might be full.

John 16:22 And ye now therefore have sorrow: but I will see you again, and your heart shall **rejoice**, and your **joy** no man taketh from you.

John 16:24 Hitherto have ye asked nothing in My Name: ask, and ye shall receive, that your **joy** may be full.

APOSTLES

Rom. 5:2 By whom also we have access by faith into this grace wherein we stand, and **rejoice** in hope of the glory of God.

Phil. 3:1 Finally, my brethren, **rejoice** in the Lord.

Phil.3:3 For we are the circumcision, which worship God in the spirit, and **rejoice** in Messiah ישוע, and have no confidence in the flesh.

Phil. 4:4 **Rejoice** in the Lord always: and again I say, **Rejoice**.

I Thess. 5:16 **Rejoice** evermore.

I Pet. 1:8 Whom having not seen, ye love; in whom, though now ye see Him not, yet believing, ye **rejoice** with **joy unspeakable** and full of glory:

125. EAT BEFORE יהוה YOUR GOD

[It appears as though יהוה wants to party with us!!!]

Deut. 12:7 And there ye shall eat [*in the Temple*] before יהוה your God, and ye shall rejoice in all that ye put your hand unto, ye and your households, wherein יהוה thy God hath blessed thee. [also in Place He shall choose, p. 154, and Rejoice, p. 186]

Deut. 12:18 But thou must eat them before יהוה thy God in the place which יהוה thy God shall choose, thou, and thy son, and thy daughter, and thy manservant, and thy maidservant, and the Levite that *is* within thy gates: and thou shalt rejoice before יהוה thy God in all that thou puttest thine hands unto. [also in Rejoice, p. 186]

Deut. 14:23 And thou shalt eat before יהוה thy God, in the place which He shall choose to place His Name there, the tithe of thy corn, of thy wine, and of thine oil, and the firstlings of thy herds and of thy flocks; that thou mayest learn to fear יהוה thy God always.

Deut. 14:26 And thou shalt bestow that money for whatsoever thy soul lusteth after, for oxen, or for sheep, or for wine, or for strong drink, or for whatsoever thy soul desireth: and thou shalt eat there before יהוה thy God, and thou shalt eat there before יהוה thy God, and thou shalt rejoice, thou, and thine household. [also in Rejoice, p. 186, and Tithe, p. 196]

Deut. 15:19-20 All the firstling males that come of thy herd and of thy flock thou shalt sanctify unto יהוה thy God: thou shalt do no work with the firstling of thy bullock, nor shear the firstling of thy sheep. Thou shalt eat it before יהוה thy God year by year in the place which יהוה shall choose, thou and thy household. [also in Firstborn animals, p. 134]

Deut. 27:7 [crossing Jordan] And thou shalt offer peace offerings, and shalt eat there, and rejoice before יהוה thy God. [also in Rejoice, p. 187]

APOSTLES

I Cor. 10:31 Whether therefore ye eat, or drink, or whatsoever ye do, do all to the glory of God.

Rev. 3:20-22 Behold, I stand at the door, and knock: if any man hear my voice, and open the door, I will come in to him, and will sup with him, and he with me. 21 To him that overcometh will I grant to sit with me in my throne, even as I also overcame, and am set down with my Father in his throne. 22 He that hath an ear, let him hear what the Spirit saith unto the churches.

126. NAZARITE VOW

*[It is very important to note that this is for a man or a **woman**.]*

Num.6:2b-4 ...When either **man or <u>woman</u>** shall separate themselves to vow a vow of a Nazarite, to separate themselves unto יהוה: 3 **He shall separate himself from wine and strong drink,** and shall drink no vinegar of wine, or vinegar of strong drink, neither shall he drink any liquor of grapes, nor eat moist grapes, or dried. 4 All the days of his separation shall he eat nothing that is made of the vine tree, from the kernels even to the husk.

Num. 6:5 All the days of the vow of his separation there shall **no razor come upon his head**: until the days be fulfilled, in the which he separateth himself unto יהוה, he shall be holy, and shall let the locks of the hair of his head grow.

Num. 6:6-10 All the days that he separateth himself unto יהוה he shall come at no dead body. 7 He shall not make himself unclean for his father, or for his mother, for his brother, or for his sister, when they die: because the consecration of his God is upon his head. 8 All the days of his separation he is holy unto יהוה. 9 And if any man die very suddenly by him, and he hath defiled the head of his consecration; then he shall shave his head in the day of his cleansing, on the seventh day shall he shave it. 10 And on the eighth day he shall bring two turtles, or two young pigeons, to the priest,... 11...for a sin offering, and ...a burnt offering, and make an atonement..., and shall hallow his head that same day. 12 And he shall consecrate unto יהוה the days of his separation, and shall bring a lamb of the first year for a trespass offering: but the days that were before shall be lost, because his separation was defiled.

ENDING THE VOW: Num. 6:13-18-20 ...when the days of his separation are fulfilled: he shall be brought unto the door of the Tabernacle.... 14 And he shall offer ...one he lamb ...for a burnt offering, and one ewe lamb ...for a sin offering, and one ram ...for peace offerings, 15 And a basket of unleavened bread, cakes of fine flour mingled with oil, and wafers of unleavened bread anointed with oil, and ...drink offerings. 16...17...18 And the Nazarite shall shave the head of his separation at the door of the Tabernacle of the congregation, and shall take the hair of the head of his separation, and put it in the fire which is under the sacrifice of the peace offerings. 19 And the priest shall take the sodden shoulder of the ram, and one unleavened cake out of the basket, and one unleavened wafer, and shall put them upon the hands of the Nazarite, after the hair of his separation is shaven: 20 And the priest shall wave them for a wave offering .... and after that the Nazarite may drink wine.

AFTER TORAH

Judges 13:3-5 [about Samson] And the angel of יהוה appeared unto the woman, ...Behold now, thou art barren, and bearest not: but thou shalt conceive, and bear a son. 4 Now therefore beware, I pray thee, and drink not wine nor strong drink, and eat not any unclean thing: 5 For, lo, thou shalt... bear a son; and no razor shall come on his head: for the child shall be a Nazarite unto God from the womb: and he shall begin to deliver Israel out of the hand of the Philistines.

Amos 2:11-16 And I raised up of your sons for prophets, and of your young men for **Nazarites**. Is it not even thus, O ye children of Israel? saith יהוה. 12 But ye gave the **Nazarites** wine to drink; and commanded the prophets, saying, Prophesy not. 13 Behold, I am pressed under

you, as a cart is pressed that is full of sheaves. 14 Therefore the flight shall perish from the swift, and the strong shall not strengthen his force, neither shall the mighty deliver himself: 15 Neither shall he stand that handleth the bow; and he that is swift of foot shall not deliver himself: neither shall he that rideth the horse deliver himself. 16 And he that is courageous among the mighty shall flee away naked in that day, saith יהוה.

Luke 1:13-16 But the angel said unto him, Fear not, Zacharias: for thy prayer is heard; and thy wife Elisabeth shall bear thee a son, and thou shalt call his name John. 14 And thou shalt have joy and gladness; and many shall rejoice at his birth. 15 For he shall be great in the sight of the Lord, and **shall drink neither wine nor strong drink;** and he shall be filled with the Holy Spirit, even from his mother's womb. 16 And many of the children of Israel shall he turn to יהוה their God.

YESHUA ישוע

Matt. 11:18-19 For John came neither eating nor drinking, and they say, He hath a devil. 19 The Son of man came eating and drinking, and they say, Behold a man gluttonous, and a winebibber....

Matt. 26:29 But I say unto you, I will not drink henceforth of this fruit of the vine, until that day when I drink it new with you in My Father's Kingdom.

Mark 14:25 Verily I say unto you, I will drink no more of the fruit of the vine, until that day that I drink it new in the Kingdom of God.

Luke 22:18 For I say unto you, I will not drink of the fruit of the vine, until the Kingdom of God shall come.

APOSTLES

Acts 18:18 And Paul ... then took his leave of the brethren, and sailed thence into Syria, ... having shorn his head in Cenchrea: for he had a vow.

Acts. 21:20-26 (RSV) ..."You see, brother, how many thousands there are among the Jews of those who have believed; they are all zealous for the law [Torah], 21 and they have been told about you that you teach all the Jews who are among the Gentiles to forsake Moses, telling them not to circumcise their children or observe the customs. 22 What then is to be done? They will certainly hear that you have come. 23 Do therefore what we tell you. We have four men who are under a vow; 24 take these men and purify yourself along with them and pay their expenses, so that they may shave their heads. Thus all will know that there is nothing in what they have been told about you but that you yourself live in observance of the law [Torah]...." 26 Then Paul took the men, and the next day he purified himself with them and went into the Temple, to give notice when the days of purification would be fulfilled and the offering presented for every one of them.

127. BEARDS

Lev 19:27 (NRSV) You shall not round off the hair on your temples or mar the edges of your beard.

128. TZIT-TZIT/TASSELS/FRINGES

[This is traditionally believed to be a commandment to men only, possibly because of the commandment that men are not to wear women's clothing and women are not to wear men's (Deut. 22:5).]

Num. 15:38-41 (TLV) Speak to Bnei-Yisrael [sons of Israel]. Say to them that they are to make for themselves tzitzit [tassels/fringes, pronounced *tseet-tseet*] on the corners of their garments **throughout their generations**, and they are to put a blue cord on each tzitzit. 39 It will be your own tzitzit—so whenever you look at them, you will remember all the mitzvot of Adonai and do them and not go spying out after your own hearts and your own eyes, prostituting yourselves. 40 This way you will remember and obey all My mitzvot and you will be holy to your God. 41 I am Adonai your God. I brought you out of the land of Egypt to be your God. I am Adonai your God."

Deut. 22:12 Thou shalt make thee fringes upon the four quarters of thy vesture, wherewith thou coverest thyself.

YESHUA ישוע

Matt. 9:20-22 And, behold, a woman, which was diseased with an issue of blood twelve years, came behind him, and touched the hem [tzit-tzit] of his garment: 21 For she said within herself, If I may but touch his garment, I shall be whole. 22 But ישוע turned him about, and when he saw her, he said, Daughter, be of good comfort; thy faith hath made thee whole. And the woman was made whole from that hour.

Matt. 23:5 But all their works they do for to be seen of men: they make broad their phylacteries, and **enlarge the borders of their garments**....

129. BIND THEM AS A SIGN

[Again, traditionally believed to be a commandment to men only.]

Ex. 13:9,16 And it shall be for a sign unto thee upon thine hand, and for a memorial between thine eyes, that יהוה's law may be in thy mouth: for with a strong hand hath יהוה brought thee out of Egypt. ... 16 And it shall be for a token upon thine hand, and for frontlets between thine eyes: for by strength of hand יהוה brought us forth out of Egypt.

Deut. 6:8 And thou shalt bind them for a sign upon thine hand, and they shall be as frontlets between thine eyes.

Deut. 11:18 Therefore shall ye lay up these my words in your heart and in your soul, and bind them for a sign upon your hand, that they may be as frontlets between your eyes.

YESHUA ישוע

Matt. 23:5 But all their works they do for to be seen of men: **they make broad their phylacteries,** and enlarge the borders of their garments....

130. CIRCUMCISION

BEFORE TORAH

Gen. 17:1-4, 10-14 And when Abram was ninety years old and nine, יהוה appeared to Abram, and said unto him, I am the Almighty God; walk before me, and be thou perfect. 2 And I will make My Covenant between Me and thee, and will multiply thee exceedingly. 3 And Abram fell on his face: and God talked with him, saying, ... 10 This is My Covenant, which ye shall keep, between Me and you and thy seed after thee; Every man child among you shall be circumcised. 11 And ye shall circumcise the flesh of your foreskin; and **it shall be a token [sign] of the covenant betwixt me and you.** 12 And he that is **eight days old** shall be circumcised among you, every man child in your generations, ... 13 He that is born in thy house, and he that is bought with thy money, must needs be circumcised: and My Covenant shall be in your flesh for an **everlasting** Covenant. 14 And the uncircumcised man child whose flesh of his foreskin is not circumcised, that soul shall be cut off from his people; he hath broken My Covenant.

TORAH

Exodus 12:44, 48 But every man's servant that is bought for money, when thou hast circumcised him, then shall he eat thereof [the Passover lamb]. ... 48 And when a stranger shall sojourn with thee, and will keep the Passover to יהוה, let all his males be circumcised, and then let him come near and keep it; **and he shall be as one that is born in the land**: for no uncircumcised person shall eat thereof. [also in Passover, p. 161 and verse 44 in Slaves, p. 71]

Lev. 12:2-3 If a woman have conceived seed, and born a man child: ... 3 And in the eighth day the flesh of his foreskin shall be circumcised.

Deut. 10:16 **Circumcise therefore the foreskin of your heart**, and be no more stiffnecked.

Deut. 30:6 And יהוה thy God will **circumcise thine heart,** and the heart of thy seed, to love יהוה thy God.... [See more in Circumcise Your Heart, p. 235.]

AFTER TORAH

Joshua 5:2-3, 5 At that time יהוה said unto Joshua, Make thee sharp knives, and circumcise again the children of Israel the second time. 3 And Joshua made him sharp knives, and circumcised the children of Israel at the hill of the foreskins. ... 5 Now all the people that came out were circumcised: but all the people that were born in the wilderness ... had not circumcised.

Jer.4:4 Circumcise yourselves to יהוה, and **take away the foreskins of your heart**, ye men of Judah and inhabitants of Jerusalem: lest my fury come forth like fire, and burn that none can quench it, because of the evil of your doings.

YESHUA

Luke 2:21 And when eight days were accomplished for the circumcising of the child, His Name was called ישוע,

Acts 15:23-24, 28-29 ...unto the brethren which are of the Gentiles 24 Forasmuch as we have heard, that certain which went out from us have troubled you with words, subverting your souls, saying, Ye must be circumcised, and keep the Torah: ... 28 For it seemed good to the Holy Spirit, and to us, to lay upon you no greater burden than these necessary things; 29 That ye abstain from meats offered to idols, and from blood, and from things strangled, and from fornication: from which if ye keep yourselves, ye shall do well.

Rom. 2:28-29 For he is not a Jew, which is one outwardly; neither is that circumcision, which is outward in the flesh: 29 But he is a Jew, which is one inwardly; and **circumcision is that of the heart, in the spirit,** and not in the letter; whose praise is not of men, but of God.

Rom. 3:29-30 Is he the God of the Jews only? is he not also of the Gentiles? Yes, of the Gentiles also: 30 Seeing it is one God, which shall justify the circumcision by faith, and uncircumcision through faith.

I Cor. 7:17-19 ...as the Lord hath called every one, so let him walk. ... 18 Is any man called being circumcised? let him not become uncircumcised. Is any called in uncircumcision? let him not be circumcised. 19 Circumcision is nothing, and uncircumcision is nothing, but the keeping of the commandments of God. *[Interesting because circumcision* **is** *a command of God, but it was determined by the Jewish leaders in Acts 15 (above) that it was only mandatory to Jewish people.]*

Gal. 5:2-4, 6 ...if ye be circumcised, Messiah shall profit you nothing. 3 For I testify again to every man that is circumcised, that he is a debtor to do the whole Torah. 4 Messiah is become of no effect unto you, **whosoever of you are justified by the law; ye are fallen from grace**. ... 6 For in ישוע Messiah neither circumcision availeth any thing, nor uncircumcision; **but faith which worketh by love.**

Gal. 6:12-15 ...they constrain you to be circumcised; only lest they should suffer persecution for the cross of Messiah. 13 For neither they themselves who are circumcised keep the Torah; but desire to have you circumcised, that they may glory in your flesh. 14 But God forbid that I should glory, save in the cross of our Lord ישוע Messiah.... 15 For in Messiah ישוע neither circumcision availeth any thing, nor uncircumcision, **but a new creature.**

Col. 2:11-13 In whom also ye are circumcised with the **circumcision made without hands,** in putting off the body of the sins of the flesh by the **circumcision of Messiah:** 12 Buried with him in baptism ... 13 And you, being dead in your sins and the **uncircumcision of your flesh,** hath he quickened together with him, having forgiven you all trespasses;

Phil. 3:2b-8 (RSV) ...look out for those who mutilate the flesh. 3 For we are the true circumcision, who worship God in spirit, and glory in Messiah Jesus, and put no confidence in the flesh. 4 ... If any other man thinks he has reason for confidence in the flesh, I have more: 5 circumcised on the eighth day, ... a Hebrew born of Hebrews; as to the law a Pharisee, 6 ... as to righteousness under the law [Torah] blameless. 7 But whatever gain I had, I counted as loss for the ... 8 ...surpassing worth of knowing Christ Jesus my Lord.

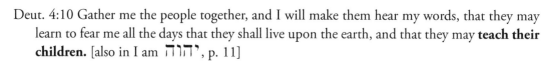

131. TEACH TO YOUR CHILDREN

Deut. 4:10 Gather me the people together, and I will make them hear my words, that they may learn to fear me all the days that they shall live upon the earth, and that they may **teach their children.** [also in I am יהוה, p. 11]

Deut. 6:6-7 And these words, which I command thee this day, shall be in thine heart: 7 And thou shalt **teach them diligently unto thy children,** and shalt talk of them when thou sittest in thine house, and when thou walkest by the way, and when thou liest down, and when thou risest up.

Deut. 6:20-25 And when thy son asketh thee in time to come, saying, What mean the testimonies, and the statutes, and the judgments, which יהוה our God hath commanded you? Then thou shalt say unto thy son, We were Pharaoh's bondmen in Egypt; and יהוה brought us out of Egypt with a mighty hand: And יהוה shewed signs and wonders ... And יהוה commanded us to do all these statutes, to fear יהוה our God, for our good always, that he might preserve us alive, as it is at this day.

Deut. 11:19 And ye shall **teach them** *[to]* **your children,** speaking of them when thou sittest in thine house, and when thou walkest by the way, when thou liest down, and when thou risest up.

Deut. 31:10-13 And Moses commanded them, saying, At the end of every seven years, in the solemnity of the year of release, in the Feast of Tabernacles [Sukkot], 11 When all Israel is come to appear before יהוה thy God in the place which He shall choose, thou shalt read this Torah before all Israel in their hearing. 12 Gather the people together, men, and women, **and children**, and thy stranger that is within thy gates, that they may hear, and that they may learn, and fear יהוה your God, and observe to <u>do all the Words of this Torah</u>: 13 And **that their children,** <u>which have not known any thing, may hear, and learn to fear</u> יהוה <u>your God</u>, as long as ye live in the land whither ye go over Jordan to possess it. [also in Keep All, p. 22, Shmitah, p. 156, and in Sukkot, p. 180]

Deut. 32:45-47 And Moses made an end of speaking all these Words to all Israel: 46 And He said unto them, Set your hearts unto <u>all the Words </u>which I testify among you this day, which <u>ye shall command</u> **your children** <u>to observe to do</u>, <u>all the Words of this Torah</u>. 47 For it is not a vain thing for you; because it is your life: and through this thing ye shall prolong your days in the land, whither ye go over Jordan to possess it. [also in Keep All, p. 22]

Ex. 12:26-27 And it shall come to pass, when **your children** shall say unto you, What mean ye by this service? 27 That ye shall say, It is the sacrifice of יהוה's Passover, who passed over the houses of the children of Israel in Egypt, when he smote the Egyptians, and delivered our houses.

Matt.18:2-6 And יֵשׁוּעַ called a little child unto him, and set him in the midst of them, 3 And said, Verily I say unto you, Except ye be converted, and become as little children, ye shall not enter into the kingdom of heaven. 4 Whosoever therefore shall humble himself as this little child, the same is greatest in the kingdom of heaven. 5 And whoso shall receive one such little child in My Name receiveth me. 6 But whoso shall offend one of these little ones which believe in me, it were better for him that a millstone were hanged about his neck, and that he were drowned in the depth of the sea.

APOSTLES

Eph. 6:4 And, ye fathers *[mothers, too],* provoke not your children to wrath: but bring them up in the nurture and admonition of the Lord.

I Tim. 3:2, 4-5 A bishop then must be ... 4 One that ruleth well his own house, having his children in subjection with all gravity; 5 (For if a man know not how to rule his own house, how shall he take care of the church of God?)

Titus 2:4 That they may teach the young women to be sober, to love their husbands, to love their children,

132. WRITE THE COMMANDMENTS ON YOUR HOUSE

Deut. 6:9 And thou shalt write them [*the commandments*] upon the posts of thy house, and on thy gates.

133. REBELLIOUS CHILD

Deut. 21:18-21 If a man have a stubborn and rebellious son, which will not obey the voice of his father, or the voice of his mother, and that, when they have chastened him, will not hearken unto them: 19 Then shall his father and his mother lay hold on him, and bring him out unto the elders of his city, and unto the gate of his place; 20 And they shall say unto the elders of his city, This our son is stubborn and rebellious, he will not obey our voice; he is a glutton, and a drunkard. 21 And all the men of his city shall stone him with stones, that he die: so shalt thou put evil away from among you; and all Israel shall hear, and fear.

YESHUA יֵשׁוּעַ

Matt. 11:18-19 For John came neither eating nor drinking, and they say, He hath a devil. 19 The Son of man came eating and drinking, and they say, Behold a man gluttonous, and a winebibber.... [also in Nazarite Vow, p. 190]

Lev. 27:30-34 And all the **tithe of the land**, whether of the seed of the land, or of the fruit of the tree, is יהוה's: it is holy unto יהוה. 31 And if a man will at all redeem ought of his tithes, he shall add thereto the fifth part thereof. 32 And concerning the **tithe of the herd**, or of the flock, even of whatsoever passeth under the rod, **the tenth shall be holy** unto יהוה. 33 He shall not search whether it be good or bad, neither shall he change it: and if he change it at all, then both it and the change thereof shall be holy; it shall not be redeemed.

Lev. 27:11-13 And if it be any unclean beast, of which they do not offer a sacrifice unto יהוה, then he shall present the beast before the priest: 12 And the priest shall value it, whether it be good or bad: as thou valuest it, who art the priest, so shall it be. 13 But if he will at all redeem it, then he shall add a fifth part thereof unto thy estimation.

Num. 15:20 Ye shall offer up a cake of **the first of your dough** for an heave offering: as ye do the heave offering of the threshingfloor, so shall ye heave it.

Num. 18:26 Thus speak unto the **Levites,** and say unto them, When ye take of the children of Israel **the tithes** which I have given you from them for your inheritance, then ye shall offer up an heave offering of it for יהוה, *even* **a tenth part of the tithe**. [also in Priests, p. 223]

Deut. 12:17 **Thou mayest not eat within thy gates the tithe** of thy corn, or of thy wine, or of thy oil, or the firstlings of thy herds or of thy flock, nor any of thy vows....

Deut. 14:22 Thou shalt truly **tithe all the increase** of thy seed, that the field bringeth forth year by year.

Deut. 14:23 And **thou shalt eat before** יהוה **thy God, in the place which He shall choose** to place His Name there, **the tithe** of thy corn, of thy wine, and of thine oil, and the firstlings of thy herds and of thy flocks; that thou mayest learn to fear יהוה thy God always.

Deut. 14:24-26 And if the way be too long for thee, so that thou art not able to carry it; or if the place be too far from thee, which יהוה thy God shall choose to set His Name there, when יהוה thy God hath blessed thee: 25 Then shalt thou turn it into money, and bind up the money in thine hand, and shalt go unto the place which יהוה thy God shall choose: 26 And thou shalt bestow that money for whatsoever thy soul lusteth after, for oxen, or for sheep, or for wine, or for strong drink, or for whatsoever thy soul desireth: and thou shalt eat there before יהוה thy God, and thou shalt rejoice, thou, and thine household.

Deut. 14:28-29 At the end of three years thou shalt **bring forth all the tithe of thine increase** the same year, and shalt lay it up within thy gates: 29 And the Levite, (because he hath no part nor inheritance with thee,) and the stranger, and the fatherless, and the widow, which are within thy gates, shall come, and shall eat and be satisfied; that יהוה thy God may bless thee in all the work of thine hand which thou doest. [also in Orphans, p. 88]

Deut. 26:12-15 When thou hast made an end of **tithing all the tithes of thine increase** the **third year, which is the year of tithing,** and hast given it unto the Levite, the stranger, the fatherless, and the widow, that they may eat within thy gates, and be filled; 13 Then thou shalt say before יהוה thy God, I have brought away the hallowed things out of mine house, and also have given them unto the Levite, and unto the stranger, to the fatherless, and to the widow, according to all Thy commandments which Thou hast commanded me: I have not transgressed Thy commandments, neither have I forgotten them: 14 I have not eaten thereof in my mourning, neither have I taken away ought thereof for any unclean use, nor given ought thereof for the dead: but I have hearkened to the voice of יהוה my God, and have done according to all that Thou hast commanded me. 15 Look down from Thy holy habitation, from heaven, and bless Thy people Israel, and the land which Thou hast given us.... [also in Poor, p. 99]

AFTER TORAH

Mal. 3:8-12 Will a man rob God? Yet ye have robbed me. But ye say, Wherein have we robbed thee? In tithes and offerings. 9 Ye are cursed with a curse: for ye have robbed Me, even this whole nation. 10 Bring ye all the tithes into the storehouse, that there may be meat in mine house, and prove Me now herewith, saith יהוה of hosts, if I will not open you the windows of heaven, and pour you out a blessing, that there shall not be room enough to receive it. 11 And I will rebuke the devourer for your sakes, and he shall not destroy the fruits of your ground; neither shall your vine cast her fruit before the time in the field, saith יהוה of hosts. 12 And all nations shall call you blessed: for ye shall be a delightsome land, saith יהוה of hosts.

YESHUA ישוע

Luke 21:1-4 [also in Mark12:41-44] And He looked up, and saw the rich men casting their gifts into the treasury. 2 And he saw also a certain poor widow casting in thither two mites. 3 And He said, Of a truth I say unto you, that this poor widow hath cast in more than they all: 4 For all these have of their abundance cast in unto the offerings of God: but she of her penury hath cast in all the living that she had.

Matt. 22:15-22 [also in Mark 12:13-18] Then went the Pharisees, and took counsel how they might entangle Him in His talk. 16 And they sent out unto Him their disciples with the Herodians, saying, Master, we know that Thou art true, and teachest the way of God in truth, neither carest Thou for any man: for Thou regardest not the person of men. 17 Tell us therefore, What thinkest Thou? Is it lawful to give tribute unto Caesar, or not? 18 But ישוע perceived their wickedness, and said, Why tempt ye Me, ye hypocrites? 19 Shew Me the tribute money. And they brought unto Him a penny. 20 And He saith unto them, Whose is this image and superscription? 21 They say unto Him, Caesar's. Then saith He unto them, **Render therefore unto Caesar the things which are Caesar's; and unto God the things that are God's**. 22 When they had heard these words, they marvelled, and left Him, and went their way.

135. TAKE CARE OF LEVITES AND PRIESTS

Deut. 12:19 Take heed to thyself that thou forsake not the Levite as long as thou livest upon the earth.

Deut. 14:27 And the Levite that is within thy gates; thou shalt not forsake him; for he hath no part nor inheritance with thee.

Num. 18:26 Thus speak unto the Levites, ... When ye take of the children of Israel the tithes which I have given you from them for your inheritance.... [also in Tithe, p. 196]

Deut. 18:3 And this shall be the priest's due from the people, from them that offer a sacrifice, whether it be ox or sheep; and they shall give unto the priest the shoulder, and the two cheeks, and the maw [NRSV: stomach]. [also in Priests, p. 221,223]

Deut.18:4 The firstfruit also of thy corn, of thy wine, and of thine oil, and the first of the fleece of thy sheep, shalt thou give him. [also in Priests, p. 223]

Deut. 18:6-8 And if a Levite come from any of thy gates out of all Israel, where he sojourned, and come with all the desire of his mind unto the place which יהוה shall choose; Then he shall minister in the Name of יהוה his God, as all his brethren the Levites do, which stand there before יהוה. They shall have like portions to eat, beside that which cometh of the sale of his patrimony.

Deut. 26:12 When thou hast made an end of tithing **all the tithes** of thine increase the third year, which is the year of tithing, and hast **given it unto the Levite**, the stranger, the fatherless, and the widow, that they may eat within thy gates, and be filled; [also in Tithe, p. 196]

YESHUA ישוע

Matt. 10:7-10 And as ye go, preach, saying, The kingdom of heaven is at hand. 8 Heal the sick, cleanse the lepers, raise the dead, cast out devils: freely ye have received, freely give. 9 Provide neither gold, nor silver, nor brass in your purses, 10 Nor scrip [money] for your journey, neither two coats, neither shoes, nor yet staves: for the workman is worthy of his meat [NKJV: food].

Luke 10:7-9 And in the same house remain, eating and drinking such things as they give: for the labourer is worthy of his hire. Go not from house to house. 8 And into whatsoever city ye enter, and they receive you, eat such things as are set before you: 9 And heal the sick that are therein, and say unto them, The kingdom of God is come nigh unto you.

APOSTLES

I Cor. 9:13-14 Do ye not know that they which minister about holy things live of the things of the Temple? and they which wait at the altar are partakers with the altar? 14 Even so hath יהוה ordained that they which preach the Gospel should live of the Gospel. [also in Wages, p. 97]

I Tim. 5:17-18 Let the elders that rule well be counted worthy of double honour, especially they who labour in the word and doctrine. 18 For the scripture saith, Thou shalt not muzzle the ox that treadeth out the corn. And, The labourer is worthy of his reward.

136. RED HEIFER

THIS IS AMAZING MEDICAL INFECTION CONTROL in 1500 B.C!! This is understanding the spread of disease from a dead body and the existence of germs!! Modern science didn't discover this until the 1900s A.D!!! This cleansing agent was apparently antiseptic—killed germs!

Num. 19:1-3 And יהוה spake unto Moses and unto Aaron, saying, 2 This is the ordinance of the Torah which יהוה hath commanded, saying, Speak unto the children of Israel, that they bring thee a red heifer without spot, wherein is no blemish, and upon which never came yoke: 3 And ye shall give her unto Eleazar the priest, that he may bring her forth without the camp, and one shall slay her before his face:

Num. 19:4 And Eleazar the priest shall take of her blood with his finger, and sprinkle of her blood directly before the Tabernacle of the congregation seven times:

Num. 19:5-8 And one shall burn the heifer in his sight; her skin, and her flesh, and her blood, with her dung, shall he burn: 6 And the priest shall take cedar wood, and hyssop, and scarlet, and cast it into the midst of the burning of the heifer. 7 Then the priest shall wash his clothes, and he shall bathe his flesh in water, and afterward he shall come into the camp, and the priest shall be unclean until the even. 8 And he that burneth her shall wash his clothes in water, and bathe his flesh in water, and shall be unclean until the even.

Num. 19:9-10 And a man that is clean shall gather up the ashes of the heifer, and lay them up without the camp in a clean place, and it shall be kept for the congregation of the children of Israel for a water of separation: it is a purification for sin. 10 And he that gathereth the ashes of the heifer shall wash his clothes, and be unclean until the even: and it shall be unto the children of Israel, and unto the stranger that sojourneth among them, for a **statute forever**.

Num. 19:11-12 **He that toucheth the dead body** of any man shall be unclean seven days. 12 He shall purify himself with it on the third day, and on the seventh day he shall be clean: but if he purify not himself the third day, then the seventh day he shall not be clean. [also in Don't Touch, p. 201]

Num. 19:14-16 This is the law, **when a man dieth in a tent**: all that come into the tent, and all that is in the tent, shall be unclean seven days. 15 And every open vessel, which hath no covering bound upon it, is unclean. 16 And whosoever toucheth one that is slain with a sword in the open fields, or a dead body, or a bone of a man, or a grave, shall be unclean seven days.

Num. 19:17-19 And for an unclean person they shall take of the ashes of the burnt heifer of purification for sin, and **running water** shall be put thereto in a vessel: 18 And a clean person shall take hyssop, and dip it in the water, and **sprinkle it upon the tent, and upon all the**

vessels, and upon the persons that were there, and upon him that touched a bone, or one slain, or one dead, or a grave: 19 And the clean person shall sprinkle upon the unclean on the third day, and on the seventh day: and **on the seventh day he shall purify himself, and wash his clothes, and bathe himself in water, and shall be clean at even.** [also in Don't Touch, p. 201, and Wash, p. 207]

Num. 19:21 And it shall be a **perpetual statute** unto them, that he that sprinkleth the water of separation shall wash his clothes; and he that toucheth the water of separation shall be unclean until even. [also in Don't Touch, p. 201]

APOSTLES

Heb. 9:13-15 For if the blood of bulls and of goats, and **the ashes of an heifer sprinkling the unclean,** sanctifieth to the purifying of the flesh: 14 How much more shall the blood of Messiah, who through the eternal Spirit offered Himself without spot to God, purge your conscience from dead works to serve the living God? 15 And for this cause He is the mediator of the New Covenant, that by means of death, for the redemption of the transgressions that were under the first Covenant, they which are called might receive the promise of eternal inheritance.

137. DON'T TOUCH ANY UNCLEAN THING

THIS IS AMAZING MEDICAL INFECTION CONTROL in 1500 B.C!! This is understanding the spread of disease and the existence of germs (!!) which modern science didn't discover until the 1900s A.D!!!

Lev. 5:2-6 If anyone becomes aware that they are guilty—if they unwittingly touch anything ceremonially unclean (whether the carcass of an unclean animal, wild or domestic, or of any unclean creature that moves along the ground) and they are unaware that they have become unclean, but then they come to realize their guilt; 3 or if they touch human uncleanness (anything that would make them unclean) even though they are unaware of it, but then they learn of it and realize their guilt; ... 5 when anyone becomes aware that they are guilty in any of these matters, they must confess in what way they have sinned. 6 As a penalty for the sin they have committed, they must bring to יהוה a female lamb or goat from the flock as a sin offering; and the priest shall make atonement for them for their sin.

Lev. 10:8-11 יהוה spake unto Aaron saying, 9 Do not drink wine nor strong drink, thou, nor thy sons with thee, when ye go into the Tabernacle of the congregation, lest ye die: it shall be a **statute forever throughout your generations**: 10 And that ye may [distinguish the] **difference between holy and unholy, and between unclean and clean;** 11 And that ye may teach the children of Israel all the statutes which יהוה hath spoken unto them by the hand of Moses.

Num. 5:2-3 Command the children of Israel, that they put out of the camp every leper, and every one that hath an issue, and whosoever is defiled by the dead: 3 Both male and female shall ye put out, without the camp shall ye put them; that they defile not their camps, in the midst whereof I dwell. [also in Bodlily discharge, p. 206, and part in Leprosy, p. 205]

Num. 19:11-12 He that toucheth the dead body of any man shall be unclean seven days. 12 He shall purify himself with it on the third day, and on the seventh day he shall be clean: but if he purify not himself the third day, then the seventh day he shall not be clean. [also in Red Heifer, p. 199]

Num. 19:13 Whosoever toucheth the dead body of any man that is dead, and purifieth not himself, defileth the Tabernacle of יהוה; and that soul shall be cut off from Israel: because the water of separation was not sprinkled upon him, he shall be unclean; his uncleanness is yet upon him.

Num. 19:14-16 This is the law, when a man dieth in a tent: all that come into the tent, and all that is in the tent, shall be unclean seven days. 15 And every open vessel, which hath no covering bound upon it, is unclean. 16 And whosoever toucheth one that is slain with a sword in the open fields, or a dead body, or a bone of a man, or a grave, shall be unclean seven days.

Num. 19:17-19 And for an unclean person they shall take of the ashes of the burnt heifer of purification for sin, and running water shall be put thereto in a vessel: 18 And a clean person shall take hyssop, and dip it in the water, and sprinkle it upon the tent, and upon all the vessels, and upon the persons that were there, and upon him that touched a bone, or one slain, or one dead, or a grave: 19 And the clean person shall sprinkle upon the unclean on the third day, and on the seventh day: and on the seventh day he shall purify himself, and wash his clothes, and bathe himself in water, and shall be clean at even. [also in Red Heifer, p. 199, and Wash, p. 207]

Num. 19:20 But the man that shall be unclean, and shall not purify himself, that soul shall be cut off from among the congregation, because he hath defiled the sanctuary of יהוה: the water of separation hath not been sprinkled upon him; he is unclean.

Num. 19:21 And it shall be a **perpetual statute** unto them, that he that sprinkleth the water of separation shall wash his clothes; and he that toucheth the water of separation shall be unclean until even. [also in Red Heifer, p. 199]

Num. 19:22 And whatsoever the unclean person toucheth shall be unclean; and the soul that toucheth it shall be unclean until even.

Deut. 14:8 And the swine ... is unclean unto you: ye shall not eat of their flesh, **nor touch their dead carcase**.

AFTER TORAH

Isaiah 52:11 Depart ye, depart ye, go ye out from thence, **touch no unclean thing**; go ye out of the midst of her; be ye clean, that bear the vessels of יהוה.

Ezek. 44:23 And they [the priests] shall teach my people the difference between the holy and profane, and cause them to **discern between the unclean and the clean.**

Hag. 2:13 Then said Haggai, If one that is unclean by a dead body touch any of these, shall it be unclean? And the priests answered and said, It shall be unclean.

APOSTLES

2 Cor. 6:14-18 Be ye not unequally yoked together with unbelievers: for what fellowship hath righteousness with unrighteousness? and what communion hath light with darkness? 15 And what concord hath Messiah with Belial? or what part hath he that believeth with an infidel? 16 And what agreement hath the Temple of God with idols? for ye are the Temple of the living God; as God hath said, I will dwell in them, and walk in them; and I will be their God, and they shall be my people. 17 Wherefore come out from among them, and be ye separate, saith the Lord, and **touch not the unclean thing**; and I will receive you, 18 And will be a Father unto you, and ye shall be my sons and daughters, saith the Lord Almighty.

138. WOMAN ON HER MENSTRAL CYCLE

THIS IS AMAZING MEDICAL understanding that blood can carry disease and is a rich source of nutrients which any germs can feed on and quickly multiply.

Lev. 15:19-23   And if a woman have an issue, and her issue in her flesh be blood, she shall be put apart seven days: and whosoever toucheth her shall be unclean until the even. 20 And every thing that she lieth upon in her separation shall be unclean: every thing also that she sitteth upon shall be unclean. 21 And whosoever toucheth her bed shall wash his clothes, and bathe himself in water, and be unclean until the even. 22 And whosoever toucheth any thing that she sat upon shall wash his clothes, and bathe himself in water, and be unclean until the even. 23 And if it be on her bed, or on any thing whereon she sitteth, when he toucheth it, he shall be unclean until the even.

Lev. 15:25-27 And if a woman have an issue of her blood many days out of the time of her separation, or if it run beyond the time of her separation; all the days of the issue of her uncleanness shall be as the days of her separation: she shall be unclean. 26 Every bed whereon she lieth ... and whatsoever she sitteth upon shall be unclean.... 27 And whosoever toucheth those things shall be unclean, and shall wash his clothes, and bathe himself in water, and be unclean until the even.

Lev. 15:28-30 But if she be cleansed of her issue, then she shall number to herself seven days, and after that she shall be clean. 29 And on the eighth day she shall take unto her two turtles, or two young pigeons, and bring them unto the priest, to the door of the Tabernacle of the congregation. 30 And the priest shall offer the one for a sin offering, and the other for a burnt offering; and the priest shall make an atonement for her before יהוה for the issue of her uncleanness.

YESHUA ישוע

*Instead of it making Him defiled and unclean, it made **her** whole and healed:*

Mark 5:25–34 (and Matt. 9:20–22 and Luke 8:43-48) And a certain woman, which had an issue of blood twelve years, 26 And had suffered many things of many physicians, and had spent all that she had, and was nothing bettered, but rather grew worse, 27 When she had heard of ישוע, came in the press behind, and touched [Matt: the hem of; Luke: the border of] His garment. 28 For she said, If I may touch but his clothes, I shall be whole. 29 And straightway the fountain of her blood was dried up; and she felt in her body that she was healed of that plague. 30 And ישוע, immediately knowing in Himself that virtue had gone out of Him, turned Him about in the press, and said, Who touched my clothes? ... 32 And he looked round about to see her that had done this thing. 33 But the woman fearing and trembling, knowing what was done in her, came and fell down before him, and told him all the truth. 34 And he said unto her, Daughter, thy faith hath made thee whole; go in peace, and be whole of thy plague.

139. DON'T SLEEP WITH WOMAN ON HER MENSTRAL CYCLE

Again, this is amazing understanding that blood can carry disease and is a rich source of nutrients in which germs can quickly multiply.

Lev. 15:24 (CJB) If a man goes to bed with her, and her menstrual flow touches him, he will be unclean seven days; and every bed he lies on will be unclean..

Lev. 18:19 Also thou shalt not approach unto a woman to uncover her nakedness, as long as she is put apart for her uncleanness.

Lev. 20:18 And if a man shall lie with a woman having her sickness, and shall uncover her nakedness; he hath discovered her fountain, and she hath uncovered the fountain of her blood: and both of them shall be cut off from among their people.

140.   WOMEN AFTER CHILDBIRTH

REST FOR THE POSTPARTUM MOTHER: Lev. 12:2-8 If a woman have conceived seed, and born a **man child:** then she shall be unclean seven days; according to the days of the separation for her infirmity shall she be unclean. 3 And in the eighth day the flesh of his foreskin shall be circumcised. 4 And she shall then continue in the blood of her purifying three and thirty days; she shall touch no hallowed thing, nor come into the sanctuary, until the days of her purifying be fulfilled. 5 But if she bear a **maid child**, then she shall be unclean two weeks, as in her separation: and she shall continue in the blood of her purifying threescore and six days. 6 And when the days of her purifying are fulfilled, for a son, or for a daughter, she shall bring a lamb of the first year for a burnt offering, and a young pigeon, or a turtledove, for a sin offering, unto the door of the Tabernacle of the congregation, unto the priest: 7 Who shall offer it before יהוה, and make an atonement for her; and she shall be cleansed from the issue of her blood. ... 8 And if she be not able to bring a lamb, then she shall bring two turtles, or two young pigeons....

(See YESHUA on the next page)

CLEAN/UNCLEAN (Infection Control)

YESHUA ישוע

Luke 2:22-24 And when the days of her purification according to the Torah of Moses were accomplished, they brought him to Jerusalem, to present him to the Lord; 23 (As it is written in the Torah of יהוה, Every male that openeth the womb shall be called holy to the Lord;) 24 And to offer a sacrifice according to that which is said in the Torah of יהוה, A pair of turtledoves, or two young pigeons.

141. MASCULINE EMISSION

Lev. 15:16 -17 And if any man's seed of copulation go out from him, then he shall wash all his flesh in water, and be unclean until the even. 17 And every garment, and every skin, whereon is the seed of copulation, shall be washed with water, and be unclean until the even.

Deut. 23:10-11 If there be among you any man, that is not clean by reason of uncleanness that chanceth him by night, then shall he go abroad out of the camp, he shall not come within the camp: 11 But it shall be, when evening cometh on, he shall wash himself with water: and when the sun is down, he shall come into the camp again.

1402 WASH AFTER HAVING SEX

Lev. 15:18 The woman also with whom man shall lie with seed of copulation, they shall both bathe themselves in water, and be unclean until the even. [also in Wash, p. 202]

143. SANITATION

Deut. 23:12-14 Thou shalt have a place also without the camp, whither thou shalt go forth abroad: 13 And thou shalt have a paddle upon thy weapon; and it shall be, when thou wilt ease thyself abroad, thou shalt dig therewith, and shalt turn back and cover that which cometh from thee: 14 For יהוה thy God walketh in the midst of thy camp, to deliver thee, and to give up thine enemies before thee; therefore shall thy camp be holy: that he see no unclean thing in thee, and turn away from thee.

144. LEPROSY / CONTAGIOUS SKIN DISEASES

AGAIN, AMAZING INFECTION CONTROL and QUARENTINE rules in 1500 B.C!!!

Lev. 13 and 14 *whole chapters. Here are portions.* Lev. 13:1-3 And יהוה spake unto Moses and Aaron, saying, 2 When a man shall have in the skin of his flesh a rising, a scab, or bright spot, and it be in the skin of his flesh like the plague of leprosy; then he shall be brought unto Aaron the priest, or unto one of his sons the priests: 3 And the priest shall look on the plague in the skin of the flesh: and when the hair in the plague is turned white, and the plague in sight be deeper than the skin of his flesh, it is a plague of leprosy: and the priest shall look on him, and pronounce him unclean.

CLEAN/UNCLEAN (Infection Control)

Lev. 13:45-46 And the leper in whom the plague is, his clothes shall be rent [NRSV: torn], and his head bare, and he shall put a covering upon his upper lip *[sounds similar to a medical mask to prevent the spread of airborne pathogens or germs!]*, and shall cry, Unclean, unclean. 46 All the days wherein the plague shall be in him he shall be defiled; he is unclean: he shall dwell alone; without the camp shall his habitation be.

Lev. 14:2-7, 9-10, 14-20 This shall be the law of the leper in the day of his cleansing: He shall be brought unto the priest: 3 And the priest shall go forth out of the camp; and the priest shall look, and, behold, if the plague of leprosy be healed in the leper; 4 Then shall the priest command to take for him that is to be cleansed two birds alive and clean, and cedar wood, and scarlet, and hyssop: ... 7 And he shall sprinkle upon him that is to be cleansed from the leprosy seven times, and shall pronounce him clean, and shall let the living bird loose into the open field. ... 9 But it shall be on the seventh day, that he shall shave all his hair off his head and his beard and his eyebrows, even all his hair he shall shave off: and he shall wash his clothes, also he shall wash his flesh in water, and he shall be clean. 10 And on the eighth day he shall take two he lambs without blemish, and one ewe lamb of the first year without blemish.... 14 And the priest shall take some of the blood of the [asham (shame, guilt)] offering, and the priest shall put it upon the tip of the right ear of him that is to be cleansed, and upon the thumb of his right hand, and upon the great toe of his right foot....20 ... and the priest shall make an atonement for him, and he shall be clean.

Num. 5:2 ...put out of the camp every leper...

Deut. 24:8-9 Take heed in the plague of leprosy, that thou observe diligently, and do according to all that the priests the Levites shall teach you: as I commanded them, so ye shall observe to do. 9 Remember what יהוה thy God did unto Miriam....

YESHUA ישוע

Matt. 10:8 Heal the sick, cleanse the lepers, raise the dead, cast out devils: freely ye have received, freely give.

Mark 1:40-44 (also in Matt. 8:2-4, Mk. 1:40-45, and Luke 5:12-14) And there came a leper to him, beseeching him, and kneeling down to him, and saying unto him, If thou wilt, thou canst make me clean. 41 And ישוע, moved with compassion, put forth his hand, and touched him, and saith unto him, I will; be thou clean. 42 And as soon as he had spoken, immediately the leprosy departed from him, and he was cleansed. 43 And he straitly charged him, and forthwith sent him away; 44 And saith unto him, See thou say nothing to any man: but go thy way, **shew thyself to the priest, and offer for thy cleansing those things which Moses commanded, for a testimony unto them.**

Luke 17:12-14 And as he entered into a certain village, there met him ten men that were lepers, which stood afar off: 13 And they lifted up their voices, and said, Jesus, Master, have mercy on us. 14 And when he saw them, he said unto them, **Go shew yourselves unto the priests.** And it came to pass, that, as they went, they were cleansed.

145. BODILY DISCHARGES

Again, this is AMAZING MEDICAL INFECTION CONTROL and UNDERSTANDING that all the BODILY DISCHARGES and fluids of an infected person can be contagious!! In 1500 B.C!! Modern science didn't discover this until the 1900s A.D!! If only they had studied the Torah! Lives would've been saved!

Lev. 15:2b-3 ... When any man hath a **running issue out of his flesh**, because of his issue he is unclean. 3 And this shall be his uncleanness in his issue: whether his flesh run with his issue, or his flesh be stopped from his issue, it is his uncleanness.

Lev. 15:4-5 **Every bed, whereon he lieth** that hath the issue, is unclean: and every thing, whereon he sitteth, shall be unclean. 5 And whosoever toucheth his bed shall wash his clothes, and bathe himself in water, and be unclean until the even.

Lev. 15:6 And he that sitteth on **any thing whereon he sat** that hath the issue shall wash his clothes, and bathe himself in water, and be unclean until the even.

Lev. 15:7 And he that toucheth **the flesh of him that hath the issue** shall wash his clothes, and bathe himself in water, and be unclean until the even.

Lev. 15:8 And if he that hath the issue **spit** upon him that is clean; then he shall wash his clothes, and bathe himself in water, and be unclean until the even.

Lev. 15:9 And **what saddle soever he rideth upo**n that hath the issue shall be unclean.

Lev. 15:10 And whosoever toucheth **any thing that was under him** shall be unclean until the even: **and he that beareth any of those things [such as blankets and sheets and clothing!!!]** shall wash his clothes, and bathe himself in water, and be unclean until the even.

Lev. 15:11 And **whomsoever he toucheth** that hath the issue, and hath not rinsed his hands in water, he shall wash his clothes, and bathe himself in water, and be unclean until the even.

Lev. 15:12 And **the vessel of earth, that he toucheth** which hath the issue, shall be broken: and every vessel of wood shall be rinsed in water.

Lev. 15:13-15 And when he that hath an issue is cleansed of his issue; then he shall number to himself seven days for his cleansing, and wash his clothes, and bathe his flesh in running water, and shall be clean. 14 And on the eighth day he shall take to him two turtledoves, or two young pigeons, and come before יהוה unto the door of the Tabernacle of the congregation, and give them unto the priest: 15 And the priest shall offer them, the one for a sin offering, and the other for a burnt offering; and the priest shall make an atonement for him before יהוה for his issue.

Lev. 15:31 Thus shall ye separate the children of Israel from their uncleanness; that they die not in their uncleanness, when they defile My Tabernacle that is among them.

Num. 5:2-3 Command the children of Israel, that they put out of the camp every leper, and every one that **hath an issue**, and whosoever is defiled by the dead: 3 Both male and female shall ye put out, without the camp shall ye put them; that they defile not their camps, in the midst whereof I dwell.

146. WASH HANDS/BODY WITH RUNNING WATER

PRIESTS IN THE TEMPLE: Ex. 30:18-21 Thou shalt also make a laver of brass, and his foot also of brass, to wash withal: ... 19 For Aaron and his sons shall wash their hands and their feet threat: 20 When they go into the Tabernacle of the congregation, they shall wash with water, that they die not; or when they come near to the altar to minister, to burn offering made by fire unto יהוה: 21 So they shall wash their hands and their feet, that they die not: and it shall be **a statute forever** to them, even to him and to his seed **throughout their generations**. [also in Tabernacle, p. 150, verse 21 in Rules for Priests, p. 222]

WHOEVER TOUCHES ANYTHING ONE WITH A DISCHARGE HAS TOUCHED:

Lev. 15:5 And whosoever toucheth his bed **shall wash his clothes, and bathe himself in water**....

Lev. 15:6 And he that sitteth on any thing whereon he sat that hath the issue **shall wash his clothes, and bathe himself in water**....

Lev. 15:7 And he that toucheth **the flesh of him** that hath the issue shall **wash his clothes, and bathe himself in wate**r....

Lev. 15:8 And if he that hath the issue **spit** upon him that is clean; then he **shall wash his clothes, and bathe himself in water**....

Lev. 15:10 And whosoever toucheth any thing that was under him shall be unclean until the even: and he that beareth any of those things [such as blankets and sheets and clothing!!!] **shall wash his clothes, and bathe himself in water**....

Lev. 15:11 And **whomsoever he toucheth** that hath the issue, and hath not **rinsed his hands in water, he shall wash his clothes, and bathe himself in water**,

WHOEVER HAS AN ISSUE OR DISCHARGE: Lev. 15:13 And when he that hath an issue is cleansed of his issue; then he shall number to himself seven days for his cleansing, and **wash his clothes, and bathe his flesh in running water,** and shall be clean.

WHOEVER HAS BEEN NEAR A DEAD BODY:

Num. 19:19 and on the seventh day he shall purify himself, and **wash his clothes, and bathe himself in water**, and shall be clean at even.

Deut. 21:6 And all the elders of that city, that are next unto the slain man, **shall wash their hands** over the heifer that is beheaded in the valley.

WHOEVER TOUCHES A WOMAN DURING HER MENSIES: *(Remember that blood can carry disease.)* Lev. 15:21-22 And whosoever toucheth her bed **shall wash his clothes, and bathe himself in water,** and be unclean until the even. 22 And whosoever toucheth any thing that she sat upon **shall wash his clothes, and bathe himself in water,** and be unclean until the even.

WHO HAD A MASCULINE EMISSION: Lev. 15:16 ...he **shall wash all his flesh in water**: [also in Masculine emission, p. 204]

AFTER HAVING SEX: Lev. 15:18 The woman also with whom man shall lie with seed of copulation, **they shall both bathe themselves in water.** [also in Wash after sex, p. 204]

YESHUA יֵשׁוּעַ

Matt. 15:18-20 But those things which proceed out of the mouth come forth from the heart; and they defile the man. 19 For out of the heart proceed evil thoughts, murders, adulteries, fornications, thefts, false witness, blasphemies: 20 These are the things which defile a man: **but to eat with unwashen hands defileth not a man.** *[It might make him sick, but it won't defile his heart. Take note that they had to wash their whole body every time they touched any unclean, infectious thing, so their hands would have been relatively clean.]*

Mark 7:1-5,9, 14-16 Then came together unto him the Pharisees, and certain of the scribes, which came from Jerusalem. 2 And when they saw some of His disciples eat bread with defiled, that is to say, with unwashen, hands, they found fault. 3 For the Pharisees, and all the Jews, except they wash their hands oft, eat not, holding the tradition of the elders. 4 And when they come from the market, except they wash, they eat not. And many other things there be, which they have received to hold, as the washing of cups, and pots, brasen vessels, and of tables. 5 Then the Pharisees and scribes asked Him, Why walk not Thy disciples according to the tradition of the elders, but eat bread with unwashen hands? ... 9 And He said unto them, Full well ye reject the commandment of God, that ye may keep your own tradition. ... 14 And when He had called all the people unto Him, He said unto them, Hearken unto Me every one of you, and understand: 15 T**here is nothing from without a man, that entering into him can defile him: but the things which come out of him, those are they that defile the man.** 16 If any man have ears to hear, let him hear. [also in What can't eat, p. 127]

147. DISINFECTING DISHES AND CLOTHING

Lev. 6:27b-28 and when there is sprinkled of the blood ... upon any garment, thou shalt wash that whereon it was sprinkled in the holy place. 28 But the **earthen vessel** wherein it is sodden shall **be broken**: and if it be sodden in a brasen pot, it shall be both **scoured, and rinsed in water.**

Lev. 15:12 And **the vessel of earth, that he toucheth** which hath the issue, **shall be broken:** and **every vessel of wood shall be rinsed** [washed?] **in water.**

Lev. 15:16-17 And if any man's seed of copulation go out from him, then he shall wash all his flesh in water, and be unclean until the even. 17 And **every garment, and every skin, whereon is the seed of copulation, shall be washed with wate**r, and be unclean until the even.

Num. 19:14-15, 18 This is the law, **when a man dieth in a tent**: all that come into the tent, and **all that is in the tent**, shall be unclean seven days. 15 And **every open vessel**, which hath no covering bound upon it, is unclean. ... 18 And a clean person shall take hyssop, and dip it in the water [of the heifer and cedar, etc., ashes], and sprinkle it upon the tent, and upon all the vessels, ... on the third day, and on the seventh day....

148. MOLD IN CLOTH

Lev. 13:47-52 The garment also that the plague of leprosy is in, whether it be a woollen garment, or a linen garment; 48 Whether it be in the warp, or woof; of linen, or of woollen; whether in a skin, or in any thing made of skin; 49 And if the plague be greenish or reddish in the garment, or in the skin, either in the warp, or in the woof, or in any thing of skin; it is a plague of leprosy, and shall be shewed unto the priest: 50 And the priest shall look upon the plague, and shut up it that hath the plague seven days: 51 And he shall look on the plague on the seventh day: if the plague be spread in the garment, either in the warp, or in the woof, or in a skin, or in any work that is made of skin; the plague is a fretting leprosy; it is unclean. 52 He shall therefore burn that garment, whether warp or woof, in woollen or in linen, or any thing of skin, wherein the plague is: for it is a fretting leprosy; it shall be burnt in the fire.... *[Continues with further detailed investigating instructions.]*

149. MOLD IN HOUSES

Lev. 14:34-54 When ye be come into the land of Canaan, which I give to you for a possession, and I put the plague of leprosy in a house of the land of your possession; 35 And he that owneth the house shall come and tell the priest, saying, It seemeth to me there is as it were a plague in the house: 36 Then the priest shall command that they empty the house, before the priest go into it to see the plague, that all that is in the house be not made unclean: and afterward the priest shall go in to see the house: 37 And he shall look on the plague, and, behold, if the plague be in the walls of the house with hollow strakes, greenish or reddish, which in sight are lower than the wall; 38 Then the priest shall ... shut up the house seven days: 39 And the priest shall come again the seventh day, and shall look: and, behold, if the plague be spread in the walls of the house; 40 Then the priest shall command that they take away the stones in which the plague is, and they shall cast them into an unclean place without the city: 41 And he shall cause the house to be scraped within round about, and they shall pour out the dust that they scrape off without the city into an unclean place: 42 And they shall take other stones, and put them in the place of those stones; and he shall take other morter, and shall plaister the house. ... 47 And he that lieth in the house shall wash his clothes; and he that eateth in the house shall wash his clothes. 48 And if the priest shall come in, and look upon it, and, behold, the plague hath not spread in the house, after the house was plaistered: then the priest shall pronounce the house clean, ... 49 And he shall take to cleanse the house two birds, and cedar wood, and scarlet, and hyssop.... 52 And he shall cleanse the house with the blood of the bird, and with the running water, ... 53 But he shall let go the living bird out of the city into the open fields, and make an atonement for the house: and it shall be clean. 54 This is the law for all manner of plague of leprosy, and scall, ...

150. SINNING IN IGNORANCE

(MERCY in the TORAH!)

[See also Sin Offerings, pp. 142-144]

Lev. 4:1-6 And יהוה spake unto Moses, saying, 2 Speak unto the children of Israel, saying, If a soul shall **sin through ignorance** against any of the commandments of יהוה concerning things which ought not to be done, and shall do against any of them: If the **priest** that is anointed do sin according to the sin of the people; then let him bring for his sin, which he hath sinned, a young bullock without blemish unto יהוה for a sin offering. 4 And he ... shall lay his hand upon the bullock's head.... 6 And the priest shall dip his finger in the blood, and sprinkle of the blood seven times before יהוה, before the veil of the sanctuary.

Lev. 4:13-14 And if the **whole congregation** of Israel **sin through ignorance,** and the thing be hid from the eyes of the assembly, and they have done somewhat against any of the commandments of יהוה concerning things which should not be done, and are guilty; When the sin, which they have sinned against it, is known, then the congregation shall offer a young bullock for the sin, ... And the priest shall dip his finger in some of the blood, and sprinkle it seven times before יהוה, even before the veil.

Lev. 4:22-24 When a **ruler** hath **sinned,** and done **somewhat through ignorance** against any of the commandments of יהוה his God concerning things which should not be done, and is guilty; 23 Or if his sin, wherein he hath sinned, come to his knowledge; he shall bring his offering, a kid of the goats, a male without blemish: 24 And he shall lay his hand upon the head of the goat, ... before יהוה: it is a sin offering.

Lev. 4:27-29,35 And if any one of the **common people sin through ignorance**, while he doeth somewhat against any of the commandments of יהוה concerning things which ought not to be done, and be guilty; 28 Or if his sin, which he hath sinned, come to his knowledge: then he shall bring his offering, a kid of the goats, a female without blemish, for his sin which he hath sinned. 29 And he shall lay his hand upon the head of the sin offering, ... 35...and the priest shall make an atonement for his sin ..., and it shall be forgiven him.

Lev. 5:4-6 Or if a soul swear, pronouncing with his lips to do evil, or to do good, whatsoever it be that a man shall pronounce with an oath, **and it be hid from him; when he knoweth of i**t, ... he shall confess that he hath sinned in that thing: 6 And he shall bring his [asham (shame, guilt)] offering unto יהוה for his sin which he hath sinned, a female from the flock, a lamb or a kid of the goats, for a sin offering; **and the priest shall make an atonement for him**...

Lev. 5:15-16 **If a soul commit a trespass, and sin through ignorance,** in the holy things of יהוה; then he shall bring ... unto יהוה a ram without blemish ... with thy estimation by shekels of silver ... for a [asham (shame, guilt)] offering: 16 And he shall make amends for the harm that he hath done in the holy thing, and shall add the fifth part thereto, and give it unto the priest: and the priest shall make an atonement for him ... and it shall be forgiven him.

Lev. 5:17-18 And if a soul sin, and commit any of these things which are forbidden to be done by the commandments of יהוה; **though he wist it not,** yet is he guilty, and shall bear his iniquity. 18 And he shall bring a ram without blemish ... with thy estimation, for a [asham (shame, guilt)] offering, unto the priest: and the priest shall make an atonement for him concerning his ignorance wherein he erred and wist it not, and it shall be forgiven him.

Num. 15:24-25 ... if ought be **committed by ignorance** without the knowledge of the congregation, that all the congregation shall offer one young bullock for a burnt offering, for a sweet savour unto יהוה... 25 And the priest shall make an atonement ... and it shall be forgiven them ... and the stranger that sojourneth among them; seeing all the people were in ignorance.

YESHUA ישוע

Luke 12:47-48 And that servant, which knew his lord's will, and prepared not himself, neither did according to his will, shall be beaten with many stripes. 48 **But he that knew not,** and did commit things worthy of stripes, shall be beaten with few stripes. For unto whomsoever much is given, of him shall be much required: and to whom men have committed much, of him they will ask the more.

APOSTLES

I John 1:7-9 But if we walk in the light, as he is in the light, we have fellowship one with another, and the blood of ישוע Messiah his Son cleanseth us from all sin. 8 If we say that we have no sin, we deceive ourselves, and the truth is not in us. 9 If we confess our sins, he is faithful and just to forgive us our sins, and to cleanse us from all unrighteousness.

151. BROTHER DIES WITHOUT CHILDREN

Deut. 25:5-6 If brethren dwell together, and one of them die, and have no child, the wife of the dead shall not marry without unto a stranger: her husband's brother shall go in unto her, and take her to him to wife, and perform the duty of an husband's brother unto her. 6 And it shall be, that the firstborn which she beareth shall succeed in the name of his brother which is dead, that his name be not put out of Israel.

Deut. 25:7-10 And if the man like not to take his brother's wife, then let his brother's wife go up to the gate unto the elders, and say, My husband's brother refuseth to raise up unto his brother a name in Israel, he will not perform the duty of my husband's brother. 8 Then the elders of his city shall call him, and speak unto him: and if he stand to it, and say, I like not to take her; 9 Then shall his brother's wife come unto him in the presence of the elders, and loose his shoe from off his foot, and spit in his face, and shall answer and say, So shall it be done unto that man that will not build up his brother's house. 10 And his name shall be called in Israel, The house of him that hath his shoe loosed.

AFTER TORAH

Gen. 38:7-9 And Er, Judah's firstborn, was wicked ... and יהוה slew him. 8 And Judah said unto Onan, Go in unto thy brother's wife, and marry her, and raise up seed to thy brother. 9 And Onan knew that the seed should not be his; and ... when he went in unto his brother's wife, ... he spilled it on the ground, lest that he should give seed to his brother. 10 And the thing which he did displeased יהוה: wherefore He slew him also.

Ruth 3:9-10 And he said, Who art thou? And she answered, I am Ruth thine handmaid: spread therefore thy skirt over thine handmaid; for thou art a near kinsman. ... 10 and he said ... howbeit there is a kinsman nearer than I. ... 4:8 ... the kinsman said [to Boaz], ... I cannot redeem it. ... Buy it for thee. So he drew off his shoe.

YESHUA ישוע

Matt. 22:23-30 The same day came to him the Sadducees, which say that there is no resurrection, and asked him, 24 Saying, Master, Moses said, If a man die, having no children, his brother shall marry his wife, and raise up seed unto his brother. 25 Now there were with us seven brethren: and the first, when he had married a wife, deceased, and, having no issue, left his wife unto his brother: 26 Likewise the second also, and the third, unto the seventh. 27 And last of all the woman died also. 28 Therefore in the resurrection whose wife shall she be of the seven? for they all had her. 29 ישוע answered and said unto them, Ye do err, not knowing the Scriptures, nor the power of God. 30 For in the Resurrection they neither marry, nor are given in marriage, but are as the angels of God in Heaven.

Luke 20:27-40 *[same story]* ... 35 ... they which shall be accounted worthy to obtain that world, and the resurrection from the dead, neither marry, nor are given in marriage: 36 Neither can they die any more: for they are equal unto the angels; and are the children of God, [and] ... Resurrection.

152. TAKE A CENSUS

Ex. 30:11-14 And יהוה spake unto Moses, saying, 12 When thou takest the sum of the children of Israel after their number, then shall they give every man a ransom for his soul unto יהוה, when thou numberest them; that there be no plague among them, when thou numberest them. 13 This they shall give, every one that passeth among them that are numbered, half a shekel after the shekel of the sanctuary: (a shekel is twenty gerahs:) an half shekel shall be the offering of יהוה. 14 Every one that passeth among them that are numbered, from twenty years old and above, shall give an offering unto יהוה. [Cont. in Temple "tax," p. 151]

Num. 1:2 Take ye the **sum** of all the congregation of the children of Israel, after their families, by the house of their fathers, with the number of *their* names, every male by their polls;

Num. 1:49 Only thou shalt not number the tribe of Levi, neither take the **sum** of them among the children of Israel:

Num. 4:2 Take the **sum** of the sons of Kohath from among the sons of Levi, after their families, by the house of their fathers,

Num. 4:22 Take also the **sum** of the sons of Gershon, throughout the houses of their fathers, by their families;

Num. 26:1-2 And it came to pass after the plague, that יהוה spake unto Moses and unto Eleazar the son of Aaron the priest, saying, 2 Take the **sum** of all the congregation of the children of Israel, from twenty years old and upward, throughout their fathers' house, **all that are able to go to war in Israel.**

Num. 26:4 **Take the <u>sum</u> of the people,** from twenty years old and upward; as יהוה commanded Moses and the children of Israel, which went forth out of the land of Egypt.

Num. 31:49 *[after a battle]* And they said unto Moses, Thy servants have taken the **sum** of the men of war which *are* under our charge, and there lacketh not one man of us.

AFTER TORAH

[David hadn't received a specific command to take a census as Moses had each time.]

I Chron. 21:1-4, 7 (and 2 Sam. 24:1-10) And Satan stood up against Israel, and provoked David to number Israel. 2 And David said to Joab and to the rulers of the people, Go, number Israel from Beersheba even to Dan; and bring the number of them to me, that I may know it. 3 And Joab answered, יהוה make His people an hundred times so many more as they be: but, my lord the king, are they not all my lord's servants? why then doth my lord require this thing? why will he be a cause of [asham (shame, guilt)] to Israel? 4 Nevertheless the king's word prevailed.... 7 And God was displeased with this thing; therefore He smote Israel. 8 And David said unto God, I have sinned greatly, because I have done this thing: but now, I beseech Thee, do away the iniquity of Thy servant; for I have done very foolishly.

153. APPORTIONING LAND AND INHERITANCE

EQUAL DISTRIBUTION: Num. 26:52-55 And יהוה spake unto Moses, saying, 53 Unto these the land shall be divided for an inheritance according to the number of names. 54 **To many** thou shalt **give the more** inheritance, and **to few** thou shalt **give the less** inheritance: to every one shall his inheritance be given according to those that were numbered of him. 55 Notwithstanding the land shall be divided by lot: according to the names of the tribes of their fathers they shall inherit. 56 According to the lot shall the possession thereof be divided between many and few.

Num. 33:54 And ye shall divide the land by lot for an inheritance among your families: and to the **more** ye shall **give the more** inheritance, and to the **fewer** ye shall **give the less** inheritance: every man's inheritance shall be in the place where his lot falleth; according to the tribes of your fathers ye shall inherit.

BORDERS: Num. 34:2 Command the children of Israel, and say unto them, When ye come into the land of Canaan; (...for an inheritance, ...with the coasts thereof:) 3 Then your south quarter shall be from the wilderness of Zin along. ... *[gives all the borders through verse 10]*

Num. 34:13-15 And Moses commanded the children of Israel, saying, This is the land which ye shall inherit by lot, which יהוה commanded to give unto the nine tribes, and to the half tribe: 14 For the tribe of ...Reuben ...and the tribe of ...Gad ...have received their inheritance; and half the tribe of Manasseh have received their inheritance: 15 The two ...and the half tribe have received their inheritance on this side Jordan near Jericho eastward, toward the sunrising.

LEADERS TO DIVIDE: Num. 34:16-18 And יהוה spake unto Moses, saying, 17 These are the names of the men which shall divide the land unto you: Eleazar the priest, and Joshua the son of Nun. 18 And ye shall take one prince of every tribe, to divide the land by inheritance.

WOMAN: Num. 27:5-11 And Moses brought their cause before יהוה. 6 And יהוה spake unto Moses, saying, 7 The **daughters** of Zelophehad speak right: thou shalt surely give them a possession of an inheritance among their father's brethren; and thou shalt cause the inheritance of their father to pass unto them. 8 And thou shalt speak unto ...saying, If a man die, and have no son, then ye shall cause his inheritance to pass unto his daughter. 9 And if he have no daughter, then ye shall give his inheritance unto his brethren. 10 And if he have no brethren, then ye shall give his inheritance unto his father's brethren. 11 And if his father have no brethren, then ye shall give his inheritance unto his kinsman that is next to him of his family, and he shall possess it: and it shall be ...a statute of judgment, as יהוה commanded....

Num. 36:5-12 And Moses commanded ...according to the Word of יהוה, saying, The tribe of the sons of Joseph hath said well. 6 This is the thing which יהוה doth command concerning the daughters of Zelophehad, saying, Let them marry to whom they think best; only to the family of the tribe of their father shall they marry. 7 So shall not the inheritance ...remove from tribe to tribe: for every one of the children of Israel shall keep himself to the inheritance of the tribe of his fathers. 8 And every daughter, that possesseth an inheritance in any tribe of the children of Israel, shall be wife unto one of the family of the tribe of her father, that the children of Israel may enjoy every man the inheritance of his fathers. 9 ...every one of the tribes of the children of Israel shall keep himself to his own inheritance. 10 Even as יהוה commanded Moses, so did the daughters of Zelophehad: ... 12 And they were married into the families of the sons of Manasseh the son of Joseph, and their inheritance remained in the tribe of the family of their father.

CITIES FOR LEVITES: Num. 35:1-7 And יהוה spake unto Moses ... near Jericho, saying, 2 Command the children of Israel, that they **give** unto **the Levites** of the inheritance of their possession **cities to dwell in;** and ... **suburbs** for the cities round about them. 3 And the **cities** ... and the **suburbs** of them shall be for their cattle, and for their goods, and for all their beasts. 4 And the suburbs of the cities, which ye shall **give** unto the Levites, shall reach from the wall ... outward a thousand cubits round about. ... 7 ... forty and eight cities.... [also in Rules for Priests, p. 223] *{In Josh. 21, these cities are given out.}*

A STATUTE FOREVER, A LIST

We have an everlasting inheritance in Torah!

KEY: *E-Everlasting, EC-Everlasting Covenant, ES-Everlasting Statute, F-Forever, SF-Statute Forever, PS-Perpetual Statute, PG-Perpetual Generations, PC-Perpetual Covenant, TYG-Throughout Your Generations, TTG-Throughout Their Generations, OF-Ordinance Forever, SF-Statute Forever, IYG-In Your Generations*

MOADIM: (p. 42, 161-184): Shabbat **TYG, PC, SF** *Ex. 31:13, 16-17*   Passover, Matzah **TYG, OF** *Ex. 12:14, 17, 24*
Firstfruits **SF, TYG** *Lev. 23:14*   Shavuot (in all your dwellings) **SF, TYG** *Lev. 23:21*
Day of Atonement **EF, SF, ES, TYG** *Lev. 16:29, 31, 34*   Sukkot **SF, IYG** *Lev. 23:41*
Jubilee, land sales only temporary **F** *Lev. 25:23*   *[Rosh Hashanah not forever? Maybe because it's prophetic?]*

PROMISES: Rainbow **E, EC, PG** *Gen. 9:12, 16*   The Land **F, E** *Gen. 13:15; Gen 48:4; Ex. 32:13; Deut. 4:40*

SET APART: Circumcision **E** *Gen. 17:7, 9, 13* (p.192)   Tzit-Tzit **TYG** *Num. 15:38* (p.191)
Eat neither fat nor blood **PS** *Lev. 3:17* (p.130)   Cities of refuge **TYG** *Num. 35:29* (p. 47)

TEMPLE: *(We are the Temple)* (p. 150): Bread of Presence **E** *Lev 24:8*   Menorah, keep lit **SF** *Ex. 27:21; Lev. 24:3*
Holy anointing oil **TYG** *Ex. 30:31*   Priest to burn incense every evening **TYG, P** *Ex. 30:8*
Daily burnt offerings by Priest **TYG** *Ex. 29:42*   Annual atonement of altar **TYG** *Ex. 30:10*
Silver trumpets, priests blow them **OF, TYG** *Num 10:8* (p.216)

SACRIFICE: *(Think spiritually):*   Peace offering **PS** *Lev. 3:17* (p.70)   Only to God **SF, TTG** *Lev. 17:7* (p.145)
Red Heifer, water for purification **SF, TYG, PS** *Num. 19:10, 21* (p. 199-201)
Burnt, freewill, Moadim offerings same for you & stranger **SF IYG** *Num. 15:15* (p.87)

PRIESTS, LEVITES: *(We are His kings and priests!)* (p.219-224):   Minister **forever** **F** *Deut.18:5*
Aaron's, priesthood **E, TYG** *Ex. 40:15*   Phinehas' priesthood **E** *Num. 25:13*
Priests ordination heave offering **SF** *Ex. 29:28*   New High Priest, day anointed offering **SF** *Lev. 6:22*
Priestly garments **SF, PS** *Ex. 28:43; Ex. 29:9*   Priests wash hands, feet to minister **SF, TTG** *Ex. 30:21*
Priests no wine or strong drink when ministering **SF, TYG** *Lev. 10:9*
Peace offering's breast, shoulder for priest to eat **SF** *Lev. 7:34, 36; 10:15*
Heave offering for priest & family to eat **OF, SF, CF** *Num. 18:8, 11, 19*
Priests eat grain offering **F** *Lev. 6:18*   Priests eat sacrifice portions in holy place **PS** *Lev. 24:9*
Levites Temple service, no inheritance **SF, TYG** *Num. 18:23*   Levite city suburbs not to be sold **P** *Lev. 25:34*

154. SILVER TRUMPETS

Num. 10:2-8 Make thee two trumpets of silver; of a whole piece shalt thou make them: that thou mayest use them for the calling of the assembly, and for the journeying of the camps. 3 And when they shall blow with them, all the assembly shall assemble themselves to thee at the door of the Tabernacle of the congregation. 4 And if they blow but with one trumpet, then the princes, which are heads of the thousands of Israel, shall gather themselves unto thee. 5 When ye blow an alarm, then the camps that lie on the east parts shall go forward. 6 When ye blow an alarm the second time, then the camps that lie on the south side shall take their journey: they shall blow an alarm for their journeys. 7 But when the congregation is to be gathered together, ye shall blow, but ye shall not sound an alarm. 8 And the sons of Aaron, the priests, shall blow with the trumpets; and they shall be to you for an **ordinance forever throughout your generations**.

Num. 10:9-10 And if ye go to war in your land against the enemy that oppresseth you, then ye shall blow an alarm with the trumpets; and ye shall be remembered before יהוה your God, and ye shall be saved from your enemies. 10 Also in the day of your gladness, and in your solemn days, and in the beginnings of your months, ye shall blow with the trumpets over your burnt offerings, and over the sacrifices of your peace offerings; that they may be to you for a memorial before your God: I am יהוה your God. [also in War, p. 116]

155. MAKE PILLARS, MT. BLESSING AND CURSING

Deut. 27:2-8 And it shall be on the day when ye shall pass over Jordan unto the land which יהוה thy God giveth thee, that thou shalt set thee up great stones, and plaister them with plaister: 3 And thou shalt write upon them all the words of this Torah, when thou art passed over, that thou mayest go in unto the land which יהוה thy God giveth thee, ... 4 Therefore it shall be when ye be gone over Jordan, that ye shall set up these stones, which I command you this day, in mount Ebal, and thou shalt plaister them with plaister. 5 And there shalt thou build an altar unto יהוה thy God, an altar of stones: ... 8 And thou shalt write upon the stones all the words of this Torah very plainly.

Deut. 27:9-15 And Moses and the priests the Levites spake unto all Israel, saying, Take heed, and hearken, O Israel; this day thou art become the people of יהוה thy God. 10 Thou shalt therefore obey the voice of יהוה thy God, and do his commandments and his statutes, which I command thee this day. 11 And Moses charged the people the same day, saying, 12 These shall stand upon mount Gerizim to bless the people, when ye are come over Jordan; Simeon, and Levi, and Judah, and Issachar, and Joseph, and Benjamin: 13 And these shall stand upon mount Ebal to curse; Reuben, Gad, and Asher, and Zebulun, Dan, and Naphtali. 14 And the Levites shall speak, and say unto all the men of Israel with a loud voice, 15 Cursed be the man. ... And all the people shall answer and say, Amen. ....

156. RULES FOR THE KING

Deut. 17:14-15a When thou art come unto the land which יהוה thy God giveth thee, and shalt possess it, and shalt dwell therein, and shalt say, I will set a king over me, like as all the nations that are about me; Thou shalt in any wise set him king over thee, whom יהוה thy God shall choose:

Deut. 17:15b ... one from among thy brethren shalt thou set king over thee: thou mayest **not set a stranger over thee**, which is not thy brother.

Deut. 17:16a But he shall **not multiply horses** to himself....

Deut. 17:17a **Neither shall he multiply wives to himself**, that his heart turn not away:

Deut. 17:17b ...**neither** shall he **greatly multiply** to himself **silver and gold**.

Deut. 17:18-20 And it shall be, when he sitteth upon the throne of his kingdom, that he shall **write him a copy of this Torah** in a book out of that which is before the priests the Levites: 19 And it shall be with him, and he shall **read therein all the days of his life:** that he may **learn to fear** יהוה **his God**, to keep all the words of this Torah and these statutes, to do them: 20 That his **heart be not lifted up above his brethren,** and that he turn not aside from the commandment, to the right hand, or to the left: to the end that he may prolong his days in his kingdom, he, and his children, in the midst of Israel.

AFTER TORAH

1 Chron. 28:9 And thou, Solomon my son, **know thou the God of thy father, and serve him** with a perfect heart [CJB: wholeheartedly] and with a willing mind: for יהוה searcheth all hearts, and understandeth all the imaginations of the thoughts: if thou seek him, he will be found of thee; but if thou forsake him, he will cast thee off **forever**.

1 Chron. 28:10b, 20 ... **be strong and act**.... 20 And David said to Solomon his son, **Be strong and of good courage,** and do it: fear not, nor be dismayed: for יהוה God, even my God, will be with thee; he will not fail thee, nor forsake thee, until thou hast finished all the work for the service of the house of יהוה. [also in Be Strong, p. 241]

Psalm 105:13-15 When they went from one nation to another, from one kingdom to another people; 14 He suffered no man to do them wrong: yea, he reproved kings for their sakes; 15 Saying, **Touch not mine anointed,** and do my prophets no harm.

YESHUA ישוע and APOSTLES

Matt. 22:21 ... Render therefore unto Caesar the things which are Caesar's; and unto God the things that are God's.

Rom. 13:1-7 (NRSV) Let every person be subject to the governing authorities; for there is no authority except from God, and those authorities that exist have been instituted by God. 2 Therefore whoever resists authority resists what God has appointed, and those who resist will incur judgment. 3 For ... if you do what is wrong, you should be afraid, for the authority does not bear the sword in vain! It is the servant of God to execute wrath on the wrongdoer.

5 Therefore one must be subject, not only because of wrath but also because of conscience. 6 For the same reason you also pay taxes, for the authorities are God's servants, busy with this very thing. 7 Pay to all what is due them—taxes to whom taxes are due, revenue to whom revenue is due, respect to whom respect is due, honor to whom honor is due.

I Tim. 2:1-4 I exhort therefore, that, first of all, supplications, prayers, intercessions, and giving of thanks, be made for all men; 2 For kings, and for all that are in authority; that we may lead a quiet and peaceable life in all godliness and honesty. 3 For this is good and acceptable in the sight of God our Saviour; 4 Who will have all men to be saved, and to come unto the knowledge of the truth.

Rev. 1:5b-6 Unto Him that loved us, and washed us from our sins in His own Blood, 6 And hath **made us kings and priests** unto God and His Father; to Him be glory and dominion **forever and ever**. Amen.

Rev. 5:9b-10 ...for Thou wast slain, and hast redeemed us to God by Thy Blood out of every kindred, and tongue, and people, and nation; 10 And hast made us unto our God **kings and priests:** and we shall reign on the earth.

157. DO NOT RETURN TO EGYPT

Deut. 17:16b **nor** *[shall the king]* **cause the people to return to Egypt,** to the end that he should multiply horses: forasmuch as יהוה hath said unto you, Ye shall henceforth return no more that way.

158. MOSES PASSING ON TO JOSHUA

Num. 27:12-21 And יהוה said unto Moses, Get thee up into this mount Abarim, and see the land which I have given unto the children of Israel. 13 And when thou hast seen it, thou also shalt be gathered unto thy people, as Aaron thy brother was gathered. 14 For ye rebelled against my commandment in the desert of Zin, in the strife of the congregation, to sanctify me at the water before their eyes: that is the water of Meribah ... 15 And Moses spake unto יהוה, saying, 16 Let יהוה, the God of the spirits of all flesh, set a man over the congregation, 17 Which may go out before them, ... that the congregation of יהוה be not as sheep which have no shepherd. 18 And יהוה said unto Moses, Take thee Joshua the son of Nun, a <u>man in whom is the spirit,</u> and lay thine hand upon him; 19 And set him before Eleazar the priest, and before all the congregation; and give him a charge in their sight. 20 And thou shalt put some of thine honour upon him, that all the congregation of the children of Israel may be obedient. 21 And he shall stand before Eleazar the priest, who shall ask counsel for him after the judgment of Urim before יהוה: at his word shall they go out, and at his word they shall come in....

Num. 27:22-23 And Moses did as יהוה commanded him: and he took Joshua, and set him before Eleazar the priest, and before all the congregation: 23 And he laid his hands upon him, and gave him a charge, as יהוה commanded by the hand of Moses.

159. RULES FOR PRIESTS AND LEVITES

THEY SERVE GOD:

Deut. 18:5 For יהוה thy God hath chosen him out of all thy tribes, to stand to minister in the name of יהוה, him and his sons **forever**.

Deut. 18:6-7 And if a Levite come from any of thy gates out of all Israel, where he sojourned, and come with all the desire of his mind unto the place which יהוה shall choose; 7 Then he shall minister in the Name of יהוה his God, as all his brethren the Levites do, which stand there before יהוה.

ITEMS OFFERED TO GOD GO TO THE PRIESTS:

Num. 5:9-10   And every offering of all the holy things of the children of Israel, which they bring unto the priest, shall be his. 10 And every man's hallowed things shall be his: whatsoever any man giveth the priest, it shall be his.

LEVITES SERVE THE PRIESTS:

Num. 3:5-9 And יהוה spake unto Moses, saying, 6 Bring the tribe of Levi near, and present them before Aaron the priest, that they may minister unto him. 7 And they shall keep his charge, and the charge of the whole congregation before the Tabernacle of the congregation, to do the service of the Tabernacle. 8 And they shall keep all the instruments of the Tabernacle of the congregation, and the charge of the children of Israel, to do the service of the Tabernacle. 9 And thou shalt give the Levites unto Aaron and to his sons....

Num. 18:6 And I, behold, I have taken your brethren the Levites from among the children of Israel: to you they are given as a gift for יהוה, to do the service of the Tabernacle....

INAUGURATING LEVITES:

Num. 8:6-15 Take the Levites from among the children of Israel, and cleanse them. 7 And thus shalt thou do unto them, to cleanse them: Sprinkle water of purifying upon them, and let them shave all their flesh, and let them wash their clothes, and so make themselves clean. 8 Then let them take a young bullock with his meat offering, even fine flour mingled with oil, and another young bullock shalt thou take for a sin offering. 9 And thou shalt bring the Levites before the Tabernacle of the congregation: and thou shalt gather the whole assembly of the children of Israel together: 10 And thou shalt bring the Levites before יהוה: and **the children of Israel shall put their hands** upon the Levites: 11 And Aaron shall offer the Levites before יהוה for an offering of the children of Israel, that they may execute the service of יהוה. 12 And the Levites shall lay their hands upon the heads of the bullocks: and thou shalt offer the one for a sin offering, and the other for a burnt offering, unto יהוה, to make an atonement for the Levites. 13 And thou shalt set the Levites before Aaron, and before his sons, and offer them for an offering unto יהוה. 14 Thus shalt thou separate the Levites from among the children of Israel: and the Levites shall be mine. 15 And after that shall the Levites go in to do the service of the Tabernacle of the congregation....

ONLY PRIESTS AND THEIR FAMILIES EAT OFFERED MEAT AND HOLY BREAD

Lev. 6:26-29 **The priest that offereth it (sin offering) for sin shall eat it:** in the holy place shall it be eaten, in the court of the Tabernacle.... 27 Whatsoever shall touch the flesh thereof shall be holy... 29 **All the males among the priests shall eat thereof:** it is most holy.

Lev. 6:30 And no sin offering, whereof any of the blood is brought into the Tabernacle of the congregation to reconcile withal in the holy place, shall be eaten: it shall be burnt in the fire.

Lev. 10:12-13 And Moses spake unto Aaron, and unto Eleazar and unto Ithamar, his sons that were left, Take the meat [grain] offering that remaineth of the offerings of יהוה made by fire, and **eat it** without leaven **beside the altar**: for it is **most holy**: 13 And ye shall **eat it in the holy place**, because it is thy due, and thy sons' due ... for so I am commanded.

Lev. 10:14-15 And the wave breast and heave shoulder shall ye **eat in a clean place**; **thou, and thy sons, and thy daughters with thee**: for they be thy due, and thy sons' due, which are given out of the sacrifices of peace offerings of the children of Israel. 15 ... it shall be thine, and thy sons' with thee, by a **statute forever.**...

Lev. 22:10-16 (NIV) No one outside a priest's family may eat the sacred offering, nor may the guest of a priest or his hired worker eat it. 11 But if a priest buys a slave with money, or if slaves are born in his household, they may eat his food. 12 If a priest's daughter marries anyone other than a priest, she may not eat any of the sacred contributions. 13 But if a priest's daughter becomes a widow or is divorced, yet has no children, and she returns to live in her father's household as in her youth, she may eat her father's food. **No unauthorized person, however, may eat it.** 14 Anyone who eats a sacred offering by mistake must make restitution to the priest for the offering and add a fifth of the value to it. 15 The priests must not desecrate the sacred offerings ... 16 by allowing them to eat the sacred offerings....

Num. 18:1a, 9-19 And יהוה said unto Aaron, Thou and thy sons and thy father's house with thee ... 9 This shall be thine of the most holy things, reserved from the fire: every oblation of theirs, every meat offering of theirs, and every sin offering of theirs, and every [asham (shame)] offering of theirs, which they shall render unto me, shall be most holy for thee and for thy sons. 10 In the most holy place shalt thou eat it; **every male shall eat it**: it shall be holy unto thee. 11 And this is thine; the heave offering of their gift, with all the wave offerings of the children of Israel: I have given them unto thee, and **to thy sons and to thy daughters with thee**, by a **statute forever**: **every one that is clean in thy house shall eat of it.** 12 All the best of the oil, and all the best of the wine, and of the wheat, the firstfruits of them which they shall offer unto יהוה, them have I given thee. 13 And whatsoever is first ripe in the land, which they shall bring unto יהוה, shall be thine; **every one that is clean in thine house shall eat of it.** 14 Every thing devoted in Israel shall be thine. 15 Every thing that openeth the matrix in all flesh, which they bring unto יהוה ... 16 ... 17 ...the firstling of a cow, or the firstling of a sheep, or the firstling of a goat, thou shalt not redeem; they are holy: thou shalt sprinkle their blood upon the altar, and shalt burn their fat for an offering made by fire, for a sweet savour unto יהוה. 18 And the flesh of them shall be thine, as the wave breast and as the right shoulder are thine. 19 All the heave offerings ... have I given **thee, and thy sons and thy daughters with thee,** by a **statute forever**: it is a **Covenant of salt forever**....

Deut. 18:1b, 3 ...they shall eat the offerings of יהוה made by fire. ... 3 And this shall be the priest's due from the people, from them that offer a sacrifice, whether it be ox or sheep; and they shall give unto the priest the shoulder, and the two cheeks, and the maw [NRSV: stomach].

APOSTLES: 1 Cor. 9:13-14 Do ye not know that they which minister about holy things live of the things of the Temple? and they which wait at the altar are partakers with the altar? 14 Even so hath יהוה ordained that they which preach the Gospel should live of the Gospel. [also p.97]

APOSTLES: Heb.13:10-13 We have an altar, whereof they have no right to eat which serve the Tabernacle. 11 For the bodies of those beasts, whose blood is brought into the sanctuary by the High Priest for sin, are burned without the camp. 12 Wherefore ישוע also, that He might sanctify the people with His own Blood, suffered without the gate. 13 Let us go forth therefore unto Him without the camp, bearing His reproach.

HOLY BREAD: Lev. 24:5 And thou shalt take fine flour, and bake twelve cakes thereof: ... 6 And thou shalt set them in two rows, six on a row, upon the pure table before יהוה. 7 And thou shalt put pure frankincense upon each row ... 8 Every sabbath he shall set it in order before יהוה continually.... 9 And it shall be Aaron's and his sons'; and they shall eat it in the holy place: for it is most holy unto him

NO WINE OR STRONG DRINK WHEN MINISTERING

Lev. 10:8-10 And יהוה spake unto Aaron, saying, 9 Do not drink wine nor strong drink, thou, nor thy sons with thee, when ye go into the Tabernacle of the congregation, lest ye die: it shall be a **statute forever throughout your generations**: 10 And that ye may put difference between holy and unholy, and between unclean and clean;

Lev. 10:8-10 (*same verses in* NIV) Then the LORD said to Aaron, 9 "You and your sons are not to drink wine or other fermented drink whenever you go into the tent of meeting, or you will die. ... 10 so that you can distinguish between the holy and the common, between the unclean and the clean...."

Lev. 10:11 And that ye may teach the children of Israel all the statutes which יהוה hath spoken unto them by the hand of Moses.

WIFE HE CHOOSES MUST BE PURE AND DAUGHTER MUST STAY PURE

Lev. 21:7-8 They shall not take a wife that is a whore, or profane; neither shall they take a woman put away from her husband: for he is holy unto his God. 8 ... for he offereth the bread of thy God: he shall be holy unto thee: for I יהוה, which sanctify you, am holy.

Lev. 21:13-15 And he shall take a wife in her virginity. 14 A widow, or a divorced woman, or profane, or an harlot, these shall he not take: but he shall take a virgin of his own people to wife. 15 Neither shall he profane his seed among his people: for I יהוה do sanctify him.

Lev. 21:9 And the **daughter** of any priest, if she profane herself by playing the whore, she profaneth her father: she shall be burnt with fire. *[Seems so barbaric. No record of it ever happening.]*

NOT TO TEAR CLOTHES OR UNCOVER HEAD OR GO NEAR THE DEAD

Lev. 10:6-7 (NIV) Then Moses said to Aaron and his sons Eleazar and Ithamar, "**Do not let your hair become unkempt** and **do not tear your clothes,** or you will die and יהוה will be angry with the whole community. But your relatives, all the Israelites, may mourn for those יהוה has destroyed by fire. 7 Do not leave the entrance to the tent of meeting or you will die, because יהוה's anointing oil is on you."

Lev. 21:10-12 And he that is the **high priest** among his brethren, upon whose head the anointing oil was poured, and that is consecrated to put on the garments, shall **not uncover his head, nor rend his clothes;** 11 Neither shall he go in to any dead body, nor defile himself for his father, or for his mother; 12 Neither shall he go out of the sanctuary, nor profane the sanctuary of his God; for the crown of the anointing oil of his God is upon him: I am יהוה.

CANNOT MOURN FOR THE DEAD EXCEPT FOR CLOSE FAMILY

Lev. 21:1-6 And יהוה said unto Moses, Speak unto the priests the sons of Aaron, and say unto them, There shall none be defiled for the dead among his people: 2 But for his kin, that is near unto him, that is, for his mother, and for his father, and for his son, and for his daughter, and for his brother, 3 And for his sister a virgin, that is nigh unto him, which hath had no husband; for her may he be defiled. 4 But he shall not defile himself, being a chief man among his people, to profane himself. 5 They shall not make baldness upon their head, neither shall they shave off the corner of their beard, nor make any cuttings in their flesh. 6 They shall be holy unto their God, and not profane the name of their God: for the offerings of יהוה made by fire, and the bread of their God, they do offer: therefore they shall be holy.

CANNOT MINISTER IF HAVE A BLEMISH OR DISABILITY

Lev. 21:17-23 Speak unto Aaron, saying, Whosoever he be of thy seed in their generations that hath any blemish, let him not approach to offer the bread of his God. 18 For whatsoever man he be that hath a blemish, he shall not approach: a blind man, or a lame, or he that hath a flat nose, or any thing superfluous, 19 Or a man that is brokenfooted, or brokenhanded, 20 Or crookbackt, or a dwarf, or that hath a blemish in his eye, or be scurvy, or scabbed, or hath his stones broken; 21 No man that hath a blemish of the seed of Aaron the priest shall come nigh to offer the offerings of יהוה made by fire: he hath a blemish; he shall not come nigh to offer the bread of his God. 22 He shall eat the bread of his God, both of the most holy, and of the holy. 23 Only he shall not go in unto the veil, nor come nigh unto the altar, because he hath a blemish; that he profane not My sanctuaries: for I יהוה do sanctify them.

CANNOT MINISTER IF THEY ARE UNCLEAN

Ex. 30:21 So they shall wash their hands and their feet, that they die not: and it shall be a **statute forever** to them, even to him and to his seed **throughout their generations.** [also in Wash, p. 207]

Lev. 22:1-9 יהוה said to Moses, 2 Tell Aaron and his sons to treat with respect the sacred offerings the Israelites consecrate to me, so they will not profane my holy name. I am יהוה. 3 Say to them: 'For the generations to come, if any of your descendants is ceremonially unclean and yet comes near the sacred offerings that the Israelites consecrate to יהוה, that person must be cut off from My presence. I am יהוה. 4 If a descendant of Aaron has a defiling skin disease or a bodily discharge, he may not eat the sacred offerings until he is cleansed. He will also be unclean if he touches something defiled by a corpse or by anyone who has an emission of semen, 5 or if he touches any crawling thing that makes him unclean, or any person who makes him unclean, whatever the uncleanness may be. 6 The one who touches any such thing will be unclean till evening. He must not eat any of the sacred offerings unless he has bathed himself with water. 7 When the sun goes down, he will be clean, and after that he may eat the sacred offerings, for they are his food. 8 He must not eat anything found dead or torn by wild animals, and so become unclean through it. I am יהוה. 9 The priests are to perform My service in such a way that they do not become guilty and die for treating it with contempt. I am יהוה, who makes them holy.

HOUSES AND CITIES, BUT NO SEPARATE LAND INHERITANCE

Lev. 25:32-34 ...the **cities** ... and the **houses** of the cities of their possession, may the Levites **redeem at any time**. 33 And if a man purchase of the **Levites**, then the house that was sold, and the city of his possession, shall go out in the year of Jubile: for the houses of the cities of the Levites are their possession.... 34 But the field of the suburbs of their cities may not be sold; for it is their **perpetual possession**. [also in Yovel/Jubilee, p. 184]

Num. 35:1-7 And יהוה spake unto Moses ... near Jericho, saying, 2 Command the children of Israel, that they **give** unto **the Levites** of the inheritance of their possession **cities to dwell in;** and ... **suburbs** for the cities round about them. 3 And the **cities** ... and the **suburbs** of them shall be for their cattle, and for their goods, and for all their beasts. 4 And the suburbs of the cities, which ye shall **give** unto the Levites, shall reach from the wall ... outward a thousand cubits round about. ... 7 ... forty and eight cities.... *{In Josh. 21, these cities are given out.]*

Deut. 18:6-8 And if a Levite come from any of thy gates out of all Israel ... with all the desire of his mind [to] ...minister ...8 [He] shall have ... that which cometh of the **sale of his patrimony.**

Deut. 18:1,2 **The priests the Levites**, and **all the tribe of Levi,** shall have **no part nor inheritance** with Israel: ... 2 יהוה is their inheritance.... *[No separate section of land for just their tribe.]*

Num. 18:20 And יהוה spake unto **Aaron**, Thou shalt have **no inheritance i**n their land, neither shalt thou have any part among them: I am thy part and thine inheritance... (See Ezek. 44:28)

LEVITES AGE TO SERVE: 30 - 50 or 25 - 50

Num. 4:46-47 All those that were numbered of the Levites.... 47 From **thirty years old** and upward even unto fifty years old, every one that came to do the service of the ministry, and the service of the burden in the Tabernacle of the congregation....

Num. 8:24-26 This is ... the Levites: from **twenty and five years old** and upward they shall go in to wait upon the service of the Tabernacle of the congregation: 25 And from the age of fifty years they shall cease ... and shall serve no more: 26 But shall minister with their brethren in the Tabernacle of the congregation, to keep the charge, and shall do no service.

BLOW THE SPECIAL SILVER TRUMPETS

Num. 10:8 And the sons of Aaron, the priests, shall blow with the trumpets; and they shall be to you for an **ordinance forever throughout your generations**

TITHE IS FOR LEVITES AND PRIESTS

Num. 18:26 Thus speak unto the Levites, and say unto them, When ye take of the children of Israel the tithes which I have given you from them for your inheritance, then ye shall offer up an heave offering of it for יהוה, even a tenth part of the tithe.   [also in Tithe, p. 196]

Deut. 18:3-4 And this shall be the priest's due from the people.... 4 The firstfruit also of thy corn, of thy wine, and of thine oil, and the first of the fleece of thy sheep, shalt thou give him.

LEVITES GIVE TITHE OF TITHE TO THE PRIESTS

Num. 18:26, 28 Thus speak unto the Levites, and say unto them, When ye take of the children of Israel the tithes ... then ye shall offer up an heave offering of it for יהוה, **even a tenth part of the tithe**. ... 28 Thus ye also shall offer an heave offering unto יהוה of all your tithes, which ye receive of the children of Israel; and ye shall give thereof יהוה's heave offering to Aaron the priest.

PHINEHAS

Num. 25:10-13 And יהוה spake unto Moses, saying, 11 Phinehas, the son of Eleazar, the son of Aaron the priest, hath turned my wrath away from the children of Israel, while he was zealous for my sake among them, that I consumed not the children of Israel in my jealousy. 12 Wherefore say, Behold, I give unto him **My Covenant of Peace**: 13 And he shall have it, and his seed after him, even the Covenant of an **everlasting** priesthood; because he was zealous for his God, and made an atonement for the children of Israel. [also in Covenant of Peace, p. 237]

AFTER TORAH

[In Ezekiel 44:21-31, you will find the above rules about purity, inheritance, etc., reiterated.]

APOSTLES

1 Cor. 9:14 (NRSV) ...those who proclaim the Gospel should get their living by the Gospel.

Gal. 6:6 (NRSV) Those who are taught the word must share in all good things with their teacher.

I Thess. 5:12-13 And we beseech you, brethren, to know them which labour among you, and are over you in the Lord, and admonish you; 13 And to esteem them very highly in love....

1 Tim. 5:17-18 Let the elders that rule well be counted worthy of double honour, especially they who labour in the word and doctrine. 18 For the scripture saith, Thou shalt not muzzle the ox that treadeth out the corn. And, The labourer is worthy of his reward.

Heb. 13:17-18 Obey them that have the rule over you, and submit yourselves: for they watch for your souls, as they that must give account, that they may do it with joy, and not with grief: for that is unprofitable for you. 18 Pray for us:

James 3:1-2 My brethren, be not many masters, knowing that we shall receive the greater condemnation. 2 For in many things we offend all. If any man offend not in word, the same is a perfect man, and able also to bridle the whole body. ...   the tongue is a little member, and boasteth great things. Behold, how great a matter a little fire kindleth!

1 Pet. 5:1-5 The elders which are among you I exhort, who am also an elder, and a witness of the sufferings of Messiah, and also a partaker of the glory that shall be revealed: 2 Feed the flock

of God which is among you, taking the oversight thereof, not by constraint, but willingly; not for filthy lucre, but of a ready mind [NKJV: not for dishonest gain but eagerly]; 3 Neither as being lords over God's heritage, but being ensamples to the flock. 4 And when the chief Shepherd shall appear, ye shall receive a crown of glory that fadeth not away. 5 Likewise, ye younger, submit yourselves unto the elder. Yea, all of you be subject one to another, and be clothed with humility: for God resisteth the proud, and giveth grace to the humble.

1 Peter 2:9 But ye are a chosen generation, a royal priesthood, an holy nation , a peculiar people....

Rev. 1:6; 5:10 And hath made us kings and priests unto God....10 ...unto our God kings and priests....

160. PROPHET LIKE MOSES – LISTEN TO HIM!

Deut. 18:15 יהוה thy God will raise up unto thee a Prophet from the midst of thee, of thy brethren, like unto me; **unto Him ye shall hearken;**

Deut. 18:18-19 I will raise them up a Prophet from among their brethren, like unto thee, and will put **My Words in His mouth**; and He shall speak unto them all that I shall command Him. And it shall come to pass, that whosoever will not **hearken** unto My Words which He shall speak in My Name, I will require it of him.

YESHUA ישוע

Matt 17:5 While He yet spake, behold, a bright cloud overshadowed them: and behold a voice out of the cloud, which said, This is My beloved Son, in whom I am well pleased; **hear ye Him.**

John 1:21b (CJB) "**Are you 'the prophet,'** the one we're expecting?" "No," [John] replied.

John 5:46 For had ye believed Moses, ye would have believed Me: for he wrote of Me.

John 7:37-46 ...ישוע stood and cried, saying, If any man thirst, let him come unto Me, and drink. 38 He that believeth on Me, as the Scripture hath said, out of his belly shall flow rivers of living water. ... 40 Many ... when they heard this saying, said, **Of a truth this is the Prophet.** 41 Others said, This is the Messiah. But some said, Shall Messiah come out of Galilee? ... 45 Then came the officers to the chief priests and Pharisees; and they said unto them, Why have ye not brought him? 46 The officers answered, **Never man spake like this man.**

John 14:24b ...and the Word which ye hear is not Mine, but the Father's which sent Me.

Acts.3:18-23 [*Peter preaching after the lame man was healed:*]... God before had shewed by the mouth of all His prophets, that Messiah should suffer, He hath so fulfilled. 19 Repent ye therefore, and be converted, that your sins may be blotted out...; 20 And He shall send ישוע Messiah, which before was preached unto you: 21 ... which God hath spoken by the mouth of all His holy prophets since the world began. 22 For Moses truly said unto the fathers, **A prophet** shall יהוה your God raise up unto you of your brethren, **like unto me**; **Him shall ye hear in all things whatsoever He shall say unto you.** 23 And it shall come to pass, that every soul, which will not hear that prophet, shall be destroyed from among the people.

161. BLESSINGS FOR OBEYING HIS COMMANDMENTS

Lev. 26:3 If ye walk in My statutes, and keep My commandments, and do them;

4-5 Then I will give you rain in due season, and the land shall yield her increase, and the trees of the field shall yield their fruit. 5 And your threshing shall reach unto the vintage [CJB: grape harvest], and the vintage shall reach unto the sowing time: and ye shall eat your bread to the full, and dwell in your land safely.

6 And I will give peace in the land, and ye shall lie down, and none shall make you afraid: and I will rid evil beasts out of the land, neither shall the sword go through your land.

7-8 And ye shall chase your enemies, and they shall fall before you by the sword. 8 And five of you shall chase a hundred, and a hundred of you shall put ten thousand to flight: and your enemies shall fall before you by the sword.

9-10 For I will have respect unto you [TLV & CJB: turn toward you], and make you fruitful, and multiply you, and establish My Covenant with you. 10 And ye shall eat old store [the old harvest], and bring forth [TLV: clear out] the old because of the new.

11-13 And I will set My Tabernacle among you: and My soul shall not abhor you. 12 And I will walk among you, and will be your God, and ye shall be My people. 13 I am יהוה your God, which brought you forth out of the land of Egypt, NIV: so that you would no longer be slaves to the Egyptians; I broke the bars of your yoke and enabled you to walk with heads held high.

Lev. 25:18 Wherefore ye shall do My statutes, and keep My judgments, and do them; and ye shall dwell in the land in safety. 19 And the land shall yield her fruit, and ye shall eat your fill, and dwell therein in safety.

Changed "thee" and "thou" and "hast" etc. from here to the end:

Deut. 8:7 For יהוה your God is bringing you into a GOOD land, a land of BROOKS OF WATER, of FOUNTAINS and depths THAT SPRING OUT of valleys and hills;

8 A land of wheat, and barley, and vines, and fig trees, and pomegranates;
   a land of olive oil, and honey;

9 A land wherein thou shalt eat bread without scarceness,
   you shalt NOT LACK ANYTHING in it;
   a land whose stones are iron, and out of whose hills thou mayest dig brass [TLV: copper].

10 When you HAVE EATEN AND ARE FULL, then you shalL BLESS יהוה your God
   for the GOOD land which He has given you.

Deut. 8:11-14 Beware that you forget not יהוה your God, in not keeping His commandments, and His judgments, and His statutes, which I command you this day: 12 Lest when you HAVE EATEN AND ARE FULL, and have BUILT GOODLY HOUSES, and dwelt therein; 13 And when your herds and your flocks multiply, and YOUR SILVER AND YOUR GOLD IS MULTIPLIED, and all that you have is multiplied; 14 Then your heart be lifted up, and you forget יהוה your God, who brought you forth out of the land of Egypt, from the house of bondage; *[and did all those things for you.]*

226

OBEY WHOLEHEARTEDLY

Deut. 8:16-17 [He] FED you in the wilderness with manna, which your fathers knew not, that He might humble you, and that He might prove you, TO DO YOU GOOD at your latter end; 17 And you say in your heart, My power and the might of my hand has gotten me this wealth.

Deut. 8:18 ... remember יהוה your God: for it is He that gives you POWER TO GET WEALTH, that He may establish HIS COVENANT...

Deut. 11:13-15 And it shall come to pass, if ye shall HEARKEN DILIGENTLY unto My commandments which I command you this day, to love יהוה your God, and to serve Him with ALL your heart and with ALL your soul, That I will give you the rain of your land in its due season, the first rain and the latter rain, that you may gather in your corn [grain], and your wine, and your oil. 15 And I will send grass in your fields for your cattle, that YOU MAY EAT AND BE FULL. [also in Love יהוה, p. 238]

Deut. 11:22-25 For if ye shall diligently keep all these commandments which I command you, to do them, to love יהוה your God, to walk in ALL His ways, and to CLEAVE unto Him; 23 Then will יהוה drive out all these nations from before you, and ye shall possess greater nations and mightier than yourselves. 24 EVERY PLACE WHEREON THE SOLES OF YOUR FEET SHALL TREAD SHALL BE YOURS: from the wilderness and Lebanon, from the river, the river Euphrates, even unto the uttermost sea shall your coast be. 25 There shall no man be able to stand before you: for יהוה your God shall lay the fear of you and the dread of you upon all the land that ye shall tread upon, as He hath said unto you. [also in Keep all, p. 21]

Deut. 28:1-2 ... if you shall HEARKEN DILIGENTLY unto the voice of יהוה your God, to observe and TO DO ALL HIS COMMANDMENTS which I command you this day, that יהוה your GOD WILL SET YOU ON HIGH ABOVE ALL NATIONS of the earth: 2 And all these blessings shall come on you, and overtake you, if you shall hearken unto the voice of יהוה your God. [also in Keep All, p. 21]

3 Blessed shall you be in the city, and blessed shall you be in the field.

4 Blessed shall be the fruit of your body, and the fruit of your ground, and the fruit of your cattle, the increase of your kine [cows], and the flocks of your sheep.

5 Blessed shall be your basket and your store.

6 Blessed shall you be when you come in, and blessed shall you be when you go out.

7 יהוה shall cause your enemies that rise up against you to be smitten before your face: they shall come out against you one way, and flee before you seven ways.

8 יהוה SHALL COMMAND THE BLESSING UPON YOU in your storehouses, and in ALL THAT YOU SET YOUR HAND UNTO; and He shall BLESS you in the land which יהוה your God gives you.

Deut. 28:9 יהוה shall establish you a holy people unto Himself, as He has sworn unto you, if you shall keep the commandments of יהוה your God, and walk in His ways.

10 And all people of the earth shall see that you are called by the Name of יהוה; and they shall be afraid of you.

11 And יהוה shall make you PLENTEOUS in GOODS [NRSV: ABOUND in PROSPERITY], in the fruit of your body, and in the fruit of your cattle, and in the fruit of your ground, in the land which יהוה sware unto your fathers to give you.

12 יהוה shall OPEN UNTO YOU HIS GOOD TREASURE, the heaven to give the rain unto your land in its season, and TO BLESS ALL THE WORK OF YOUR HAND:

12b and you shall LEND unto many nations, and you shall NOT BORROW.

13 And יהוה shall make you THE HEAD, and NOT THE TAIL; and you shalt be ABOVE only, and you shall NOT be BENEATH;

13b —if that you HEARKEN UNTO the COMMANDMENTS of יהוה your God, which I command you this day, to observe and to do them: 14 And *[if]* you shall not go aside from any of the Words which I command you this day, to the right hand, or to the left....

Deut. 30:9-10 And יהוה your God will make you PLENTEOUS in EVERY work of your hand, in the fruit of your body, and in the fruit of your cattle, and in the fruit of your land, for good: for יהוה will again REJOICE OVER YOU for good, as He rejoiced over your fathers: 10 **If** you shall hearken unto the voice of יהוה your God, to keep His commandments and His statutes which are written in this book of the TORAH, and if you turn unto יהוה your God with ALL your heart, and with ALL your soul. [also in Keep All, p. 22, Love יהוה, p. 238]

AFTER TORAH

Psalms 1:1,2,3 Blessed is the man *(person) [whose]* ... delight is in the TORAH of יהוה; and in His TORAH doth he meditate day and night. ...WHATSOEVER he does shall PROSPER.

Mal. 3:10-11 (TLV) Bring the whole tithe into the storehouse. Then ... test Me in this"—says Adonai-Tzva'ot—"if I will not open for you the windows of heaven, and pour out blessing for you, until no one is without enough. 11 I will rebuke the devouring pest for you, so it will not destroy.... 12 All the nations will call you blessed. For you will be a land of delight,".....

YESHUA ישוע and APOSTLES

Matt. 5:17-20 Think not that I am come to destroy the Torah, or the Prophets: I am not come to destroy, but to fulfill. 18 For verily I say unto you, till heaven and earth pass, one jot or one tittle shall in no wise pass from the Torah, till all be fulfilled. 19 ... whosoever shall do and teach them [commandments], the same shall be called great in the Kingdom of Heaven. 20 For I say unto you, That except your righteousness shall exceed the righteousness of the scribes and Pharisees, ye shall in no case enter into the Kingdom of Heaven. [also in Keep All, p. 23]

Matt. 6:25, 35 ...Take no thought for your life, what ye shall eat, ... drink ... put on. ... 33 But seek ye first the kingdom of God, and His righteousness; and all these things shall be added unto you.

James 1:25 But whoso looketh into the perfect Torah of liberty, and continueth therein, he being not a forgetful hearer, but a doer of the work, this man shall be blessed in his deed.

2 Cor. 9:7b-8 (TLV) God loves a cheerful giver. 8 And God is able to make all grace overflow to you, so that by always having enough of everything, you may overflow in every good work.

Heb. 11:6 ... he that comes to God must believe that He is, and that He is a rewarder of them that diligently seek Him

162. PUNISHMENT FOR DISOBEYING

If we have any of these things in our lives, we might should look closer at our obedience of Torah.

Lev. 26:14-16a But if ye will not hearken unto Me, and will not do all these commandments; 15 And if ye shall despise My statutes, or if your soul abhor My judgments, so that ye will not do all My commandments, but that ye break My Covenant: 16 I also will do this unto you;

16b I will even appoint over you terror, consumption [TLV: wasting disease], and the burning ague [TLV: fever], that shall consume the eyes, and cause sorrow of heart:

16c and ye shall sow your seed in vain, for your enemies shall eat it.

17 And I will set My face against you, and ye shall be slain before your enemies: they that hate you shall reign over you; and ye shall flee when none pursueth you.

18 And if ye will not yet for all this hearken unto Me, then I will punish you seven times more....

19 And I will break the pride of your power; and I will make your heaven as iron, and your earth as brass:

20 And your strength shall be spent in vain: for your land shall not yield her increase, neither shall the trees of the land yield their fruits.

21 And if ye walk contrary unto Me, and will not hearken unto Me; I will bring seven times more plagues upon you according to your sins.

22 I will also send wild beasts among you, which shall rob you of your children, and destroy your cattle, and make you few in number; and your high ways shall be desolate.

23 And if ye will not be reformed by Me by these things, but will walk contrary unto Me; 24 Then will I also walk contrary unto you, and will punish you yet seven times for your sins.

25 And I will bring a sword upon you, that shall avenge the quarrel of My Covenant: and when ye are gathered together within your cities, I will send the pestilence among you; and ye shall be delivered into the hand of the enemy.

26 And when I have broken the staff of your bread, ten women shall bake your bread in one oven, and they shall deliver you your bread again by weight: and ye shall eat, and not be satisfied.

27 And if ye will not for all this hearken unto Me, but walk contrary unto Me; 28 Then I will walk contrary unto you also in fury; and I, even I, will chastise you seven times for your sins.

29 And ye shall eat the flesh of your sons, and ... your daughters.... Ezek. 5:9-10 CJB: ...because of all your disgusting practices, NRSV: I will do to you what I have never yet done, and ... **will never do again**. 10 ...parents shall eat their children, and children ... their parents! *[It happened so it's done.]*

30-32 And I will destroy your high places, and cut down your images, and cast your carcases upon the carcases of your idols, and My soul shall abhor you. 31 And I will make your cities waste, and bring your sanctuaries unto desolation, and I will not smell the savour of your sweet odours. 32 And I will bring the land into desolation: and your enemies which dwell therein shall be astonished at it.

33-34 And I will scatter you among the heathen, and will draw out a sword after you: and your land shall be desolate, and your cities waste. 34 Then shall the land enjoy her Sabbaths, as long as it lieth desolate, and ye be in your enemies' land; even then shall the land rest, and enjoy her sabbaths. ...

Lev. 26:36-37 And upon them that are left alive of you I will send a faintness into their hearts in the lands of their enemies; and the sound of a shaken leaf shall chase them; and they shall flee, as fleeing from a sword; and they shall fall when none pursueth. 37 And they shall fall one upon another, as it were before a sword, when none pursueth: and ye shall have no power to stand before your enemies.

38-39 And ye shall perish among the heathen, and the land of your enemies shall eat you up. 39 And they that are left of you shall pine away in their iniquity in your enemies' lands; and also in the iniquities of their fathers shall they pine away with them.

Num. 15:30-31 But the **soul that doeth ought presumptuously** [CJB: **intentionally**], whether he be born in the land, or a stranger, the same reproacheth יהוה; and that soul **shall be cut off from among his people.** 31 Because he hath despised the Word of יהוה, and hath broken His commandment, that soul shall utterly be cut off; his iniquity shall be upon him.

Deut. 28:15 on *[changing thou and thee to you, etc.]* But it shall come to pass, if you will not hearken unto the voice of יהוה your God, to observe to do all His commandments and His statutes which I command you this day; that all these curses shall come upon you, and overtake you: [also in Keep All, p. 22]

16-17 Cursed shall you be in the city, and cursed shall you be in the field. 17 Cursed shall be your basket and your store.

18 Cursed shall be the fruit of your body, and the fruit of your land, the increase of your [cattle], and the flocks of your sheep.

19 Cursed will you be when you come in, and cursed shalt thou be when you go out.

20 יהוה shall send upon you cursing, vexation, and rebuke, in all that you set your hand ... to do, until you be destroyed, and until you perish quickly; because of the wickedness of your doings, whereby you have forsaken Me.

21 יהוה shall make the pestilence cleave unto you, until *[it has]* consumed you from off the land....

22 יהוה shall smite you with a consumption, and with a fever, and with an inflammation, and with an extreme burning, and with the sword, and with blasting, and with mildew; and they shall pursue you until you perish.

23-24 And your heaven that is over your head shall be brass, and the earth that is under you shall be iron. 24 יהוה shall make the rain of your land powder and dust: from heaven shall it come down upon you, until you be destroyed.

25-26 יהוה shall cause you to be smitten before your enemies: you shall go out one way against them, and flee seven ways before them: and shall be removed into all the kingdoms of the earth. 26 And your carcase shall be meat unto all fowls of the air, and unto the beasts of the earth, and no man shall fray them away.

Deut. 28:27 יהוה will smite you with the botch [TLV: boils] of Egypt, and with emerods [TLV: hemorrhoids] and with the scab, and with the itch, whereof you can not be healed.

35 יהוה shall smite you in the knees, and in the legs, with a sore botch [TLV: severe boils] that cannot be healed, from the sole of your foot unto the top of your head.

28-29 יהוה shall smite you with madness, and blindness, and astonishment of heart [CJB: confusion]: 29a And thou shalt grope at noonday, as the blind grope in darkness,

29b and you shall not prosper in your ways: and you shall be only oppressed and spoiled evermore, and no man shall save you.

30 You shall betroth a wife, and another man shall lie with her:
you shall build a house, and you shall not dwell therein:
you shall plant a vineyard, and shall not gather the grapes thereof.

31 Your ox shall be slain before your eyes, and you shall not eat thereof: your [donkey] shall be violently taken away from before your face, and shall not be restored to you: your sheep shall be given unto your enemies, and you shall have none to rescue them.

32 Your sons and your daughters shall be given unto another people, and your eyes shall look, and fail with longing for them all the day long: and there shall be no might in your hand.

41 You shall beget sons and daughters, but you shall not enjoy them; for they shall go into captivity.

33-34 The fruit of your land, and all your labor, shall a nation which you know not eat up; and you shall be only oppressed and crushed alway: 34 So that you shall be mad [insane] for the sight of your eyes which you shall see. ...

36 יהוה shall bring you, and your king which you shall set over you, unto a nation which neither you nor your fathers have known; and there shall you serve other gods, wood and stone.

37 And you shall become an astonishment, a proverb, and a byword, among all nations whither יהוה shall lead you.

38 You shall carry much seed out into the field, and shall gather but little in; for the locust shall consume it.

39-40 You shall plant vineyards, and dress them, but shall neither drink of the wine, nor gather the grapes; for the worms shall eat them. 40 You shall have olive trees throughout all your coasts, but you shall not anoint yourself with the oil; for TLV: your olives will drop off.

42 All your trees and fruit of your land shall the locust consume.

43 The stranger [among you] shall get up above you very high; and you shall come down very low.

44 He shall lend to you, and you shall not lend to him: he shall be the head, and you shall be the tail.

45-47 Moreover all these curses shall come upon you, and shall pursue you, and overtake you, till you be destroyed; because you hearkened not unto the voice of יהוה your God, to keep His commandments and His statutes which He commanded you: 46 And they shall be upon you for a sign and for a wonder, and upon your seed **forever**. 47 Because you served not יהוה your God **with joyfulness, and with gladness of heart**, for the abundance of all things;

Deut. 28:48-50 *[changing thou and thee to you, etc.]* Therefore shall you serve your enemies which יהוה shall send against you, in hunger, and in thirst, and in nakedness, and in want of all things: and he shall put a yoke of iron upon your neck, until he have destroyed you. 49 יהוה shall bring a nation against you from far, from the end of the earth, as swift as the eagle flieth; a nation whose tongue you shall not understand; 50 **A nation of fierce countenance, which shall not regard ... the old, nor show favor to the young**:

51-52 And he shall eat the [offspring] of your cattle, and the fruit of your land, until you be destroyed: which also shall not leave you either [grain], wine, or oil, or the increase of your cattle or flocks ... until he have destroyed you. 52 And he shall besiege you in all your gates, until your high and fenced walls come down, wherein you trusted, throughout all your land ... which יהוה your God has given you.

53-57 And you shall eat the fruit of your own body, the flesh of your sons and of your daughters, which יהוה your God has given you, in the siege, and in the straitness, wherewith your enemies shall distress you: 54 So that the man that is tender among you, and very delicate, his eye shall be evil toward his brother, and toward the wife of his bosom, and toward the remnant of his children which he shall leave: 55 So that he will not give to any of them of the flesh of his children whom he shall eat: because he hath nothing left him in the siege.... 56 The tender and delicate woman among you, which would not adventure to set the sole of her foot upon the ground for delicateness and tenderness, her eye shall be evil toward the husband of her bosom, and toward her son, and toward her daughter, 57 And ... toward her children which she shall bear: for she shall eat them for want of all things secretly in the siege and straitness, wherewith your enemy shall distress you in your gates [towns]. *[This happened during the siege of Jerusalem, and God said He will never do it again. See Lev. 26:29 and Ezek, 5:9-10, p. 229.]*

58 If you will not observe to do all the Words of this Torah that are written in this book, that you may fear this glorious and fearful Name, יהוה your God;

59-61 Then יהוה will make your plagues, and the plagues of your seed TLV: extraordinary—terrible and prolonged plagues, severe and prolonged illnesses. SNB: 60 Moreover He will bring upon you all the diseases of Egypt, which you were afraid of; and they shall cleave unto you. 61 Also every sickness, and every plague, which is not written in the book of this Torah, them will יהוה bring upon you, until you be destroyed.

62 And ye shall be left few in number, whereas ye were as the stars of heaven for multitude; because you would not obey the voice of יהוה your God.

63 And it shall come to pass, that as יהוה rejoiced over you to do you good, and to multiply you; so יהוה will rejoice over you to destroy you, and to bring you to nought; and ye shall be plucked from off the land....

Deut. 28:64-65a And יהוה shall scatter you among all people, from the one end of the earth even unto the other; and there you shall serve other gods, which neither you nor your fathers have known, even wood and stone. 65 And among these nations shall you find no ease, neither shall the sole of your foot have rest: [verses 58-64 also in Keep All, p. 22]

Deut. 28:65b-67 but יהוה shall give you there a trembling heart, and failing of eyes, and sorrow of mind: 66 And your life shall hang in doubt before you; and you shall fear day and night, and shall have none assurance of your life: 67 In the morning you shall say, If only it were evening! and at evening you shall say, If only it were morning! for the fear of your heart wherewith you shall fear, and for the sight of your eyes which you shall see.

68 And יהוה shall bring you into Egypt again with ships, by the way whereof I spoke unto you, you shall see it no more again: and there ye shall be sold unto your enemies for bondmen and bondwomen, and no man shall buy you.

Deut. 30:17-18 But if your heart turn away, so that you will not hear, but shall be drawn away, and worship other gods, and serve them; 18 I denounce unto you this day, that ye shall surely perish, and that ye shall not prolong your days upon the land.... [also in Obey, p. 27 and in No other gods, p. 35]

Deut. 8:19-20 And it shall be, if you do at all forget יהוה your God, and walk after other gods, and serve them, and worship them, I testify against you this day that ye shall surely perish. 20 As the nations which יהוה destroys before your face, so shall ye perish; **because ye would not be obedient** unto the voice of יהוה your God. [also in No other gods, p. 31]

AFTER TORAH: 1 Chron. 28:9b ...but if thou forsake Him, He will cast thee off **forever**.

YESHUA: Matt. 5:19- 20 <u>Whosoever therefore shall break one of these least commandments,</u> and shall teach men so, he <u>shall be called the least in the Kingdom of Heaven:</u> ... 20... except your righteousness shall exceed the righteousness of the scribes and Pharisees, ye shall in no case enter into the Kingdom of Heaven. [also in Keep All, p. 23]

APOSTLES: Gal. 3:13 Messiah hath redeemed us from the curse of the Torah, being made a curse for us: for it is written, Cursed is every one that hangeth on a tree: [also in Trees p. 133]

REPENTANCE BRINGS BACK BLESSINGS:

Lev. 26:40-42 If they shall **confess their iniquity,** and the iniquity of their fathers, with their trespass which they trespassed against Me, and that also they have walked contrary unto Me; 41 And that I also have walked contrary unto them, and have brought them into the land of their enemies; if then their uncircumcised hearts be humbled, and they then accept of the punishment of their iniquity: 42 Then will I remember My Covenant with Jacob, and ... Isaac, and ... Abraham ... and I will remember the land. 43 ...and they shall accept of the punishment of their iniquity: because ... they despised My judgments, and because their soul abhorred My statutes. 44 And yet for all that, when they be in the land of their enemies, I will not cast them away, neither will I abhor them, to destroy them utterly, and to break My Covenant with them: for I am יהוה their God. 45 But I will for their sakes remember the Covenant of their ancestors ... that I might be their God: I am יהוה.[also in Obey, p. 24]

Deut. 30:1-5a *[changing thou and thee to you, etc.]* 1 And it shall come to pass, when all these things are come upon you, the blessing and the curse, which I have set before you, and you shall call them to mind among all the nations, whither יהוה your God hath driven you, 2 And **shall return** unto יהוה your God, and shall obey His voice according to all that I

OBEY WHOLEHEARTEDLY

REPENTANCE BRINGS BACK BLESSINGS (cont.)

(cont.) command you this day, you and your children, with all your heart, and with all your soul; 3 That then יהוה your God will turn your captivity, and have compassion upon you, and will return and gather you from all the nations, whither יהוה your God has scattered you. 4 If any of you be driven out unto the outmost parts of heaven, from thence will יהוה your God gather you, and from thence will He fetch you: 5a And יהוה your God will bring you into the land which your fathers possessed, and you shall possess it; [also in Obey, p. 26; verse 2 also in Love יהוה, p. 238]

Deut. 30:5b *[changing thou and thee to you, etc.]* and He will **do you good**, and **multiply you above your fathers.**

6 And יהוה your God will circumcise your heart, and the heart of your [children], to love יהוה your God with all your heart, and with all your soul, that you may live. [also in Circumcise your heart, p. 235 and Love יהוה, p. 238]]

7 And יהוה your God will put all these curses upon your enemies, and on them that hate you, which persecuted you.

AFTER TORAH: 2 Chron. 30:9 For if ye turn again unto יהוה, your brethren and your children shall find compassion before them that lead them captive, so that they shall come again into this land: for יהוה your God is gracious and merciful, and will not turn away His face from you, if ye return unto Him.

Ezek. 18:21-23, 30-32 But if the wicked will **turn from all his sins** that he hath committed, and keep all My statutes, and do that which is lawful and right, he shall surely live, he shall not die. 22 All his transgressions that he hath committed, they shall not be mentioned unto him: in his righteousness that he hath done he shall live. 23 Have I any pleasure at all that the wicked should die? saith Adonai יהוה: and not that he should **return from his ways, and live**? ... 30 Therefore I will judge you, O house of Israel, every one according to his ways, saith [Adonai] יהוה. **Repent, and turn yourselves from all your transgressions;** so iniquity shall not be your ruin. 31 **Cast away from you all your transgressions,** whereby ye have transgressed; and make you a new heart and a new spirit: for why will ye die, O house of Israel? 32 For I have no pleasure in the death of him that dieth, saith [Adonai] יהוה: wherefore **turn yourselves,** and live ye.

163. DON'T THINK THAT IT IS FOR YOUR RIGHTEOUSNESS

Deut. 9:4-8 Speak not thou in thine heart, after that יהוה thy God hath cast them out from before thee, saying, For my righteousness יהוה hath brought me in to possess this land: but for the wickedness of these nations יהוה doth drive them out from before thee. 5 **Not for thy righteousness,** or for the uprightness of thine heart, dost thou go to possess their land: but for the wickedness of these nations יהוה thy God doth drive them out from before thee, and that He may perform the Word which יהוה sware unto thy fathers, Abraham, Isaac, and Jacob. 6 Understand therefore, that יהוה thy God giveth thee not this good land to possess it for thy righteousness; for thou art a stiffnecked people. 7 Remember, and forget not, how thou provoked יהוה thy God to wrath in the wilderness:....

164. CIRCUMCISE YOUR HEART

Deut. 10:16 **Circumcise therefore the foreskin of your heart**, and be no more stiffnecked.

Deut. 30:6 And יהוה thy God will **circumcise thine heart**, and the heart of thy [children], to love יהוה thy God with all thine heart, and with all thy soul, that thou mayest live.

Lev. 26:40 ...if then their **uncircumcised hearts** be humbled, and they then accept of the punishment of their iniquity: 42 Then will I remember My Covenant....

AFTER TORAH

Jer.4:4 **Circumcise yourselves** to יהוה, and take away **the foreskins of your heart**, ye men of Judah and inhabitants of Jerusalem: lest my fury come forth like fire, and burn that none can quench it, because of the evil of your doings.

Jer. 9:25-26 Behold, the days come, saith יהוה, that I will punish all them which are circumcised with the uncircumcised; 26 Egypt, and Judah, and Edom, and the children of Ammon, and Moab, and all that are in the utmost corners, that dwell in the wilderness: for all these nations are uncircumcised, and all the house of Israel are **uncircumcised in the heart**.

Joel 2:13 (CJB) **Tear your heart**, not your garments; and turn to ADONAI your God. For He is merciful and compassionate, slow to anger, rich in grace, and willing to change His mind about disaster.

APOSTLES

Acts. 7:51 Ye stiffnecked and **uncircumcised in hear**t and ears, ye do always resist the Holy Ghost: as your fathers did, so do ye.

Rom. 2:28-29 For he is not a Jew, which is one outwardly; neither is that circumcision, which is outward in the flesh: 29 But he is a Jew, which is one inwardly; and **circumcision is that of the heart**, in the spirit, and not in the letter; whose praise is not of men, but of God.

Col. 2:11,13 In whom also ye are circumcised with the circumcision made without hands, in **putting off the body of the sins of the flesh by the circumcision of Messiah**: ... 13 And you, being dead in your sins and the uncircumcision of your flesh, hath he quickened together with Him, **having forgiven you all trespasses...**

165. CHOOSE LIFE, BLESSINGS

Deut. 11:26-28 **Behold, I set before you this day a blessing and a curse;** 27 a blessing, if ye obey the commandments of יהוה your God, which I command you this day: 28 And a curse, if ye will not obey the commandments of יהוה your God, but turn aside out of the way which I command you this day, to go after other gods, which ye have not known.

Deut. 30:15-19 **See, I have set before you this day life and good, and death and evil**; 16 In that I command you this day to love יהוה your God, to walk in His ways, and to keep His commandments and His statutes and His judgments, **that you may live** and multiply: and יהוה your God shall bless you in the land whither you go to possess it. 17 But if your heart turn away, so that you will not hear, but shall be drawn away, and worship other gods, and serve them; 18

I denounce unto you this day, that ye shall surely perish.... 19 I call heaven and earth to record this day against you, that **I have set before you life and death, blessing and cursing: therefore choose life**, that both you and your [children] may live: [also in Obey, p. 27]

166. BE PERFECT / HOLY

Lev. 11:44-45 For I am יהוה your God: ye shall therefore sanctify yourselves, and **ye shall be holy; for I am holy:** neither shall ye defile yourselves with any manner of creeping thing that creepeth upon the earth. For I am יהוה that bringeth you up out of the land of Egypt, to be your God: ye shall therefore **be holy, for I am holy.**

Lev. 19:2 Speak unto all the congregation of the children of Israel, and say unto them, **Ye shall be holy: for I** יהוה **your God am holy.**

Lev. 20:7 Sanctify yourselves therefore, and **be ye holy: for I am** יהוה **your God**.

Lev. 20:26 And **ye shall be holy unto Me: for I** יהוה **am holy**, and have severed you from other people, that ye should be Mine.

Num. 15:40 That ye may remember, and do all My commandments, and **be holy unto your God.**

Deut. 18:13 **Thou shalt be perfect** with יהוה thy God. [also in Don't imitate, p. 102]

YESHUA ישוע and APOSTLES

Matt. 5:48 **Be ye therefore perfect**, even as your Father which is in Heaven is perfect.

Phil. 3:13-15 ...forgetting those things which are behind, and reaching forth unto those things which are before, 14 I press toward the mark for the prize of the high calling of God in Messiah ישוע. 15 Let us therefore, as many as **be perfect,** be thus minded: and if in any thing ye be otherwise minded, God shall reveal even this unto you.

I Pet. 1:14-19 As obedient children, not fashioning yourselves according to the former lusts...: 15 But as He which hath called you is holy, so **be ye holy in all manner of conversation** [NRSV: conduct]; 16 Because it is written, **Be ye holy; for I am holy.** 17 And if ye call on the Father, who without respect of persons judgeth according to every man's work, pass the time of your sojourning here in fear: 18 Forasmuch as ye know that ye were not redeemed with corruptible things, as silver and gold, from your vain conversation received by tradition from your fathers; 19 But with the precious blood of Messiah, as of a lamb without blemish and without spot:

2 Pet. 3:10-12a But the day of the Lord will come as a thief in the night; in the which the heavens shall pass away with a great noise, and the elements shall melt with fervent heat, the earth also and the works that are therein shall be burned up. 11 Seeing then that all these things shall be dissolved, what manner of persons ought ye to be **in all holy conversation** and godliness, 12 Looking for and hasting unto the coming of the day of God,

167. COVENANT OF PEACE/SHALOM

[In this whole section, replacing "peace" with "shalom."]

Lev. 26:6 And I will give **shalom** in the land, and ye shall lie down, and none shall make you afraid....

Num. 6:26 יהוה lift up His countenance upon thee, and give thee **shalom**.

Num. 25:10-13 And יהוה spake..., 11 Phinehas, the son of Eleazar, the son of Aaron the priest, hath turned My wrath away..., while he was zealous for My sake..., that I consumed not the children of Israel in My jealousy. 12 ... Behold, I give unto him **My Covenant of Shalom**: 13 And he shall have it, and his seed after him, even the Covenant of an **everlasting** priesthood; *[We are kings & priests!]* because he was zealous for his God... [complete in Rules for Priests, p. 224]

PSALMS, PROPHETS,

Ps. 119:165 Great **shalom** have they which love Thy Torah: and nothing shall offend them.

Isaiah 9:7 Of the increase of His government and **shalom** there shall be no end....

Isaiah 54:10 For the mountains shall depart, and the hills be removed; but My kindness shall not depart from thee, neither shall the **Covenant of My Shalom** be removed, saith יהוה that hath mercy on thee.

Ezek. 34:25 And I will make with them a **Covenant of Shalom,** and will cause the evil beasts to cease out of the land: and they shall dwell safely in the wilderness, and sleep in the woods.

Ezek. 37:26 Moreover I will make a **Covenant of Shalom** with them; it shall be an **everlasting** covenant with them: and I will place them, and multiply them, and will set My sanctuary in the midst of them for evermore.

Mal. 2:5 My **Covenant was with him** (Levi) **of Life and Shalom;** and I gave them to him for the fear wherewith he feared Me, and was afraid before My Name. 6 The Torah of Truth was in his mouth, and iniquity was not found in his lips: he walked with Me in shalom and equity, and did turn many away from iniquity.

YESHUA ישוע and APOSTLES

John 14:27 **Shalom** I leave with you, My **shalom** I give unto you: not as the world giveth, give I unto you. Let not your heart be troubled, neither let it be afraid. [also in Shelem offering, p. 70]

John 16:33 These things I have spoken unto you, that in Me ye might have **shalom**. In the world ye shall have tribulation: but be of good cheer; I have overcome the world.

Mar 5:34; Luk 7:50; 8:48 Go in **shalom.** Luke 24:36; John 20:19,20,26 **Shalom** be unto you.

1 Cor. 7:15b God hath called us to **shalom**. Col. 1:20 And, having made **shalom** through the Blood of His Cross, by Him to reconcile all things unto Himself....

2 Cor 13:11 Finally, brethren, ...live in **shalom**; and the God of love and **shalom** shall be with you.

Col 3:15 And let the **shalom** of God rule in your hearts, ... and be ye thankful. [also in Shelem, p. 70]

Phil. 4:7 And the **shalom** of God, which passeth all understanding, shall keep your hearts and minds through Messiah ישוע. [also in Shelem offering, p. 70]

Rom. 16:20 (TLV) Now the God of **shalom** will soon crush satan under your feet. May the grace of our Lord Yeshua ישוע be with you. *[See more shalom Bible verses on page 250-255.]*

168. LOVE יהוה YOUR GOD
(WITH ALL YOUR HEART AND SOUL)

We love Him, because He first loved us. I John 4:19

(Thee, thou, thine to you, your etc.) Deut. 4:29 But if from thence you shalt seek יהוה your God, you shall find Him, if you seek Him **with all your heart and with all your soul.**

Deut. 6:4-6 Hear, O Israel: יהוה our Elohim, יהוה is one: 5 And **you shall love יהוה your God with all your heart, and with all your soul, and with all your might.** 6 And these words, which I command you this day, shall be in your heart:

Deu 7:6,8 ... יהוה your God has chosen you to be a special people unto Himself, above all people that are upon the face of the earth. ... 4 ...because יהוה loved you,

Deut. 10:12-13 And now, Israel, what does יהוה your God require of you, but to fear יהוה your God, to walk in all His ways, and to l**ove Him**, and to serve יהוה your God **with all your heart and with all your soul,** 13 To keep the commandments of יהוה ... for your good?

Deut. 11:1,8 Therefore you shall **love יהוה your God**, and keep His charge, and His statutes, and His judgments, and His commandments, alway. ... 8 ...that ye may be strong....

Deut. 11:13-14,18 And it shall come to pass, if ye shall hearken diligently unto My commandments which I command you this day, to **love יהוה your God**, and to serve Him **with all your heart and with all your soul,** 14 That I will give you the rain of your land in his due season, the first rain and the latter rain, that you may gather in your [grain], and your wine, and your oil. ... 18 Therefore shall ye lay up these My Words **in your heart and in your soul**....

Deut. 11:22-23a For if ye shall diligently keep all these commandments which I command you, to do them, to **love יהוה your God**, to walk in all His ways, and to cleave unto Him; 23 Then [*blessings*].... [also in Keep all, p. 21 and Blessings for obedience, p. 227]

Deut. 13:3 You shall not hearken unto the words of that [false] prophet, or that dreamer of dreams: for יהוה your God [TLV: is testing] you, to know whether ye **love יהוה your God with all your heart and with all your soul**.

Deu 19:9 If you shalt keep all these commandments ... to **love יהוה your God**, and to walk ever in His ways; then shall you add three cities more.... {also in Keep all, p. 21]

Deut. 30:2,6 And shalt return unto יהוה your God, and shalt obey His voice according to all that I command you this day, you and your children, **with all your heart, and with all your soul**; ... 6 And יהוה your God will circumcise your heart, and the heart of your [children], to **love יהוה your God with all your heart and with all your soul,** that you may live.

Deu 30:9, 10, 16, 20 ... for יהוה will again rejoice over thee ... 10 ...if thou turn unto יהוה thy God **with all thine heart, and with all thy soul.** ... 16 ...I command you this day to **love יהוה your God,** to walk in His ways ... that you may live and multiply: and יהוה your God shall bless thee....20 That you may **love יהוה your God**, and that you may obey His voice, and that you may cleave unto Him: for He is your life.... [also in Keep All, p. 22 and Obey, p.27]

OBEY WHOLEHEARTEDLY

Josh. 22:5 But take diligent heed to do the commandment and the Torah, which Moses the servant of יהוה charged you, to **love יהוה your God**, and to walk in all His ways, and to keep His commandments, and to cleave unto Him, and to serve Him **with all your heart and with all your soul.**

Josh. 23:11 Take good heed therefore unto yourselves, that **ye love יהוה your God.**

1 Chron. 28:9 And you, Solomon my son, know you the God of your father, and **serve Him with a perfect heart** [CJB: wholeheartedly] **and with a willing mind**: for יהוה searches all hearts, and understands all the imaginations of the thoughts: if you seek Him, He will be found by you; but if you forsake Him, He will cast you off **forever**.

2 Chron. 15:15 And all Judah rejoiced ... for they had sworn with **all their heart**, and sought Him with their **whole desire**; and He was found of them: and יהוה gave them rest round about.

2 Kings 23:25 And like unto him [Josiah] was there no king before him, that turned to יהוה **with all his heart, and with all his soul, and with all his might**, according to all the Torah of Moses; neither after him arose there any like him.

Psalm 9:1; 111:1; 138:1 I will praise You, O יהוה, with my **whole heart**....

Psa 116:1 I love יהוה, because He has heard my voice and my supplications.

Psalm 119:2 Blessed are they that keep His testimonies, and that seek Him with the **whole heart**.

Psalm 119:10, 34, 69 With my **whole heart** have I sought You: O let me not wander from Your commandments. ... 34 Give me understanding, and I shall keep Your Torah; yea, I shall observe it with my **whole heart**. ... 69 ...I will keep Your precepts with my **whole heart**. [also in Obey, p. 27]

Psalm 146:8 יהוה opens the eyes of the blind: יהוה raises them that are bowed down: יהוה **loves the righteous:**

Psa 145:20a יהוה preserves all them that **love Him**....

Pro 3:12 For whom יהוה loves He corrects; Heb 12:6 For whom the Lord loves He chastens, and scourges every son whom He receives.

Jer. 24:7 And I will give them a **heart** to know Me, that I am יהוה: and they shall be My people, and I will be their God: for they shall return unto Me with their **whole heart**.

Jer 31:3 יהוה hath appeared of old unto me, saying, Yea, **I have loved you** with an **everlasting** love: therefore with lovingkindness have I drawn you.

YESHUA ישוע

Matt. 22:36-40 Master, which is the great[est] commandment in the Torah? 37 ישוע said unto him, You shall **love יהוה your God with all your heart, and with all your soul, and with all your mind**. 38 This is the first and great[est] commandment. 39 And the second is like unto it, You shall love your neighbour as yourself. 40 On these two commandments hang all the Torah and the prophets. [also in First and Second Command, p. 9]

Mark 12:28-30 And one of the scribes came, and having heard them reasoning together, ... asked Him, Which is the first commandment of all? 29 And ישוע answered him, The first of all the commandments is, **Hear, O Israel;** יהוה **our Elohim,** יהוה **is one**: 30 And thou shalt **love** יהוה **thy God with all thy heart, and with all thy soul, and with all thy mind, and with all thy strength:** this is the first commandment. [also in First Command, p. 9]

Luke 10:27-28 ... Thou shalt **love** יהוה **thy God with all thy heart, and with all thy soul, and with all thy strength, and with all thy mind;** and thy neighbour as thyself. 28 And He [ישוע] said unto him, Thou hast answered right: this do, and thou shalt live.

Luke 7:47b ... to whom little is forgiven, the same loveth little.

John 14:15, 21 If ye love Me, keep My commandments. ... :21 He that hath My commandments, and keepeth them, he it is that loveth Me: and he that loveth Me shall be loved of My Father, and **I will love him**, and will manifest Myself to him.

John 14:23-24 ישוע answered ... If a man love Me, he will keep My Words: and **My Father will love him**, and We will come unto him, and make our abode *[home]* with him. 24 He that loveth Me not keepeth not My sayings....

John 15:13 Greater love hath no man than this, that a man lay down his life for his friends.

John 16:27 For the Father Himself loveth you, because ye have loved Me, and have believed that I came out from God.

APOSTLES

1 John 4:10, 19 **Herein is love, not that we loved God, but that He loved us**, and sent His Son.... 19 **We love Him, because He first loved us.**

Rom. 5:6-8 (NRSV) For while we were still weak, at the right time Christ [Messiah] died for the ungodly. 7 Indeed, rarely will anyone die for a righteous person—though perhaps for a good person someone might actually dare to die. 8 But **God proves His love for us in that while we still were sinners Christ [Messiah] died for us.**

1 John 4:15-17 Whosoever shall confess that ישוע is the Son of God, God dwelleth in him, and he in God. 16 And we have known and believed the love that God hath to us. **God is love**; and **he that dwelleth in love dwelleth in God**, and God in him. 17 Herein is our love made perfect, that we may have boldness in the day of judgment: because as He is, so are we in this world.

1 John 4:8 He that loveth not knoweth not God; for **God is love.**

1 John 4:18 There is no fear in love; but **perfect love casteth out fear:** because fear hath torment. He that feareth is not made perfect in love.

1 John 4:20b-21 ...he that loveth not his brother whom he hath seen, how can he love God whom he hath not seen? 21 And this commandment have we from Him, That he who loveth God love his brother also. [also in Love thy neighbor, p. 96]

1 John 5:1b ... every one that loveth Him that begat *[God]* loveth Him also that is begotten of Him.

2 John 1:6 And this is love, that we **walk after His commandments.** [also in Obey, p. 29]

169. BE STRONG, HE WILL NEVER LEAVE YOU

Deut. 31:1,6-8 And Moses went and spake these words unto all Israel. ... 6 **Be strong and of a good courage, fear not, nor be afraid** of them: for יהוה thy God, He it is that doth go with thee; He will not fail thee, nor forsake thee. 7 And Moses called unto Joshua, and said unto him in the sight of all Israel, **Be strong and of a good courage:** for thou must go with this people unto the land which יהוה hath sworn unto their fathers to give them; and thou shalt cause them to inherit it. 8 And יהוה, He it is that doth go before thee; **He will be with thee, He will not fail thee, neither forsake thee:** fear not, neither be dismayed.

AFTER TORAH

Josh 1:6 **Be strong and of a good courage**: for unto this people shalt thou divide for an inheritance the land, which I sware unto their fathers to give them.

Josh 1:7 Only **be thou strong and very courageous,** that thou mayest observe to do according to all the Torah, which Moses my servant commanded thee: turn not from it to the right hand or to the left, that thou mayest prosper whithersoever thou goest.

Josh. 1:9 Have not I commanded thee? **Be strong and of a good courage; be not afraid**, neither be thou dismayed: for יהוה thy God is with thee whithersoever thou goest.

1 Chron. 28:10b, 20 ... **be strong and act**.... **Be strong and of good courage,** ... **fear not**, nor be dismayed: for יהוה God, even my **God, will be with thee; He will not fail thee, nor forsake thee,** until thou hast finished all the work for the service of the house of יהוה. [also in Rules for the King, p. 217]

Isaiah 41:9-10 Thou whom I have taken from the ends of the earth, and called thee from the chief men thereof, and said unto thee, Thou art My servant; I have chosen thee, and not cast thee away. 10 **Fear thou not; for I am with thee: be not dismayed; for I am thy God**: I will strengthen thee; yea, I will help thee; yea, I will uphold thee with the right hand of My righteousness.

Psalm 27:14 (ASV) Wait for Jehovah: **Be strong**, And let thy heart **take courage**; Yea, wait thou for Jehovah.

YESHUA ישוע and APOSTLES

Matt. 28:19-20 Go ye therefore, and teach all nations, baptizing them in the Name of the Father, and of the Son, and of the Holy Spirit: 20 Teaching them to observe all things whatsoever I have commanded you: and, **lo, I am with you alway, even unto the end of the world.** Amen

Heb. 13:5b-6 ...**for He hath said, I will never leave thee, nor forsake thee.** 6 So that we may boldly say, The Lord is my helper, and I will not fear what man shall do unto me.

170. GRACE IN THE TORAH

["Grace" and "gracious" in Hebrew: חֵן khen, חָנַן khanan, חָנוּן khanun, חָנֹת khanot, and חֶסֶד khesed.]

BEFORE TORAH

Gen 6:8 But Noah found GRACE in the eyes of יהוה.

Gen. 19:19 Behold now, Thy servant hath found GRACE in Thy sight, and Thou hast magnified Thy mercy, which Thou hast shewed unto me in saving my life....

Gen. 43:29 (NRSV) God be GRACIOUS to you, my son!

TORAH

Ex 33:13 Now therefore, I pray Thee, if I have found GRACE in Thy sight, shew me now Thy way, that I may know Thee, that I may find GRACE in Thy sight:

Ex. 33:16 For wherein shall it be known here that I and Thy people have found GRACE in Thy sight? Is it not in that Thou goest with us?

Ex. 33:17 And יהוה said unto Moses, I will do this thing also that thou hast spoken: for thou hast found GRACE in My sight, and I know thee by name.

Ex. 33:18-19 And he said, I beseech Thee, shew me Thy Glory. 19 And He said, I will make all My goodness pass before thee, and I will proclaim the Name of יהוה before thee; and will be GRACIOUS to whom I will be GRACIOUS, and will shew mercy on whom I will shew mercy.

Ex. 34:6-7 And יהוה passed by before him, and proclaimed, יהוה, יהוה אל (God) merciful and GRACIOUS, (NRSV) slow to anger, and abounding in steadfast love and faithfulness, 7 keeping steadfast love for the thousandth generation, forgiving iniquity and transgression and sin, yet by no means clearing the guilty,

Ex. 34:9 If now I have found GRACE in Thy sight, O [Adonai], let my [Adonai], I pray Thee, go among us;

Numbers 6:23-27 Speak unto Aaron and ...sons, saying, On this wise ye shall bless the children of Israel, saying..., 24 יהוה bless thee, and keep thee: 25 יהוה make His face shine upon thee, and be GRACIOUS unto thee: 26 יהוה lift up His countenance upon thee, and give thee **shalom**. 27 And they shall **put My Name** upon the children of Israel; and I will bless them.

AFTER TORAH

2 Kings 13:23 And יהוה was GRACIOUS unto them, and had compassion on them,

2 Chron. 30:9 (NRSV) For as you return to the LORD, your kindred and your children will find compassion with their captors, and return to this land. For the LORD your God is GRACIOUS and merciful, and will not turn away His face from you, if you return to Him.

Ezra 8:22 (NRSV) ...the hand of our God is GRACIOUS [KJV: good; Hebrew: tov טוֹב] to all who seek Him, but His power and His wrath are against all who forsake Him.

Neh 2:8 (NRSV) ...the king granted me what I asked, for the GRACIOUS [KJV: good; Hebrew: tov טוב] hand of my God was upon me.

Neh 9:17, 31 ...but Thou art a God ready to pardon, GRACIOUS and merciful, slow to anger, and of great kindness, and forsook them not. ... 31 Nevertheless for Thy great mercies' sake Thou didst not utterly consume them, nor forsake them; for Thou art a GRACIOUS and merciful God.

PSALMS AND PROVERBS

Psalms 4:1 (NRSV) Answer me when I call, O God of my right! You gave me room when I was in distress. Be GRACIOUS to me, and hear my prayer.

Psalms 6:2 (NRSV) Be GRACIOUS to me, O LORD, for I am languishing; O LORD, heal me, for my bones are shaking with terror.

Psalms 9:13 (NRSV) Be GRACIOUS to me, O LORD. See what I suffer from those who hate me; you are the one who lifts me up from the gates of death,

Psalms 25:16 (NRSV) Turn to me and be GRACIOUS to me, for I am lonely and afflicted.

Psalms 26:11 (NRSV) But as for me, I walk in my integrity; redeem me, and be GRACIOUS to me.

Psalms 45:2 GRACE is poured into thy lips: therefore God hath blessed thee **forever**.

Psalms 67:1 (NRSV) May God be GRACIOUS to us and bless us and make His face to shine upon us, (Selah)

Psalms 84:11 For יהוה God is a sun and shield: יהוה will give GRACE and glory: no good thing will He withhold from them that walk uprightly.

Psalms 86:15 But thou, O [Adonai], art a God full of compassion, and GRACIOUS, longsuffering, and plenteous in mercy and truth.

Psalms 103:8 יהוה is merciful and GRACIOUS, slow to anger, and plenteous in mercy.

Psalms 116:5 GRACIOUS is יהוה, and righteous; yea, our God is merciful.

Psalms 145:8 יהוה is GRACIOUS, and full of compassion; slow to anger, and of great mercy.

Prov. 1:8-9 My son, hear the instruction of thy father, and forsake not the Torah of thy mother: 9 For they shall be an ornament of GRACE unto thy head, and chains about thy neck.

Prov. 3:21-22 My son, ... keep sound wisdom and discretion: 22 So shall they be life unto thy soul, and GRACE to thy neck.

Prov. 3:34 Surely He scorneth the scorners: but He giveth GRACE unto the lowly .

Prov. 4:7-9 Wisdom is the principal thing; therefore get wisdom: and with all thy getting get understanding. 8 Exalt her, and she shall promote thee: she shall bring thee to honour, when thou dost embrace her. 9 She shall give to thine head an ornament of GRACE: a crown of glory shall she deliver to thee.

Prov. 22:11 He that loveth pureness of heart, for the GRACE of his lips the king shall be his friend.

PROPHETS

Isaiah 30:18 And therefore will יהוה wait, that He may be GRACIOUS unto you, and therefore will He be exalted, that He may have mercy upon you: for יהוה is a God of judgment: blessed are all they that wait for Him.

Isaiah 30:19 For the people shall dwell in Zion at Jerusalem: thou shalt weep no more: He will be very GRACIOUS unto thee at the voice of thy cry; when He shall hear it, He will answer thee..

Isaiah 63:7 I will mention the lovingkindnesses (GRACIOUSNESS) of יהוה, and the praises of יהוה, according to all that יהוה hath bestowed on us, and the great goodness toward the house of Israel, which He hath bestowed on them according to His mercies, and according to the multitude of His lovingkindnesses (GRACIOUSNESS).

Joel 2:12-14 Therefore also now, saith יהוה, turn ye even to Me with all your heart, and with fasting, and with weeping, and with mourning: 13 And rend your heart, and not your garments, and turn unto יהוה your God: for He is GRACIOUS and merciful, slow to anger, and of great kindness, and [NRSV: relents from punishing]. 14 Who knoweth if He will return and [comfort], and leave a blessing behind Him; ....

Amos 5:15 Hate the evil, and love the good, and establish judgment in the gate: it may be that יהוה God of hosts will be GRACIOUS unto the remnant of Joseph.

Jonah 4:2 ...Thou art a gracious God, and merciful, slow to anger, and of great kindness, and [NRSV: relents from punishing].

Zech. 12:10 And I will pour upon the house of David, and upon the inhabitants of Jerusalem, the spirit of GRACE and of supplications: and they shall look upon Me whom they have pierced, and they shall mourn for Him, as one mourneth for his only son, and shall be in bitterness for Him, as one that is in bitterness for his firstborn.

Zech 4:7 Who art thou, O great mountain? before Zerubbabel thou shalt become a plain: and he shall bring forth the headstone thereof with shoutings, crying, GRACE, GRACE unto it.

YESHUA ישוע

John 1:14 And the Word was made flesh, and dwelt among us, (and we beheld His glory, the glory as of the only begotten of the Father,) full of GRACE and truth.

John 1:16 (NRSV) From His fullness we have all received, **GRACE upon GRACE.**

John 1:17 For the Torah was given by Moses, *but* **GRACE and truth** came by ישוע Messiah.

Luke 2:40 And the child grew, and waxed strong in spirit, filled with wisdom: and the GRACE of God was upon Him.

Luke 4:22 And all ... wondered at the GRACIOUS Words which proceeded out of His mouth.

Matt. 11:25-26 (NRSV) At that time Jesus said, "I thank You, Father, Lord of heaven and earth, because You have hidden these things from the wise and the intelligent and have revealed them to infants; 26 yes, Father, for such was Your GRACIOUS will.

Luke 10:21 (NRSV) At that same hour Jesus rejoiced in the Holy Spirit and said, "I thank You, Father, Lord of heaven and earth, because You have hidden these things from the wise and the intelligent and have revealed them to infants; yes, Father, for such was Your GRACIOUS will.

APOSTLES

Acts 4:33 And with great power gave the apostles witness of the Resurrection of Adonai ישוע: and great GRACE was upon them all.

Acts 11:23 (NRSV) When he (Barnabas) came and saw the GRACE of God, he rejoiced, and he exhorted them all (the Hellenist Jews) to remain faithful to the LORD with steadfast devotion;

Acts 13:43 Now when the congregation was broken up, many of the Jews and religious proselytes followed Paul and Barnabas: who, speaking to them, persuaded them to continue in the GRACE of God.

Acts 14:3 (NRSV) So they remained for a long time, speaking boldly for the Lord, who testified to the Word of His GRACE by granting signs and wonders to be done through them.

Acts 15:11 But we believe that through the GRACE of Adonai ישוע Messiah we shall be saved, even as they.

Acts 15:40 And Paul chose Silas, and departed, being recommended by the brethren unto the GRACE of God.

Acts 18:27 ...when he was ...to pass into Achaia, the brethren wrote, exhorting the disciples to receive him: who, when he was come, helped them much which had believed through GRACE:

Acts 20:24 But none of these things move me, neither count I my life dear unto myself, so that I might finish my course with joy, and the ministry, which I have received of Adonai ישוע, to testify the Gospel of the GRACE of God.

Acts 20:32 And now, ...I commend you to God, and to the Word of His GRACE, which is able to build you up, and to give you an inheritance among all them which are sanctified.

Romans 1:3-5 Concerning His Son ישוע Messiah our Lord, ... 4 declared to be the Son of God with power, according to the Spirit of holiness, by the resurrection from the dead: 5 By whom we have received GRACE and apostleship, for obedience to the faith among all nations, for His Name:

Romans 3:21-25 But now the righteousness of God TLV: apart from the Torah has been revealed, to which the Torah and the Prophets bear witness; SNB: 22 Even the righteousness of God which is by faith of ישוע Messiah unto all and upon all them that believe: for there is no difference: 23 For all have sinned, and come [fall] short of the glory of God; 24 Being justified freely by His GRACE through the redemption that is in Messiah ישוע: 25 Whom God hath set forth to be [the atonement] through faith in His Blood, to declare His righteousness for the remission of sins that are past, through the forbearance of God;

Romans 4:16 (NRSV) For this reason it depends on faith, in order that the promise may rest on GRACE and be guaranteed to all his descendants, not only to the adherents of the law [Torah] but also to those who share the faith of Abraham....

Romans 5:2 By whom also we have access by faith into this GRACE wherein we stand, and rejoice in hope of the glory of God.

Romans 5:15 But ... much more the GRACE of God, and the gift by GRACE, which is by one man, ישוע Messiah, hath abounded unto many.

Romans 5:17 ...much more they which receive abundance of GRACE and of the gift of righteousness shall reign in life by one, ישוע Messiah.

Romans 5:20   ...But where sin abounded, GRACE did much more abound:

Romans 5:21 even so might GRACE reign through righteousness unto eternal life by ישוע Messiah our Lord.

Romans 6:14 For sin shall not have dominion over you: for ye are not under the law, but under GRACE.

Romans 11:5 (NRSV) So too at the present time there is a remnant, chosen by GRACE.

Romans 11:6 (NRSV) But if it is by GRACE, it is no longer on the basis of works, otherwise GRACE would no longer be GRACE.

Romans 12:6 (NRSV) We have gifts that differ according to the GRACE given to us.

Romans 16:20 The GRACE of our Adonai ישוע Messiah be with you.

I Cor. 3:10 According to the GRACE of God which is given unto me, as a wise masterbuilder, I have laid the foundation, and another buildeth thereon. But let every man take heed how he buildeth thereupon.

I Cor. 15:10 But by the GRACE of God I am what I am: and His GRACE which was bestowed upon me was not in vain; but I laboured more abundantly than they all: yet not I, but the GRACE of God which was with me.

I Cor. 16:23 The GRACE of our Adonai ישוע Messiah be with you.

2 Cor 1:12 (TLV) ... we behaved in the world, and most especially toward you, with simplicity and Godly sincerity—not by human wisdom but by the GRACE of God ....

2 Cor. 8:1 (NRSV) We want you to know, brothers and sisters, about the GRACE of God that has been granted to the churches of Macedonia.

2 Cor. 6:1 We then, as workers together with Him, beseech you also that ye receive not the GRACE of God in vain.

2 Cor. 8:7 Therefore, as ye abound in every thing, in faith, and utterance, and knowledge, and in all diligence, and in your love to us, see that ye abound in this GRACE also.

2 Cor. 8:9 For ye know the GRACE of our Adonai ישוע Messiah that, though He was rich, yet for your sakes He became poor, that ye through His poverty might be rich.

2 Cor. 8:19 ...with this GRACE, which is administered by us to the glory of the same Lord....

2 Cor. 9:8 And God is able to make all GRACE abound toward you; that ye, always having all sufficiency in all things, may abound to every good work:

2 Cor. 9:14 (NRSV) the surpassing GRACE of God that He has given you.

2 Cor. 12:9 **My GRACE is sufficient for thee:** for My strength is made perfect in weakness. Most gladly therefore will I rather glory in my infirmities, that the power of Messiah may rest upon me.

2 Cor. 13:14 The GRACE of Adonai ישוע Messiah, the love of God, and the communion of the Holy Spirit be with all of you. Amen.

Gal 1:6 ...Him that called you into the GRACE of Messiah....

Gal 1:15 ...and called me by His GRACE....

Gal 2:9 (NRSV) When James and Cephas and John, who were acknowledged pillars, recognized the GRACE that had been given to me, they gave to Barnabas and me the right hand of fellowship....

Gal 2:21 (NRSV) I do not nullify the GRACE of God; for if justification comes through the law, then Christ died for nothing.

Gal 5:4 Messiah is become of no effect unto you, whosoever of you are justified by Torah; ye are fallen from GRACE.

Gal 6:18 ...the GRACE of our Adonai ישוע Messiah be with your spirit. Amen.

Eph. 1:6 To the praise of the glory of His GRACE, wherein He hath made us accepted in the Beloved.

Eph. 1:7 In whom (Him) we have redemption through His Blood, the forgiveness of sins, **according to the riches of His GRACE.**

Eph. 2:5 ...**by GRACE ye are saved**....

Eph. 2:7 That in the ages to come He might shew the exceeding [NRSV: immeasurable] riches of His GRACE in His kindness toward us through Messiah ישוע.

Eph. 2:8 (NRSV) **For by GRACE you have been saved through faith, and this is not your own doing; it is the gift of God—**

Eph. 3:2 (NRSV) ...for surely you have already heard of the commission of God's GRACE that was given me for you,

Eph. 3:7 Whereof I was made a minister, according to the gift of the GRACE of God given unto me by the effectual working of His Power.

Eph. 3:8 Unto me, who am less than the least of all saints, is this GRACE given, that I should preach among the Gentiles the unsearchable riches of Messiah;

Eph. 4:7 But unto every one of us is given GRACE according to the measure of the gift of Messiah.

Eph. 4:29 (NRSV) Let no evil talk come out of your mouths, but only what is useful for building up, as there is need, so that your words may give GRACE to those who hear.

Eph. 6:24 GRACE be with all them that love our Adonai ישוע Messiah in sincerity. Amen.

Phil. 1:7 (NRSV) ...for all of you share in God's GRACE with me, both in my imprisonment and in the defense and confirmation of the Gospel.

Phil. 4:23   The GRACE of Adonai ישוע Messiah be with you all. Amen.

Col. 1:6 (NRSV) Just as it is bearing fruit and growing in the whole world, so it has been bearing fruit among yourselves from the day you heard it **and truly comprehended the GRACE of God**.

Col. 4:18b   GRACE be with you. Amen.

I Thess. 5:28   The GRACE of our Adonai ישוע Messiah be with you.

2 Thess. 1:11-12 (ASV) To which end we also pray always for you, that our God may count you worthy of your calling, and fulfill every desire of goodness and [every] work of faith, with power; 12 that the Name of our Lord [ישוע]may be glorified in you, and ye in Him, according to the GRACE of our God and the Lord [ישוע Messiah].

2 Thess. 2:16-17 Now our Adonai ישוע Messiah Himself, and God, even our Father, which hath loved us, and hath given us **everlasting** consolation and good hope through GRACE, 17 comfort your hearts, and stablish you in every good word and work.

2 Thess. 3:18   The GRACE of our Adonai ישוע Messiah be with you all. Amen.

I Tim. 1:14 And the grace of our Lord was exceeding abundant with faith and love which is in Messiah ישוע.

I Tim. 6:21   GRACE be with thee. Amen.

2 Tim. 1:8-9 (NKJV) Therefore do not be ashamed of the testimony of our Lord, nor of me His prisoner, but share [NRSV: join] with me in the sufferings for the Gospel according to [NRSV: relying on] the power of God, 9 who has saved us and called us with a holy calling, not according to our works, but according to His own purpose and GRACE which was given to us in Christ Jesus before time began,

2 Tim. 2:1 [You then, my child], **be strong in the GRACE that is in Messiah ישוע**;

2 Tim. 4:22 Adonai ישוע Messiah be with thy spirit. GRACE be with you. Amen.

Titus 2:11-13 For the GRACE of God that bringeth salvation hath appeared to all men, 12 **Teaching us** that, denying ungodliness and worldly lusts, we should live soberly, righteously, and Godly, in this present world; 13 Looking for that blessed hope, and the glorious appearing of the great God and our Saviour ישוע Messiah....

Titus 3:4-7 But after that the kindness and love of God our Saviour toward man appeared, 5 Not by works of righteousness which we have done, but according to His mercy He saved us, by the washing of regeneration, and renewing of the Holy Spirit; 6 Which He shed on us abundantly through Jesus Christ our Saviour; 7 That being **justified by His GRACE**, we should be made heirs according to the hope of eternal life.

Titus 3:15 GRACE be with you all. Amen.

Heb. 2:9   But we see Jesus, who was made a little lower than the angels for the suffering of death, crowned with glory and honour; that He by the GRACE of God should taste death for every man.

Heb. 4:16 Let us therefore come boldly unto the throne of GRACE, that we may obtain mercy, and **find GRACE to help in time of need.**

GRACE AND SHALOM

Heb. 10:29 (NRSV) How much worse punishment do you think will be deserved by those who have spurned the Son of God, profaned the Blood of the Covenant by which they were sanctified, and outraged the Spirit of GRACE?

Heb. 12:15 (NRSV) **See to it that no one fails to obtain the GRACE of God;** that no root of bitterness springs up and causes trouble, and through it many become defiled.

Heb. 12:28 Wherefore we receiving a Kingdom which cannot be moved, let us have GRACE, whereby we may serve God acceptably with reverence and Godly fear:

Heb. 13:9 (TLV) Do not be carried away by all kinds of strange teachings, for it is good for the heart to **be strengthened by GRACE**—not by foods that have not benefited those occupied by them.

Heb. 13:25 GRACE be with you all. Amen.

James 4:6 But He giveth more GRACE. Wherefore He saith, God resisteth the proud, but giveth GRACE unto the humble.

I Pet. 1:10 (NRSV) Concerning this salvation, the prophets who prophesied of the GRACE that was to be yours made careful search and inquiry,

I Pet. 1:13 (NRSV) Therefore prepare your minds for action; discipline yourselves; **set all your hope on the GRACE that Jesus Christ** will bring you when He is revealed.

I Pet. 3:7 Likewise, ye husbands, dwell with them according to knowledge, giving honour unto the wife, as unto the weaker vessel, and as being heirs together of the GRACE of life; that your prayers be not hindered.

I Pet. 4:10 (NRSV) Like good stewards of the manifold GRACE of God, serve one another with whatever gift each of you has received.

I Pet. 5:5 Likewise, ye younger, submit yourselves unto the elder. Yea, all of you be subject one to another, and be clothed with humility: for God resisteth the proud, and giveth GRACE to the humble.

I Pet. 5:10 (NRSV) And after you have suffered for a little while, **the God of all GRACE,** who has called you to His eternal Glory in Christ, will Himself restore, support, strengthen, and establish you. SNB: But **the God of all GRACE,** who hath called us unto His eternal Glory by Messiah יֵשׁוּעַ, after that ye have suffered a while, make you perfect, stablish, strengthen, settle you.

I Pet. 5:12 (NRSV) I have written this short letter to encourage you and to testify that this is the true GRACE of God. **Stand fast in it.**

2 Pet. 3:18 But **grow in GRACE** and in the knowledge of our Lord and Saviour יֵשׁוּעַ Messiah. To Him be Glory both now and **forever**. Amen.

Jude 1:4 (NRSV) For certain intruders have stolen in among you, people who long ago were designated for this condemnation as ungodly, who pervert the GRACE of our God into licentiousness and deny our only Master and Lord, Jesus Christ.

Rev. 22:21 The GRACE of our Adonai יֵשׁוּעַ Messiah be with you all. Amen

171. SHALOM IN THE TORAH

The Hebrew word, Shalom שלום *means: completeness, soundness, welfare, peace, health, prosperity, quiet, tranquillity, contentment, serenity, well-being, all needs met, The Hebrew word picture is: destroy the authority attached to chaos. Shalom is one of the goals and affects of the Gospel.*

TORAH

Numbers 6:23-27 Speak unto Aaron and unto his sons, saying, On this wise ye shall bless the children of Israel, saying unto them, 24 יהוה bless thee, and keep thee: 25 יהוה make His face shine upon thee, and be gracious unto thee: 26 יהוה lift up His countenance upon thee, and give thee **shalom**. 27 And they shall **put My Name** upon the children of Israel; and I will bless them.

Lev. 26:6 And I will give **shalom** in the land, and ye shall lie down, and none shall make you afraid....

PSALMS, PROVERBS, PROPHETS

Psalm 4:8 I will both lay me down in **shalom**, and sleep: for Thou, יהוה, only makest me dwell in safety.

Psalm 29:11 יהוה will give strength unto His people; יהוה will bless His people with **shalom**.

Psalm 34:14 Depart from evil, and do good; seek **shalom**, and pursue it.

Psalm 35:27 Let them shout for joy, and be glad, that favour My righteous cause: yea, let them say continually, Let יהוה be magnified, which hath pleasure in the **shalom** of His servant.

Psalm 37:11 But the meek shall inherit the earth; and shall delight themselves in the abundance of **shalom**.

Psalm 37:37 Mark the perfect man, and behold the upright: for the end of that man is **shalom**.

Psalm 119:165 Great **shalom** have they which love Thy Torah: and nothing shall offend them.

Psalm 122:6-9 Pray for the **shalom** of Jerusalem: they shall prosper that love thee. 7 **Shalom** be within thy walls, and prosperity within thy palaces. 8 For my brethren and companions' sakes, I will now say, **Shalom** be within thee. 9 Because of the house of יהוה our God I will seek thy good.

Psalm 147:14 He maketh **shalom** in thy borders, and filleth thee with the finest of the wheat.

Prov. 3:1-2 My son, forget not My Torah; but let thine heart keep My commandments: 2 For length of days, and long life, and **shalom**, shall they add to thee.

Isaiah 9:6-7 For unto us a child is born, unto us a Son is given: and the government shall be upon His shoulder: and His Name shall be called Wonderful, Counsellor, The mighty God, The **everlasting** Father, The Prince of **Shalom**. 7 Of the increase of His government and **shalom** there shall be **no end**....

Isaiah 26:3 Thou wilt keep him in **shalom**, **shalom**, whose mind is stayed on Thee: because he trusteth in Thee. 4 Trust ye in יהוה **forever**: for in Yah יהוה יה is **everlasting** strength:

Isaiah 26:12 יהוה, Thou wilt ordain **shalom** for us: for Thou also hast wrought all our works in us.

Isaiah 32:17 And the work of righteousness shall be **shalom**; and the effect of righteousness quietness and assurance **forever**. And My people shall dwell in a **shalom** habitation, and in sure dwellings, and in quiet resting places;

Isaiah 48:18 O that thou hadst hearkened to My commandments! then had thy **shalom** been as a river, and thy righteousness as the waves of the sea:

Isaiah 52:7 How beautiful upon the mountains are the feet of him that bringeth good tidings, that publisheth **shalom**; that bringeth good tidings of good, that publisheth salvation; that saith unto Zion, Thy God reigneth!

Isaiah 53:5 But He was wounded for our transgressions, He was bruised for our iniquities: the chastisement of our **shalom** was upon Him; and with His stripes we are healed.

Isaiah 54:13 And all thy children shall be taught of יהוה; and great shall be the **shalom** of thy children.

Isaiah 55:12 For ye shall go out with joy, and be led forth with **shalom**: the mountains and the hills shall break forth before you into singing, and all the trees of the field shall clap their hands.

Isaiah 57:1b-2 …the righteous is taken away from the evil to come. 2 He shall enter into **shalom**: they shall rest in their beds, each one walking in His uprightness.

Isaiah 57:19 I create the fruit of the lips; **Shalom**, **shalom** to him that is far off, and to him that is near, saith יהוה; and I will heal him.

Isaiah 66:12 …Behold, I will extend **shalom** to her like a river….

Jer. 29:11 (TLV) For I know the plans that I have in mind for you," declares Adonai, "plans for **shalom** and not calamity—to give you a future and a hope.

Jer 33:9 And it shall be to Me a name of joy, a praise and an honour before all the nations of the earth, which shall hear all the good that I do unto them: and they shall fear and tremble for all the goodness and for all the prosperity (**shalom**) that I procure unto it.

Nahum 1:15 Behold upon the mountains the feet of him that bringeth good tidings, that publisheth **shalom**! O Judah, keep thy solemn feasts, perform thy vows: for the wicked shall no more pass through thee; he is utterly cut off.

Haggai 2:9 The glory of this latter house shall be greater than of the former, saith יהוה of hosts: and in this place will I give **shalom**, saith יהוה of hosts.

Zech. 8:19 [the fasts] …shall be to the house of Judah joy and gladness, and cheerful feasts; therefore love the Truth and **shalom**.

Zech. 9:10b … and He shall speak **shalom** unto the heathen: and His dominion shall be from sea even to sea, and from the river even to the ends of the earth.

YESHUA ישוע

Mark 4:39 And He arose, and rebuked the wind, and said unto the sea, **Shalom**, be still. And the wind ceased, and there was a great calm.

Mark 5:34 And He said unto her, Daughter, thy faith hath made thee whole; **go in shalom**, and be whole of thy plague.

Luke 1:79 To give light to them that sit in darkness and in the shadow of death, to guide our feet into the way of **shalom**.

Luke 7:50 And He said to the woman, Thy faith hath saved thee; **go in shalom**.

Luke 8:48 And He said unto her, Daughter, be of good comfort: thy faith hath made thee whole; **go in shalom**.

Luke 19:42 Saying, If thou hadst known, even thou, at least in this thy day, the things which belong unto thy **shalom**! but now they are hid from thine eyes.

Luke 24:36 And as they thus spake, ישוע Himself stood in the midst of them, and saith unto them, **Shalom** be unto you. [Hebrew: Shalom alekhem! שלום אלכם]

John 14:27 **Shalom** I leave with you, My **shalom** I give unto you: not as the world giveth, give I unto you. Let not your heart be troubled, neither let it be afraid.

John 16:33 These things I have spoken unto you, that in Me ye might have **shalom**. In the world ye shall have tribulation: but be of good cheer; I have overcome the world.

John 20:19 ... came ישוע and stood in the midst, and saith unto them, **Shalom** be unto you. [Hebrew: Shalom alekhem! שלום אלכם]

John 20:21 Then said ישוע to them again, **Shalom** be unto you [Shalom alekhem! אלכם שלום]: as my Father hath sent Me, even so send I you.

John 20:26 ...then came ישוע, the doors being shut, and stood in the midst, and said, **Shalom** be unto you. [Shalom alekhem! שלום אלכם]

APOSTLES

Act 10:36 The Word which God sent unto the children of Israel, preaching **shalom** by ישוע Messiah: (He is Lord of all:)

Rom 2:10 But glory, honour, and **shalom**, to every man that worketh good, to the Jew first, and also to the Gentile:

Rom 5:1 Therefore being justified by faith, we have **shalom** with God through our Adonai ישוע Messiah:

Rom 8:6 For to be carnally minded is death; but to be spiritually minded is life and **shalom**.

Rom 14:17 For the Kingdom of God is not meat and drink; but righteousness, and **shalom**, and joy in the Holy Ghost.

Rom 14:19 Let us therefore follow after the things which make for **shalom**, and things wherewith one may edify another.

Rom 15:13 Now the God of hope fill you with all joy and **shalom** in believing, that ye may abound in hope, through the power of the Holy Spirit.

Rom 15:33 Now the God of **shalom** be with you all. Amen.

Rom 16:20 And the God of **shalom** shall bruise Satan under your feet shortly. The grace of our Adonai יֵשׁוּעַ Messiah be with you. Amen.

1 Cor. 7:15 ...but God hath called us to **shalom**.

1 Cor 14:33 For God is not the author of confusion, but of **shalom**,

2 Cor 13:11 Finally, brethren, farewell. Be perfect, be of good comfort, be of one mind, live in **shalom**; and the God of love and **shalom** shall be with you.

Gal 5:22 But the fruit of the Spirit is love, joy, **shalom**, longsuffering, gentleness, goodness, faith, 23 Meekness, temperance: **against such there is no law**. 24 And they that are Messiah's have crucified the flesh with the affections and lusts. 25 If we live in the Spirit, let us also walk in the Spirit.

Eph. 2:14-17 For He is our **shalom**, who hath made both one, ... 15 ... for to make in Himself of twain one new man, so making **shalom**; 16 And that He might reconcile both unto God in one body by the Cross, having slain the enmity thereby: 17 And came and preached **shalom** to you which were afar off, and to them that were nigh.

Eph. 4:3 Endeavouring to keep the unity of the Spirit in the bond of **shalom**.

Eph. 6:15 And your feet shod with the preparation of the Gospel of **shalom**;

Eph. 6:23 **Shalom** be to the brethren, and love with faith, from God the Father and Adonai יֵשׁוּעַ Messiah.

Phil. 4:6-7 Be careful [anxious] for nothing; but in everything by prayer and supplication with thanksgiving let your requests be made known unto God. 7 And the **shalom** of God, which passeth all understanding, shall keep your hearts and minds through Messiah יֵשׁוּעַ. 8 Finally, brethren, whatsoever things are true, whatsoever things are honest, whatsoever things are just, whatsoever things are pure, whatsoever things are lovely, whatsoever things are of good report; if there be any virtue, and if there be any praise, think on these things. 9 … and the God of **shalom** shall be with you.

Col. 1:20 And, having made **shalom** through the Blood of His Cross, by Him to reconcile all things unto Himself; by Him, I say, whether they be things in earth, or things in heaven.

Col 3:15 And let the **shalom** of God rule in your hearts, to the which also ye are called in one body; and be ye thankful.

1 Thess. 5:23 And the very God of **shalom** sanctify you wholly; and I pray God your whole spirit and soul and body be preserved blameless unto the coming of our Adonai יֵשׁוּעַ Messiah.

GRACE AND SHALOM

2 Thess. 3:16 Now the Lord of **shalom** Himself give you **shalom** always by all means. The Lord be with you all.

Heb. 12:14 Follow **shalom** with all men, and holiness, without which no man shall see the Lord:

Heb. 13:20-21 Now the God of **shalom**, that brought again from the dead our Adonai יֵשׁוּעַ, that great Shepherd of the sheep, through the Blood of the **everlasting Covenant**, Make you perfect in every good work to do His will, working in you that which is well-pleasing in His sight, through יֵשׁוּעַ Messiah; to whom be glory **forever** and ever. Amen.

James 3:18 And the fruit of righteousness is sown in **shalom** of them that make **shalom**.

1 Pet. 3:10-11 For he that will love life, and see good days, let him refrain his tongue from evil, and his lips that they speak no guile: 11 Let him eschew evil, and do good; let him seek **shalom**, and ensue it.

1 Pet. 5:14 … **Shalom** be with you all that are in Messiah יֵשׁוּעַ. Amen.

2 Pet. 3:14 Wherefore, beloved, …be diligent that ye may be found of Him in **shalom**, without spot, and blameless.

Jude 1:2 Mercy unto you, and **shalom**, and love, be multiplied.

172. GRACE AND SHALOM

Numbers 6:25-26 יהוה make His face shine upon thee, and be GRACIOUS unto thee: 26 יהוה lift up His countenance upon thee, and give thee **shalom**.

Rom. 1:7 To all that be in Rome, beloved of God, called to be saints: GRACE to you and **shalom** from God our Father, and Adonai ישוע Messiah.

I Cor. 1:3-4 GRACE be unto you, and **shalom**, from God our Father and from Adonai ישוע Messiah. 4 I thank my God always on your behalf, for the GRACE of God which is given you by ישוע Messiah;

2 Cor. 1:2 GRACE be to you and **shalom** from God our Father and from Adonai ישוע Messiah.

Gal 1:3 GRACE be to you and **shalom** from God the Father, and from our Adonai ישוע Messiah.

Eph. 1:2 GRACE be to you and **shalom**, from God our Father, and Adonai ישוע Messiah.

Phil. 1:2 GRACE be unto you, and **shalom**, from God our Father, and from Adonai ישוע Messiah.

Col. 1:2 GRACE be unto you, and **shalom**, from God our Father and Adonai ישוע Messiah.

I Thess. 1:1b GRACE be unto you, and **shalom**, from God our Father, and Adonai ישוע Messiah.

2 Thess. 1:2 GRACE unto you, and **shalom**, from God our Father and Adonai ישוע Messiah.

I Tim. 1:2 ...Grace, mercy, and **shalom**, from God our Father and ישוע Messiah our Lord.

2 Tim. 1:2 ...GRACE, mercy, and **shalom**, from God the Father and Messiah ישוע our Lord.

Titus 1:4 ...GRACE, mercy, and **shalom**, from God the Father and Adonai ישוע Messiah our Saviour.

Philemon 1:3,25 GRACE to you, and **shalom**, from God our Father and Adonai ישוע Messiah. ... 25 The GRACE of Adonai ישוע Messiah be with your spirit. Amen.

I Pet. 1:1-2 (NRSV)... To the exiles of the Dispersion ... 2 who have been chosen and destined by God the Father and sanctified by the Spirit to be obedient to Jesus Christ and to be sprinkled with His Blood: May GRACE and **shalom** be yours **in abundance**.

2 Pet. 1:2-3 GRACE and **shalom** be **multiplied** unto you through the knowledge of God, and of ישוע our Lord, 3 According as His divine power hath given unto us all things that pertain unto life and Godliness, through the knowledge of Him that hath called us to glory and virtue....

2 John 1:3 GRACE be with you, mercy, and **shalom**, from God the Father, and from Adonai ישוע Messiah, the Son of the Father, in truth and love.

Rev. 1:4 (TLV) GRACE to you and **shalom** from Him who is and who was and who is to come, as well as from the seven spirits who are before His throne....

173. THAT IT MAY GO WELL WITH YOU

[Most also in Keep All, p. 20-23 or Obey, p.24-29]

Deut. 4:40 ...keep therefore His statutes, and His commandments, which I command thee this day, **that it may go well with thee**, and with thy children after thee, and that thou mayest **prolong thy days upon the earth**, which יהוה thy God giveth thee, **forever**.

Deut. 5:16 Honour thy father and thy mother, as יהוה thy God hath commanded thee; that thy days may be prolonged, and **that it may go well with thee**, in the land which יהוה thy God giveth thee.

Deut. 5:33 Ye shall walk in all the ways which יהוה your God hath commanded you, that ye may live, and **that it may be well with you**, and that ye may **prolong your days** in the land....

Deut. 5:29 O that there were such an heart in them, that they would fear Me, and keep all My commandments always, **that it might be well with them,** and with their children **forever**!

Deut. 6:1-2 Now these are the commandments, the statutes, and the judgments, which יהוה your God commanded to teach you, that ye might do them...: 2 That thou mightest fear יהוה thy God, to keep all His statutes and His commandments, which I command thee, thou, and thy son, and thy son's son, all the days of thy life; and **that thy days may be prolonged**

Deut. 6:3 Hear therefore, O Israel, and observe to do it; **that it may be well with thee,** and that **ye may increase mightily,** as יהוה God of thy fathers hath promised thee, in the land that floweth with milk and honey.

Deut. 6:18 And thou shalt do that which is right and good in the sight of יהוה: **that it may be well with thee**....

Deut. 6:24 And יהוה commanded us to do all these statutes, to fear יהוה our God, **for our good always,** that He might **preserve us alive**, as it is at this day.

Deut. 7:12-13 ...if ye hearken to these judgments, and keep, and do them, that יהוה thy God shall keep unto thee the Covenant and the mercy which He sware unto thy fathers: 13 And **He will love thee, and bless thee, and multiply thee:** He will also bless the fruit of thy womb,...of thy land, thy corn,...wine, ...oil, ...kine (cattle), and ...sheep, in the land....

Deut. 8:1-3 All the commandments which I command thee this day shall ye observe to do, **that ye may live,** and multiply, and go in and possess the land which יהוה sware unto your fathers. NRSV: 2 Remember the long way that the LORD your God has led you these forty years in the wilderness, in order to humble you, testing you to know what was in your heart, whether or not you would keep His commandments. **3** He humbled you by letting you hunger, then by feeding you with manna, with which neither you nor your ancestors were acquainted, in order to make you understand that one does not live by bread alone, SNB: but by every Word that proceedeth out of the mouth of יהוה...

Deut. 10:12-13 And now, Israel, what doth יהוה thy God require of thee, but to fear יהוה thy God, to walk in all His ways, and to love Him, and to serve יהוה thy God with all thy heart and with all thy soul, To keep the commandments of יהוה, and His statutes, which I command thee this day **for thy good?**

Deut. 11:8-9 ...keep all the commandments which I command you this day, **that ye may be strong**, and go in and possess the land, whither ye go to possess it; 9 And that ye may **prolong your days** in the land, which יהוה sware unto your fathers to give unto them and to their seed, a land that floweth with milk and honey.

Deut. 12:28 Observe and hear all these words which I command thee, **that it may go well with thee, and with thy children** after thee **forever**, when thou doest that which is good and right in the sight of יהוה thy God.

Deut. 29:9 Keep therefore the Words of this Covenant, and do them, that ye may **prosper in all that ye do.**

Deut. 30:19 (NRSV) I call heaven and earth to witness against you today that I have set before you **life** and death, blessings and curses. **Choose life** so that **you and your descendants may live**, [Also in Choose Life, p. 235]

FOR INDIVIDUAL COMMANDMENTS: Deut. 12:23-25 Only be sure that thou eat not the blood: for the blood is the life.... 24 ...thou shalt pour it upon the earth as water. 25 Thou shalt not eat it; **that it may go well with thee, and with thy children** after thee, when thou shalt do that which is right in the sight of יהוה. [also in Don't eat, p. 131]

Deut. 19:13 Thine eye shall not pity him, but thou shalt put away the guilt of innocent blood from Israel, that it **may go well with thee**. [also in No killing, p. 48 and Cities of Refuge p. 50]

Deut. 22:7 (NRSV) Let the mother go, taking only the young for yourself, in order that it **may go well with you** and you may **live long**. *(So birds do not go extinct! So we always have the beauty of birds and their songs!)* [also in Prevent extinction, p. 83]

AFTER TORAH, ישוע YESHUA, and APOSTLES

Josh. 1:8 This book of the Torah ... thou shalt meditate therein day and night, that thou mayest observe to do ...all that is written therein: for then thou shalt make thy way **prosperous,** and then thou shalt have **good success**.

Psalm 1:2,3 But his delight is in the Torah of יהוה; and in His Torah doth he meditate day and night. 3 And he shall be like a tree planted by the rivers of water, that bringeth forth his fruit in his season; his leaf also shall not wither; and **whatsoever he doeth shall prosper**.

Prov. 13:13 ...he that feareth the commandment shall be **rewarded**.

Matt. 19:17b ...if thou wilt **enter into Life**, keep the commandments.

John. 15: 7 "If ye abide in Me, and My Words abide in you, ye shall ask what ye will, and it shall be done unto you."

Eph. 6:2-3 Honour thy father and mother; (which is the first commandment with promise;) 3 That it may **be well with thee,** and thou mayest **live long** on the earth. [also in Honor, p. 46]

3 John 1:2 (NRSV and TLV) Beloved, I pray that all **may go well** with you and that you may be in good health, just as it is **well** with your soul.

APPENDIX A: WHAT IS TORAH?

(TORAH תורה in Hebrew means INSTRUCTION)

*The Torah is the **glorious** Word of God, spoken from the mouth of God. Yeshua is the Word that was in the beginning with God and was God—the Word that became flesh and dwelt among us (from John 1:1- 2,14). He is the <u>Word of God, which includes the **Torah**</u>, dwelling in us! So the Torah, like the rest of the Word is an infinite treasure of Truth and Wisdom and the **Light of Life**. The Torah is part of our **Manna from Heaven** (John 6:33) and our **Living Water** (John 4:10b). We will find amazing blessings by studying it and knowing it, and perhaps even following it because we want all of the Word to abide in us—not for our salvation, not in a rigid, legalistic, or condescending way, not in a controlling way, that tells others they must follow it, but **in Spirit and in Truth** (John4:24), **walking in the Spirit, not in the flesh** (from Rom. 8:4)*

Rom. 7:6b ...we should serve **in newness of spirit,** and not in the oldness of the letter.

2 Cor. 3:6   [He] has made us competent to be ministers of a New Covenant, **not of letter but of Spirit**; for the letter kills, but the **Spirit gives life.**

Can we *completely* know God without studying His *whole* Word?

Eph. 1:17-18 That the God of our Lord ישוע Messiah, the Father of glory, may give unto you the Spirit of wisdom and revelation in the **knowledge of Him:** 18 The eyes of your **understanding** being **enlightened**; that ye may **know** what is the hope of His calling, and what the riches of the glory of **His inheritance in the saints....**

*Who are the **saints** in Apostle Paul's mind? The faithful Israelites!:*

Eph. 2:12-13, 19 At that time ye were without Messiah, being **aliens from the commonwealth of Israel,** and **strangers from the Covenants of promise,** having no hope, and without God in the world: 13 But now in Messiah ישוע ye who sometimes were far off are made nigh by the Blood of Messiah. ... 19 Now therefore ye are no more strangers and foreigners, but **fellow citizens** with the **saints....**

But wasn't the Law abolished and done away with?

Heb. 9:11-15a But Messiah being come an high priest of good things to come, by a greater and more perfect Tabernacle, not made with hands ... **by His own Blood He entered in once into the Holy Place, having obtained eternal redemption for us.** 13 For if the blood of bulls and of goats, and the ashes of an heifer sprinkling the unclean, sanctifieth to the purifying of the flesh: 14 **How much more shall the blood of Messiah, who through the eternal Spirit offered Himself without spot to God,** purge your conscience from dead works to serve the living God? 15 And for this cause He is the mediator of the New Covenant....

Col. 2:13-14 And you, being dead in your sins ... hath He quickened together with Him, **having forgiven you all trespasses;** 14 **Blotting out the handwriting of ordinances** that was against us ... and took it out of the way, **nailing it to His Cross;**

Heb. 10:19-22 Having therefore, brethren, boldness to enter into the holiest by the **blood of** ישוע 20 By a new and living way, which He hath consecrated [NRSV: opened] for us, through the veil [curtain], that is to say, **[through] His flesh....** 22 Let us draw near with a true heart in full assurance of faith, having our hearts sprinkled from an evil conscience, and our bodies washed with pure water.

Eph. 2:14-15 For He is our peace, who hath made both one, and hath broken down the middle wall of partition between us; 15 **Having abolished in His flesh the enmity, even the law of**

commandments contained in ordinances; for to make in Himself of twain one new man, so making peace; *[Could the "middle wall" be the Temple **curtain** that separated us from Him!? Now He has abolished those Temple laws. Now we can all come directly to Him as new creations!! Now **we are His Temple!!**]*

Gal. 3:13 (NRSV) Christ redeemed us from the curse of the law by becoming a curse for us—for it is written, "Cursed is everyone who hangs on a tree" (Deut. 21:23). *[The curse of Torah is that death was the only penalty for breaking many of its commandments. (See list, p. 121.)]*

Rom. 10:4 (NRSV) For Christ is the end [SNB: end; NIV: culmination; CJB: **goal**] of the law so that there may be righteousness for everyone who believes. *[Messiah brought an end to the curse and the sacrifices.]*

Gal. 5:4-5 Messiah is become of no effect unto you, **whosoever of you are justified by the law; ye are fallen from grace**. 5 For we through the Spirit wait for the hope of righteousness by faith. *[We can no longer be justified by animal sacrifices.]*

Rom. 7:6 But now we are **delivered from the law,** that being dead wherein we were held; that we should serve in newness of spirit, and not in the oldness of the letter. *[We are delivered from the death penalty! (See list, p. 121.)]*

What was abolished?

1. *Gone is the part of the Torah that required us to go through a priest (cohen), sacrificing animals to have our sins forgiven and to connect to God. NOW: The way is open for us to go directly to God ourselves, individually, through Messiah Yeshua.*

2. *Gone is the part in which many sins required we be put to death. (See list, p.121.) That deadly part— the curse of the Torah—has been "nailed to the Cross." NOW: We can find forgiveness for even the worst of sins. NOW: Through Yeshua's sacrifice on the Cross, the Holy Spirit gives us power to resist temptation and to obey the Torah with joy and grace, not in sour, rigid, controlling legalism.*

*The Torah is still in place. It is **still __not okay__** to commit adultery, or kill or steal or rape or commit incest or be mean to the unfortunate. We are still supposed to be kind to strangers and the blind and take care of widows and orphans. **There are so many laws from the Torah that definitely still apply.** Without God's Torah, upon what would we base right and wrong? Surely not the world's changing standard that today says we must be kind to wolves, but it's okay to kill our unborn babies!!*

The Torah is an amazing, glorious gift from God!

Rom. 3:31 Do we then make void the Torah through faith? God forbid: yea, **we establish the Torah**.

Rom. 3:1-2 What advantage then hath the Jew? ... Much in every way: chiefly, because **that unto them were committed the oracles of God**.

Rom. 9:4-5 (NRSV) **They are Israelites, and to them belong** the adoption, **the GLORY, the Covenants, the giving of the Law [Torah],** the worship, and the promises; 5 to them belong the patriarchs [*Abraham, Isaac, and Jacob*], and from them, according to the flesh, comes the **MESSIAH**, who is over all, God blessed **forever**.

2 Cor. 3:7, 11 ...the ministration of death, written and engraven in stones, was **glorious.**... For if that which is done away *was* **glorious**, much more that which remaineth *is* **glorious**.

2 Cor. 3:9-10 (NRSV) For if there was glory in the ministry of condemnation [*the death penalty*], much more does the ministry of justification abound in **GLORY!** ...10 Indeed, what once had **glory** has lost its glory because of the **GREATER GLORY**.

APPENDIX B:
YESHUA AND TORAH AND HIS COMMANDMENTS

Yeshua and His parents kept Torah

Luke 2:21-24 And when eight days were accomplished for the circumcising of the child, His Name was called ישוע, which was so named of the angel before he was conceived in the womb. 22 And when the days of her purification according to the Torah of Moses were accomplished, they brought him to Jerusalem, to present him to יהוה; 23 (As it is written in the Torah of יהוה, Every male that openeth the womb shall be called holy to יהוה;) 24 And to offer a sacrifice according to that which is said in the Torah of יהוה, A pair of turtledoves, or two young pigeons.

Luke 2:39 And when they had performed all things according to the Torah of יהוה, they returned into Galilee, to their own city Nazareth.

Luke 2:41 Now his parents went to Jerusalem every year at the feast of the Passover.

John 2:13 ...Passover was at hand, and ישוע went up to Jerusalem.

John 7:2-3,10 (NRSV) Now the Jewish festival of Booths was near. 3 So his brothers said to him, "Leave here and go to Judea so that your disciples also may see the works you are doing; ... 10 But after his brothers had gone to the festival, then he also went, not publicly but as it were in secret.

Luke 4:15-16 (NRSV) He began to teach in their synagogues and was praised by everyone. 16 When he came to Nazareth, where he had been brought up, he went to the synagogue on the Sabbath day, as was his custom. He stood up to read...."

His View of the Torah Commandments

Matt. 5:17-20 Think not that I am come to destroy the Torah, or the prophets: I am not come to destroy, but to fulfil. 18 For verily I say unto you, Till heaven and earth pass, one jot or one tittle shall in no wise pass from the Torah, till all be fulfilled. 19 Whosoever therefore shall break one of these least commandments, and shall teach men so, he shall be called the least in the kingdom of heaven: but whosoever shall do and teach them, the same shall be called great in the kingdom of heaven. 20 For I say unto you, That except your righteousness shall exceed the righteousness of the scribes and Pharisees, ye shall in no case enter into the kingdom of heaven.

Matt. 22:36-40 Master, which is the great[est] commandment in the Torah? 37 ישוע said unto him, **Thou shalt love יהוה thy Elohim with all thy heart, and with all thy soul, and with all thy mind**. 38 This is the first and great[est] commandment. 39 And the second is like unto it, Thou shalt love thy neighbour as thyself. 40 **On these two commandments hang all the Torah and the prophets.**

Mark 12:28-31 And one of the scribes came, and ... asked Him, Which is the first commandment of all? 29 And ישוע answered him, **The first of all the commandments is, Hear, O Israel; יהוה our Elohim יהוה is one** [changed a bit to match the Hebrew]: 30 **And thou shalt love יהוה thy Elohim with all thy heart, and with all thy soul, and with all thy mind, and with all thy strength: this is the first commandment.** 31 And the second is like, namely this, Thou shalt love thy neighbour as thyself. There is none other commandment greater than these.

Matt. 19:16-21   ... Good Master, what good thing shall I do, that I may have eternal life? 17 ...if thou wilt enter into life, keep the commandments. 18 He saith unto him, Which? ישוע said, Thou shalt do no murder, Thou shalt not commit adultery, Thou shalt not steal, Thou shalt not bear false witness, 19 Honour thy father and thy mother: and, Thou shalt love thy neighbour as thyself. ... 21 ישוע said unto him, If thou wilt be perfect, go and sell that thou hast, and give to the poor, and thou shalt have treasure in heaven: and come and follow me.

Luke 10:25-28, 36-37 And, behold, a certain lawyer stood up, and tempted [NRSV: test] him, saying, Master, what shall I do to inherit eternal life? 26 He said unto him, **What is written in the Torah**? how readest thou? 27 And he answering said, Thou shalt love the Lord thy God with all thy heart, and with all thy soul, and with all thy strength, and with all thy mind; and thy neighbour as thyself. 28 And He said unto him, Thou hast answered right: this do, and thou shalt live. ... *[Then* ישוע *tells the Good Samaritan story where the priest and levite passed by the wounded man.]* 36 Which now of these three, thinkest thou, was neighbour unto him that fell among the thieves? 37 And he said, He that shewed mercy on him. Then said ישוע unto him, Go, and do thou likewise.

Matt. 15:1-3, 6-11, 18 (NRSV) Then Pharisees and scribes came ... and said, 2 "Why do your disciples break the tradition of the elders? For they do not wash their hands before they eat." 3 He answered them, "And why do you break the commandment of God for the sake of your tradition? ... 6 So, for the sake of your tradition, you make void the Word of God. 7 You hypocrites! Isaiah prophesied rightly about you when he said: 8 'This people honors Me with their lips, but their hearts are far from Me; 9 in vain do they worship Me, teaching human precepts as doctrines.'" 10 Then He called the crowd to Him and said to them, "Listen and understand: 11 it is not what goes into the mouth that defiles a person, but it is what comes out of the mouth that defiles. ... 18 ... what comes out of the mouth proceeds from the heart, and this is what defiles."

Matt. 23:2-5, 23 (NRSV) The scribes and the Pharisees sit on Moses' seat; 3 therefore, do whatever they teach you and follow it *[They taught the Torah!!]*; but do not do as they do, for they do not practice what they teach. 4 They tie up heavy burdens, hard to bear, and lay them on the shoulders of others; ... 5 They do all their deeds to be seen by others; for they make their phylacteries broad and their fringes long. ... 23 Woe to you, scribes and Pharisees, hypocrites! For you tithe mint, dill, and cummin, and have neglected the weightier matters of the law [Torah]: justice and mercy and faith. It is **these you ought to have practiced** without neglecting the others.

Matt. 13:51-52 (NRSV) "Have you understood all this?" They answered, "Yes." 52 And He said to them, "Therefore every scribe who has been trained for the kingdom of heaven is like the master of a household who brings out of his treasure what is new and what is old."

His Commandments

Unless marked, NRSV with ישוע

John 3:7 ... You must be born from above.

John 14:15 **If you love Me, you will keep My commandments.**

John 14:21a (SNB) **He that hath My commandments, and keepeth them, he it is that loveth Me:**

Luke 6:46 Why do you call Me "Lord, Lord," and do not do what I tell you?

John 14:23 (SNB) ... If a man love Me, he will keep My Words: *[The Torah is also His Word.]*

John 15:14 (SNB) Ye are My friends, if ye do whatsoever I command you.

John 14:24 (SNB) He that loveth Me not keepeth not My sayings....

John 15:10 (SNB) **If ye keep My commandments, ye shall abide in My love;**

John 5:14 See, you have been made well! Do not sin anymore so that nothing worse happens to you.

YESHUA SAYS DISOBEYING TORAH STARTS IN OUR THOUGHTS:

Yeshua came to pay the penalty for our sins (including our sins of breaking Torah). He also came in part to <u>explain</u> the Torah to us. He showed us the Spirit and the intent of Torah. He taught us that sin begins in our thoughts. He made some Torah commandments a lot harder, not easier. His additional commandments are much tougher because they have to do with our thoughts and words and attitudes.

Matt. 5:21-22 You have heard that it was said to those of ancient times, "<u>You shall not murder</u>"; and "whoever murders shall be liable to judgment." 22 <u>But I say</u> to you that if you are angry with a brother or sister, you will be liable to judgment; and if you insult a brother or sister, you will be liable to the council; and if you say, "You fool," you will be liable to the hell of fire.

Matt. 5:27-28 You have heard that it was said, "<u>You shall not commit adultery</u>." 28 <u>But I say</u> to you that everyone who looks at a woman with lust has already committed adultery with her in his heart.

Matt. 5:31 It was also said, "Whoever divorces his wife, let him give her a certificate of divorce." 32 <u>But I say</u> to you that anyone who divorces his wife, except on the ground of unchastity, causes her to commit adultery; and whoever marries a divorced woman commits adultery.

Matt. 19:7-12 They said to Him, "Why then did Moses command us to give a certificate of dismissal and to divorce her?" 8 He said to them, "It was because you were so hard-hearted that Moses allowed you to divorce your wives, <u>but from the beginning it was not so.</u> 9 And I say to you, whoever divorces his wife, except for unchastity, and marries another commits adultery." 10 His disciples said to Him, "If such is the case of a man with his wife, it is better not to marry." 11 But he said to them, "Not everyone can accept this teaching, but only those to whom it is given. 12 For there are eunuchs who have been so from birth, and there are eunuchs who have been made eunuchs by others, and there are eunuchs who have made themselves eunuchs for the sake of the kingdom of heaven. Let anyone accept this who can."

Matt. 5:33-34 Again, you have heard that it was said to those of ancient times, "You shall not swear falsely, but carry out the vows you have made to the Lord." 34 <u>But I say</u> to you, Do not swear at all....

Matt. 5:38-39 You have heard that it was said, "An eye for an eye and a tooth for a tooth." 39 <u>But I say</u> to you, Do not resist an evildoer.

LOVE YOUR ENEMIY: Matt. 5:43-44 You have heard that it was said, "You shall love your neighbor and hate your enemy." 44 <u>But I say</u> to you, Love your enemies and pray for those who persecute you, ...

Luke 6:27-28,35 Love your enemies, do good to those who hate you, 28 bless those who curse you, pray for those who abuse you. ... 35 But love your enemies, do good, and lend, expecting nothing in return. Your reward will be great, and you will be children of the Most High; for he is kind to the ungrateful and the wicked.

Luke 6:29-30 ...and from anyone who takes away your coat do not withhold even your shirt. Give to everyone who begs from you; and if anyone takes away your goods, do not ask for them again.

Matt. 5:25 Come to terms quickly with your accuser while you are on the way to court with him,

Matt. 5:23-24 (SNB) Therefore if thou bring thy gift to the altar, and there rememberest that thy brother hath ought against thee; 24 Leave there thy gift ... first be reconciled to thy brother, and then come and offer thy gift.

YESHUA'S COMMANDMENTS

LOVE ONE ANOTHER: John 13:34-35 (SNB) A new commandment I give unto you, That ye <u>love one another; as I have loved you</u>, that ye also <u>love one another</u>. 35 By this shall all men know that ye are My disciples, if ye have love one to another.

John 15:12-14 (SNB) This is My commandment, That ye <u>love one another, as I have loved you</u>. 13 Greater love hath no man than this, that a man lay down his life for his friends. 14 Ye are my friends, if ye do whatsoever I command you. *[Yeshua died for us while we were filthy sinners.]*

John 13:14-15 So if I, your Lord and Teacher, have washed your feet, you also ought to <u>wash one another's feet</u>. 15 For I have set you an example, that you also should do as I have done to you.

Matt 7:12-16 In everything do to others as you would have them do to you; <u>for this is the law [Torah] and the prophets</u>. 13 Enter through the narrow gate; for the gate is wide and the road is easy that leads to destruction, and there are many who take it. 14 For the gate is narrow and the road is hard that leads to life, and there are few who find it.

Luke 13:24a Strive to enter through the narrow door; for many, I tell you, will try to enter and will not be able.

Luke 6:31-33 (SNB) And as ye would that men should do to you, do ye also to them likewise. 32 For if ye love them which love you, what thank have ye? For sinners also love those that love them. 33 And if ye do good to them which do good to you, what thank have ye? For sinners also do even the same.

DO NOT JUDGE: Matt. 7:1 <u>Do not judge</u>, so that you may not be judged. 2 For with the judgment you make you will be judged….

Luke 6:37 <u>Do not judge</u>, and you will not be judged; do not condemn, and you will not be condemned. Forgive, and you will be forgiven; … 41 Why do you see the speck in your neighbor's eye, but do not notice the log in your own eye?

BEWARE OF FALSE PEOPLE: Matt. 7:15 <u>Beware of false prophets</u>, who come to you in sheep's clothing but inwardly are ravenous wolves. 16 You will know them by their fruits. Are grapes gathered from thorns, or figs from thistles?

Matt. 7:6 Do not give what is holy to dogs; and do not throw your pearls before swine…

NO HYPOCRISY, BE HUMBLE: Matt. 6:1, 3-4 Beware of practicing your piety before others <u>in order to be seen</u> by them; for then you have no reward from your Father in heaven. … 3 But when you give alms, do not let your left hand know what your right hand is doing, 4 so that your alms may be done in secret; and your Father who sees in secret will reward you.

Matt. 6:5-6 And whenever you pray, do not be like the hypocrites; for they love to stand and pray in the synagogues and at the street corners, <u>so that they may be seen by others</u>. … 6 But whenever you pray, go into your room and shut the door and pray to your Father who is in secret; and your Father who sees in secret will reward you. 7 When you are praying, do not heap up empty phrases….

Matt. 6:16-17 And whenever you fast, do not look dismal, … 17 But when you fast, put oil on your head and wash your face, 18 <u>so that your fasting may be seen not by others</u>….

Luke 12:1b-2 Beware of the yeast of the Pharisees, that is, <u>their hypocrisy</u>. 2 Nothing is covered up that will not be uncovered, and nothing secret that will not become known. 3 Therefore whatever you have said in the dark will be heard in the light, and what you have whispered behind closed doors will be proclaimed from the housetops.

Matt. 5:20 For I tell you, unless your righteousness exceeds that of the scribes and Pharisees, you will never enter the kingdom of heaven.

Matt. 5:16 … let your light shine before others, so that they may see your good works and give glory to your Father in heaven.

Luke 17:10 …when you have done all that you were ordered to do, say, "We are worthless slaves; we have done only what we ought to have done!"

NO GREED: Luke 12:15 Take care! Be on your guard against all kinds of greed; for one's life does not consist in the abundance of possessions.

Matt. 6:19-21 Do not store up for yourselves treasures on earth, where moth and rust consume and where thieves break in and steal; 20 but store up for yourselves treasures in heaven, where neither moth nor rust consumes and where thieves do not break in and steal. 21 For where your treasure is, there your heart will be also.

Luke 12:20-21 But God said to him, "You fool! This very night your life is being demanded of you. And the things you have prepared, whose will they be?" 21 So it is with those who store up treasures for themselves but are not rich toward God."

GIVE TO THE POOR: Luke 14:12-14; 12:33 When you give a luncheon or a dinner, do not invite your friends or your brothers or your relatives or rich neighbors, in case they may invite you in return, and you would be repaid. 13 But when you give a banquet, invite the poor, the crippled, the lame, and the blind. 14 And you will be blessed, because they cannot repay you, for you will be repaid at the resurrection of the righteous. …12: 33 Sell your possessions, and give alms.

Luke14:33 …none of you can become my disciple if you do not give up all your possessions.

Matt. 19:21 … If thou wilt be perfect, go and sell that thou hast, and give to the poor, and thou shalt have treasure in heaven: and come and follow me.

NO WORRYING: Matt. 6:25-34 Therefore I tell you, do not worry about your life, what you will eat or what you will drink, or about your body, what you will wear. Is not life more than food, and the body more than clothing? … 31 Therefore do not worry, … 33 But strive first for the kingdom of God and his righteousness, and all these things will be given to you as well. 34 So do not worry about tomorrow….

Luke 12:22-34 …do not worry about your life, what you will eat, or about your body, what you will wear. 23 For life is than food, and the body more than clothing. … 29 And do not keep striving for what you are to eat and what you are to drink, and do not keep worrying. … 31 Instead, strive for his kingdom, and these things will be given to you as well. 32 Do not be afraid, little flock, for it is your Father's good pleasure to give you the kingdom. 33 Sell your possessions, and give alms. Make purses for yourselves that do not wear out, an unfailing treasure in heaven…. 34 For where your treasure is, there your heart will be also.

Luke 10:41-42 But the Lord answered her, "Martha, Martha, you are worried and distracted by many things; 42 there is need of only one thing. Mary has chosen the better part, which will not be taken away from her."

John 6:27-29 "Do not work for the food that perishes, but for the food that endures for eternal life, which the Son of Man will give you. …" 28 Then they said to Him, "What must we do to perform the works of God?" 29 יֵשׁוּעַ answered them, "This is the work of God, that you believe in him whom he has sent."

HOW TO BE BLESSED: Matt: 5:3-10 (SNB) <u>Blessed</u> are the poor in spirit: for theirs is the kingdom of heaven. 4 <u>Blessed</u> are they that mourn: for they shall be comforted. 5 <u>Blessed</u> are the meek: for they shall inherit the earth. 6 <u>Blessed</u> are they which do hunger and thirst after righteousness: for they shall be filled. 7 <u>Blessed</u> are the merciful: for they shall obtain mercy. 8 <u>Blessed</u> are the pure in heart: for they shall see God. 9 <u>Blessed</u> are the peacemakers: for they shall be called the children of God. 10 <u>Blessed</u> are they which are persecuted for righteousness' sake: for theirs is the kingdom of heaven.

Luke 6:20-26 <u>Blessed</u> are you who are poor, for yours is the kingdom of God. 21 <u>Blessed</u> are you who are hungry now, for you will be filled. <u>Blessed</u> are you who weep now, for you will laugh. 22 <u>Blessed</u> are you when people hate you, and when they exclude you, revile you, and defame you on account of the Son of Man. 23 Rejoice... 24 But woe to you who are rich, for you have received your consolation. 25 Woe to you who are full now, for you will be hungry. Woe to you who are laughing now, for you will mourn and weep. 26 Woe to you when all speak well of you, for that is what their ancestors did to the false prophets.

LOVE AND ABIDE IN YESHUA: John 15:4-5, 7-8 <u>Abide in Me</u> as I abide in you. ... 5 ... Those who abide in Me and I in them bear much fruit ... 7 If you abide in Me and My Words abide in you, ask for whatever you wish, and it will be done for you. 8... that you bear much fruit.

John 6:53-56 Very truly, I tell you, unless you eat the flesh of the Son of Man and drink His <u>Blood,</u> you have no life in you. 54 Those who eat My flesh and drink My Blood have eternal life, and I will raise them up on the last day; 55 for My flesh is true food and My Blood is true drink. 56 Those who eat My flesh and drink My Blood abide in Me, and I in them.

Luke 12:8-9 ...everyone who acknowledges Me before others, the Son of Man also will acknowledge before the angels of God; 9 but whoever denies Me before others will be denied before the angels of God.

Luke 14:26-27 Whoever comes to Me and does not hate father and mother, wife and children, brothers and sisters, yes, and even life itself, cannot be My disciple. 27 Whoever does not carry the cross and follow Me cannot be My disciple.

PROTECT CHILDREN: Matt. 18:6-9 (SNB) But whoso shall offend one of these little ones which believe in Me, it were better for him that a millstone were hanged about his neck, and that he were drowned in the depth of the sea. 7 ... woe to that man by whom the offence cometh! ... 8 ... it is better for thee to enter into life halt or maimed, rather than having two hands or two feet to be cast into **everlasting** fire. 9 ... it is better for thee to enter into life with one eye, rather than having two eyes to be cast into hell fire.

Matt. 18:10 (SNB) Take heed that ye despise not one of these little ones; for I say unto you, That in heaven their angels do always behold the face of my Father which is in heaven.

Matt. 18:14 (SNB) Even so it is not the will of your Father which is in heaven, that one of these little ones should perish.

Mark 9:42-48 (SNB) And whosoever shall offend one of these little ones that believe in Me, it is better for him that a millstone were hanged about his neck, and he were cast into the sea. 43 And if thy hand offend thee, cut it off: it is better for thee to enter into life maimed, than having two hands to go into hell, into the fire that never shall be quenched: 44 Where their worm dieth not, and the fire is not quenched. 45 And if thy foot offend thee, cut it off: ... 47 And if thine eye offend thee, pluck it out: it is better for thee to enter into the kingdom of God with one eye [or one foot], than having two eyes [or feet] to be cast into hell fire: 48 Where their worm dieth not, and the fire is not quenched.

DO NOT FEAR PERSECUTION, EXPECT IT: Luke 12:11-12 When they bring you before the synagogues, the rulers, and the authorities, <u>do not worry</u> about how you are to defend yourselves or what you are to say; 12 for the Holy Spirit will teach you at that very hour what you ought to say.

Luke 12:4 … <u>do not fear</u> those who kill the body, and after that can do nothing more.

Luke 6:22-23 (and Matt. 5:11-12) <u>Blessed</u> are you when people hate you, and when they exclude you, revile you, and defame you on account of the Son of Man. 23 Rejoice in that day and leap for joy, for surely your reward is great in heaven; for that is what their ancestors did to the prophets.

BE ALERT, READY, AND WORKING: Luke 21:34-36 Be on guard so that your hearts are not weighed down with dissipation and drunkenness and the worries of this life, and that day does not catch you unexpectedly, 35 like a trap. For it will come upon all who live on the face of the whole earth. 36 Be alert at all times, praying that you may have the strength to escape all these things that will take place, and to stand before the Son of Man.

Luke 12:35, 37, 40 Be dressed for action and have your lamps lit; 36 be like those who are waiting for their master to return from the wedding banquet, … 37 Blessed are those slaves whom the master finds alert when he comes; … 40 You also must be ready, for the Son of Man is coming at an unexpected hour. … 43 Blessed is that slave whom his master will find at work when he arrives.

KNOW OUR POWER AND AUTHORITY IN YESHUA: Luke 10:19 "See, I have given you authority to tread on snakes and scorpions, and over all the power of the enemy; and nothing will hurt you. 20 Nevertheless, do not rejoice at this, that the spirits submit to you, but <u>rejoice that your names are written in heaven</u>." 21 At that same hour ישוע rejoiced in the Holy Spirit.

Matthew 28:18-20 And ישוע came and said to them, "All authority in heaven and on earth has been given to me. 19 Go therefore and make disciples of all nations, baptizing them in the name of the Father and of the Son and of the Holy Spirit, 20 and teaching them to obey everything that I have commanded you. And remember, I am with you always, to the end of the age."

SPREAD THE GOSPEL: Mark 16:15-16 (SNB) Go ye into all the world, and preach the Gospel to every creature. 16 He that believeth and is baptized shall be saved;

Luke 24:45-49 (SNB) Then opened He their understanding, that they might understand the Scriptures, 46 And said unto them, Thus it is written, and thus it behooved Messiah to suffer, and to rise from the dead the third day: 47 And that repentance and remission of sins should be preached in His Name among all nations, beginning at Jerusalem. 48 And ye are witnesses of these things. 49 And, behold, I send the promise of My Father upon you: but tarry ye in the city of Jerusalem, until ye be endued [NRSV: clothed] with power from on high.

Acts 1:8 (SNB) But ye shall receive power, after that the Holy Spirit is come upon you: and ye shall be witnesses unto Me both in Jerusalem, and in all Judaea, and in Samaria, and unto the uttermost part of the earth.

John 21:15-22 Feed My lambs. … Tend My sheep. … Feed My sheep. … Follow Me!

YESHUA'S COMMANDMENTS

YESHUA about His Kingdom and Judgment

Unless marked, NRSV with ישוע

Matt. 8:10-12 When ישוע heard him, He was amazed and said to those who followed Him, "Truly I tell you, in no one in Israel have I found such faith. 11 I tell you, <u>many will come from east and west and will eat with Abraham and Isaac and Jacob in the kingdom of heaven, 12 while the heirs of the kingdom will be thrown into the outer darkness,</u> where there will be weeping and gnashing of teeth."

Luke 13:28 There shall be weeping and gnashing of teeth, when ye shall see Abraham, and Isaac, and Jacob, and all the prophets, in the kingdom of God, and you yourselves thrust out.

Matt. 21:31-32 ישוע said to them, "Truly I tell you, the tax collectors and the prostitutes are going into the kingdom of God ahead of you. 32 For John came to you in the way of righteousness and you did not believe him, but the tax collectors and the prostitutes believed him; and even after you saw it, you did not change your minds and believe him.

Matt. 21:43 Therefore I tell you, the kingdom of God will be taken away from you and given to a people that produces the fruits of the kingdom.

Matt 7:19-23 Every tree that does not bear good fruit is cut down and thrown into the fire. 20 Thus you will know them by their fruits. 21 Not everyone who says to Me, "Lord, Lord," will enter the kingdom of heaven, but only the one who does the will of My Father in heaven. 22 On that day many will say to Me, "Lord, Lord, did we not prophesy in Your Name, and cast out demons in Your Name, and do many deeds of power in Your Name?" 23 Then I will declare to them, "I never knew you; go away from Me, <u>you evildoers</u>." *[The Greek word for "evildoers" is "anomia": "without law" ie: "without Torah."]*

Luke 13:26-28 Then you will begin to say, "We ate and drank with You, and You taught in our streets." 27 But He will say, "I do not know where you come from; go away from Me, all you evildoers!" 28 There will be weeping and gnashing of teeth when you see Abraham and Isaac and Jacob and all the prophets in the kingdom of God, and you yourselves thrown out. 29 Then people will come from east and west, from north and south, and will eat in the kingdom of God.

Matt. 23:13 But woe to you ... <u>hypocrites!</u> For you lock people out of the kingdom of heaven. For you do not go in yourselves, and when others are going in, you stop them.

Matt. 12:36-37 But I say unto you, That every idle word that men shall speak, they shall give account thereof in the day of judgment. 37 For <u>by thy words thou shalt be justified, and by thy words thou shalt be condemned.</u>

Matt. 5:29; 18:9b (SNB) And if thy right eye offend thee, pluck it out, and cast it from thee: for it is profitable for thee that one of thy members should perish, and not that thy whole body should be cast into hell. ... 18:9b ...it is better for thee to enter into life with one eye, rather than having two eyes to be cast into hell fire.

Matt. 10:28 (SNB) And fear not them which kill the body, but are not able to kill the soul: but rather fear Him [God?] which is able to destroy both soul and body in hell.

YESHUA on Forgiveness

Unless marked, NRSV with ישוע

Matt. 12:31 Therefore I tell you, people will be forgiven for every sin and blasphemy, but....

Matt. 16:18-19 ...on this rock I will build My church, and the gates of Hades will not prevail against it. 19 I will give you the keys of the kingdom of heaven, and <u>whatever you bind on earth will be bound in heaven, and whatever you loose on earth will be loosed in heaven."</u>

Matt. 18:15- 21 If another member of the church sins against you, go and point out the fault when the two of you are alone. If the member listens to you, you have regained that one. ... 17 If the member refuses to listen to them, tell it to the church; and if the offender refuses to listen even to the church, let such a one be to you as a Gentile and a tax collector. 18 Truly I tell you, <u>whatever you bind on earth will be bound in heaven, and whatever you loose on earth will be loosed in heaven.</u> 19 Again, truly I tell you, if two of you agree on earth about anything you ask, it will be done for you by My Father in Heaven. 20 For where two or three are gathered in My Name, I am there among them. 21 Then Peter came and said to Him, "Lord, if another member of the church sins against me, how often should I <u>forgive</u>? As many as seven times?" 22 ישוע said to him, "Not seven times, but, I tell you, seventy-seven times." *[Then tells the parable of the unforgiving servant.]*

John 20:21-23 Peace be with you. As the Father has sent Me, so I send you. ... Receive the Holy Spirit. 23 <u>If you forgive the sins of any, they are forgiven them; if you retain the sins of any, they are retained."</u>

Luke 17:3-4 Be on your guard! If another disciple sins, you must rebuke the offender, and if there is repentance you must forgive. 4 And if the same person sins against you seven times a day, and turns back to you seven times and says, "I repent," you must <u>forgive.</u>

Mark 11:25-26 (SNB) And when ye stand praying, <u>forgive</u>, if ye have ought against any: that your Father also which is in heaven may forgive you your trespasses. 26 But if ye do not forgive, neither will your Father which is in Heaven forgive your trespasses. *[Observant Jewish people stand to pray the Amidah (Standing) Prayer three times a day.]*

Matt. 6:14 For if you <u>forgive</u> others their trespasses, your Heavenly Father will also forgive you; 15 but if you do not forgive others, neither will your Father forgive your trespasses.

Luke 6:37b <u>Forgive</u>, and you will be forgiven;

Luke 6:36 Be merciful, just as your Father is merciful.

Matt. 9:12-13 (SNB) They that be whole need not a physician, but they that are sick. 13 But go ye and learn what that meaneth, I will have <u>mercy, and not sacrifice</u>: for <u>I am not come to call the righteous, but sinners to repentance.</u>

Luke 5:31-32 Those who are well have no need of a physician, but those who are sick; 32 I have come to call <u>not the righteous but sinners to repentance.</u>

And beginning at Moses [the Torah]
and all the prophets,
He expounded unto them
in all the Scriptures [including the Torah]
the things concerning Himself.
...
And He said unto them,
These are the Words which I spake unto you,
while I was yet with you,
that all things must be fulfilled,
which were written in the Torah of Moses,
and in the Prophets, and in the Psalms,
concerning Me.
Then opened He their understanding,
that they might understand
the Scriptures....

Luke 24:27, 44-45

APPENDIX C: APOSTLES AND TORAH

All NRSV unless marked.

For Torah

Rom. 15:4 (SNB) For whatever was written in former days **was written for our instruction,** so that by steadfastness and by the encouragement of the Scriptures we might have hope.

Rom. 3:1-2 (SNB) What advantage then hath the Jew? ... 2 Much in every way: chiefly, because **that unto them were committed the oracles of God.**

Rom. 9:4-5 **They are Israelites, and to them belong** the adoption, **the glory, the Covenants, <u>the giving of the Torah,</u>** the worship, and the promises; 5 to them belong the patriarchs, and from them, according to the flesh, comes the Messiah, who is over all, God blessed **forever**.

Rom. 15:27 (SNB) and indeed they [Gentiles] owe it to them [Jewish people]; for if the Gentiles have come to share in their spiritual blessings, they ought also to be of service to them in material things.

Rom. 3:31 (SNB) Do we then make void the Torah through faith? God forbid: yea, **we establish the Torah.**

Rom. 7:13 (SNB) the **Torah is holy, and the commandment holy, and just, and good.**

Rom. 7:22 (SNB)...the **Torah is spiritual** ... I **delight** in the **Torah of God**....

Rom. 7:25b (SNB) with the mind **I myself serve the Torah of God**....

Rom. 8:2 (SNB) For the Torah of the Spirit of life in Messiah יֵשׁוּעַ [*God's Law*] hath made me free from the law of sin and death *[the law of our sinful flesh]*.

Rom. 8:4,7 (SNB) That the **righteousness of the Torah** might be fulfilled in us, who walk not after the flesh, but after the Spirit. ... 7 Because the carnal mind is enmity against God: for it is not subject to the Torah of God, neither indeed can be.

1 Cor. 9:20b-21 (SNB) ...to them that are under the Torah, [*I become*] as under the Torah, that I might gain them that are under the Torah; 21 To them that are without Torah, as without Torah, (**being not without Torah to God, but under Torah to Messiah**,) that I might gain them that are without Torah.

2 Thess. 2:15 (SNB) ...stand fast, and hold the **traditions** which ye have been taught....

James 1:25 (SNB) But whoso looketh into the **perfect Torah of liberty,** and continueth therein, he being not a forgetful hearer, but a doer of the work, this man shall be blessed in his deed.

James 2:8-12 (SNB) If ye fulfill the **royal Torah** according to the Scripture *[The only Scripture at the time was the Old Testament]*, Thou shalt love thy neighbour as thyself, ye do well: 9 But if ye have respect to persons, ye commit sin, and are convinced [ASV: convicted] of the Torah as transgressors. For whosoever shall **keep the whole Torah,** and yet offend in one point, he is guilty of all. 11 For he that said, Do not commit adultery *[which Yeshua said is also just lusting]*, said also, Do not kill *[which Yeshua said is also just being angry]*. Now if thou commit no adultery, yet if thou kill, thou art become a transgressor of the Torah. 12 <u>So speak ye, and so do, as they that shall be judged by the</u> **Torah of liberty.**

James 4:12 (NASB) **There is only one Lawgiver** and Judge, the One who is able to save and to destroy

2 Thess 3:6 (SNB) We command you, brethren, in the Name of our Lord יֵשׁוּעַ Messiah, that ye withdraw yourselves from every brother that walketh disorderly, and not after the **tradition** which he received of us.

Following Torah is NOT FOR SALVATION!!!

Apostle Paul followed Torah: Phil. 3:6 ...as to righteousness under the law [Torah], blameless. Acts 18:21 (SNB) I must by all means keep this feast.... Acts 21:24 *[James speaking to Paul]* You yourself observe and guard the law [Torah]. Acts 28:17 (SNB) I have committed nothing against the people, or customs of our fathers.... 2 Tim. 1:3 I am grateful to God—whom I worship with a clear conscience, as my ancestors did. *[His ancestors were Torah following Jewish people.]*

We can follow Torah only through faith: Rom. 9:31-32 Israel, who did strive for the righteousness that is based on the law [Torah], did not succeed in fulfilling that law. 32 Why not? Because they did not strive for it **on the basis of faith**, but as if it were based on works.

Following Torah is NOT FOR SALVATION!!!

[For some of these verses, it is hard to know for sure if the word "law" means Torah, or law of sin or oral law, etc.]

Gal. 1:6 I am astonished that you are so quickly deserting the one who called you in the grace of Messiah and are turning to a different gospel ... there are some who are confusing you and want to pervert the Gospel of Christ [Messiah].

Romans 6:12-14 Therefore, do not let sin exercise dominion in your mortal bodies, to make you obey their passions. 13 No longer present your members to sin as instruments of wickedness, but present yourselves to God as those who have been brought from death to life, and present your members to God as instruments of righteousness. 14 For <u>sin will have no dominion over you</u>, since you are not under law but <u>under grace</u>.

Gal 2:1-4 Then after fourteen years I went up again to Jerusalem with Barnabas, taking Titus along with me. 2 I went up in response to a revelation. Then I laid before them (though only in a private meeting with the acknowledged leaders) the Gospel that I proclaim among the Gentiles, in order to make sure that I was not running, or had not run, in vain. 3 But even Titus, who was with me, was not compelled to be circumcised, though he was a Greek. 4 But because of false believers secretly brought in, who slipped in to spy on the freedom we have in Christ Jesus, so that they might enslave us— 5 we did not submit to them even for a moment, so that the truth of the Gospel might always remain with you.

Gal 2:7 ...when they saw that I had been entrusted with the Gospel for the uncircumcised, just as Peter had been entrusted with the Gospel for the circumcised ....

Acts 15:1-5, 7-11 Then certain individuals came down from Judea and were teaching the brothers, "<u>Unless you are circumcised according to the custom of Moses, you cannot be saved.</u>" 2 And after Paul and Barnabas had <u>no small dissension and debate with them</u>, Paul and Barnabas and some of the others were appointed to go up to Jerusalem <u>to discuss this question</u> with the apostles and the elders. ... they reported the conversion of the Gentiles, and brought great joy to all the believers. 4 When they came to Jerusalem, they were welcomed by the church and the apostles and the elders, and they reported all that God had done with them. 5 But some believers who belonged to the sect of the Pharisees stood up and said, "<u>It is necessary for them to be circumcised and ordered to keep the law [Torah] of Moses.</u>" ... 7 After there had been much debate, Peter stood up and said to them, "... Now therefore why are you putting God to the test by placing on the neck of the disciples a yoke that neither our ancestors nor we have been able to bear? 11 On the contrary, <u>we believe that we will be saved through the grace of the Lord Jesus, just as they will.</u>"

Acts 15:13-20 (TLV) After they finished speaking, Jacob answered, "Brothers, listen to me. ... 15 The words of the Prophets agree, as it is written: 16 'After this I will return and rebuild the fallen Tabernacle of David.I will rebuild its ruins and I will restore it, 17 so that <u>the rest of humanity may seek the Lord— namely all the Gentiles who are called by My name</u>—says ADONAI....' 19 Therefore, I judge <u>not to trouble those from among the Gentiles who are turning to God</u>— 20 but to write to them to abstain from the contamination of idols, and from sexual immorality, and from what is strangled, and from blood."

Gal 2:15-16 <u>We</u> ourselves <u>are Jews</u> by birth and not Gentile sinners; 16 <u>yet we know that a person is justified not by the works of the law but through faith in Jesus Christ</u>. And we have come to believe in Christ Jesus, so that we might be <u>justified by faith</u> in Christ, and not by doing the works of the law, <u>because no one will be justified by the works of the law</u>.

Gal 3:10-13 (CJB) For everyone who depends on legalistic observance of Torah commands lives under a curse, since it is written, "Cursed is everyone who does not keep on doing everything written in the Scroll of the Torah." (Deut. 27:26) 11 Now it is evident that no one comes to be declared righteous by God through legalism, since "The person who is righteous will attain life by trusting and being faithful." 12 Furthermore, legalism is not based on trusting and being faithful, but on [a misuse of] (sic) the text that says, "Anyone who does these things will attain life through them."(Lev. 18:5) 13 The Messiah redeemed us from the curse pronounced in the Torah by becoming cursed on our behalf....

> *[So, this is what we see here. The Torah does not emphasize believing. Does it ever say "believe in ...."? The Torah is about <u>doing</u>! The New Covenant is about <u>believing,</u> then doing!! It's about God writing the laws on our hearts! The point is, keeping Torah is <u>not for our salvation</u>!! It never was! There always had to be sacrifices to cover continual sinning. Salvation only comes through <u>believing in and followingYeshua</u>!! We keep Torah because Yeshua did. It is the lifestyle God designed, therefore it is good! It is His Word! We do it to understand some deeper things about Yeshua and His Word and to receive the tremendous blessings it brings. But it is not anything we can boast about! And never dare we ever feel like it lifts us above other believers. Neither does it degrade us (See Col. 2:16-17 on page 267).]*

Gal 2:19-21 For through the law I died to the law, so that I might live to God. I have been crucified with Christ; 20 and it is no longer I who live, but it is Christ who lives in me. And the life I now live in the flesh I live by faith in the Son of God, who loved me and gave Himself for me. 21 I do not nullify the grace of God; <u>for if justification comes through the law, then Christ died for nothing</u>.

Gal 2:11-14 But when Cephas came to Antioch, I opposed him to his face, because he stood self-condemned; 12 for until certain people came from James, <u>he used to **eat** with the Gentiles</u>. But after they came, he drew back and kept himself separate for fear of the circumcision faction. 13 And the other Jews joined him in this hypocrisy, so that even Barnabas was led astray by their hypocrisy. 14 But when I saw that they were not acting consistently with the truth of the Gospel, I said to Cephas before them all, "<u>If you, though a Jew, live like a Gentile and not like a Jew, how can you compel the Gentiles to live like Jews</u>?" *[This is referring to eating only, not to sexual sins or breaking any other commandments.]*

Rom.14:1 Welcome those who are weak in faith, but not <u>for the purpose of quarreling</u> over opinions.

Rom. 14:17 For the <u>kingdom of God is not food and drink</u> but righteousness and peace and joy in the Holy Spirit. *[Again, this is referring to eating, not to helping the poor or any other commandments.]*

YESHUA ON WORKS: Matt. 5:16 … let your light shine before others, so that they may see <u>your good works</u> and give glory to your Father in heaven.

Rom. 4:2-9a, 11-16, 23-25 (CJB) …<u>if Avraham came to be considered righteous by God because of legalistic observances, then he has something to boast about. But this is not how it is before God!</u> 3 For what does the Tanakh *[Sripture]* say? **"Avraham put his trust in God, and it was credited to his account as righteousness".** (Gen. 15:6) 4 Now the account of someone who is working is credited not on the ground of grace but on the ground of what is owed him. 5 However, in the case of one who is not working but rather is trusting in Him who makes ungodly people righteous, his trust is credited to him as righteousness. 6 In the same way, the blessing which David pronounces is on those whom God credits with righteousness apart from legalistic observances: 7 "Blessed are those whose transgressions are forgiven, whose sins are covered over; 8 Blessed is the man whose sin ADONAI will not reckon against his account." 9 Now is this blessing for the circumcised only? … 11…while he was still uncircumcised. This happened so that he could be the father of every uncircumcised person who trusts..... 12 and at the same time be the father of every circumcised person who ... follows in the footsteps of the trust which Avraham avinu had when he was still uncircumcised. 13 For the promise to Avraham and his **seed** that he would inherit the world <u>did not come through legalism but through the righteousness that trust produces. 14 For if the heirs are produced by legalism, then trust is pointless and the promise worthless.</u> 15 For what law brings is punishment. But where there is no law, there is also no violation. 16 The reason the promise is based on trusting is so that it may come as God's free gift, a promise that can be relied on by all the seed, not only those who live within the framework of the Torah, but also those with the kind of trust Avraham had.... 23 But the words, "it was credited to his account . . . ," were not written for him only. 24 They were written also for us, who will certainly have our account credited too, because we have trusted in Him who raised Yeshua our Lord from the dead — 25 Yeshua, who was delivered over to death because of our offences and raised to life in order to make us righteous.

[So, righteousness is by trusting in faith, but we still are not allowed to covet or lie or mistreat orphans and strangers and the blind. The Torah still applies, but our salvation and forgiveness is no longer through animal sacrifices, but only through believing in Yeshua's sacrifice on the Cross.]

[James gives us the balance, as does Yeshua (see above), to Apostle Paul's teaching on faith and legalism.]

James 2:14a, 21-26 What good is it, my brothers and sisters, if you say you have faith but do not have <u>works</u>? … 21 Was not our ancestor Abraham justified by works when he offered his son Isaac on the altar? 22 <u>You see that faith was active along with his works, and faith was brought to completion by the works.</u> 23 Thus the scripture was fulfilled that says, "Abraham believed God, and it was reckoned to him as righteousness," and he was called the friend of God. 24 You see that <u>a person is justified by works and not by faith alone.</u> 25 Likewise, was not Rahab the prostitute also justified by works when she welcomed the messengers and sent them out by another road? 26 For just as the body without the spirit is dead, so faith without works is also dead.

Ephesians 2:8-8 <u>For by grace you have been saved through faith, and this is not your own doing; it is the gift of God— 9 not the result of works, so that no one may boast.</u>

Do Not Judge and Do Not Offend (mostly concerning kosher food)

Rom 14:5-6 Some judge <u>one day to be better than another</u>, while <u>others judge all days to be alike</u>. Let all be fully convinced in their own minds. 6 Those who observe the day, observe it in honor of the Lord. Also those who eat, eat in honor of the Lord, since they give thanks to God;

Rom.14:2-4 Some believe in eating anything, while the weak eat only vegetables. 3 Those who eat must not despise those who abstain, and those who abstain <u>must not pass judgment</u> on those who eat; for God has welcomed them. 4 Who are you to pass judgment on servants of another?

Rom. 14:6-7 … those who abstain, abstain in honor of the Lord and give thanks to God. 7 We do not live to ourselves, and we do not die to ourselves.

Rom. 14:14 I know and am persuaded in the Lord Jesus that nothing is unclean in itself; but it is unclean for anyone who thinks it unclean. *[He's talking about food here, not bodily discharges.]*

Rom. 14:20-21 Everything is indeed clean, but it is wrong for you to make others fall by what you eat; 21 it is good not to eat meat or drink wine or do anything that makes your brother or sister stumble.

I Tim. 4:1-5 Now the Spirit expressly says that in later times some will renounce the faith by paying attention to deceitful spirits and teachings of demons, 2 through the hypocrisy of liars whose consciences are seared with a hot iron. 3 They forbid marriage <u>and demand abstinence from foods</u>, which God created to be received with thanksgiving by those who believe and know the truth. 4 <u>For everything created by God is good, and nothing is to be rejected, provided it is received with thanksgiving; 5 for it is sanctified by God's word and by prayer.</u>

I Cor. 6:12 "All things are lawful for me," but not all things are beneficial. "All things are lawful for me," but I will not be dominated by anything. 13 "<u>Food is meant for the stomach and the stomach for food,</u> <u>and God will destroy both one and the other.</u> The body is meant not for fornication but for the Lord, and the Lord for the body.

I Cor. 10:23-24 "All things are lawful," but not all things are beneficial. "All things are lawful," but not all things build up. Do not seek your own advantage, but that of the other.
[He obviously doesn't mean that it is lawful now to take revenge or use bribery or assault people—all of which are parts of the Torah! He is referring only to food here.]

I Cor. 8:1 Now concerning food sacrificed to idols: … 8 "<u>Food will not bring us close to God.</u>" We are no worse off if we do not eat, and no better off if we do.

I Cor. 8:9, 13 But take care that this liberty of yours does not somehow become a stumbling block to the weak. … 13 Therefore, if food is a cause of their falling, I will never eat meat, so that I may not cause one of them to fall.

Rom. 14:23 But <u>those who have doubts are condemned</u> if they eat, because they do not act from faith; for whatever does not proceed from faith is sin.

I Cor. 10:30 If I partake with thankfulness, why should I be denounced because of that for which I give thanks?

I Cor. 10:31 So, <u>whether you eat or drink, or whatever you do,</u> **do everything for the glory of God.**

I Cor. 10:32-33 (CJB) <u>Do not be an obstacle to anyone</u> 33 … so that they may be saved;

Rom 14:15-17 If your brother or sister is being injured by what you eat, you are no longer walking in love. Do not let what you eat cause the ruin of one for whom Christ died. 16 So do not let your good be spoken of as evil. 17 For the <u>kingdom of God is not food and drink but righteousness and peace and joy in the Holy Spirit.</u>

Rom. 14:20 **<u>Do not, for the sake of food, destroy the work of God.</u>**

James 2:12-13 (SNB) So speak ye, and so do, as they that shall be judged by the Torah of liberty. (NRSV) 13 For judgment will be without mercy to anyone who has shown no mercy; mercy triumphs over judgment.

I Cor. 5:11 But now I am writing to you not to associate with anyone who bears the name of brother or sister who is sexually immoral or greedy, or is an idolater, reviler, drunkard, or robber. Do not even eat with such a one. *[In other words, someone who violates Torah. A Torah believer wouldn't be doing those things.]*

Cannot Perfect

Gal. 3:21 Is the law then opposed to the promises of God? Certainly not! For <u>if a law had been given that could make alive, then righteousness would indeed come through the law.</u>
[If a law could make alive, God would have given it!!! No law can make alive!! Apparently, though, it could bring a certain righteousness, if you obeyed all, including making sacrifices for sins. See next verse.]

Luke 1:5-6 … there was a priest named Zechariah ….. His wife was … Elizabeth. 6 Both of them were <u>righteous before God</u>, living blamelessly according to all the commandments and regulations of the Lord.

Rom. 2:13-15 (SNB) For not the hearers of Torah are just before God, but the doers of Torah shall be justified. 14 For when the Gentiles, which have not the Torah, do by nature the things contained in the Torah, these, having not Torah, are a Torah unto themselves: 15 Which shew the work of Torah written in their hearts....

Rom. 8:3-4 (SNB) For what the Torah could not do, in that it was weak through the flesh, God sending His own Son in the likeness of sinful flesh, and for sin, condemned sin in the flesh: 4 That the <u>righteousness of Torah</u> might be fulfilled in us, who walk not after the flesh, but after the Spirit.

Heb. 7:19 (SNB) For the Torah made nothing perfect, but the bringing in of a better hope did; by the which we draw nigh unto God.

Heb. 8:8-12 God finds fault with them *[former Covenant and promises]* when he says: "The days are surely coming, says the Lord, when I will establish a new covenant with … Israel and … Judah; 9 not like the covenant that I made with their ancestors, … for they did not continue in my covenant *[quoting Jer. 31:31-32]*…. 10 This is the covenant … I will put **my laws** *[the same laws not different ones!!]* in their minds, and write them on their hearts, and I will be their God, and they shall be my people *[quoting Jer. 31:33]*. And they shall not teach one another or say to each other, "Know the Lord," for they shall all know me, from the least of them to the greatest *[quoting Jer. 31:34a]*. *[Has this truly happened yet?]* For I will be merciful toward their iniquities, and I will remember their sins no more *[Jer.31:34b]*.

Heb. 9:9-10 This is a symbol of the present time, during which gifts and sacrifices are offered <u>that cannot perfect the conscience of the worshiper,</u> 10 but deal only with food and drink and various baptisms, regulations for the body imposed until the time comes to set things right. *[The Torah deals with much more than those few things!]*

Col. 2:20-23 If with Christ you died to the elemental spirits of the universe, why do you live as if you still belonged to the world? Why do you submit to regulations, 21 "Do not handle, Do not taste, Do not touch"? 22 All these regulations refer to things that perish with use; they are simply human commands and teachings. *[Can he be referring to the Torah? It was not human but from God Himself!!!]* 23 These have indeed an appearance of wisdom in <u>promoting self-imposed piety, humility, and severe treatment of the body, but they are of no value in checking self-indulgence.</u> *[This doesn't sound like Torah! Sounds more like other religions. But, this is the whole point! Keeping laws <u>does not change the heart</u>! Only in Yeshua is our heart changed.]*

Heb. 13:9b (ASV) ...it is good that the heart be established by grace; not by meats, wherein they that occupied themselves were not profited.

Rom. 2:17-24 (CJB) But if you ... rest on Torah and boast about God 18 and know His will and give your approval to what is right, because you have been instructed from the Torah; 19 and if you have persuaded yourself that you are a guide to the blind, a light in the darkness, 20 an instructor for the spiritually unaware and a teacher of children, since in the Torah you have the embodiment of knowledge and truth; 21 then, you who teach others, don't you teach yourself? Preaching, "Thou shalt not steal," do you steal? 22 Saying, "Thou shalt not commit adultery," do you commit adultery? Detesting idols, do you commit idolatrous acts? 23 You who take such pride in Torah, do you, by disobeying the Torah, dishonor God? — 24 as it says in the Tanakh *[Scriptures]*, "It is because of you that God's name is blasphemed...."

Miscellaneous

Gal. 3:24 (SNB) Wherefore Torah was our schoolmaster to bring us unto Messiah....

Gal. 3:25 (SNB) But after that faith is come, we are no longer under a schoolmaster.

Gal. 4:4 But when the fullness of time had come, God sent His Son, born of a woman, <u>born under the law [Torah]</u>, 5 in order to redeem those who were under the law [Torah] ....

Gal 3:17 My point is this: the law [Torah], which came four hundred thirty years later, **does not annul a covenant previously ratified by God**, so as to nullify the promise.

Gal 3:19 Why then the law [Torah]? It was **added because of transgressions, until the offspring *[Yeshua]*** would come ....

Phil. 3:8-9 (SNB) ... that I may win Messiah, 9 And be found in Him, not having mine own righteousness, which is of the Torah, but that which is through the faith of Messiah, the righteousness which is of God by faith....

Col. 2:2-3 (TLV) ... have all the riches of the full assurance of understanding, leading to a true knowledge of the mystery of God—that is, Messiah. 3 In Him all the treasures of wisdom and knowledge are hidden.

Col. 2:9-12 For in Him the whole fullness of deity dwells bodily, 10 and you have come to fullness in Him, who is the head of every ruler and authority. 11 In Him also you were <u>circumcised with a spiritual circumcision</u>, by putting off the body of the flesh in the circumcision of Christ; 12 when you were buried with Him in baptism, you were also raised with Him through faith in the power of God, who raised Him from the dead.

Col. 2:13-15   … He forgave us all our trespasses, 14 erasing the record that stood against us with its <u>legal demands</u>. He set this aside, nailing it to the cross. 15 He disarmed the rulers and authorities and made a public example of them, triumphing over them in it.

Col. 2:18 Do not let anyone disqualify you, insisting on self-abasement and worship of angels, <u>dwelling on visions</u> *[This is not Torah. The Torah forbids these things!]*, puffed up without cause by a human way of thinking *[The Torah is not human! It is from the mouth of Elohim Himself!]*, 19 and not holding fast to the head (Yeshua) ….

1 Tim. 6:13b-14 I charge you 14 to keep the commandment without spot or blame until the manifestation of our Lord Jesus Christ…. [Greek: τηρῆσαί σε τὴν ἐντολὴν *"keep you the commandment." Is it referring to the Torah?!]*

2 Tim. 3:15-17 (SNB) And that from a child thou hast known the Holy Scriptures, which are able to make thee wise unto salvation through faith which is in Messiah יֵשׁוּעַ. 16 All Scripture *[Torah is Scripture!]* is given by inspiration of God, and is profitable for doctrine, for reproof, for correction, for instruction in righteousness: 17 That the man of God may be perfect, thoroughly furnished unto all good works.

Torah is a shadow of the Heavenly Temple!

Heb. 8:1-2 Now the main point in what we are saying is this: we have such a high priest, one who is seated at the right hand of the throne of the Majesty in the heavens, 2   a minister in the sanctuary and the true tent [Tabernacle] <u>that the Lord, and not any mortal, has set up</u>.

Heb. 8:4-5 … there are priests who offer gifts according to the law [Torah]. 5 They offer worship in a sanctuary that is a sketch and shadow of the heavenly one; for Moses, when he was about to erect the tent, was warned, "See that you make everything according to the pattern that was shown you on the mountain." *[This is the Messianic point: The Torah gives us a glimpse of what is to come. There is a Heavenly Temple and a Heavenly Jerusalem. By studying the Holy Days, the Tallit, etc.—keeping them as part of the study of them—we can come to understand better our Messiah and the awesomeness of what awaits us in Heaven!!!]*

Col. 2:16-17   Therefore <u>do</u> <u>not let anyone condemn you in matters of food and drink or of observing festivals, new moons, or Sabbaths.</u> 17 These are only <u>a shadow of what is to come</u>, but the substance belongs to Christ. *[So Torah gives us a glimpse of what is to come!]*

Heb. 10:1 …the law [Torah] has only <u>a shadow of the good things to come</u> and not the true form of these realities,

Rev. 8:3 Another angel with a golden censer came and stood at the altar ….

Heb. 9:11-12 (SNB) But Messiah being come an High Priest of good things to come, by a greater and more perfect Tabernacle, not made with hands, that is to say, not of this building; 12 Neither by the blood of goats and calves, but <u>by His own Blood He entered in once into the Holy Place</u>, having obtained eternal Redemption for us.

Heb. 9:14-15   … how much more will the blood of Christ, who through the eternal Spirit offered Himself without blemish to God, purify our conscience from dead works to worship the living God! 15 For this reason He is the mediator of a new covenant, so that those who are called may receive the promised eternal inheritance, because a death has occurred that redeems them <u>from the transgressions under the first covenant</u>. *[See, our transgressions are based on the Torah Covenant!!]*

Heb. 9:22-24 ... without the shedding of blood there is no forgiveness of sins. 23 Thus it was necessary for the sketches of the heavenly things to be purified with these rites, but the heavenly things themselves need better sacrifices than these. 24 <u>For Christ did not enter a sanctuary made by human hands, a mere copy of the true one, but he entered into heaven itself</u>, now to appear in the presence of God on our behalf.

Heb. 10:19-20 Therefore, my friends, since we have confidence to <u>enter the sanctuary</u> by the blood of Jesus ישוע, 20 by the new and living way that he opened for us <u>through the curtain</u> (that is, through His flesh), 21 and since we have a great priest over the house of God....

Heb.12:22 But you have come to Mount Zion and to the city of the living God, the <u>heavenly Jerusalem</u>, and to innumerable angels in <u>festal gathering</u>,

Abolish?

Heb. 10:8-9 When he said above, "You have neither desired nor taken pleasure in sacrifices and offerings and burnt offerings and sin offerings" (these are offered according to the law), 9 then he added, "See, I have come to do your will." He <u>abolishes the first in order to establish the second</u>. *[Remember, he is referring to the sacrificial part of the Torah here, not the rest of Torah.]*

Matt. 5:17-20 "Do not think that I have come to abolish the law [Torah] or the prophets; <u>I have come not to abolish</u> **but to fulfill**. 18 For truly I tell you, until heaven and earth pass away, not one letter, not one stroke of a letter, will pass from the law until all is accomplished."

Heb. 8:13 In speaking of "a new covenant," he has made the first one obsolete. And what is obsolete and growing old will soon disappear. *[The sacrificial laws have disappeared. The Temple was destroyed and sacrifices therefore had to cease just a few years after this was written.]*

1 John 2:3-6 (SNB) And hereby we do know that we know Him, if we keep His commandments. 4 He that saith, I know Him, and keepeth not His commandments, is a liar, and the truth is not in him. 5 But whoso keepeth His word, in him verily is the love of God perfected: hereby know we that we are in Him. 6 He that saith he abideth in Him ought himself also so to walk, even as He walked. *[Yeshua kept Torah.]* ... 3:24 And he that keepeth His commandments dwelleth in Him, and He in him.

The New Covenant is no less harsh for those who disobey

Rom. 2:8-9, 12 ... for those who are self-seeking and who obey not the truth but wickedness, there will be wrath and fury. 9 There will be anguish and distress for everyone who does evil.... 12 (CJB) All who have sinned outside the framework of Torah will die outside the framework of Torah; and all who have sinned within the framework of Torah will be judged by Torah.

Rom. 2:16 God, through Jesus Christ, will judge the secret thoughts of all. [SNB: secrets of men.]

2 Thess. 2:12 ...all who have not believed the truth but took pleasure in unrighteousness will be condemned.

Heb. 2:1 (NASB) we must pay much closer attention to what we have heard, so that we do not drift away from it. 2 For if the word spoken through angels proved unalterable, and every transgression and disobedience received a just penalty, 3 **how will we escape if we neglect so great a salvation**? After it was at the first spoken through the Lord, it was confirmed to us by those who heard, 4 God also testifying with them, both by signs and wonders and by various miracles and by gifts of the Holy Spirit according to His own will.

Heb.10:24-31   And let us consider how to provoke one another to love and good deeds, 25 not neglecting to meet together, as is the habit of some, but encouraging one another, and all the more as you see the Day approaching. 26 For **if we willfully persist in sin** after having received the knowledge of the truth, there no longer remains a sacrifice for sins, 27 but **a fearful prospect of judgment**, and a fury of fire that will consume the adversaries. 28 Anyone who has violated the law [Torah] of Moses dies without mercy "on the testimony of two or three witnesses." 29 **How much worse punishment do you think** will be deserved by those who have spurned the Son of God, profaned the blood of the covenant by which they were sanctified, and outraged the Spirit of grace? 30 For we know the one who said, "Vengeance is mine, I will repay." And again, "The Lord will judge His people." 31 It is a fearful thing to fall into the hands of the living God.

Heb. 11:6 (NKJV) But without faith it is **impossible** to please Him [God], for he who comes to God must believe that He is, and that He is a rewarder of those who diligently seek Him.

Heb. 12:14 (NKJV) Pursue peace with all people, and holiness, without which **no one** will see the Lord:

Heb. 12:25,29 (NKJV) See that you do not refuse Him who speaks. For if they did not escape who refused Him who spoke on earth, much more shall we not escape if we turn away from Him who speaks from heaven.... For our God is a consuming fire.

James 4:17 ...whoever knows the right thing to do and fails to do it, for him it is sin.

2 Pet. 2:4-6,9,17-21 (ASV) For if God spared not angels when they sinned, but cast them down to hell, and committed them to pits of darkness, to be reserved unto judgment; 5 and spared not the ancient world, but preserved Noah with seven others, a preacher of righteousness, when he brought a flood upon the world of the ungodly; 6 and turning the cities of Sodom and Gomorrah into ashes condemned them with an overthrow, having made them an example unto those that should live ungodly; ... 9 the Lord knoweth how to deliver the [G]odly out of temptation, and to keep the unrighteous under punishment unto the day of judgment.... 17 These are springs without water, and mists driven by a storm; for whom the blackness of darkness hath been reserved. 18 For, uttering great swelling [words] of vanity, they entice in the lusts of the flesh, by lasciviousness, those who are just escaping from them that live in error; 19 promising them liberty, while they themselves are bondservants of corruption; for of whom a man is overcome, of the same is he also brought into bondage. 20 For if, after they have escaped the defilements of the world through the knowledge of the Lord and Saviour Jesus Christ, they are again entangled therein and overcome, the last state is become worse with them than the first. 21 For it were better for them not to have known the way of righteousness, than, after knowing it, to turn back from the holy commandment *[Torah?!]* delivered unto them.

Rev. 20:11-15 Then I saw a great white throne and Him who sat upon it; from His presence earth and sky fled away, and no place was found for them. 12 And I saw the dead, great and small, standing before the throne, and books were opened. Also another book was opened, which is the book of life. And the dead were judged by what was written in the books, by what they had done. 13 And the sea gave up the dead in it, Death and Hades gave up the dead in them, and all were judged by what they had done. ... 15 and if any one's name was not found written in the book of life, he was thrown into the lake of fire.

APPENDIX D: SINS LISTED IN THE NEW COVENANT

For those who want to believe that the whole Torah is abolished, we ask, Why then does the New Covenant list as immoral and sinful, things also considered so in the Torah (underlined) plus so many more?!

NRSV unless marked

Mark 7:21-23 For it is from within, from the human heart, that evil intentions come: **<u>fornication</u>, <u>theft</u>, <u>murder</u>,** 22 **<u>adultery</u>, avarice, wickedness, <u>deceit</u>, licentiousness, <u>envy</u>, <u>slander</u>, pride, folly.** 23 All these evil things come from within, and they defile a person."

2 Tim. 3:1-5 You must understand this, that in the last days distressing times will come. 2 For people will be **lovers of themselves, lovers of money, boasters, arrogant, abusive, disobedient to their parents, ungrateful, unholy,** 3 **inhuman, implacable, slanderers, profligates, brutes, haters of good,** 4 **treacherous, reckless, swollen with conceit, lovers of pleasure** rather than lovers of God, 5 holding to the outward form of godliness but denying its power. Avoid them!

Rom. 1:18 For the wrath of God is revealed from heaven against all ungodliness and wickedness of men who by their wickedness suppress the truth. ... 29 Being filled with all unrighteousness, **<u>fornication</u>, wickedness, covetousness, maliciousness; full of <u>envy</u>, <u>murder</u>, debate, <u>deceit</u>, malignity; whisperers,** 30 **backbiters, haters of God, despiteful, proud, boasters, inventors of evil things, disobedient to parents,** 31 **without understanding, covenant breakers, without natural affection, implacable, unmerciful:** 32 Who knowing the judgment of God, that they which commit such things are worthy of death, not only do the same, but have pleasure in them that do them.

Rom. 13:13 (NKJV) Let us walk properly, as in the day, not in **revelry** [CJB: **partying**] and **drunkenness,** not in **lewdness** *[indecency]* and **lust,** not in **strife** and **envy.** 14 But put on the Lord Jesus Christ, and make no provision for the flesh, to fulfill its lusts.

1 Cor. 5:11 (SNB) ... I have written unto you not to keep company, if any man that is called <u>a brother</u> be a **<u>fornicator</u>, or <u>covetous</u>, or an <u>idolater</u>,** or a railer, or a drunkard, or an extortioner; with such an one do not eat.

1 Cor 6:9-11a (NIV) Or do you not know that wrongdoers will not inherit the kingdom of God? Do not be deceived: Neither the <u>**sexually immoral**</u> nor <u>**idolaters**</u> nor <u>**adulterers**</u> nor <u>**homosexual offenders,**</u> nor <u>**thieves**</u> **nor the greedy nor drunkards nor slanderers nor swindlers** will inherit the kingdom of God. And that is what some of you were.

I Cor. 13:4-8 (TLV) Love is patient, love is kind, it does not **<u>envy</u>,** it does not **brag,** it is not **puffed up,** 5 it does not **behave inappropriately,** it does not **seek its own way,** it is not **provoked,** it **<u>keeps</u> no <u>account of wrong</u>,** 6 it does not **rejoice over injustice** but rejoices in the truth;

Gal 5:19-21 The acts of the flesh are obvious: <u>**sexual immorality,**</u> **impurity and debauchery** *[perversion]*; <u>**idolatry**</u> **and** <u>**witchcraft**</u>**; hatred, discord, jealousy, fits of rage, selfish ambition, dissensions, factions and <u>envy</u>; drunkenness, orgies,** and the like. I warn you, as I did before, that those who live like this will not inherit the kingdom of God.

Eph. 4:17b-19 ...henceforth walk not as other Gentiles walk, in the **vanity of their mind,** 18 Having the **understanding darkened,** being **alienated from the life of God** through the **ignorance** that is in them, because of the **blindness of their heart:** 19 Who being **past feeling** have given themselves over unto **lasciviousness** *[dirty mindedness]*, to work all **uncleanness** with **greediness.**

Eph. 4:31 (RSV) Let all **bitterness** and **wrath** and **anger** and **clamor** [other versions: **loud quarelling, backbiting, violent assertiveness**], and **slander** be put away from you, with all **malice** *[<u>hatred</u>]*,

Eph 5:3-7 But among you there **must not be even a hint of <u>sexual immorality</u>, or of any kind of impurity, or of greed**, because these are improper for God's holy people. Nor should there be **obscenity, foolish talk or coarse joking,** which are out of place, but rather thanksgiving. For of this you can be sure: **No <u>sexually immoral</u>, impure or greedy person—such a person is an <u>idolater</u>—** has any inheritance in the kingdom of Christ and of God. ...because of such things God's wrath comes on those who are **disobedient**. Therefore do not be partners with them.

Eph. 5:11-12 (SNB) And have no fellowship with the unfruitful works of darkness, but rather reprove them. 12 For it is a shame even to speak of those things which are done of them in secret.

Col. 3:5-8 Put to death, therefore, whatever in you is earthly: **<u>fornication</u>, impurity, passion, evil desire, and greed (which is idolatry).** 6 On account of these the wrath of God is coming on those who are disobedient. 7 These are the ways you also once followed, when you were living that life. 8 But now ye also put off all these; **anger, wrath, malice, blasphemy, filthy communication out of your mouth.**

I Tim. 1:9-10 ...the law is laid down not for the innocent but for the lawless and disobedient, for the godless and sinful, for the unholy and profane, for those who **<u>kill</u>** their father or mother, for **<u>murderers</u>,** 10 **<u>fornicators</u>, <u>sodomites</u>, slave traders, <u>liars</u>, <u>perjurers</u>,** and whatever else is contrary to the sound teaching;

1 Tim. 6:4-5 (RSV) ...**<u>envy</u>, dissension, <u>slander</u>, base suspicions**, 5 and **wrangling**....

Titus 1:7b,10 ...he must not be **arrogant or quick-tempered or addicted to wine or violent or greedy for gain**; ... **rebellious people, idle talkers** and **<u>deceivers</u>**.... 2:3 ...**<u>slanderers</u>** or **slaves to drink**....

I Pet. 2:1-2 (SNB) Wherefore laying aside all **malice**, and all **guile**, and **hypocrisies**, and **<u>envies</u>**, and all **evil speakings**, 2 as newborn babes, desire the sincere milk of the word, that ye may grow thereby:

1 Pet. 4:2-3 (NASB) ...live the rest of the time in the flesh no longer for the lusts of men, ... **sensuality, lusts, drunkenness, carousing, drinking parties** and **abominable <u>idolatries</u>.**

2 Pet. 2:9-15 (NASB) ...the Lord knows how to rescue the godly from temptation, and to keep the unrighteous under punishment for the day of judgment, 10 and especially those who **indulge the flesh** in its **corrupt desires** and **despise authority**. **Daring**, **self-willed**, they do not tremble when they revile angelic majesties, ... 12 But these, like unreasoning animals, born as creatures of instinct to be captured ... 13 They count it a pleasure to **revel** in the daytime. They are stains and blemishes, **reveling in their deceptions**, as they **carouse** with you, 14 having eyes full of **<u>adultery</u>** that never cease from sin, enticing unstable souls, having a heart trained in **greed**, accursed children; 15 forsaking the right way, they have gone astray....

Rev. 21:7-8 (SNB) He that overcometh shall inherit all things; and I will be his God, and he shall be My son. 8 But the **fearful**, and **unbelieving**, and the **abominable**, and **<u>murderers</u>**, and **whoremongers**, and **<u>sorcerers</u>**, and **<u>idolaters</u>**, and all **<u>liars</u>**, shall have their part in the lake which burneth with fire and brimstone: which is the second death.

Rev. 22:12-15 (SNB) And, behold, I come quickly; and My reward is with Me, to give every man according as his work shall be. 13 I am Alpha and Omega, the beginning and the end, the first and the last. 14 Blessed are they that do His commandments, that they may have right to the tree of life, and may enter in through the gates into the city. 15 For without are dogs, and **<u>sorcerers,</u>** and **whoremongers,** and **<u>murderers</u>**, and **idolaters**, and **whosoever loveth and maketh a <u>lie</u>**.

APPENDIX E: COMMANDMENTS IN THE EPISTLES

These are rules/commandments in the New Covenant! And some are not easy to obey! The New Covenant is stricter than the Torah! Really!

All as marked.

REPENT   Acts 2:38b, 40b (SNB) Repent, and be baptized every one of you in the name of יֵשׁוּעַ Messiah for the remission of sins, and ye shall receive the gift of the Holy Spirit. ... Save yourselves from this untoward [NRSV: corrupt] generation.   Acts 3:19-20a (CJB) Therefore, repent and turn to God, so that your sins may be erased [SNB: blotted out; NRSV: wiped out]; 20 so that times of refreshing may come from the Lord's presence....   Rev. 2:5,16 (SNB) Remember therefore from whence thou art fallen, and repent.... Therefore repent....   Rev. 3:3 (ASV) Remember therefore how thou hast received and didst hear; and keep *it*, and repent. Rev. 3:19b (SNB) ...be zealous therefore, and repent.

STRIP OFF OLD NATURE: Eph. 4:22 (CJB) ...strip off your old nature....   Eph. 4:17 (CJB) ...do not live any longer as the pagans live.... *(They resist God's will. They live by sensuality, all kinds of impurity, and greed)* Eph. 4:31 *Summary:* Get rid of bitterness, rage, anger, violence, slander, spitefulness. 2 Cor. 13:11a (RSV) Mend your ways....   2 Cor. 7:1 (SNB) ...let us cleanse ourselves from all filthiness of the flesh and spirit, perfecting holiness in the fear of God.   Heb. 3:12-13 (NASB) Take care ... that there not be in any one of you an evil, unbelieving heart that falls away from the living God. But encourage one another day after day, as long as it is still called "Today," so that none of you will be hardened by the deceitfulness of sin. Heb. 12:1-2 (SNB) ...let us lay aside every weight, and the sin which doth so easily beset us, and let us run with patience the race that is set before us, Looking unto יֵשׁוּעַ the author and finisher of our faith....   James 4:8 (SNB) ...purify your hearts....   1 Pet. 1:14 (NASB) ...do not be conformed to the former lusts which were yours in your ignorance....   1 Pet. 2:11 (SNB) ...abstain from fleshly lusts, which war against the soul....   1 Pet. 3:11 (ASV) ...turn away from evil, and do good ... seek peace, and pursue it.

BE HOLY: 1 Pet. 1:15 (NASB) ...but like the Holy One who called you, be holy yourselves also in all your behavior....   2 Pet. 3:13-14 (SNB) Nevertheless we, according to His promise, look for new heavens and a new earth, wherein dwelleth righteousness. 14 Wherefore, beloved, seeing that ye look for such things, be diligent that ye may be found of Him in peace, without spot, and blameless.

LIVE/WALK IN THE LIGHT: Eph. 5:8-9 (NRSV) Live as children of light. The fruit of light is in every kind of goodness, rightness, and truth. 1 John 1:9 (SNB) ...walk in the light, as He is in the light....

DO NOT CONFORM TO THIS WORLD: Rom.12:2 (SNB) Be not conformed to this world.... 2 Cor. 6:14 (SNB) Be ye not unequally yoked together with unbelievers....   2 Tim. 1:8 (SNB) Be not thou therefore ashamed of the testimony of our Lord, nor of me His prisoner: but be thou partaker of the afflictions of the Gospel according to the power of God....   Heb. 13:12-13 (NASB) Jesus ... suffered outside the gate. So, let us go out to Him outside the camp, bearing His reproach. James 1:27 (RSV) ...keep oneself unstained from the world. 1 John 2:15-17 (SNB) Love not the world, neither the things that are in the world. If any man love the world, the love of the Father is not in him. 16 For all that is in the world, the lust of the flesh, and the lust of the eyes, and the pride of life, is not of the Father, but is of the world. 17 And the world passeth away, and the lust thereof: but he that doeth the will of God abideth **forever**.

FIND OUT WHAT PLEASES GOD: Rom. 12:2b (SNB) ...be ye transformed by the renewing of your mind, that ye may prove what is that good, and acceptable, and perfect, will of God. Eph. 5:10 Try to determine what will please the Lord. 1 Pet. 3:15 (RSV) ...reverence Christ as Lord.

PRESENT YOURSELF TO GOD: Rom. 12:1 (SNB) I beseech you therefore, brethren, by the mercies of God, that ye present your bodies a living sacrifice, holy, acceptable unto God. Rom. 12:11 (NIV) Never be lacking in zeal, but keep your spiritual fervor, serving the Lord. Rom. 6:19b For just as you once presented your members as slaves to impurity and to greater and greater iniquity, so now present your members as slaves to righteousness for sanctification. 1 Cor. 7:23 (ASV) Ye were bought with a price; become not bondservants of men. Eph. 5:1 (SNB) Be ye therefore followers of God, as dear children.... Heb. 10:22 (RSV) ...let us draw near with a true heart in full assurance of faith, with our hearts sprinkled clean from an evil conscience and our bodies washed with pure water. James 4:7 (SNB) Submit yourselves therefore to God. Resist the devil, and he will flee from you. James 4:8 (RSV) Draw near to God and He will draw near to you.

SPREAD THE GOSPEL: 1 Pet. 3:15b (NASB) ...always being ready to make a defense to everyone who asks you to give an account for the hope that is in you, yet with gentleness and reverence....

BE RENEWED: Rom. 12:2b (SNB) ...be ye transformed by the renewing of your mind, that ye may prove what is that good, and acceptable, and perfect, will of God. Eph. 4:23 *Summary:* Keep renewing your spirit and your mind. Eph. 4:24 (CJB) Clothe yourself in the new nature ... in righteousness and holiness. 2 Tim. 1:6 (RSV) ...rekindle the gift of God that is within you....

BE FILLED: Eph. 5:18 (CJB) Keep on being filled with the Holy Spirit. Rev. 2:17b (also 29b; 3:6,13, and 22) (NRSV) ...listen to what the Spirit is saying....

DO NOT GRIEVE THE SPIRIT: Eph. 4:30 (SNB) And grieve not the holy Spirit of God.... I Thess. 5:19 (SNB) Quench not the Spirit.

DO NOT FEAR: I Pet. 3:6 (NRSV) ...never let fears alarm you. I Pet. 3:6 (CJB) ...do not succumb to fear. 1 Pet. 3:14b (NRSV) ... Do not fear what they fear, and do not be intimidated.... Rev. 2:10 (ASV) Fear not....

DON'T BE DECEIVED: Eph. 5:6 (RSV) Let no one deceive you with empty words.... Eph. 4:14 (ASV) ...be no longer children, tossed to and fro and carried about with every wind of doctrine, by the sleight of men, in craftiness, after the wiles of error. Gal. 6:7 (SNB) Be not deceived; God is not mocked: for whatsoever a man soweth, that shall he also reap. Col. 2:8 (SNB) Beware lest any man spoil you through philosophy and vain deceit, after the tradition of men, after the rudiments of the world, and not after Messiah. 2 Thess. 2:3 (RSV) Let no one deceive you in any way. Heb. 13:9 (ASV) Be not carried away by divers and strange teachings: James 1:16 (ASV) Be not deceived.... 2 Pet. 3:17-18 (SNB) Ye therefore, beloved, seeing ye know these things before, beware lest ye also, being led away with the error of the wicked, fall from your own stedfastness. 18 But grow in grace, and in the knowledge of our Lord and Saviour ישוע Messiah. To Him be glory both now and **forever**. Amen. 1 John 4:1-3 (SNB) Beloved, believe not every spirit, but try the spirits whether they are of God: because many false prophets are gone out into the world. 2 Hereby know ye the Spirit of God: Every spirit that confesseth that ישוע Messiah is come in the flesh is of God: 3 And every spirit that confesseth not that ... is not of God.... 2 John 1:7-8 (NASB) For many deceivers have gone out into the world, those who do not acknowledge Jesus Christ as coming in the flesh. This is the deceiver and the antichrist. 8 Watch yourselves....

BE HUMBLE, GENTLE, KIND: Eph. 4:2 *Summary:* Be humble, gentle, and patient. Eph. 4:32 (SNB) And be ye kind one to another, tenderhearted.... Gal. 6:1 (SNB) if a man be overtaken in a fault, ye which are spiritual, restore such an one in the spirit of meekness; considering thyself, lest thou also be tempted. Phil. 2:3-5 (NASB) Do nothing from selfishness or empty conceit, but with humility of mind regard one another as more important than yourselves; 4 do not merely look out for your own personal interests, but also for the interests of others. 5 Have this attitude in yourselves which was also in Christ Jesus.... Col. 3:12 (NRSV) ...clothe yourselves with compassion, kindness, humility, meekness, and patience. James 4:10 (SNB) Humble yourselves in the sight of the Lord, and He shall lift you up. James 4:13-16 *Summary:* Don't boast about what you will do tomorrow or next year. 1 Pet. 5:5-6 (SNB) Yea, all of you be subject one to another, and be clothed with humility: for God resisteth the proud, and giveth grace to the humble. 6 Humble yourselves therefore under the mighty hand of God, that He may exalt you in due time....

DO NOT THINK TOO HIGHLY OF YOURSELF: Rom. 12:3 I say to everyone among you not to think of yourself more highly than you ought to think, but to think with sober judgment, each according to the measure of faith that God has assigned. Rom. 12:16b ...do not be haughty, but associate with the lowly; do not claim to be wiser than you are. Phil. 2:12-13 (SNB) ...work out your own salvation with fear and trembling. 13 For it is God which worketh in you both to will and to do of His good pleasure.

LOVE: Rom. 12:9 (NIV) Let love be without hypocrisy. Rom. 12:10 (SNB) Be kindly affectioned one to another with brotherly love; in honour preferring one another.

1 Cor. 13 *(whole chapter) Summary;* If you do anything without love, it is worth nothing.

1 Cor. 14:1 (NASB) Pursue love....

Eph. 4:2,15 (NRSV) Bear with one another in love. ... Speak the truth in love.

Eph. 5:2 (NRSV) Live a life of love. [SNB & CJB: Walk in love.]

I Thess. 4:9b (SNB) Love one another.

Col. 3:14 (NRSV) Above all, clothe yourselves with love....

Heb. 13:1-3 (NRSV) Let mutual love continue. 2 Do not neglect to show hospitality to strangers.... 3 Remember those who are in prison....

I Pet. 1:22b (SNB) ...see that ye love one another with a pure heart fervently

1 Pet. 2:17 (NRSV) Honor everyone. Love the family of believers.

1 Pet. 4:8 (RSV) Above all hold unfailing your love for one another, since love covers a multitude of sins.

1 John 2:10-11 (NASB) The one who loves his brother abides in the Light and there is no cause for stumbling in him. 11 But the one who hates his brother is in the darkness and walks in the darkness, and does not know where he is going because the darkness has blinded his eyes.

1 John 3:11,14,18,23 (ASV) ...love one another ... 14 We know that we have passed out of death into life, because we love ... 18 ...let us not love in word, neither with the tongue *[only]*; but in deed and truth. ... 23 And this is His commandment, that we should believe in the Name of His Son Jesus Christ, and love one another....

1 John 4:7-12, 16-21 (SNB) Beloved, let us love one another: for love is of God; and every one that loveth is born of God, and knoweth God. 8 He that loveth not knoweth not God; for God is love. 9 In this was manifested the love of God toward us, because that God sent His only begotten Son into the world, that we might live through Him. 10 Herein is love, not that we loved God, but that He loved us, and sent His Son to be the propitiation for our sins.

11 Beloved, if God so loved us, we ought also to love one another. 12 No man hath seen God at any time. If we love one another, God dwelleth in us, and His love is perfected in us. ... 16 ...God is love; and he that dwelleth in love dwelleth in God, and God in him. ... 18 There is no fear in love; but perfect love casteth out fear.... He that feareth is not made perfect in love. 19 We love Him, because He first loved us. 20 If a man say, I love God, and hateth his brother, he is a liar: for he that loveth not his brother whom he hath seen, how can he love God whom he hath not seen? 21 And this commandment have we from Him, That he who loveth God love his brother also.

2 John 1:5-6 (SNB) ...love one another. 6 And this is love, that we walk after His commandments.

GIVE: Rom. 12:13 (NIV) Share with the Lord's people who are in need. Practice hospitality. 2 Cor. 9:7 (NRSV) ...give as you have made up your mind, not reluctantly or under compulsion, for God loves a cheerful giver. Heb. 13:16 (RSV) Do not neglect to do good and to share what you have, for such sacrifices are pleasing to God.

BEAR EACH OTHER'S BURDENS: Gal. 6:2 (SNB) Bear ye one another's burdens, and so fulfill the Torah of Messiah.

SPEAK TRUTH: Eph. 4:15 Speak the truth in love. Eph. 4:25 Speak the truth. Eph. 4:25 Strip off all falsehood. 1 Pet. 3:10 (CJB) Whoever wants to love life and see good days must keep his tongue from evil and his lips from speaking deceit....

SPEAK ONLY GOOD WORDS: Eph. 4:29 (SNB) Let no corrupt communication proceed out of your mouth, but that which is good to the use of edifying, that it may minister grace unto the hearers. Eph. 5:4 Speak no obscene or stupid talk. Eph. 5:4 Speak no coarse language. I Thess. 4:18 (NRSV) ...encourage one another.... James 4:11 (SNB) Speak not evil one of another....

UNIFY: Rom. 12:16 (SNB) Be of the same mind one toward another. Rom. 12:18 (SNB) If possible, so far as it depends upon you, live peaceably with all. Rom. 14:19 (RSV) Let us then pursue what makes for peace and for mutual upbuilding. Rom. 15:1 (RSV) We who are strong ought to bear with the failings of the weak.... 1 Cor. 1:10 (NRSV) I appeal to you, brothers and sisters, by the name of our Lord Jesus Christ, that all of you be in agreement and that there be no divisions among you, but that you be united in the same mind and the same purpose. 2 Cor. 13:11b (SNB) ...be of one mind, live in peace.... Eph. 4:3 (SNB) Endeavouring to keep the unity of the Spirit in the bond of peace. Eph. 5:21 (SNB) Submitting yourselves one to another in the fear of God. Col. 3:15 (SNB) let the peace of God rule in your hearts, to the which also ye are called in one body; Heb. 11:14 (NKJV) Pursue peace with all people, and holiness....

EDIFY EACH OTHER: Rom. 15:2,5 (SNB) Let every one of us please his neighbour for his good to edification *[building up]*. ... 5 ...be likeminded one toward another according to Messiah יֵשׁוּעַ: 1 Cor. 14:26 (SNB) when ye come together, every one of you hath a psalm, hath a doctrine, hath a tongue, hath a revelation, hath an interpretation. Let all things be done unto edifying. Eph. 4:12 (CJB) ... equip God's people for the work of service that builds the body of the Messiah. 1 Thess. 5:14 (RSV) ... encourage the fainthearted, help the weak, be patient with them all. Heb. 10:24-25 (RSV) ...stir up one another to love and good works, 25 not neglecting to meet together, ...encouraging one another. 1 Pet. 4:10-11 (SNB) As every man hath received the gift, even so minister the same one to another, as good stewards of the manifold grace of God. 11 If any man speak, let him speak as the oracles of God; if any man minister, let him do it as of the ability which God giveth: that God in all things may be glorified through יֵשׁוּעַ Messiah.... Jude 1:20 (RSV) ...build yourselves up on your most holy faith....

MARRIAGE and SEXUAL PURITY:

1 Cor. 6:18 (SNB) Flee fornication.

1 Cor. 7:10b,11b, 15 (RSV) ...the wife should not separate from her husband ... and that the husband should not divorce his wife. ... 15 But if the unbelieving partner desires to separate, let it be so; in such a case the brother or sister is not bound. For God has called us to peace.

Eph. 5:3 *Summary:* No sexual immorality or impurity or greed (SNB: covetousness).

Eph. 5:21 (SNB) Submitting yourselves one to another in the fear of God.

Eph. 5:22 (SNB) Wives, submit yourselves unto your own husbands, as unto the Lord. Col. 3:18 (SNB) Wives be subject to your husbands.

Eph. 5:25 *Summary:* Husbands love your wives. Give yourself up for her in order to set her apart for God. Feed her and take care of her.

Col. 3:19 (NRSV) Husbands love your wives and never treat them harshly.

Eph. 5:31 *Summary:* Husband: Leave your father and mother and cleave to your wife.

Eph. 5:33 *Summary:* Wife: Respect your husband.

I Thess. 4:3b-5 (CJB) keep away from sexual immorality, 4 ... manage [your] sexual impulses in a holy and honorable manner, 5 without giving in to lustful desires.

Heb. 13:4 (NASB) Marriage is to be held in honor among all, and the marriage bed is to be undefiled; for fornicators and adulterers God will judge.

I Pet. 3:1-4 (NASB) In the same way, you wives, be submissive to your own husbands so that even if any of them are disobedient to the word, they may be won without a word by the behavior of their wives, 2 as they observe your chaste and respectful behavior. 3 Your adornment must not be merely external ... 4 but let it be the hidden person of the heart, with the imperishable quality of a gentle and quiet spirit, which is precious in the sight of God.

I Pet. 3:7 (CJB) You husbands, likewise, conduct your married lives with understanding. Although your wife may be weaker physically, you should respect her as a fellow-heir of the gift of Life. If you don't, your prayers will be blocked [SNB: that your prayers be not hindered].

WORK: 1 Cor. 15:58 (SNB) ...be ye stedfast, unmoveable, always abounding in the work of the Lord, forasmuch as ye know that your labour is not in vain in the Lord. Eph. 4:28 (NRSV) Work honestly with [your] own hands, so as to have something to share with the needy. 1 Thess. 4:11-12 (SNB) Work with your own hands, as we commanded you; ... that ye may have lack of nothing. 2 Thess. 3:12b ...work quietly and earn [your] own living. 1 Thess. 5:14 (RSV)...admonish the idlers.... 2 Thess. 3:6 (NRSV) ...keep away from believers who are living in idleness and not according to the tradition.... 1 Tim. 5:8 (RSV) If any one does not provide for his relatives, and especially for his own family, he has disowned the faith and is worse than an unbeliever. 1 Cor. 9:10b (RSV) the plowman should plow in hope and the thresher thresh in hope of a share in the crop.

PAY TAXES, HONOR GOVERNMENTS: Rom. 13:1-4 (CJB) Everyone is to obey the governing authorities. For there is no authority that is not from God, and the existing authorities have been placed where they are by God. ... 3 For rulers are no terror to good conduct, but to bad. ... for he is God's servant, there as an avenger to punish wrongdoers. Rom. 13:7 (RSV) Pay all of them their dues, taxes to whom taxes are due, revenue to whom revenue is due, respect to whom respect is due, honor to whom honor is due. 1 Pet. 2:13-14,17b (SNB) Submit yourselves to every ordinance of man for the Lord's sake: whether it be to the king, as supreme; 14 Or unto governors, as unto them that are sent by Him for the punishment of evildoers, and for the praise of them that do well. ... 17... Honour the king.

Appendix E: Commandments in the Epistles (cont.)

RICHES ARE FUTILE, BE CONTENT:

1 Tim. 6:17-19 (RSV) As for the rich in this world, charge them not to be haughty, nor to set their hopes on uncertain riches but on God who richly furnishes us with everything to enjoy. 18 They are to do good, to be rich in good deeds, liberal and generous, 19 thus laying up for themselves a good foundation for the future, so that they may take hold of the life which is life indeed [NRSV: life that really is life].

1 Tim. 6:9-10 (RSV) ...those who desire to be rich fall into temptation, into a snare, into many senseless and hurtful desires that plunge men into ruin and destruction. 10 For the love of money is the root of all evils; it is through this craving that some have wandered away from the faith and pierced their hearts with many pangs [SNB: sorrows].

1 Tim. 6:6-8 (SNB) ... **Godliness with contentment is great gain.** 7 For we brought nothing into this world, and it is certain we can carry nothing out. 8 And having food and raiment let us be therewith content.

Heb. 13:5 (ASV) Be ye free from the love of money; content with such things as ye have....

James 1:9-11 (RSV) Let the lowly brother boast in his exaltation, 10 and the **rich** in his humiliation, because like the flower of the grass he will pass away. 11 For the sun rises with its scorching heat and withers the grass; its flower falls, and its beauty perishes. So will the **rich** man fade away in the midst of his pursuits.

James 5:1-5 (CJB) Next, a word for the rich: weep and wail over the hardships coming upon you! 2 Your riches have rotted, and your clothes have become moth-eaten; 3 your gold and silver have corroded, and their corrosion will be evidence against you and will eat up your flesh like fire! This is the acharit-hayamim [last days], and you have been storing up wealth! 4 Listen! The wages you have fraudulently withheld from the workers who mowed your fields are calling out against you, and the outcries of those who harvested have reached the ears of ADONAI-Tzva'ot. 5 You have led a life of luxury and self-indulgence here on earth—in a time of slaughter, you have gone on eating to your heart's content.

DEFUSE ANGER: Eph. 4:26-27 (SNB) Be ye angry, and sin not: let not the sun go down upon your wrath: 27 Neither give place to the devil. James 1:19-20 (NASB) ....everyone must be quick to hear, slow to speak and slow to anger; 20 NRSV: for your anger does not produce God's righteousness.

NO REVENGE: Rom. 12:19 (RSV) Beloved, never avenge yourselves [See more in the Torah section, p. 91.]

FORGIVE: Eph. 4:32 (NRSV) ...forgiving one another, as God in Christ has forgiven you. Col. 3:13 (NRSV) ...forgive each other; just as the Lord has forgiven you....

DON'T BE FOOLISH: Eph. 5:17 (RSV) ...do not be foolish.... 2 Tim. 2:23 Have nothing to do with stupid and senseless controversies; you know that they breed quarrels. 1 Pet. 2:15 (SNB) For so is the will of God, that with well doing ye may put to silence the ignorance of foolish men....

DON'T GET DRUNK: Rom. 13:13 (RSV) let us conduct ourselves becomingly as in the day, not in reveling and drunkenness.... Eph. 5:18 (CJB) Don't get drunk with wine, because it makes you lose control. 1 Thess. 5:6b, 8 (RSV) ...keep awake and be sober. ... let us be sober.... 1 Pet. 1:13b (ASV) Be sober. 1 Pet. 4:2-3 (NASB) ...live ... no longer for the lusts of men, ... 3 ...drunkenness, carousing, drinking parties....

BE WISE: Rom. 16:19 (NASB) ...be wise in what is good and innocent in what is evil. James 1:5-6 (NASB) if any of you lacks wisdom, let him ask of God, who gives to all generously and without reproach, and it will be given to him. 6 But he must ask in faith without any doubting.... 1 Pet. 1:13 (NASB) Therefore, prepare your minds for action, keep sober in spirit, fix your hope completely on the grace to be brought to you at the revelation of Jesus Christ. 2 Pet. 3:8a (SNB) ...be not ignorant....

NO STEALING: Eph. 4:28 (SNB) ...steal no more: [See more in the Torah section, p. 52.]

NO IDOLS: 1 Cor. 10:14 (NRSV) Flee from the worship of idols. Eph. 5:5 (SNB) ...nor covetous man, who is an idolater, hath any inheritance in the Kingdom of Messiah... [See more in the Torah sections, pp. 35, 38.]

CONDUCT YOURSELVES:

Eph. 4:1 (ASV) ...walk worthily of the calling wherewith ye were called....

Eph. 5:15 (CJB) Pay careful attention to how you conduct your life.

Eph. 5:15-17 (NRSV) Be careful then how you live, not as unwise people but as wise, 16 making the most of the time, because the days are evil.

Col. 3:17 (SNB) And whatsoever ye do in word or deed, do all in the name of the Lord יֵשׁוּעַ...

Eph. 5:11-12 (SNB) And have no fellowship with the unfruitful works of darkness, but rather reprove them. 12 For it is a shame even to speak of those things which are done of them in secret.

I Thess. 5:22 (SNB) **Abstain from all appearance of evil.**

I Thess. 4:11 (SNB) Study to be quiet, and ... [mind] your own business.

I Thess. 5:13, 15b (SNB) ...be at peace among yourselves.... [don't] render evil for evil unto any man.

I Thess. 4:6b (NIV) No one should wrong or take advantage of a brother or sister.

Rom. 12:9b (NKJV) Abhor what is evil. Cling to what is good.

1 Cor. 10:31-32 (SNB) Whether therefore ye eat, or drink, or whatsoever ye do, do all to the glory of God. 32 Give none offence, neither to the Jews, nor to the Gentiles, nor to the church....

Gal. 5:16 (NASB) ...walk by the Spirit, and you will not carry out the desire of the flesh.

I Tim. 4:12,16 (RSV) ...set the believers an example in speech and conduct, in love, in faith, in purity. ... Take heed to yourself....

I Tim. 5:1b-2 (RSV) ...treat younger men like brothers, 2 older women like mothers, younger women like sisters, in all purity.

1 Tim. 6:11 (NRSV) ...pursue righteousness, godliness, faith, love, endurance, gentleness.

2 Tim. 2:22-26 (NRSV) Shun youthful passions and pursue righteousness, faith, love, and peace ... 24 And the Lord's servant must not be quarrelsome but kindly to everyone, an apt teacher, patient, 25 correcting opponents with gentleness. God may perhaps grant that they will repent and come to know the truth, 26 and that they may escape from the snare of the devil, having been held captive by him to do his will.

James 5:7-8 (NRSV) Be patient.... 8 You also must be patient.

1 Pet. 3:16 (NASB) ...keep a good conscience....

2 Pet. 1:5-10 (RSV) *Summary* ...make every effort to supplement [NRSV: support] your faith with virtue, knowledge, self-control, steadfastness, godliness, love. 8 For if these things are yours and abound, they keep you from being ineffective or unfruitful in ... our Lord Jesus Christ. 9 For whoever lacks these things is blind and shortsighted ... be the more zealous to confirm your call and election, for if you do this you will never fall....

DON'T WORRY: Phil. 4:6a (NRSV) Do not worry about anything. [RSV: Have no anxiety about anything.] 1 Pet. 5:7 (NRSV) Cast all your anxiety on Him, because He cares for you.

DON'T COMPLAIN: 1 Cor. 10:10 (NRSV) And do not complain.... Phil. 2:14-15 (NRSV) Do all things without murmuring and arguing, 15 so that you may be blameless and innocent, children of God without blemish in the midst of a crooked and perverse generation, in which you shine like stars in the world. James 5:9 (TLV) Do not grumble against one another, brothers and sisters, so that you may not be judged. 1 Pet. 4:16 (SNB) Yet if any man suffer as a Christian, let him not be ashamed; but let him glorify God on this behalf.

BE THANKFUL: Eph. 5:4 *Summary:* Give thanks.   Eph. 5:20 (SNB) Giving thanks always for all things unto God.... Col. 3:15b (SNB) ...and be ye thankful. 1 Thess. 5:18 (SNB) In every thing give thanks.... Heb. 12:28 (NRSV) ...let us give thanks, by which we offer to God an acceptable worship with reverence and awe....   Heb. 13:15 (ASV) ...let us offer up a sacrifice of praise to God continually....

REJOICE: Rom. 12:12 (NIV) Be joyful in hope, patient in affliction, faithful in prayer. Rom. 12:15 (SNB) Rejoice with them that do rejoice, and weep with them that weep. Phil. 3:1 (SNB) Rejoice in the Lord. Phil. 4:4 (SNB) Rejoice in the Lord alway: and again I say, Rejoice. I Thess. 5:16 (SNB) Rejoice evermore. James 1:2-4 (NASB) Consider it all joy, my brethren, when you encounter various trials, 3 knowing that the testing of your faith produces endurance. 4 ... so that you may be perfect and complete, lacking in nothing. 1 Pet. 4:12-14 (SNB) Beloved, think it not strange concerning the fiery trial which is to try you, as though some strange thing happened unto you: 13 But rejoice, inasmuch as ye are partakers of Messiah's sufferings; that, when His glory shall be revealed, ye may be glad also with exceeding joy. 14 If ye be reproached for the name of Messiah, happy are ye; for the spirit of glory and of God resteth upon you

SING: Eph. 5:19 (NRSV) ...sing psalms and hymns and spiritual songs among yourselves, singing and making melody to the Lord in your hearts.... James 5:13b (ASV) Is any cheerful? Let him sing praise.

KEEP ALERT: Eph. 6:18 (NRSV) ...keep alert and always persevere.... Phil. 3:2-3 (NASB) Beware of the dogs, beware of the evil workers, beware of the false circumcision; 3 for we are the true circumcision, who worship in the Spirit of God and glory in Christ Jesus and put no confidence in the flesh, 1 Pet. 5:8-11 (TLV) Stay alert! Watch out! Your adversary the devil prowls around like a roaring lion, searching for someone to devour. 9 Stand up against him, firm in your faith, knowing that the same kinds of suffering are being laid upon your brothers and sisters throughout the world. 10 After you have suffered a little while, the God of all grace—who has called you into His eternal glory in Messiah—will Himself restore, support, strengthen, and establish you. 11 All power to Him **forever**! Amen. Rev. 3:2 (CJB) Wake up, and strengthen what remains....

PRAY: Rom. 12:12 (NRSV) Persevere in prayer.
> Eph. 6:18 (NRSV) Pray in the Spirit at all times in every prayer and supplication. ...keep alert and always persevere in supplication for all....
> Phil. 4:6b (SNB) in every thing by prayer and supplication with thanksgiving let your requests be made known unto God.
> Col. 4:2 Devote yourselves to prayer ... with thanksgiving.
> I Thess. 5:17 (SNB) Pray without ceasing.
> I Tim. 2:1,8 (SNB) first of all, supplications, prayers, intercessions, and giving of thanks, be made for all men.... 8 ...pray every where, lifting up holy hands, without wrath and doubting.
> James 5:13-16 (ASV) Is any among you suffering? Let him pray. 14 Is any among you sick? Let him call for the elders of the church; and let them pray over him, anointing him with oil in the name of the Lord: 15 and the prayer of faith shall save him that is sick, and the Lord shall raise

him up; and if he have committed sins, it shall be forgiven him. 16 Confess therefore your sins one to another, and pray one for another, that ye may be healed. The supplication of a righteous man availeth much in its working.

Jude 1:20 (RSV) ...pray in the Holy Spirit....

PROPHESY: 1 Cor. 12:31 (NASB) ...earnestly desire the greater gifts. 1 Cor. 14:1 (NASB) Pursue love, yet desire earnestly spiritual gifts, but especially that you may prophesy. 1 Cor. 14:39-40 (NASB) ...desire earnestly to prophesy, and do not forbid to speak in tongues. I Thess. 5:20-21 (SNB) Despise not prophesyings. 21 Prove all things; hold fast that which is good.

GUARD YOUR THOUGHTS: Rom. 2:16 (NRSV) God, through Jesus Christ, will judge the secret thoughts of all. [SNB: God shall judge the secrets of men by ישוע Messiah.] I Cor. 4:5 (RSV) ...before the Lord comes, who ... will disclose the purposes of the heart. Phil 4:8 *Summary:* Think about good things. Col. 3:1-2 (RSV) seek the things that are above, where Christ is, seated at the right hand of God. 2 Set your minds on things that are above, not on things that are on earth. Heb. 4:12 (SNB) For the Word of God is ... a discerner of the thoughts and intents of the heart.

USE GOD'S ARMOR: Rom. 13:12 (RSV) The night is far gone, the day is at hand. Let us then cast off the works of darkness and put on the armor of light. Eph. 6:11-17 *Summary:* Use all the armor and weaponry that God provides: Truth, righteousness, Gospel, salvation (deliverance), faith, prayer. 1 Thess. 5:8 (RSV) ...put on the breastplate of faith and love, and for a helmet the hope of salvation. 1 Tim. 1:18-19 (SNB) ...war a good warfare; 19 Holding faith, and a good conscience; which some having put away concerning faith have made shipwreck.... 1 Tim. 6:12 (SNB) Fight the good fight of faith, lay hold on eternal life.... 2 Tim. 1:14 (NRSV) Guard the good treasure entrusted to you, with the help of the Holy Spirit living in us.

BE STRONG IN THE LORD: 1 Cor. 16:13 (RSV) Be watchful, stand firm in your faith, be courageous, be strong. Eph. 6:10 (SNB) ...be strong in the Lord, and in the power of His might.

Gal. 5:1 (NASB) ...keep standing firm and do not be subject again to a yoke of slavery.

Gal. 6:9 (SNB) And let us not be weary in well doing: for in due season we shall reap, if we faint not.

Phil. 4:1 (NRSV) ...stand firm in the Lord....

Col. 2:6-7 (SNB) As ye have therefore received Messiah ישוע the Lord, so walk ye in Him: 7 Rooted and built up in Him, and stablished in the faith, as ye have been taught, abounding therein with thanksgiving.

2 Thess. 2:15 (RSV) ...stand firm and hold to **the traditions**....

2 Thess. 3:13 (SNB) ... be not weary in well doing.

2 Tim. 2:1 (NRSV) Be strong in the grace that is in Christ Jesus....

Heb. 10:23 (NKJV) Let us hold fast the confession of our hope without wavering, for He who promised is faithful.

Heb. 10:35-36 (NRSV) Do not, therefore, abandon that confidence of yours.... 36 For you need endurance, so that when you have done the will of God, you may receive what was promised.

Heb. 12:3 (NASB) ...consider Him who has endured such hostility by sinners against Himself, so that you will not grow weary and lose heart.

Heb. 12:7 (NRSV) Endure trials for the sake of discipline.

Heb. 12:12-13 (RSV) ...lift your drooping hands and strengthen your weak knees, 13 and make straight paths for your feet....

James 5:8 (NASB) ... strengthen your hearts for the coming of the Lord is near.

Rev. 2:10b, 25b (SNB) ...be thou faithful unto death.... 25 ... hold fast till I [ישוע] come.

Rev. 3:11 (SNB) ...hold that fast which thou hast, that no man take thy crown.

ABIDE IN THE WORD: 1 Cor. 4:6b (RSV) ...learn by us not to go beyond what is written.... Col 3:16 (SNB) Let the Word of Messiah dwell in you richly ... teaching and admonishing one another... I Tim. 4:13 (CJB) ...pay attention to the public reading of the Scriptures. James 1:21-22 (SNB) ...receive with meekness the engrafted word, which is able to save your souls. 22 But be ye doers of the word, and not hearers only, deceiving your own selves. 2 Pet. 3:2 (NASB) remember the words spoken beforehand by the holy prophets and the commandment of the Lord and Savior spoken by your apostles. 1 John 2:24 (ASV) ...let that abide in you which ye heard from the beginning. If that which ye heard from the beginning abide in you, ye also shall abide in the Son, and in the Father.

DO NOT JUDGE:

Rom. 2:1-5 (RSV) Therefore you have no excuse, O man, whoever you are, when you judge another; for **in passing judgment** upon him **you condemn yourself**, because you, the judge, are doing the very same things. ... 3 Do you suppose, O man, that when you judge those who do such things and yet do them yourself, you will escape the judgment of God? 4 Or do you presume upon the riches of His kindness and forbearance and patience? Do you not know that God's kindness is meant to lead you to repentance? 5 But by your hard and impenitent heart you are storing up wrath for yourself on the day of wrath when God's righteous judgment will be revealed.

Rom. 14:4 (RSV) **Who are you to pass judgment** on the servant of another? It is before his own master that he stands or falls. And he will be upheld, for the Master is able to make him stand.

Rom. 14:10 (NKJV) But why do you judge your brother? Or why do you show contempt for your brother? For we shall all stand before the judgment seat of Christ.

Rom. 14:12-13 (SNB) So then every one of us shall give account of himself to God. 13 Let us not therefore judge one another any more: but judge this rather, that no man put a stumblingblock or an occasion to fall in his brother's way.

I Cor. 4:3-5a (RSV) ...I do not even judge myself. 4 I am not aware of anything against myself, but I am not thereby acquitted. It is the Lord who judges me. 5 Therefore do not pronounce judgment before the time, before the Lord comes, who will bring to light the things now hidden in darkness and will disclose the purposes of the heart.

James 4:11-12 (NASB) He who speaks against a brother or judges his brother, speaks against the law [Torah] and judges the law [Torah]; but if you judge the law [Torah], you are not a doer of the law [Torah] but a judge of it. 12 There is only one Lawgiver and Judge, the One who is able to save and to destroy; but who are you who judge your neighbor?

1 Pet. 4:15 (SNB) But let none of you suffer as a ... busybody in other men's matters.

BUT THERE MUST BE DISCERNMENT: Titus 1:13b-14 (CJB) *[To Titus, a leader]* ...rebuke those who have followed this false teaching, so that they will come to be sound in their trust [faith] 14 and no longer pay attention to Judaistic myths or to the commands of people who reject the truth.

Titus 3:9-10 (TLV) ...avoid foolish controversies and genealogies and strife and **disputes about Torah**, for they are unprofitable and useless. 10 Dismiss a quarrelsome person after a first and second warning,

Thy Torah is the Truth....
The sum of Thy Word is Truth....
Psalm 119:142 (SNB), 160 (ASV)

And ye shall know the Truth,
and the Truth shall make you Free.
John 8:32

For whatever was written in former days
was written for our Instruction, [Torah means "instruction"]
so that by steadfastness and by the encouragement
of the Scriptures we might have hope.
Romans 15:4.

... that keep the commandments of God, and
hold the testimony of Jesus: ...they that keep the
commandments of God, and the faith of Jesus. ... And
they sing the song of Moses ... and ... of the Lamb....
Revelation 12:17b; 14:12; 15:3a (ASV)

The Torah of יהוה is perfect,
converting the soul:
The testimony of יהוה is sure,
making wise the simple.
The statutes of יהוה are right,
rejoicing the heart:
The commandment of יהוה is pure,
enlightening the eyes. ...
More to be desired are they than gold,
yea, than much fine gold:
sweeter also than honey and the honeycomb.
Moreover by them is thy servant warned:
and in keeping of them
there is **great reward.**
Psalm 19:7-8,10-11

AARONIC, PRIESTLY BLESSING

Num. 6:22-26 And יהוה spake unto Moses, saying, 23 Speak unto Aaron and unto his sons, saying, On this wise ye shall bless the children of Israel, saying unto them,

יהוה

bless thee, and keep thee:

יהוה

make His face shine upon thee,
and be gracious unto thee:

יהוה

lift up His countenance upon thee,
and give thee peace [shalom].

And they shall put My Name
upon the children of Israel;
and I will bless them.

Psalm 4:6b יהוה, lift thou up the light of Thy countenance upon us.

Psalm 31:16 Make Thy face to shine upon Thy servant: save me for Thy mercies' sake.

Psalm 67:1 (NRSV) May God be gracious to us and bless us and make His face to shine upon us, (Selah)

Psalm 80:3,7,19 Turn us again, O God, and cause Thy face to shine; and we shall be saved.

Psalm 89:15 Blessed is the people that know the joyful sound: they shall walk, O יהוה, in the light of Thy countenance.

Psalm 119:135 Make Thy face to shine upon Thy servant; and teach me Thy statutes.

Prov. 16:15 In the light of the king's countenance is life; and His favour is as a cloud of the latter rain.

Dan. 9:17 (CJB) Therefore, our God, listen to the prayer and pleadings of Your servant; and cause Your face to shine on Your desolated Sanctuary, for Your own sake.

Luke 9:29 And as He prayed, the fashion of His countenance was altered, and His raiment was white and glistening.

Matt. 17:2 And was transfigured before them: and His face did shine as the sun, and His raiment was white as the light.

Acts 2:28 Thou hast made known to me the ways of life; Thou shalt make me full of joy with Thy countenance.

2 Cor. 4:6 For God, who commanded the Light to shine out of darkness, hath shined in our hearts, to give the light of the knowledge of the Glory of God in the face of ישוע Messiah.

Rev. 1:16 (NRSV) In His right hand He held seven stars, and from His mouth came a sharp, two-edged sword, and His face was like the sun shining with full force.

Ingram Content Group UK Ltd.
Milton Keynes UK
UKHW031836060323
418105UK00011B/1208